Neoliberalism and the Moral Economy of Fraud

There is evidence that economic fraud has, in recent years, become routine activity in the economies of both high- and low-income countries. Many business sectors in today's global economy are rife with economic crime.

Neoliberalism and the Moral Economy of Fraud shows how neoliberal policies, reforms, ideas, social relations and practices have engendered a type of socio-cultural change across the globe which is facilitating widespread fraud. This book investigates the moral worlds of fraud in different social and geographical settings, and shows how contemporary fraud is not the outcome of just a few 'bad apples'. Authors from a range of disciplines including sociology, anthropology and political science, social policy and economics, employ case studies from the Global North and Global South to explore how particular values, morals and standards of behaviour rendered dominant by neoliberalism are encouraging the proliferation of fraud.

This book will be indispensable for those who are interested in political economy, development studies, economics, anthropology, sociology and criminology.

David Whyte is Professor of Socio-legal Studies at the University of Liverpool, UK.

Jörg Wiegratz is Lecturer in Political Economy of Global Development at the University of Leeds, UK.

Routledge Frontiers of Political Economy

For a complete list of titles in this series please visit www.routledge.com/books/series/SE0345.

201. **Economics, Culture and Development**
Eiman O. Zein-Elabdin

202. **Paradigms in Political Economy**
Kavous Ardalan

203. **The Economics of Voting**
Studies of self-interest, bargaining, duty and rights
Dan Usher

204. **The Political Economy of Food and Finance**
Ted P. Schmidt

205. **The Evolution of Economies**
An alternative approach to money bargaining
Patrick Spread

206. **Representing Public Credit**
Credible commitment, fiction, and the rise of the financial subject
Natalie Roxburgh

207. **The Rejuvenation of Political Economy**
Edited by Nobuharu Yokokawa, Kiichiro Yagi, Hiroyasu Uemura and Richard Westra

208. **Macroeconomics After the Financial Crisis**
A post-Keynesian perspective
Edited by Mogens Ove Madsen and Finn Olesen

209. **Structural Analysis and the Process of Economic Development**
Edited by Jonas Ljungberg

210. **Economics and Power**
A Marxist critique
Giulio Palermo

211. **Neoliberalism and the Moral Economy of Fraud**
Edited by David Whyte and Jörg Wiegratz

Neoliberalism and the Moral Economy of Fraud

Edited by David Whyte and Jörg Wiegratz

LONDON AND NEW YORK

First published 2016
by Routledge
2 Park Square, Milton Park, Abingdon, Oxon OX14 4RN

and by Routledge
711 Third Avenue, New York, NY 10017

First issued in paperback 2017

Routledge is an imprint of the Taylor & Francis Group, an informa business

© 2016 selection and editorial matter, David Whyte and Jörg Wiegratz; individual chapters, the contributors

The right of the editors to be identified as the author of the editorial material, and of the authors for their individual chapters, has been asserted in accordance with sections 77 and 78 of the Copyright, Designs and Patents Act 1988.

All rights reserved. No part of this book may be reprinted or reproduced or utilised in any form or by any electronic, mechanical, or other means, now known or hereafter invented, including photocopying and recording, or in any information storage or retrieval system, without permission in writing from the publishers.

Trademark notice: Product or corporate names may be trademarks or registered trademarks, and are used only for identification and explanation without intent to infringe.

British Library Cataloguing in Publication Data
A catalogue record for this book is available from the British Library

Library of Congress Cataloging in Publication Data
Names: Whyte, David, 1968- editor. | Wiegratz, Jörg, editor.
Title: Neoliberalism and the moral economy of fraud / edited by David Whyte and Jörg Wiegratz.
Description: Abingdon, Oxon ; New York, NY : Routledge, [2016]
Identifiers: LCCN 2015050394| ISBN 9781138930377 (hardback) | ISBN 9781315680545 (ebook)
Subjects: LCSH: Neoliberalism—Moral and ethical aspects. | Fraud—Economic aspects. | Economics—Moral and ethical aspects.
Classification: LCC HB95 .N435 2016 | DDC 364.16/3—dc23
LC record available at http://lccn.loc.gov/2015050394

ISBN 13: 978-1-138-05805-7 (pbk)
ISBN 13: 978-1-138-93037-7 (hbk)

Typeset in Times New Roman
by FiSH Books Ltd, Enfield

Contents

Tables

Acknowledgements

This book would not have been possible without the inspiration and support from a very large number of organisations and individuals. We are grateful to countless friends and colleagues who we have discussed the themes of this project with over the years. James Carrier in particular was instrumental in providing ideas and a draft proposal at the early stages of the project. We also thank the University of Leeds, School of Politics and International Studies (POLIS) and Centre for African Studies (LUCAS) for providing funds that allowed us to hold the international workshop on 'Neoliberalism, fraud and moral economy' at the University of Leeds on 2 May 2014, where the contributors first presented papers that ended up in this book. We also thank colleagues who have been part of the project along the way, but in the end were unable to contribute to the book. Those colleagues include Gerhard Anders, Chloé Buire, Jose Maria Munoz and Matthew Watson. We also wish to acknowledge Laura Johnson and Andy Humphries at Routledge for their commitment to, and enthusiasm for, the project and support through the commissioning and production process. Thank you to all of the contributors of this volume for rising to both the practical demands and intellectual framing of their chapters, and for sticking with us on this project, even when our demands as editors might have at times seemed pedantic. Without their commitment and willingness to speak to the volume themes it would not be the book it is. We hope it has all been worth it in the end. A project like this takes up a lot of time and energy and involves sitting alone in libraries and offices for far too long. So we are most grateful to our families and friends for putting up with us through what is a profoundly anti-social process and always providing crucial moral support whenever and wherever it was needed.

Contributors

Georgios A. Antonopoulos obtained his doctorate from the University of Durham in 2006. He is currently Professor of Criminology at the School of Social Sciences, Business and Law of Teesside University. His teaching and research interests include 'organised crime'/illegal markets, the criminality, criminalisation and victimisation of minority ethnic groups, and qualitative research methods. He is an associate of the *Cross-Border Crime Colloquium*, associate editor of the journal *Trends in Organised Crime* and member of the editorial boards of the journals *Global Crime*, *Journal of Financial Crime*, *Journal of Money Laundering Control* and the *British Journal of Criminology*.

Erik Bähre (Institute of Cultural Anthropology and Development Sociology, Leiden University) specialises in economic anthropology. He has conducted ethnographic fieldwork, as well as conducted surveys, in the townships and squatter settlements of Cape Town and fieldwork in Brasília and The Netherlands. One of his research interests is how rapid economic change realigns personal relations (kin, neighbours, fellow migrants, friends). He has published on topics that include, among others, financial mutuals, commercial insurance, social grants, debt, violence, entrepreneurship and ethnography.

James G. Carrier has taught and done research in Papua New Guinea, the United States and Great Britain, and is presently Research Associate at Oxford Brookes University, Adjunct Professor of Anthropology at the University of Indiana and Associate at the Max Planck Institute for Social Anthropology. His main interest is economy and society: *Wage, Trade and Exchange in Melanesia* (California, 1989, with A.H. Carrier), *Gifts and Commodities: Exchange and Western Capitalism Since 1700* (Routledge, 1995), *Meanings of the Market* (Berg, 1997, ed.), *A Handbook of Economic Anthropology* (Edward Elgar, 2005, 2012, ed.) and *Anthropologies of Class* (Cambridge, 2015, ed. with D. Kalb).

John Christensen directs the Tax Justice Network, an expert network that leads research and advocacy effort to expose the corrupt activities of tax havens and their users. Having trained as both a forensic auditor and as an economist, he has spent a large part of his career investigating offshore tax havens, including a period working for Deloittes (a global accounting firm), and 11 years working as economic adviser to the government of Jersey, a prominent tax haven closely linked to the City of London. His work is largely focused on the evolution of financial capitalism since the 1980s, and the phenomenon known as the Finance Curse. His most recent book is titled *The Greatest Invention: Tax and the Campaign for a Just Society* (Commonwealth Publishing, 2015)

Matías Dewey is a Senior Researcher in the Sociology of Illegal Markets project area at the Max Planck Institute for the Study of Societies, Germany. He studied sociology in Argentina and received his PhD in Germany. His research areas are illegal markets, economic sociology, informal institutions, social theory and qualitative sociology. As a visiting scholar, he has spent time at the University of Oxford, at the MaxPo in Paris and recently at the Department of Sociology at the University of Texas at Austin. He has received grants from the Alexander von Humboldt and Volkswagen foundations.

David Ellis is a Postdoctoral Research Associate in the School of Law and Social Justice at the University of Liverpool. His primary research interests focus on political economy, social policy, the welfare state, personal finance and the historic growth of personal indebtedness in the UK. David has also collaborated in major research projects with organisations such as Democratic Audit and the Law Commission.

Maritza Felices-Luna is Associate Professor in the Department of Criminology, at the University of Ottawa, in Ottawa, Canada. She came from Peru to study Criminology at the University of Montreal where she conducted her master's and PhD research on internal armed conflict in Peru and Belfast. Her research and teaching areas of interest are political violence, armed conflict, qualitative methodology and North–South relations of domination. She is currently researching security walls (anti-immigration, anti-terrorism, anti-trafficking) as the embodiment of ideologies of national security aiming to monitor and restrict the mobility of certain populations construed as dangerous bodies.

Steve Hall is Professor of Criminology at Teesside University and co-founder of the Teesside Centre for Realist Criminology. In the 1970s he was a musician. In the 1980s he worked with young offenders in the de-industrialising north-east of England. In the 1990s he began teaching, researching and publishing in the fields of criminology, sociology, history and philosophy. He is author of *Theorizing Crime and Deviance* (Sage, 2012), co-editor of *New Directions in Criminology* (Routledge, 2012) and co-author of *Violent Night* (Berg, 2006), *Criminal Identities and Consumer Culture* (Routledge, 2008), *Rethinking Social Exclusion*, (Sage, 2013), *Revitalizing Criminological Theory* (Routledge, 2015) and *Riots and Political Protest* (Routledge, 2015).

Chris Holden is Reader in International Social Policy at the University of York, UK. He has published widely on the relationships between the global economy, transnational corporations and health and social policy. Specific research has involved investigation of transnational tobacco companies, including their relationships to the illicit trade in tobacco products. He has been a member of the ditorial Board of the *Journal of Social Policy* and of the International Advisory Board of the journal *Global Social Policy*. He co-edited *The Global Social Policy Reader* (2009) and *Social Policy Review (2009–2011)*.

Paul Jones is a Senior Lecturer in Sociology at the University of Liverpool. In general his research centres on the political economy of the urban; recently this has included studies of architecture and the built environment, digital models, regeneration photography and – with Michael Mair – the Private Finance Initiative, supermarkets and state reform.

Michael Mair is a Senior Lecturer in the Department of Sociology, Social Policy and Criminology at the University of Liverpool. Michael's most recent research falls into two main areas: politics, government and the state; and the methodology and philosophy of research. The focus of that work includes the politics of accountability in different settings, with an emphasis on statecraft, market formation and the political economy of the local, as well as methodological practice in the social sciences.

Nicolette Makovicky is Lecturer in Russian and East European Studies at the University of Oxford. Her research considers the impact of socio-economic reforms and European Union integration policies on historically embedded modes of economic activity in Central Europe, including artisanal crafts and food production. She has a particular theoretical interest in processes of value creation, work ethics, entrepreneurialism, gender and citizenship in post-socialist society. Makovicky is the editor of *Neoliberalism, Personhood, and Postsocialism: Enterprising Selves in Changing Economies* (Ashgate, 2014) and co-editor of *Economies of Favour After Socialism* (University of Oxford Press, 2016).

Sitna Quiroz is a lecturer in the Study of Religion at Durham University. She is a social anthropologist and specialises in the study of religion, particularly of Christianity. She has carried out long-term ethnographic fieldwork in the Benin Republic, West Africa, and Mexico. She is currently preparing a monograph on her most recent research on Pentecostalism in the Benin Republic, which explores ruptures and continuities in kinship and gender relations, and their influence in people's everyday political and economic lives.

Balihar Sanghera is a Senior Lecturer in Sociology at the University of Kent's School of Social Policy, Sociology and Social Research. His main interests are political economy, social theory and ethics. His research explores how social class and power intertwine with the ethics of everyday life and social justice. Currently, he is writing papers on several research projects, including social class, charitable giving and philanthropic foundations in the UK and the rentier class, neoliberal judges and internal migrants in Kyrgyzstan. His papers have appeared in *Theory and Society*, *The Sociological Review*, *Cambridge Journal of Economics*, *International Sociology* and *Europe-Asia Studies*.

Andrew Sayer is Professor of Social Theory and Political Economy at Lancaster University. Over the last 15 years his work has focused on inequality and moral economy, and on ethics in everyday life. Recent books include *Why Things Matter to People: Social Science, Values and Ethical Life* (Cambridge University Press, 2011) and *Why We Can't Afford the Rich* (Policy Press, 2015).

Christopher S. Swader is an Associate Senior Lecturer with the Lund University Sociology Department. His recent book is entitled *The Capitalist Personality: Face-to-Face Sociality and Economic Change in the Post-Communist World* (Routledge, 2013). In recent years, he has developed projects on anomie in post-Soviet countries, on compensated dating and on the intersection between state violence, individual violence and gender polarization. He is currently planning a comparative multi-method investigation on loneliness in mega-cities. Overall he explores the connection between intimacy and normative order, and he has developed themes close to family sociology, economic sociology, anomie, the commodification of sex, post-socialism and the life course.

Steve Tombs is Professor of Criminology at the Open University. He has a long-standing interest in the incidence, nature and regulation of corporate and state crime and harm, and has published widely in these areas. His most recent publications are *Social Protection After the Crisis: Regulation Without Enforcement* (Policy Press, 2016) and, with David Whyte, *The Corporate Criminal: Why Corporations Must be Abolished* (Routledge, 2015). He has long worked closely with the Hazards movement in the UK, and is a Board Member and Trustee of INQUEST.

David Whyte is Professor of Socio-legal Studies at the University of Liverpool where he teaches and researches on the relationship between corporate power and law. His most recent publications are *How Corrupt is Britain?* (Pluto, 2015, ed.), *The Corporate Criminal* (Routledge, 2015, with Steve Tombs) and *The Mythology of Business* (Institute of Employment Rights, 2015). He is an Executive Committee member of the Institute of Employment Rights and an Advisory Board member of Corporate Watch.

Jörg Wiegratz is Lecturer in Political Economy of Global Development at the University of Leeds. He researches the political economy and moral economy of neoliberalism in Africa and elsewhere, with a focus on the topics of moral restructuring, economic fraud, anti-fraud measures and populism. In the past he has researched global value chains and industrial development, predominantly with an empirical focus on Uganda where he has worked as consultant and researcher. He is a member of the editorial working group of *Review of African Political Economy*; here, he coordinates the project on *Economic trickery, fraud and crime in Africa*. He is the author of Uganda's *Human Resource Challenge: Training, Business Culture and Economic Development* (Fountain Publishers, 2009) and *Neoliberal Moral Economy: Capitalism, Socio-cultural Change and Fraud in Uganda* (Rowman & Littlefield International, 2016), and co-editor of *Neoliberal Uganda* (Zed Books, forthcoming, with Giuliano Martiniello and Elisa Greco).

1 Neoliberalism, moral economy and fraud

David Whyte and Jörg Wiegratz

> [H]igher immorality is a systematic feature of the American elite; its general acceptance is an essential feature of the mass society.
>
> (C. Wright Mills, *The Power Elite*)

> Politicians can only take money because people picture their corruption as being altogether finer and nobler than it really is.
>
> (Berthold Brecht, *Threepenny Novel*)

Introduction

Various forms of fraud and corruption are not just present, but are widespread in the economies of both income-rich and income-poor countries. As this book goes to press, the Volkswagen defeat device scandal is the most widely publicised example of fraud in a key sector of the global economy. Yet, the automobile industry is only one of a number of industrial sectors, such as oil and gas, financial products, the arms industry and pharmaceuticals, in which fraud scandals have become commonplace (Braithwaite, 1984; Andvig, 1995; Chwastiak, 1998; Rosoff *et al.*, 2002; Briody, 2005; Qureshi *et al.*, 2012). Indeed, it is no exaggeration to say that many of the key business sectors in the global economy are rife with fraud. Certain practices and norms that many people in the Global North considered 'shocking' and 'unthinkable' only a while ago have become routinized in public life or have been institutionalised as the 'new normal' (Wiegratz, 2014; Whyte, 2015). This book brings a wide range of contributions together that show collectively how the practices of fraud and corruption are encouraged by a *moral* culture, i.e. a distinct set of ideas, norms and values that has social currency in contemporary capitalist societies.

That said, it is noteworthy that public and policy discussions of one of the most significant phenomena of pre- and post-crash capitalism – economic fraud – is barely informed by any empirical knowledge-base, particularly concerning the socio-cultural underpinning of fraud. Some studies do provide empirical evidence of this type (for example Whyte, 2007b; Wiegratz, 2010; Swader, 2013; Dewey, 2014), but the number of available studies is very small in comparison to the significance of the phenomenon. Moreover, the available material constitutes a very small fraction of the data that are produced and used – mostly by scientists based in the Global North – to discuss topics such as democracy and elections, political parties, security and terrorism, economic reform and structural adjustment, in terms often very narrowly prescribed by key state institutions and think tanks and thus supported via research and consultancy funding. But the failure to explore the incidence and production of corporate fraud *empirically* by much of the social sciences is not just a function of funding and priority dynamics 'outside' academia, but is also related to longer-term trends concerning how social sciences understand and research matters of the economy. The empirical study of economic practice (and its making) in modern capitalism, until recently, has been a marginal affair in a number of disciplines including political economy and sociology (for example Lie, 1997; Carrier, 1997; Carrier and Miller, 1998; Callon, 1998; Beckert, 2009), as the empirical study of corporate and white-collar crime generally has been (Tombs and Whyte, 2003).

There has clearly been a hesitation by the academic community in the North to study the crimes of the powerful – the practices of the economic and political establishment – in their own backyard rather than in distant places in the South. One reason for the lack of research data and debate on corporate fraud in the South is the almost exclusive focus of the international donor and aid community over the last two decades on matters of political corruption (as part of the concern with 'governance' and the state). Research agendas tend to be organized around dominant definitions that focus on the 'corruption of public office' (Wedel, 2015), and therefore leave off the radar the whole issue of private sector fraud, especially in everyday sectors such as health, education, food and agriculture. This situation has slightly changed recently given the string of revelations about financial sector fraud, tax evasion, production and trade of substandard goods, and official concerns about money laundering and 'terrorism financing'. Some of those issues are beginning to attract official attention; for instance the illicit financial flows agenda (www.uneca.org/iff). That said, for the purposes of this book, we adopt a broad definition of the term fraud: the use of deception to make an economic gain, a practice that thus harms those who are being defrauded or those who ultimately have to pay the costs of the fraud.

Yet, where research agendas have taken private sector fraud seriously, they tend to frame the problem from a highly partisan and epistemologically restrictive perspective. Mainstream debates in Western academic scholarship on the complex relationship between neoliberalism and fraud have tended to make a common, over-simplified, assumption. This assumption is that 'corruption' and 'fraud' are likely to diminish in the current, neoliberal, period as global markets 'liberalize' and become more 'open', 'competitive' and 'efficient', and polities adopt liberal forms of democracy, transparency and accountability. This line of argument supposes that eventually, the dynamics of liberal market and polity will punish 'wrong-doing' (fraudsters lose customers or voters) and thus reinforce incentives for honesty and accountability. Thus, one key contribution asserts that although in the short term, structural adjustment policies and the globalization of trade may – because of the 'openness' and transparency of economic liberalization – heighten perceptions of corruption in a given economy: '[t]he spread of democratization and market reforms should reduce corruption in the long run' (Ann Elliot, 1997: 176). The assumption that corruption and fraud are cured by more market discipline, and more structural adjustment – in other words, *more* neoliberal capitalism – has for many years been part of the common sense in much of what passes for academic literature on the subject (for example, Shleifer and Vishny, 1993; Rose-Ackerman, 1999) not to mention the intellectual output of international financial institutions (IFIs) (for a typical articulation of this position, see Stapenhurst and Kpundeh, 1999; and Abed and Davoodi, 2000).

Crucially, guarantees that counter-corruption measures are in place are now used prescriptively as a precondition of grant aid, debt relief or of membership of international bodies. Counter-corruption policy in this form is often imposed by the same international institutions (such as the World Bank and the United Nations Development Programme) (Shore and Haller, 2005; Le Billon, 2005) that advance structural adjustment policies that demand the removal of protective economic policies and encourage privatization and 'market' reform. This contemporary counter-corruption movement – and the more recent counter-fraud movement concerning for instance fake agro inputs and pharmaceuticals in some African countries (for the cases of Nigeria and Uganda, see e.g. Nandudu and Baguma, 2014; Tibyangye, 2015; Yeebo, 2015) – therefore involves a much larger enterprise that goes beyond the eradication of corruption in business and political life per se. Increasingly, this movement can be understood not only as a political-economic programme that demands restructuring of the state and economy in the South but also as a moral crusade that organizes international opposition to what is framed as non-mainstream or deviant economic practices carried out by particular actors. The world of counter-corruption for instance is, in Sampson's (2005: 129) terms, a 'stage in which moral projects are intertwined with money and power'. In other words, it is a place where political economy and moral economy intersect. The IFI agenda on corruption can therefore be read as an attempt to organize a consensus around the need to reform states and economies that are targeted for structural adjustment. Being against 'corruption' and 'fraud' (and by implication being against opaque markets and opaque relations between technocrats, politicians and business actors) allows state officials to construct a moral narrative that legitimates all manner of political interventions at local, national and global levels (Gupta, 2005).

Yet, in contra-distinction to the position that fraud is a residual effect of pre-neoliberal forms of capitalism or, in Eastern Europe, socialism, the apparent rapid rise in a range of business and consumer frauds in many countries can be explained simply as a direct consequence of the liberalization of market, the re-regulation of particular economic sectors and the restructuring of the state in line with IFI structural adjustment principles (for a review of the evidence, see Karstedt, 2015). As the chapters in this book collectively show, the assumption that fraud and corruption will be cured by more market discipline is decisively challenged by our real, lived experience of the rampant opportunities for old and new forms of bribery and deception that have flourished in liberalized economies.

The evidence assembled in this book therefore demands that we reject the hegemonic (and often racist) assumptions that: (1) fraud is a problem of only the Global South, i.e. of regions and countries that are not yet sufficiently capitalist (and for this read 'Westernised'); and (2) that the Global North sets the standards and is a force of clean business ethics and transparency around the world (Whyte, 2007a). In so doing, the chapters in this book collectively represent a way in to understanding and responding to fraud as a problem that is rooted in neoliberal capitalist economic relationships and in related political-economic and socio-cultural practices.

Neoliberalism's moral project

Neoliberalism is a contested concept that tries to make sense of an empirically varied reality. However, we view neoliberalism as an analytical category which describes a set of policies that that seek the creation of fully fledged market societies across the globe. As part of this aim, these policies encourage the marketization of all social relations, a general empowerment of capital in the form of large private corporations, and the corresponding restructuring of people's subjectivities, relationships and everyday practices (Harrison, 2005, 2010). Neoliberalism has been advanced via policy, programme and discourse (individual freedom, self-interest, free markets), and has usually triggered changes not only in the economy, but also polity, society and culture (Bush, 2007; Harvey, 2007; Mirowski, 2013). Importantly, 'neoliberalism' – that is the repercussion of neoliberal reform – becomes present and embodied especially in social practice and discourse (Harrison, 2010: 29). The process of neoliberal reform raises important questions related to the effect of neoliberalism on prevailing moral economies (Wiegratz and Cesnulyte, 2016): How do people in neoliberalized societies think about themselves and others, or their relationships with money? What set of social practices – as well as values and norms – is dominant, and why? What do people consider to be acceptable, proper, or necessary ways of earning a living, and treating others in the process?

This book analyses, in a wide range of different contexts, the process by which neoliberal reforms and resulting dynamics have changed not only the affected political economies but also respective moral economies. The book therefore asks what is regarded as acceptable and unacceptable, proper and improper, legitimate and illegitimate practice in contemporary societies, and whether there has been a recent change concerning notions of what is proper practice (Keller, 2006; Wiegratz, 2010)? Analytically, we perceive the phenomenon of fraud to be linked to the phenomenon of this neoliberal *moral* change. This moral change is closely linked to the political-economic change that neoliberalism brought about (Wiegratz, 2012). In that sense we understand contemporary fraud to be a phenomenon of both neoliberal moral economy and neoliberal political economy. This interaction in neoliberal society between political and moral economy – or the material and socio-cultural – and the resulting fostering of fraud will be analysed in this book.

Our book differs from dominant understandings of fraud that tend to project causal explanations that show deception and criminality to be a manifestation of the *weakening* of morals (due, for example, to the crowding out of nonmarket norms by market values; Sandel, 2012) or the *absence* of morals ('bankers have lost their moral compass'). Those position typically suggests that people who harm others through fraudulent practices have either 'lost' their values or have no morals, or that practices such as bribery and fraud 'undermine moral values' and produce 'moral costs' (Della Porta and Vannucci, 2012: 59).

In some of the least sophisticated analyses, it is assumed that in a battle between 'good' and 'evil', corruption is simply 'bad', or a pathological flaw or 'a symptom that something has gone wrong in the management of a state' (Rose-Ackerman, 1999: 9). For many analysts this flaw is made worse simply because academics find it difficult to intervene on the side of the 'good'. Thus, as Rose-Ackerman (2006: xiv) has noted regretfully, 'writing on corruption often stakes out a moral high ground, but economists are reluctant to sermonize about right or wrong'. For us, this is hardly the point. Economic and more broadly social practices are, for us, always supported empirically by a set of core moral understandings and claims advanced by social actors. And, together, the case studies in this book provide ample evidence of the moral economy that always stands somewhere in the shadows of fraud. This book thus conceives fraud as in part shaped by the acting out or operationalization of particular moral values and norms in a particular political economic context.

Counter to the dominant claims we find in much of the academic literature, then, we cannot assume that concepts of moral actor or moral economy automatically refer to pro-social practice, or our own, subjective, divisions between honest or 'good' and dishonest or 'bad' practice (Olivier de Sardan, 1999; Wiegratz, 2012). Fraudulent economic and political actors (e.g. fraudulent bankers, traders, peasants or politicians, and even those who are war criminals) construct what they do within a particular set of morals and norms. Rather than having no moral system to draw upon at all, fraudulent practices are guided by (interpretations of) particular values (say, personal success, materialism, enjoyment, power and self-direction) that for instance advance self-interest, require cutting corners and so on. Thus an oversimplified suggestion that a renewed focus on socially neutral 'morals' or 'values' will resolve the fraud problem makes little sense unless the content of the values and the link between values and political economy are specified.

Take the example of the banking sector in the US, the UK or Germany – riddled for years now by extensive and escalating fraud, or to use that analytically very ambiguous term, 'malpractice'. We learn very little about the specific dynamics of fraud in a neoliberal society if we continue to simply refer to the age-old explanations for such money-making methods: greed, selfishness, ruthlessness. We claim that the action logics and justifications, including moral logics that underpin fraud in banking and elsewhere are a lot more complex and nuanced, and an outcome of a longer-term, multi-layered, collective, social process – rather than the 'animal instincts' of a lone actor who 'messed up' and 'failed' (e.g. the society/community). Yet, very few studies have to date explored via qualitative research the dominant norms, values and practices related to these structures of routine fraud (e.g. Honegger *et al.*, 2010), let alone the political-economic and socio-cultural making of these norms, values and practices. It is this direction of enquiry that this book seeks to advance.

This book aims to show how, in a range of very different contexts, the neoliberal project is partly a project that provides moral leadership in contemporary capitalist societies, and is also a project that has triggered and facilitated moral transformation in those societies. Neoliberalism advances, directly and indirectly, certain moral values at the expense of others; moral values that, in turn, are conducive to fostering fraudulent motivation and practice (Wiegratz, 2010). For instance, the counter-corruption discussed above is a *moral* undertaking; it is a key source of legitimacy for IFIs and the dominant economies of the Global North in seeking the development and promotion of neoliberal social and economic policies.

The moral project provides hegemonic leadership to economic policies and practices, and a moral rationale for their coruscating social effects: the freeing of capital from societal constraints, the concentration of wealth and the deepening of poverty and inequality across neoliberal economies. One of the functions of this project is to provide a rationale and set of narratives that connect the macro structure of economics and politics to the everyday practices of various key actors, including politicians, bureaucrats, business executives, market traders and so on. This moral project is closely intertwined with the political-economic project of neoliberalism since both aim at, or bring about, the introduction and consolidation of fully fledged market societies across the globe (Harrison, 2005).

A higher morality?

That said, capitalism's normative structure does not just come about due to top-down processes – via a dominant 'project' – but also, amongst others, relevant local, grass-root and bottom-up dynamics that are prevalent in neoliberal societies. It is only by setting out a detailed understanding of what the dominant moralities and moral economies in neoliberal social formations are, how and why they have become dominant, how they work and what social consequences they bring about, that we can understand the routine and institutional nature of fraud in neoliberalized societies. In other words, we understand that neoliberal fraud is not simply, as some argue, an outcome of material desperation (aka, crimes of the poor), or the action of some errant, misbehaving, unscrupulous individuals (aka greedy bankers), but instead is the outcome of a broader process that has restructured the entire assemblage of power relations, accumulation imperatives, subjectivities, common sense and modes of thinking, as well as material incentives and disincentives in a way that makes fraud a more common practice across sectors and classes, in a range of countries. Thus, we argue that fraud is not merely an epiphenomenon but is a core feature of the structure of neoliberal capitalism.

The core argument, then, that runs through the chapters in this book, albeit using a range of very different approaches, is that the policies, principles, logics and practices underpinning neoliberalism, often dismissed by critical scholars as 'amoral' or 'immoral', have a *moral* core or character. To say that – and to describe and analyse this moral character of neoliberalism – is not to sanction or endorse this morality. Instead, to speak of and investigate the moral core of neoliberalism – this particular view of the world and set of action justifications – demands that we explore this key socio-cultural element of the current social order, show the political nature and socially harmful character of this moral core, and lay it open for discussion, critique and attack.

It is the recognition of this moral core – the recognition that all economies and actors are moral, in one way or another – that needs to be taken seriously since, as the chapters will show, the morality of neoliberalism is central to providing a credible basis for the *legitimacy* of policy development concerning both economy and society, and also for the (self-claimed) legitimacy and routine character of the business operations and practices of concern. Moreover, the morality of neoliberalism is able to confront other moralities and give impetus to a process of substantial and lasting moral change. It is a moral project that, we argue, has socially devastating consequences, in so far as the moral economy (in interaction with the political economy) of neoliberalism shapes the structures and practices of accumulation and making a living. In so far as this moral economy encourages the institutionalization of routine fraud and corruption in both the Global North and the Global South, it is a project that is not merely 'cultural', but is a key state-corporate strategy of power mongering in contemporary capitalist economies (Whyte, 2007b; Wiegratz and Cesnulyte, 2016).

The process of ensuring that corporate and political elites remain dominant in society has a deep cultural impact upon the way that powerful elites construct their normative worlds. Thus, according to C. Wright Mills, in his classic study, *The Power Elite*, the morality of the ruling class – their understanding of what is legitimate, acceptable, normal, good practice – is a morality that serves the interests of this class, rather than any general social or public interest. Yes, this morality *claims* (in public) to serve the general (public) interest: 'Every such naked interest, every new, unsanctioned power of corporation, farm bloc, labor union, and governmental agency that has risen in the past two generations has been clothed with morally loaded slogans. For what is not done in the name of the public interest?' (Wright Mills, 2000: 344).

In reality the morality of the ruling class reproduces very particular sets of norms and values in which 'the pursuit of the moneyed life is the commanding value' (Wright Mills, 2000: 346), a value that is projected in socially beneficial terms. It is a morality that, for Mills, remains concerned with how moral values are used – quite cynically and instrumentally – as a strategy of dominance by the power elite.

A genre of reportage that has become popular in revealing the culture of the finance sector in recent years has been the insider account. And it is apposite for our purposes here that very often those insider accounts are *moral* tales. Geraint Anderson in *Cityboy* consistently puts the loose morality of city traders in the context of government light-touch policy and an unmoderated economic system.

Yet at the same time, Anderson notes, city traders understand their industry's privileged status in policy as resulting from its social contribution. City traders believe their industry is left relatively untouched by regulation because 'it brings in shedloads of tax revenue for hospitals and schools' (Anderson, 2009: 396). Essentially, here we find a connection made between a certain world view (i.e. actor's perception and interpretation of the world operating around them) and notions of one's actions bringing about wider good results (for company, exchequer, common good etc.), action justifications and practice.

Seth Freedman's 'Binge Trading' develops a moral tale of excess that sacrifices collective human values in the pursuit of a hyper-individualised hedonism. He also reveals, in one fascinating discussion of the charitable works of city traders, how they construct their own moral universe (Freedman, 2009: 79–84). It is a moral universe where various good causes benefit from organized 'charitable trading days' in which traders donate their proceeds, and where traders' wives volunteer without payment for the charity of their choice. It becomes clear from Freedman's account that this, almost Victorian portrayal of philanthropy, is a significant source of self-justification for the astronomical commissions and obscenely lavish lifestyles of these traders and their families (see also Thompson, 2010). Again, here, money making and morality among these professionals are interlinked in all sorts of ways in the actual world that people live in and create at a cultural and economic level.

That said, those insider accounts penetrate the moral universe of key actors in the financial markets by describing the subculture of the City of London as one that is distinct and in various ways different from the general culture. Those accounts reveal value systems that are fundamentally separated and isolated from the value systems 'normal' people share. Key academic studies of the moral universe of the financial world approach the problem from a similar angle: as a subculture that is cut off and, though it is encouraged by government policy, regulation and a culture of impunity, has a moral compass that is not connected to the norms and values that ordinary people hold. Similarly, there are academic accounts that uncover the morality of the Wall Street trader in meticulous detail, but do not consider how those values are shared across the wider social body (for example, Ho, 2009).

What is missing from those insider accounts are detailed insights into how the dominant class bid to have their values, norms and moral justifications accepted more generally in popular and public debate and discourse; in Gramscian terms, how ideas can provide moral leadership to subdominant social classes as part of a more general process of hegemonic rule. The morals that guide the conduct of Wright Mills' elite, for example, constituted sets of values and norms that express desirable objectives and draw lines across what is acceptable and unacceptable, proper and improper, behaviour (i.e. common sense) for *all* social groups. For us, the norms and moral assertions about economic practices do not merely operate, in Wright Mills' terms, as a 'higher morality'; nor do they merely serve a cynical or instrumental function for corporate and government elites. But rather, sets of moral claims and assertions guide economic practices – for instance at the level of motivation and sense making – at every level of a given society. In this sense, morals in various shades can shape and change the cultures and practices of all social groups in every sphere of economic activity.

In banking, for example, dominant norms (moral, professional, social, operative etc.) can sanction exploitation, destructive and harmful trading practices: e.g. fleecing pensioners, mis-selling insurances, misinforming customers about risks, helping criminal organizations and individuals to transfer, wash and hide their money, eliminating rivals, deceiving a trading rival or rival company, in order to advance sales, take commissions and survive and prosper, to advance the power and wealth of oneself and/or one's own company and so on (Wiegratz 2012).

Further, as MacLennan (1997: 198) has noted as part of her inquiry into the culture of Wall Street traders:

> the ethnographer's inquiry into corporate corruption must also entertain questions pertaining to the market values of twenty-first century capitalist society. To what extent are corporate values mirror images of the market values that permeate social institutions in the wider society?

Elsewhere she has described how such values were critical to the rise of the corporate anti-regulation movement in the US (MacLennan, 2005). Specifically she has noted how the language of the market was used to encourage a way of thinking, a controlling process that translated societal values into market terms.

Here, we begin to explore the spectrum of forces and processes that advance moral change in capitalist society. The connections between the dominant values that are found in finance industry and other sections of society could only be insignificant if we accepted that the values of the city trader or the hedge fund manager are produced solely by the subculture they operate in. But clearly they are not. Value systems are learned in a range of social institutions and human relationships: at home, in connection with peers, in schooling, media, in commercial places like supermarkets, shopping malls and so on, as well as in the workplace. Moreover, the value systems that come to dominate particular workplaces also have their origins in a wider set of social relationships.

Moral economy and class contradiction

In this context, we should not underestimate the unrivalled cultural impact of the corporation (Tombs and Whyte, 2015). In his account of the development of modern corporate capitalism, Johnson (2010), argues that the "commercial morality" that is dominant in modern day financial systems was crucially shaped by the evolution of a particular model of corporate capitalism in the 19th century. It is only by understanding the dilemmas and ambiguities that were created by a new model of corporate capitalism that we can understand the time-space specific dominance of particular norms and values in capitalist societies and related matters of moral change (see also Carrier, 1997).

It is for this reason that the book explores how cultural norms and values spread through a given society, and not merely how they develop in a particular elite subculture. We are therefore not *merely* interested in the subcultures that exist within particular sectors of the economy, no matter how central to the economy those sectors are. We are interested in a much broader set of questions. What makes values and norms – especially those that are connected to the political economy – socially dominant in capitalist society? How do dominant values and norms in a given society reach into particular social relationships and institutions? How far are those dominant values universal or fragmented across a given society? What is the link between dominant values and norms and fraudulent (and thus other harming) practices; and how does social class shape related morals and practice? How easy can alternative sets of values be developed to challenge the dominant moralities? The concern of this book is to investigate these questions in the realm of economy, the sphere where a lot is at stake for all sorts of people; the sphere that connects fortune and misery, opulence and poverty, flourishing and suffering in a highly specific and human way.

As the preceding section has begun to argue, all actors – regardless of the social group or social class they belong to – are moral actors (Polanyi, 1957; Thompson, 1971; Watson, 2005); their identities, motives, actions and relationships have a necessary moral connotation and are guided by specific sets of norms. Any economic practice – not just those in the elite corporate world – can be related analytically to notions of what constitutes acceptable or unacceptable practice, and to standards of interaction regarding others' welfare (for example, the competitor who does not get the contract; the pensioner who loses pension to due to fraudulent banking practices; or the road user who gets killed in an accident because the road built by fraudulent contractors is of poor standard).

Analytically speaking, we can assume that every economic practice is underpinned by a specific action justification that has some sort of moral connotation. Thus, for instance, it is justifiable to use substandard materials in my construction business – and thus to cut costs and increase profits – because I need to feed my family, be a providing parent and spouse, and make my loved ones proud because of my business success. Self-interest or the need to feed the family might be invoked when justifying actions of taking advantage of a vulnerable person or overcharging someone. Thus, in a descriptive-interpretative analysis, the existence of fraudulent (and what some regard as immoral) practice does not signal the absence of moral norms but, on the contrary, signifies the presence of specific moral views, norms, priorities and judgements concerning acceptable practice and a standard of the treatment of others. In other words, fraudsters have a moral compass too (Wiegratz, 2015a, 2015b).

The study of moral economy is typically set up as the study of pro-social values and practices such as care, solidarity, reciprocity and decency. This emphasis on 'good' values and practices is partly due to the scholarly origin of the term moral economy in the study of the (customary) moral views of subaltern classes. It was actually coined by E.P. Thompson (1971) and further popularized by James Scott (1979), who analysed the moral expectations and priorities concerning proper economic order, relationships and practices of 'the poor' in eighteenth century England and 'peasants' in South-East Asia, respectively. Thompson directly referred to 'the moral economy of the poor' and analysed their actions to defend and keep socially relevant their customary economic practices in the face of pressures on the moral order brought about by the rise of capitalist economy. His study showed how economic relationships and practices are shaped by sets of class-specific norms that bring about particular understandings of what constitutes appropriate, acceptable and good practice. There can be contestation over what is acceptable practice, and this conflict can be coloured by class contradictions. Thus, matters of the economy – ranging from economic order, relationships and practices to outcomes including the distribution of wealth, poverty and harm – have a *moral* character that is subject to change and conflict, especially in times of economic crisis and change (see also Sayer, 2010; Wiegratz and Cesnulyte, 2016).

Particularly apposite in this account was Thompson's observation that, as capitalism advances, profiteering from the vulnerability of others, and crisis in society more generally, had to be naturalized so as expand and reproduce a capitalist economy and society. During the time of Thompson's 'crowd' there was still 'a deeply-felt conviction that prices *ought*, in times of dearth, to be regulated, and that the profiteer put himself outside of society' (Thompson, 1971: 112, italics in original). Intimidating profiteering and reigning in on 'extortionate mechanisms' was important because these were existential matters: 'high prices meant swollen bellies and sick children whose food was coarse bread made up from stale flour' (Thompson, 1971: 134, cited in Wiegratz and Cesnulyte, 2016). The fact that price regulation is hardly existent in the moral economy of today's global capitalism shows that Thompson identified a key trend that is advanced by powerful actors in political economy: the normalization of both, maximizing the exploits of one's market power regardless of social consequences, and profiteering from other's vulnerability. Those points offer insights that can be used to study today's moral economies, for instance, the idea that the moral economy of the dominant classes aimed to rehabilitate and bring the profiteer back into acceptable society. More generally, a particular type of moral change and resulting moral structure – with all sorts of characteristics regarding what and who is good and bad – is in the interest of dominant classes.

Conclusion

The analytical term moral economy is nowadays adopted to a wider range of subject matters, including the moral views of various social actors and the moral dimensions of various industries, professions or social phenomena (Edelman, 2012). Empirical studies of moral economies of neoliberalism remain rare though. That said, we can find recent indications of a rising and systematic interest in the broad subject of *moral economy* in anthropology, sociology, economics and moral psychology (Gintis *et al.*, 2006; Heintz, 2009; Doris and the Moral Psychology Research Group, 2010; Hitlin and Vaisey, 2010; Sayer, 2011; Fassin, 2012). Yet, qualitative research that investigates the moral economy of capitalist class relations remains rare (Mandel and Humphrey, 2002; Browne and Milgram, 2009).

Some scholars have given attention to the issue of moral change in rapidly transforming societies, especially in formerly socialist countries and regions (Sanghera *et al.*, 2006; Zigon, 2010; Swader, 2013). In area studies too, there is an emerging research into moral economy dynamics; regarding Africa, studies explore the moral economy of corruption for instance (Olivier de Sardan, 1999). Notably, the term moral economy is now used to study not only the moral grammar of 'good', i.e. pro-social behaviour but also harmful or deceptive practice, e.g. the moral views and logics of violent or fraudulent actors (e.g. Olivier de Sardan, 1999; Bouhana and Wikström, 2008; Wiegratz, 2010; Karandinos *et al.*, 2014).

With this book we seek to move beyond the dominant understanding of the term moral economy that has restricted its application mostly to cases of pro-social (aka customary and traditional) values, relationships and practices – that are typically set up analytically in opposition to immoral/amoral capitalism. We see the study of moral economy as generally concerned with social practices (from 'good' to 'bad') and the moral norms, beliefs, evaluations and priorities, as well as values, emotions and material structures that underpin them (Sayer, 2007; Hann, 2010; Wiegratz and Cesnulyte, 2016). We conceptualize the term moral economy in wide terms: as a context (i.e. time and space) specific set of social actors that are, directly and indirectly, in an economic relationship to each other that connects their respective lives and thus their welfare (i.e. economic fortunes and misfortunes). These relationships and welfare interconnections (e.g. benefit–harm pattern) are embedded in a particular social and political setting, including power structure. Of course, different actors in a moral economy have divergent power resources. There are some who can advance their moral views concerning economic order and practice better than others and thus have more influence regarding the actual outcome of prevaling practice in a given moral economy. Power asymmetry and inter-actor conflicts regarding moral issues of the economy are thus another key element of our schematic moral economy (Wiegratz, 2016).

In this book we seek to trace what can be called the neoliberalization of fraud. In doing so, we explore the way in which neoliberal policies, reforms, material practices and transformations have left a particular 'neoliberal footprint' or character that has shaped the structure and form of the moral economies of fraud and corruption. Few social scientists have traced key processes related to this aspect of neoliberal societal engineering – and its drivers, characteristics and repercussions – via extensive empirical studies.

Together, the contributions to this book therefore seek to contribute more widely to an understanding of the socio-cultural dynamics, conflicts and struggles around the production and distribution of wealth and harm in neoliberal society, and to uncover a key aspect of its cultural political economy. The book thus complements theoretical and desk-based analyses of the moral characteristics of neoliberal theory, ideology and society (e.g., Sayer 2007, 2011; Sandel, 2012; Rodrigues, 2013) that have recently emerged in the social science and public debates. For the reasons spelt out in this introduction we aim to open up the terrain of analysis on matters of moral economy, fraud and neoliberalism in significant ways. We hope to challenge a number of mainstream positions in the scholarship on related matters and thus encourage more debate and scholarship in future. We are convinced that this can yield better understandings of neoliberal capitalism in particular and the human condition in general.

References

Abed, G. and Davoodi, H. (2000) *Corruption, Structural Reforms, and Economic Performance in the Transition Economies*, IMF Working Paper No. 00/132, New York: International Monetary Fund Fiscal Affairs Department.

Andvig, J. (1995) Corruption in the North Sea oil industry: issues and assessments, *Crime, Law and Social Change*, vol. 23, no. 4: 289–313.

Ann Elliot, K. (1997) Corruption as an international policy problem: overview and recommendations, in Ann Elliot, K (ed.) *Corruption and the Global Economy*, Washington: Institute for International Economics.

Anderson, G. (2009) *Cityboy: Beer and Loathing in the Square Mile*, London: Headline.

Beckert, J. (2009) The social order of markets, *Theory and Society*, vol. 38, no. 3: 245–269.

Bouhana, N. and Wikström, P.-O. (2008) *Theorising Terrorism: Terrorism as Moral Actions*, London: Jill Dando Institute.

Braithwaite, J. (1984) *Corporate Crime in the Pharmaceutical Industry*, London: Routledge and Kegan Paul.

Brecht, B. (1979) *Threepenny Novel*, Harmondsworth, Middlesex: Penguin.

Briody, D. (2005) *The Halliburton Agenda: The Politics of Oil and Money: The Politics of Oil and Money*, New York: Briody.

Browne, K.E. and Milgram, B.L. (2009) *Economics and Morality: Anthropological Approaches*, Society for Economic Anthropology Monographs, Plymouth: Alta Mira Press.

Bush, R. (2007) *Poverty and Neoliberalism: Persistence and Reproduction in the Global South*, London: Pluto.

Callon, M. (1998) Introduction: The embeddedness of economic markets in economics, in Callom, M. (ed.) *The Laws of the Markets*, Oxford: Blackwell.

Carrier, J. (ed.) (1997) *Meanings of the Market: the free market in Western culture*, Oxford: Berg.

Carrier, J.G. and Miller, D. (eds) (1998) *Virtualism: A New Political Economy*, Oxford: Berg.

Chwastiak, M. (1998) Star wars at the bottom line: The accounting forum for defense contractors, *Accounting, Organizations and Society*, vol. 23, no. 4: 343–360.

Dewey, M. (2014) *Crisis and the Emergence of Illicit Markets: A Pragmatist View on Economic Action outside the Law*, MPIfG Discussion Paper 14/6, Köln: MPIfG.

Della Porta, D. and Vannucci, A. (2012) *The Hidden Order of Corruption: an institutional approach*, Farnham, Surrey: Ashgate.

Doris, J. and the Moral Psychology Research Group (2010) *The Moral Psychology Handbook*, Oxford: Oxford University Press.

Edelman, M. (2012) E.P. Thompson and moral economies, in D. Fassin (ed.) *A Companion to Moral Anthropology*, Malden: Wiley-Blackwell.

Fassin, D. (ed.) (2012) *A Companion to Moral Anthropology*, Malden: Wiley-Blackwell.

Freedman, S. (2009) *Binge Trading: the real inside story of cash, cocaine and corruption in the City*, London: Penguin.

Gintis, H., Boyd, R. and Fehr, E. (eds) (2006) *Moral Sentiments and Material Interests: The Foundations of Cooperation in Economic Life*, Chicago: MIT Press.

Gupta, A. (2005) Narrating the state of corruption, in Haller, D. and Shore, P. (eds) *Corruption: anthropological perspectives*, London: Pluto.

Hann, C. (2010) Moral economy, in K. Hart, J.-L. Laville and A.D. Cattani (eds) *The Human Economy*, Cambridge: Polity.

Harrison, G. (2005) Economic faith, social project, and a misreading of African society: the travails of neoliberalism in Africa, *Third World Quarterly*, vol. 26, no. 8: 1303–1320.

Harrison, G. (2010) *Neoliberal Africa: The Impact of Global Social Engineering*, London: Zed Books.

Harvey, D. (2007) *A Brief History of Neoliberalism*, London: Oxford University Press.

Heintz, M. (ed.) (2009) *The Anthropology of Moralities*, Oxford: Berghahn Books.

Hitlin, S. and Vaisey, S (eds) (2010) *Handbook of the Sociology of Morality*, New York: Springer.

Ho, K. (2009) *Liquidated: An Ethnography of Wall Street*, Durham, North Carolina: Duke University Press.

Honegger, C., Neckel, S. and Magnin, C. (2010) *Strukturierte Verantwortungslosigkeit. Berichte aus der Bankenwelt*, Berlin: Suhrkamp.

Johnson, P. (2010) *Making the Market: Victorian Origins of Corporate Capitalism*, Cambridge: Cambridge University Press.

Karandinos, G., *et al.* (2014) The moral economy of violence in the US inner city, *Current Anthropology*, vol. 55, no. 1: 1–22.

Karstedt, S. (2015) Charting Europe's moral economies: citizens, consumers, and the crimes of everyday life, in van Erp, J, Huisman, W. and Vande Walle, G. (eds) *The Routledge Handbook of White-Collar and Corporate Crime in Europe*, London: Routledge.

Keller, B. (2006) The development of obligations and responsibilities in cultural context, in Smith, L. and Vonèche, J. (eds) *Norms in Human Development*, London: Cambridge University Press.

Le Billon, P. (2005) Corruption, reconstruction and oil governance in Iraq, *Third World Quarterly*, vol. 26, no. 4–5: 685–703.

Lie, J. (1997) Sociology of markets, *Annual Review of Sociology*, vol. 23: 341–360.

Mandel, R. and Humphrey, C. (eds) (2002) *Markets and Moralities – Ethnographies of Post-socialism*, Oxford: Berg.

MacLennan, C. (1997) Democracy under the influence of cost-benefit analysis in the United States, in Carrier, J (ed.) *Meanings of the Market: The Free Market in Western Culture*, Oxford: Berg.

MacLennan, C. (2005) Corruption in corporate America: Enron – before and after, in Haller, D. and Shore, C. (eds) *Corruption: Anthropological Perspectives*, London: Pluto.

Mirowski, P. (2013) *Never Let a Serious Crisis Go to Waste: How Neoliberalism Survived the Financial Meltdown*, London: Verso.

Nandudu, P. and Baguma, R. (2014) Government moves to curb fake agro-inputs, *New Vision* 9 July 2014 www.newvision.co.ug/news/657340-government-moves-to-curb-fake-agro-inputs

Olivier de Sardan, J.-P. (1999) A moral economy of corruption in Africa? *The Journal of Modern African Studies*, vol. 37, no. 1: 25–52.

Polanyi, K. (1957) [1944] *The Great Transformation*, Boston, MA: Beacon.

Qureshi, Z., Sartor, O., Xirasagar, S., Liu, Y. and Bennett, C. (2012) Pharmaceutical fraud and abuse in the United States, *Archives of Internal Medicine*, vol. 171, no. 16: 1503–1506.

Rodrigues, J. (2013) The political and moral economies of neoliberalism: Mises and Hayek, *Cambridge Journal of Economics*, vol. 37, no. 5: 1001–1017.

Rose-Ackerman, S. (1999) *Corruption and Government: Causes, Consequences and Reform*, Cambridge: Cambridge University Press.

Rose-Ackerman, S. (2006) Introduction and overview, in Rose-Ackerman, S. (ed.) *International Handbook of the Economics of Corruption*, Cheltenham: Edward Elgar.

Rosoff, S., Pontell, H. and Tillman, R. (2002) *Profit Without Honor: White-Collar Crime and the Looting of America*, 2nd ed., Upper Saddle River, NJ: Prentice Hall.

Sampson, S. (2005) Integrity warriors: global morality and the anticorruption movement in the Balkans, in Haller, D. and Shore, P. (eds) *Corruption: anthropological perspectives*, London: Pluto.

Sanal, A. (2011) *New Organs Within Us: Transplants and the Moral Economy*, Durham: Duke University Press.

Sandel, M. (2012) *What Money Can't Buy: The Moral Limits of Markets*, London: Allen Lane.

Sanghera, B., Ilyasov, A. and Satybaldieva, E. (2006) Understanding the moral economy of post-Soviet societies: an investigation into moral sentiments and material sentiments in Kyrgyzstan, *International Social Science Journal*, vol. 58: 715–727.

Sayer, A. (2007) Moral economy as critique, *New Political Economy*, vol. 12, no. 2: 261–270.

Sayer, A. (2010) Class and morality, in Hitlin, S. and Vaisey, S. (eds) *Handbook of the Sociology of Morality*, New York: Springer.

Sayer, A. (2011) *Why Things Matter to People: Social Science, Values and Ethical Life*, Cambridge: Cambridge University Press.

Scott, J.C. (1979) *The Moral Economy of the Peasant: Rebellion and Subsistence in Southeast Asia*, New Haven: YUP.

Shore, P. and Haller, D. (2005) Sharp practice: anthropology and the study of corruption, in Haller, D. and Shore, P. (eds) *Corruption: Anthropological Perspectives*, London: Pluto.

Stapenhurst, R. and Kpundeh, S. (eds) (1999) *Curbing Corruption: Toward a Model for Building National Integrity*, Washington D.C.: The World Bank.

Swader, C.S. (2013) *The Capitalist Personality: Face-To-Face Sociality and Economic Change in the Post-Communist World*, New York: Routledge.

Thompson, E.P. (1971) The moral economy of the English crowd in the eighteenth century, *Past and Present*, vol. 50: 76–136.

Thompson, V. (2010) *Gross Misconduct: My Year of Excess in the City*, London: Simon and Schuster.

Tibyangye, O. (2015) Progress in fight against fake seeds, *Daily Monitor*, 9 September, www.monitor.co.ug/Magazines/Farming/-Progress-fight-against-fake-seeds-/-/689860/2862736/-/7iqmu2z/-/index.html

Tombs, S. and Whyte, D. (2003) Unmasking the crimes of the powerful: establishing some rules of engagement, in Tombs, S. and Whyte, D. (eds) *Unmasking the Crimes of the Powerful: Scrutinising States and Corporations*, New York: Peter Lang.

Tombs, S. and Whyte, D. (2015) *The Corporate Criminal: Why the Corporation Must be Abolished*, London: Routledge.

Watson, M. (2005) *Foundations of International Political Economy*, Basingstoke: Palgrave.

Wedel, J. (2015) High priests and the gospel of anti-corruption, *Challenge*, vol. 58, no. 1: 4–22.

Whyte, D. (2007a) Hire an American! Tyranny and corruption in occupied Iraq, *Social Justice*, vol. 35, no. 4: 153–168.

Whyte D. (2007b) The crimes of neo-liberal rule in occupied Iraq, *British Journal of Criminology*, vol. 47, no. 2: 177–195.

Whyte, D. (2015) Introduction, in Whyte, D. (ed.) *How Corrupt is Britain?* London: Pluto.

Wiegratz, J. (2010) Fake capitalism? The dynamics of neoliberal moral restructuring and pseudo-development: the case of Uganda, *Review of African Political Economy*, vol. 37, no 124: 123–137.

Wiegratz, J. (2012) The neoliberal harvest: the proliferation and normalisation of economic fraud in a market society, in Winlow, S. and Atkinson, R. (eds) *New Directions in Crime and Deviancy*, London: Routledge.

Wiegratz, J. (2014) The arrival of the New Normal, *Le Monde diplomatique*, 9 April.

Wiegratz, J. (2015a) The New Normal: moral economies in the 'Age of Fraud', in Whyte, D. (ed.) *How Corrupt is Britain?*, London: Pluto.

Wiegratz, J. (2015b) Bankers have a moral compass, it just may not look like yours, *The Conversation*, 3 March.

Wiegratz, J. (2016) *Neoliberal Moral Economy: Capitalism, Socio-cultural Change and Fraud in Uganda*, London: Rowman & Littlefield International.

Wiegratz, J. and Cesnulyte, E. (2016) Money talks: moral economies of earning a living in neoliberal East Africa, *New Political Economy*, 21(1), 1–25.

Wright Mills, C. (2000) *The Power Elite*, Oxford: Oxford University Press.

Yeebo, Y. (2015) The African startup using phones to spot counterfeit drugs: a Ghanaian entrepreneur thinks he has the answer to Africa's fake medicine problem, *Bloomberg*, 31 July, 2015, www.bloomberg.com/news/features/2015-07-31/the-african-startup-using-phones-to-spot-counterfeit-drugs

Zigon, J. (2010) *Making the New Post-Soviet Person: Narratives of Moral Experience in Contemporary Moscow*, Leiden: Brill Publishing.

2 Economic wrong and economic debate in the neoliberal era

James G. Carrier

Economic wrong-doing doubtless has been around for as long as some people have had things that other people want. To say that this has always been with us is not, however, to say that the form it takes and the ways that people think about it have always been the same.

Until fairly recently, the form of economic wrong-doing that attracted the most attention was bribery. Commonly, bribery was seen to characterise the world beyond the modern West. It was a feature of what used to be called the Third World, 'a pathology endemic to "backward" developing countries' (Shore, 2004, p. 36), and of the former Second World of post-socialist countries, still suffering the consequences of the old command economy (see Wedel, 2012, pp. 454–55). Those areas are easy to identify, for they are the ones coloured deep red on Transparency International's world corruption map. This was a comforting occidentalist (Carrier, 1995b) view of the West as the seat of probity, coupled with an orientalist (Said, 1978) view of the rest as lands of the venal and self-serving.

However, that comfort turned cold with the turmoil that began in the financial markets in 2007 and the turmoil in the global economy, the Great Recession, that quickly followed. Those events suggested that economic probity may not, in fact, reign so thoroughly in the West, and they did so in a way that cast doubt on the wisdom of the neoliberalism that had dominated much economic thinking and policy since the closing decades of the twentieth century. Moreover, because newspaper stories told us regularly of activities that seemed dubious at best but were legal, as well as of activities that seemed illegal but led to no prosecutions, those events raised questions about what 'right' and 'wrong' in the economic sphere might mean. As a consequence, it seems appropriate here to use 'deviance' to describe both economic crime and wrong-doing. That is because the idea of deviance reminds us that crime and wrong need not be the same, that different sets of people can define different sorts of things as wrong for different reasons and that defining crime, the province of government, is a function of the political process.

I said that the financial turmoil of 2007 and its aftermath raised doubts not only about the assumed economic probity of the West, but also about the wisdom of neoliberalism as a form of economic thought and a basis for economic policy. Those doubts spring from the fact that neoliberalism revolves around the idea of the free market. This in turn implies an assumption that when markets are fairly free and people can act as they chose, they will be fairly honest in their dealings with each other.

The words of Alan Greenspan indicate that, at least in retrospect, this assumption looks shaky. Greenspan was a strong neoliberal, and in his tenure as the head of the Federal Reserve in the US in the years before 2007 he was influential in shaping government economic policy to bring it into line with his neoliberal orientation. Testifying before a House committee, he expressed his 'shocked disbelief' (Andrews, 2008) at the mess that American financial institutions made of things when left to their own devices. Instead of the Western probity that both neoliberalism and the common view of corruption assumed, there turned out to be economic deviance on an industrial scale, especially in the financial sector. The US and many other Western countries paid heavily for it.

Accounting for deviance

As Whyte and Wiegratz note in the first chapter in this volume, there is a common view that people use to account for that sort of deviance, one that invokes the image of the rotten apple in a barrel of otherwise healthy ones. It holds that deviants are people who are deficient, for they lack a moral compass. That view is illustrated, and justified, by a tale told about a famous American economic deviant, Willie Sutton, who was renowned as a bank robber. When asked why he robbed banks, it is reported that he replied: 'Because that's where the money is'. It is illustrated and justified as well by Nick Leeson, who fits the image of an important type of rotten apple in the financial world, the rogue trader. He worked at Barings, a British merchant bank, in the 1990s, and his lies about the losses he made trading with other people's money brought the bank down (Stevenson, 1995).

This view is attractive for many reasons. Not the least of these is its individualistic orientation, which resonates with important elements of Anglo-American thought and of neoliberalism, as well as the neoclassical economics that is its intellectual foundation. However, the deviant economic practices revealed since 2007 indicate that such a view is simplistic to the point of being misleading. That is because its focus on individuals ignores the fact that individuals live in a social world that makes it more or less likely that they will deviate. One reason this is so is that people's values are shaped by their socialisation, so that they will vary in what they see as proper and what as wrong. Another reason is that the different social situations in which people find themselves will make it more or less difficult to behave properly.

It is, then, inadequate to approach economic deviance as an individual fact, a fact about one person or another, in the manner of the rotten apple. While there are such apples, we need also to approach economic deviance as a social fact, a fact about the social world. Such an approach went out of fashion in many branches of the social sciences in the closing decades of the twentieth century (see Carrier, 2012a), which means that many are likely to have forgot that we have long had the intellectual resources for such an approach. For instance, well over a century ago Emile Durkheim provided one such resource, in his consideration of a different deviant act, suicide (1951 [1897]). In that work, he said that the likelihood that people will commit suicide is a function of the situation in which they find themselves, especially the degree to which it encourages people to conform to the social values that condemn suicide.

Forty years later, Robert Merton (1938) applied Durkheim's approach in *Suicide* to another form of deviance. He did so when he considered economic deviance in terms of the relationship between two values that are common in American society. One of these reflects the group: it is good to play by society's rules and conform to people's expectations in one's endeavours. The other reflects the individual: it is good to make money through one's own efforts. Merton argued that the likelihood of economic deviance is a function of the relative strength of these two values, and especially of the degree to which their relative strength is different from what is conventional. It may be, for instance, that in some groups in society those values have strengths that are different from what they have more generally. Equally, it may be that their relative strengths are affected by extraordinary events that affect a number of sections of society. In either case, the result is that sets of people will be more likely to think and act in their economic lives in ways that appear deviant to more conventional people in more conventional times. Such thinking and acting is the sort of thing that John Maynard Keynes referred to as the animal spirits that move market traders. It is also the sort of thing a neighbour of mine referred to when he spoke of the bigger fool theory: however much one pays for a house in a booming market, there is always a bigger fool who you can sell your house to for more.

This view helps us begin to make sense of the surprising amount of economic deviance among firms in the financial sector that occurred during the bubble in the housing market in the US that preceded, and helped bring about, the economic turmoil that began in 2007 (for an extended discussion, see Lewis, 2011). I want to show how that view can help in making sense. In doing so, I do not claim to offer a thorough, much less definitive, analysis. Rather, I seek only to sketch the general outline of what such a view might reveal.

Prior to that turmoil, there was a lot of questionable activity in the financial sector, but what attracted the most attention was the issuing of mortgages, the bundling of them together into collateralised debt obligations (CDOs) and the certification of those CDOs by rating agencies. After the bubble burst, it became apparent that some mortgages were being issued without verifying that the would-be borrower earned enough money to make the mortgage payments or that the property was worth what that borrower claimed. Appropriately, these were called 'liar loans' and a number of companies issued them (Corkery and Protess, 2014; Morgenson, 2014), though Countrywide Financial was renowned for doing so (Morgenson, 2012). The resulting CDOs were complex to the point of being opaque, even to those who sold them. However, they were given good marks by the rating agencies, which were paid by the firms that wanted to sell them and which seemed happy to do what those firms wanted, which was to make assumptions that would justify those good marks (Krugman, 2010; Norris, 2014).

In more dispassionate times, these sorts of activities would look foolhardy and wrong. Who, after all, would want to issue a mortgage without being confident that the borrower is likely to be able to repay the loan and that the property that serves as collateral is worth enough to pay off the balance if the borrower defaults? However, for those in the financial side of the housing sector, the bubble in which they occurred was a time of something that Alan Greenspan (1996) had warned us about earlier, 'irrational exuberance'. It seemed that people were doing extraordinary things and getting richer and richer and no one was getting hurt. The old rules, that is, seemed to make less and less sense. And because this was a social phenomenon, it had social corollaries that justified and even encouraged that economic deviance.

One of those was that firms that wanted to maintain their reputation and income were under pressure to continue to make deals even if they would have hesitated to do so in more conventional circumstances. Citibank was heavily involved in CDOs and similar instruments, and when those were beginning to look problematic the head of Citibank's parent company, Charles O. Prince, captured that competitive pressure when he said: 'As long as the music is playing, you've got to get up and dance' (Dealbook, 2007). Another social corollary was the spread of ideas that justified those activities and the wealth that they produced. One such idea was that those in the financial sector could see things that ordinary people could not, because they were extraordinarily intelligent (Ho, 2009, Chapters 1, 2). Related to this was the idea that what people in the sector were doing was more important than ordinary people understood. That is because it was central to the rational allocation of capital and the benefits that would result. As the head of Goldman Sachs, Lloyd Blankenfein, put it, they were 'Doing God's work' (Dealbook, 2009).

Like Durkheim before him, Merton treated deviance as a social fact, arguing that in extraordinary times people are more prone to behave in extraordinary ways, and so deviate from the ordinary rules. As well, of course, in such times people are unusually receptive to ideas and attitudes, like the need to keep dancing and the doing of God's work, that justify that deviation. The bubble in the housing market was an extraordinary moment. I have indicated how Merton's framework can help us to make sense of the economic deviance in the financial sector that accompanied it, and do so without recourse to rotten apples.

Economic deviance and economic debate

What Merton had to say points to more than how economic deviance can be approached as a social fact. In addition, it points to a distinction between two realms of contemporary societies, which I shall call the economic and the social. These two realms are both objective aspects of life and cultural understandings of them (see Carrier, 2012b, pp. 3–7). For Merton, the rules of the group that people are expected to follow are an aspect of the social realm and the activities by which people acquire wealth are an aspect of the economic.

The nature of that relationship is important for understanding economic deviance. Perceiving an economic activity as deviance is an assessment of an aspect of the economic realm in terms of an aspect of the social realm. Similarly, making that assessment stick, perhaps by embodying it in law, reflects the relative strengths of those two realms in society. As should be clear, Merton's model assumes that the relationship is likely to vary over the course of time and across groups. In this assumption, Merton drew once more from Durkheim, this time from his *The Division of Labour in Society* (Durkheim, 1984 [1893]). That was Durkheim's sustained consideration of the relationship between the nature of economic activity, in this case the division of labour, and the nature of moral systems, including their institutional force. Durkheim argued that increasing the division of labour leads to increasing fragmentation of the moral system, and this process is associated with a decline in its institutional force: criminal law, which he said expresses shared moral values, gives way to civil law, especially contract law. The latter is a process concerned with assuring that people are compensated if others fail to fulfil their agreements with them or, in modern commercial parlance, with making people whole.

This aspect of Merton's approach can be applied usefully to economic deviance in the time of neoliberal ascendancy. That is because the rise of neoliberalism late in the twentieth century was attended by changes in those social and economic values and relationships, as well as by conscious efforts to bring about such changes. That rise was associated with assertions of the virtue of free markets and market rationality, and with efforts to extend those markets and that rationality into areas of life and society where hitherto they had been fairly unimportant. Similarly, it was associated with assertions that people need to rely more on themselves and less on social and political institutions and relationships, and with efforts to induce that self-reliance by undercutting those institutions and relationships. In some ways, however, those changes look more like the return to something old than the advocacy of something new. Attending to those changes, both the old and the new, helps make sense of what people were doing in the boom years before the bubble burst, and of reactions to it.

The predominant political-economic orientation in Western societies at the end of the Second World War was broadly that of Keynesian macroeconomics, an orientation that is an important part of what some call Fordism. Keynes and his followers saw their job as learning about the nature and processes of a country's economic system, and saw the job of government as using the resulting knowledge to see if there were policies that could make things better for the citizenry.

Keynesianism became ascendant during the Great Depression, but by the 1950s it began to be challenged by those who argued for a return to the older classical and marginalist view (Cockett, 1994), with 'neoclassical economics' being the common name for the resurrected economics and 'neoliberalism' being the common name for the resurrected political orientation associated with it. The prefix that they share indicates that they are not the same as their ancestral forms from the nineteenth century, but it also indicates that they had much in common with them (important elements of which are described in Carrier, 1997).

Those older forms of economics began to emerge in Britain late in the eighteenth century, a period that saw the continued development and spread of a capitalist market, with increasing, and increasingly centralised, manufacturing and increasing long-distance trade (Carrier, 1995a, pp. 63–69). One intellectual accompaniment to this was the Scottish Enlightenment, and many who were part of it argued that material and moral progress would come if the economic and social realms of life were untangled and kept separate, for that would allow people freedom in both their economic and social dealings (e.g. Silver, 1990). The result would be not just greater prosperity. In addition, the passions and constraints that characterised the old order would be replaced by 'la douce commerce' in the economic realm (Hirschman, 1977) and in the social realm people could be true to their natures and so better able to perceive and evaluate their worlds (Carrier, 1995a, pp. 160–66).

The emergence of new economic forms, practices and beliefs faced resistance, and E.P. Thompson (1971) described the nature of that resistance and the beliefs that motivated it in his treatment of what he calls the English crowd. That crowd was made up of English peasants and villagers, and Thompson says that in the second half of the eighteenth century they often rejected the emerging notion that the social and the economic should be kept separate. Rather, it appears that they saw the two as intertwined in a particular way. In principle, if not always in practice, those who behaved in the appropriate ways could expect a reasonable livelihood. Those appropriate ways were what some called a 'conscionable course of dealing' (Everitt, 1967, p. 569), and they included making a proper effort in one's own activities as well as dealing properly with one's fellows, dealings that had both social and economic aspects.

Adam Smith, one of the leading members of the Scottish Enlightenment, wrote at length about what concerned Thompson's crowd, the nature of economy and society and their relationship, but of his work, the one that had the most influence on economics is *The Wealth of Nations*. That book reflected what I said was the view common in the Scottish Enlightenment, that the two should be kept separate. Thus, he rejected the idea that the basis of people's economic activities and rewards lay in their relationship with their fellows, in the expectations about how they should behave or in the rewards that would follow. As he (1976 [1776], p. 18) put it, 'It is not from the benevolence of the butcher, the brewer, or the baker, that we expect our dinner, but from their regard to their own interest', so that, in our dealings with our fellows, 'We address ourselves, not to their humanity, but to their self-love, and never talk to them of our own necessities, but of their advantages'.

In stressing the importance of the self-interested individual free of collective, social bonds and expectations, Smith was advocating what Karl Polanyi (1957 [1944]) called the disembedding of economy from society that occurred in Britain in the nineteenth century. Marx and Engels (1948 [1848], p. 11) presaged Polanyi's argument when they said that the emergence of capitalism torn asunder the motley feudal ties that bound man to his 'natural superiors', and has left no other bond between man and man than naked self-interest, than callous 'cash payment'. It has drowned the most heavenly ecstasies of religious fervour, of chivalrous enthusiasm, of philistine sentimentalism, in the icy water of egotistical calculation has pitilessly.

Thompson's peasants did not simply dissent from this emerging view. In addition, they held that those who acted in accord with it were violating important moral values. At times they responded to those violations with force, becoming Thompson's crowd that sought to punish those deviants and enforce their own moral values. Of course, the adherents of the emerging liberal order thought that Thompson's peasants were wrong. What those peasants saw as rough justice intended to impose conformity to proper values, those adherents saw as crime, mob violence that needed to be suppressed and punished, the view that, Thompson (1971, pp. 76–79) said, coloured the treatment of those crowds ever since.

This tale of economic, intellectual and political changes around the start of the nineteenth century is useful for identifying the broad outlines of the classic economics and liberalism that are the ancestral forms of the neoclassical economics and neoliberalism that replaced Keynesianism. It is useful also for illustrating two of the aspects of Merton's approach to economic deviance. One of those is that people's values and orientations, which shape both their economic activities and their moral assessment of those activities, can vary significantly across groups and over time. The idea of liberal economy that Smith promoted was gaining strength in certain sectors of the British population, and as it did so a different sector, Thompson's peasants, found itself increasingly isolated.

The other aspect of Merton's approach that this tale illustrates is his rejection of the usefulness of the idea of the isolated, self-regarding individual. Thompson was concerned with the values and orientations of his peasants, but those who embraced the new order had values and orientations of their own. They were articulated by Smith and others in the Scottish Enlightenment and expressed in the spread of liberal capitalist economic practice. To say that both the crowd and the liberals had their own moral view of economy, society and their relationship does not, of course, mean that their views were the same. Clearly they were not, and Polanyi's notion of disembedding points to an important difference. For those peasants, the economic activities of the production and circulation of things were inseparable from the social relationships, expectations and obligations of which they were a part, and for them it was right that they were so. For Smith and the others, however, economic activities should be carried out by autonomous individuals free of all links to their fellows, other than those that are forged when they transact and that dissolve once the transaction is complete (Carrier, 1995a, pp. 31–35).

Economic deviance and neoliberalism

I said that the rise of neoliberalism and neoclassical economics in the final third of the last century looks more like the return to something old than the advocacy of something new. That is, while the circumstances are very different, the positions of those in the Scottish Enlightenment and in Thompson's English crowd, which I sketched in the preceding paragraphs, resemble positions being taken in the present. I turn now to some of the central political and economic arguments of neoliberals and their allies, the broad outline of which should be familiar.

Politically, advocates argued that the free market is crucial for the maintenance of personal freedom. This position was put forward forcefully by Friedrich von Hayek, who was awarded a Nobel prize in economics in 1974. He (1944, p. 204) had told those of an earlier generation that the economic realm was complex to the point of incomprehensibility, so that governments need to resist 'the craving for intelligibility' about how the economy operates and why. Any attempt to shape the economy to serve social ends marks the failure to resist that craving and puts countries on *The Road to Serfdom* (Hayek, 1944). What he said gained force as the rhetoric of the Cold War linked Soviet central economic planning to the loss of political freedom. The most rigorous defence against starting down this road was to have an anarchic, wholly unfettered economic realm, the position of the anarcho-capitalists (Brown, 1977). Such a position would seem to offer no secure defence against economic wrong-doing, and in fact it is not clear that the concept of such wrong-doing, as distinct from personal dissatisfaction with the behaviour of others, makes sense in such a conception of economy.

Economically, the advocates said that we should let the market regulate itself. Some who put forward this position echoed Hayek's (1974) argument that the economy is so complex that we cannot adequately understand it. Others put forward a somewhat different position, one that asserts market rationality (see Fox, 2009). They argued that the market is the result of the decisions of a mass of individuals, and thus it reflects an intelligence far greater than what could be found in any government ministry, much less in any individual. As is the case with the anarcho-capitalists, the extreme advocates of liberal economy, it is not clear that this neoliberal and neoclassical-economic approach to the economy allows for the idea of economic wrong-doing. That is because it construes the world as populated only by those in the market seeking to transact according to their preferences and resources, both of which are taken as given and hence not to be explained. That is, this approach to economy seems to eliminate the idea of wrong and replace it with cost: the deception or fraud that would be wrong-doing seems to be treated only as a risk of loss. Market actors take that risk into account when deciding whether to deal with one counter-party or another, and transact accordingly, with the result that the market, with its collective intelligence, ends up regulating itself.

Those who were doubtful of the benefits of free markets full of calculating individuals, or those who became doubtful following the onset of the Great Recession, do not resemble Thompson's English peasants. However, in some regards the general thrust of their arguments was not all that different.

The tone of those arguments is expressed in what Steven Sampson (2005, p. 105) said about those seeking to eliminate corruption, a problem that was seen as the most important form of economic deviance before the Great Recession. Sampson said that they are seeking 'to restore standards that were lost, the standards of morality and responsibility which connote what we call "community"'. After the onset of the Great Recession, this invocation of society and social obligation, and its role as a counter to the untrammelled self-interest of the free market, appeared elsewhere, in places that many had thought were committed to a neoliberal view of the world. One of those places was the Bank of England. Mark Carney, its Governor, stressed the importance of the sort of standards that Sampson described, when he said that if the economic system is to survive, 'individuals and their firms must have a sense of their responsibilities for the broader system' (Carney, 2014). Another of those places is the International Monetary Fund. Christine Lagarde, its head, said that a healthy economy requires that we protect and strengthen 'the principles of solidarity and reciprocity that bind societies together' (Lagarde, 2014).

I said that modern positions are not the same as those of the Scottish Enlightenment or Thompson's peasants, but they share significant features. Neoliberals and classic liberals share the assumption that individuals should be free to transact as they want, guided only by their desires and resources, and they share condemnation of those who dissent. For the classic liberals, the peasants who dissented were ignorant, and occasionally violent, hindrances to progress. For the neoliberals, those who dissent lack initiative and are free riders carried along by those who create wealth or, if they are in what used to be called the Second World, are victims of a lingering socialist mentality, and are hindrances to progress.

The peasants and the modern critics of neoliberalism share the assumption that people have obligations that should constrain the ways that they deploy their resources to satisfy their desires. However, they differ in the nature of those obligations. For Thompson's peasants, those obligations appear to spring from their routine interactions with other people, and so reflect their relationships with those people. For the modern critics the obligations are to something that is less personal and more amorphous, like community, the broader system and the principles that bind societies together, the things that, Durkheim argued, become less salient with an increase in the division of labour. This decreasing attention to personality and greater attention to systems and principles, moreover, diverts attention from what concerned Thompson's peasants. As I indicate below, that is the question of who benefits and who suffers from economic activity.

These two different positions imply different views of the economic world, and associated with those views are guides for action, and hence criteria for assessing action as deviant or not. So, for those I have called the critics of neoliberalism and of classic liberalism, the economic world is not sharply defined, in the sense that its boundary with the broader social world occasionally is unclear and often it does not need to be policed rigorously. Indeed, for Thompson's peasants, as I have indicated, it is not clear that there is a boundary worthy of the name. For the modern critics there is a boundary, but it is crossed every time governments act in the economic realm. This is so even if that action is intended to protect the economic system, for that protection is justified by the benefits that the system is said to bring to society as a whole. Equally, crossing that boundary occurs in a different way every time the critics urge market actors to temper their self-interest with a sense of responsibility, solidarity and reciprocity.

For both Thompson's peasants and those critics, then, individuals' economic actions can be seen to be wrong, but the basis of that assessment does not appear to be the same. For the peasants, as I have presented them, the wrong is the violation of a moral code that springs from and reflects interactions between people and the expectations that arise from them. This is the sort of thing that J.E. Crowley (1974, p. 6) described in his analysis of economic thought in early colonial America: 'It was the traditional view that exchange … was a social matter involving reciprocity and redistribution: competition, in the sense of one man's gaining at the expense of another, was a violation of this traditional ethic'. For the modern critics, the wrong is more abstract and impersonal, revolving around concepts like reciprocity and responsibility for the larger system. For them, it appears, economic actions are to be judged in terms of their effects on that system, effects illustrated by the way that the activities of banks before the financial crisis increased the risk that the financial system would cease to function adequately as a result of unanticipated events (such as the ending of the bubble in the housing market).

Alternatively, the neoliberals and classic liberals see an economic world made up of individuals endowed with desires and resources who transact with each other impersonally, and for those like the anarcho-capitalists, that is all there is. The decisions of such actors can be criticised as silly, for instance paying too much for something, but there is no moral basis for assessing them. Market actors are, as I noted already, possessed of their preferences and resources, both of which are simply taken as given and are expressed when those actors decide to buy one thing rather than another, or to buy nothing at all. For the less extreme, there appears also to be a system, which must be obeyed and protected. However, that system must not, indeed cannot, be governed, nor must we interfere with it, as the discredited Keynesians sought to do and as some of the critics seek to do. That system is implicit in the assumption that free markets lead to the rational allocation of capital. That allocation can lead to hardship for some, which may be unfortunate, but it is not a wrong, for it is justified by the collective benefit that follows from that allocation. This is illustrated by the words of an investment banker that Karen Ho (2012, p. 420) reports: 'Inefficiency requires reallocation of assets. That includes people, and that can be painful, especially if you are one of the people. But society as a whole is still, without question, better off'.

I have described some of the key differences between the classic liberals and neoliberals on the one hand, and on the other their critics, as I have described some of the ways that the modern and ancestral positions have changed. For the advocates of all of these positions, some economic activities are better and some are worse. However, the bases and justifications of those assessments vary, so much so that in some cases, as I have noted, it is not clear that the idea of economic deviance, in the sense of reprehensible economic behaviour, has much meaning. This, of course, makes it easier for people to adopt what is described by Whyte and Wiegratz (this volume) in their discussion of C. Wright Mills's 'higher immorality'.

Among the moderns this appears to be the case most clearly with the anarcho-capitalists. It also appears to be the case for Adam Smith in *The Wealth of Nations*. In his other main work, *The Theory of Moral Sentiments* (1984 [1759]), he put forward another influential argument, which resembles to a degree the position of some of the neoliberals. That is because both he and they assert that there is an overarching mechanism that is beyond our understanding, is impossible for us to influence and is beneficial. For Smith it was the invisible hand (Lubasz, 1992); for those neoliberals it is the economic system in a free economy. For neither, then, is it clear that the notion of economic deviance makes much sense. Equally, it is worth noting that, for both, the benefit that these mechanisms produce is as impersonal as are the mechanisms themselves. All that we can do, as Hayek urged, is try to assure that we do not interfere with the operation of those mechanisms.

This impersonality points to an important difference between Thompson's peasants and the modern critics, and hence the notion of economic deviance that these two positions allow. For those peasants, the rules of economic behaviour spring from direct interpersonal relations and the expectations associated with them. Violating those rules is a wrong, and it is carried out by one person against another. For the modern critics, economic deviance would seem to be possible, as deviants are those who shirk their responsibilities to the system and ignore the imperatives of reciprocity. However, these are fairly bloodless wrongs: the system or our generic fellows may suffer, but the suffering and the victims are abstract.

Conclusion

The financial crisis of 2007 and its aftermath revealed massive amounts of economic wrong-doing, especially in the financial sector in the US. In suggesting how we might approach that, I have invoked the conceptual framework of scholars who are long dead. Those frameworks are sociological, in the sense that they lead us to see that economic deviance as a social phenomenon, perhaps carried out by individuals but made more likely by changes in the financial sector in general and society as a whole. As well, those frameworks are unusually general, and in that generality they encourage us to look for other circumstances that might resemble the rise of neoliberalism and the economic deviance that, events revealed, was associated with it. The other circumstance, suggested by the very name of neoliberalism, was the rise of liberal market economy, especially in Britain late in the eighteenth century.

Certainly there are important similarities between the two periods. In each, I have argued, an emerging orientation toward economy and society held that the economic realm and the people in it should operate free from social constraint. Also in each, advocates of the emerging order offered similar justifications for that order. In both periods, those advocates asserted the existence of processes and predilections that are beyond what people can comprehend and hence beyond their control. For the early British liberals, the most striking of these is Smith's invisible hand, predilections so basic that they appear natural and unavoidable; for the neoliberals there is the rational market, the product of economic processes that are complex beyond human understanding. In each case, any effort to shape the economy so that it might reflect collective values is folly, for it is bound to fail. The wisest and most beneficial thing that people can do is to let the market run. If there is virtue, then, it lies in doing nothing but minding one's own business.

I described how the rise of liberal and neoliberal systems were met with dissent from adherents of the old order. There are similarities in that dissent from both periods. The most obvious of these is the assertion that people are not wholly autonomous, self-regarding individuals who are the only proper judge of their own interests. Rather, the collectivity should have a say, perhaps to the extent that it overrules individual desires: the rough justice of Thompson's crowd; the stress tests and capital requirements of the Basel Committee on Banking Supervision, the Bank of England and the Federal Reserve.

However, as I have described them, these two bodies of dissent differ in important ways. The expectations and values by which Thompson's peasants judged their fellows were social and even personal. The idea of a conscionable course of dealing and the expectation that people engage in it emerged from social interactions over an extended period. The modern dissenters in Basel and at the Bank and the Federal Reserve appear to hold no such view. For them, rather, it is the system that must be protected. In some ways this system resembles the neoliberal vision of the market economy with its collective rationality. However, it differs in that the market system, or at least important parts of it, is not beyond human understanding and intervention. So, this modern dissent differs from the liberal and neoliberal positions in that it assumes that people's collective action make a difference, whether that be for ill in the case of those who turn liar loans into dubious CDOs or for good in the case of those who seek to regulate markets and their actors to reduce systematic risk. In spite of their differences, then, Thompson's peasants and the modern dissenters unite in asserting that there is a place on which to stand, a perspective rooted outside the impersonal transactions of the market, one that allows assessment of those transactions in terms of something other than market rationality.

References

Andrews, Edmund L. (2008) 'Greenspan concedes error on regulation', *The New York Times*, 24 October.

Brown, Susan Love (1997) 'The free market as salvation from government: the anarcho-capitalist view', in Carrier, James G. (ed.) *Meanings of the Market*. Oxford: Berg, pp. 99–128.

Carney, Mark (2014) 'Inclusive capitalism: creating a sense of the systemic', The Conference on Inclusive Capitalism, London, 27 May. www.bankofengland.co.uk/publications/Documents/speeches/2014/speech731.pdf (accessed 18 August 2015).

Carrier, James G. (1995a) *Gifts and Commodities: Exchange and Western Capitalism since 1700*. London: Routledge.

Carrier, James G. (1995b) 'Introduction', in Carrier, J.G. (ed.) *Occidentalism: Images of the West*. Oxford: Oxford University Press, pp. 1–32.

Carrier, James G. (1997) 'Introduction', in Carrier, J.G. (ed.) *Meanings of the Market*. Oxford: Berg, pp. 1-67.

Carrier, James G. (2012a) 'Anthropology after the crisis', *Focaal*, 64, pp. 115–28.

Carrier, James G. (2012b) 'Introduction', in Carrier, J.G. and Luetchford, Peter (eds) *Ethical Consumption: Social Value and Economic Practice*. New York: Berghahn, pp. 1–35.

Cockett, Richard (1994) *Thinking the Unthinkable: Think-Tanks and the Economic Counter-Revolution, 1931–83*. London: Harper-Collins.

Corkery, Michael and Protess, Ben (2014) 'Bank of America papers show conflict and trickery in mortgages', *The New York Times*, 21 August.

Crowley, J.E. (1974) *This Sheba, Self: The Conceptualization of Economic Life in Eighteenth Century America*. Baltimore: Johns Hopkins University Press.

Dealbook (2007) 'Citi chief on buyouts: "We're still dancing"', *The New York Times*, 10 July.

Dealbook (2009) 'Blankfein says he's just doing "God's work"', *The New York Times*, 9 November.

Durkheim, Emile (1951 [1897]) *Suicide: A Study in Sociology*. New York: The Free Press.

Durkheim, Emile (1984 [1893]) *The Division of Labour in Society*. London: Routledge & Kegan Paul.

Everitt, Alan (1967) 'The marketing of agricultural produce', in Thirsk, Joan (ed.) *The Agrarian History of England and Wales, vol. IV, 1500–1640*. Cambridge: Cambridge University Press, pp. 466–592.

Fox, Justin (2009) *Myth of the Rational Market*. New York: Harper Business.

Greenspan, Alan (1996) 'The challenge of central banking in a democratic society', Francis Boyer Lecture, the American Enterprise Institute for Public Policy Research, Washington, DC, 5 December. www.federalreserve.gov/boarddocs/speeches/1996/19961205.htm (accessed 18 August 2015).

Hayek, Friedrich A. von (1944) *The Road to Serfdom*. London: Routledge.

Hayek, Friedrich A. von (1974) 'The pretence of knowledge', Nobel prize lecture, 11 December. www.nobelprize.org/nobel_prizes/economics/laureates/1974/hayek-lecture.html (accessed 18 August 2015).

Hirschman, Albert O. (1977) *The Passions and the Interests*. Princeton: Princeton University Press.

Ho, Karen (2009) *Liquidated: An Ethnography of Wall Street*. Durham, NC: Duke University Press.

Ho, Karen (2012) 'Finance', in Fassin, Didier (ed.) *A Companion to Moral Anthropology*. Malden, MA: Wiley-Blackwell pp. 413–31.

Krugman, Paul (2010) 'Berating the raters', *The New York Times*, 25 April.

Lagarde, Christine (2014) 'Economic inclusion and financial integrity', The Conference on Inclusive Capitalism. Washington, DC: International Monetary Fund. www.imf.org/external/np/speeches/2014/052714.htm (accessed 18 August 2015).

Lewis, Michael (2011) *The Big Short: Inside the Doomsday Machine*. London: Penguin.

Lubasz, Heinz (1992) 'Adam Smith and the invisible hand – of the market?', in Dilley, Roy (ed.) *Contesting Markets*. Edinburgh: Edinburgh University Press, pp. 37–56.

Marx, Karl and Engels, Frederick (1948 [1848]) *Manifesto of the Communist Party*. New York: International Publishers.

Merton, Robert K. (1938) 'Social structure and anomie', *American Sociological Review*, 3 (5), pp. 672–82.

Morgenson, Gretchen (2012) 'Bank settles over loans in Nevada', *The New York Times*, 23 October.

Morgenson, Gretchen (2014) 'Credit Suisse documents point to mortgage lapses', *The New York Times*, 9 March.

Norris, Floyd (2014) 'Regulators struggle with conflicts in credit ratings and audits', *The New York Times*, 21 August.

Polanyi, Karl (1957 [1944]) *The Great Transformation*. Boston: Beacon Press.

Said, Edward (1978) *Orientalism*. Harmondsworth: Penguin.

Sampson, Steven (2005) 'Integrity warriors: global morality and the anti-corruption movement in the Balkans', in Haller, Dieter and Shore, Cris (eds) *Corruption: Anthropological Perspectives*. London: Pluto, pp. 103–30.

Shore, Cris (2004) 'Corruption scandals in America and Europe: Enron and EU fraud in comparative perspective', in Gledhill, John (ed.) *Corporate Scandal: Global Corporatism Against Society*. Oxford: Berghahn, pp. 29–39.

Silver, Allan (1990) 'Friendship in commercial society: eighteenth-century social theory and modern sociology', *American Journal of Sociology*, 95 (6), pp. 1474–504.

Smith, Adam (1976 [1776]) *An Inquiry into the Nature and Causes of the Wealth of Nations*. Chicago: University of Chicago Press.

Smith, Adam (1984 [1759]) *The Theory of Moral Sentiments*. Indianapolis: Liberty Fund.

Stevenson, Richard W. (1995) 'Breaking the bank – a special report. Big gambles, lost bets sank a venerable firm', *The New York Times*, 3 March.

Thompson, E.P. (1971) 'The moral economy of the English crowd in the eighteenth century', *Past and Present*, 50, pp. 76–136.

Wedel, Janine R. (2012) 'Rethinking corruption in an age of ambiguity', *Annual Review of Law and Social Science*, 8, pp. 453–98.

3 'After' the crisis

Morality plays and the renewal of business as usual

Steve Tombs

Introduction: the moral capital of capital under neo-liberalism

It is commonly observed that central to neo-liberal political economy are claims that markets are best when 'freer', that state and public sector activity are relatively inefficient, and that states' attempts to regulate private economic activity should be kept to a minimum. If these claims have political and economic dimensions, their key *moral* dimensions are less often subject to comment. Moreover, as noted by Whyte and Wiegratz (this volume), it is crucial to understand the ways in which market values are translated into, and then reproduced through, societal values – and that is precisely one focus of this chapter. More specifically, following MacLennan (cited in ibid.), it seeks to show how this dominance of market values as societal values is key to understanding the power of 'anti-regulation' sentiments and practices.

Specifically, the chapter considers, with reference to the UK, some of the fall-out from the financial then economic crises that erupted across much of the world from 2007 onwards. Here I wish to consider the various ways in which the crisis has been politically and popularly framed in the UK – ways that have allowed business-more-or-less-as-usual to proceed in its aftermath. The focus is upon various discursive initiatives and narratives that were constructed and utilised as, and since, the crisis unfolded. A starting point is with the claim that, 'Narratives are important instruments … because they co-construct and legitimize regimes by framing the way we see the world. Narratives are not author-less discourses, but represent specific, powerful interests' (Hansen, 2014: 636). Moreover, narratives are an element of the discursive ways (Wiegratz and Cesnulyte, 2016) through which moral economies are constructed and reconstructed.

Elsewhere, I have discussed the emergence and consolidation of the 'moral capital of capital' under conditions of emergent and then dominant neo-liberalism (Tombs, 2001). There is no doubt that the economic and political changes that represented the emergence of neo-liberalism amounted to an increase in the structural power of capital (Gill and Law, 1993: 104). But an often-overlooked aspect to this augmented power was an increase in private capital's social importance. Indeed, there was a clear *moral* aspect to the new status of private capital – an elevation that simultaneously encouraged and fed from a sustained attack on state, public and regulatory activity. As Snider (2000) has demonstrated, the phraseology of 'burdens on business' and 'red tape' to refer to laws designed to regulate economic activity had become common currency, the unquestioned implication being that such burdens should be reduced as far as possible – since they no longer express any public good. The renewed moral status of private capital – to emphasise, not to particular businesses (a task that would be difficult given the evidence of a-morality, immorality or criminality on the part of individual business organisations) but to business, or rather 'capital', as a whole – was partly a function of it *not* being the 'other', that is, wasteful, inefficient and intrusive public sector bodies. Thus a key triumph of neo-liberalism was to connect with many peoples' (negative) experiences of state monopolies in the provision of goods and services and at the same time to equate such experiences with the values that had helped create those forms of public provision – notably a moral collectivism. Further, for neo-liberal discourse, it is not simply that state and public provision is inefficient – through their very existence they thwart individual and institutional innovation and competitiveness. Private enterprise, entrepreneurship, risk-taking, the pursuit of wealth, and the 'market' all become valorised not just as the most effective means to certain ends - profits, taxation, wages, or various socially necessary and (perhaps) socially useful goods and services - but *as ends in themselves*. Thus, neo-liberalism was and remains more than an economic or political project: it also has a moral core (Amable, 2011), albeit one beset by what are tensions and contradictions (see Shorthose, 2011).

At the most general level, we can understand this valorisation of private economic activity in terms of two well-documented processes that characterise capitalism from the late twentieth century onwards, namely marketisation and financialisation of economy, society and culture; indeed, these processes also demonstrate the mutually reinforcing effects of the ideological and the material. Together, these were central to instituting the dominance of a (greater or lesser) neo-liberal rationality through all aspects of social life; social relations have increasingly become economic relations, with individuals interpellated as entrepreneurial subjects in ever-more aspects of their lives, responsibilised and free from the state (Giroux, 2008: 172).

This elevated moral capital of private capital in general cannot simply be understood as pure 'ideology', but is a product – while giving further impetus to – material changes in the organisation of economic and social life; in short, the fortunes of private capital are much more closely tied to many of our fates, from cradle to grave, than was the case forty years ago. In fact, it is the combination of the ideological strength and thoroughgoing material basis for the elevated moral status of private capital that makes 'freedom' for capital not just difficult to resist, but increasingly so in the 'post-crisis' settlement.

Crisis, whose crisis? Discursive frames and morality plays

The crisis was framed in a variety of ways, which varied across nation-states, in ways which had more or less 'success', and which took a variety of forms.

However, paying particular attention to the UK, many of these framings contained an implicit or explicit moral element – and moral narratives were *necessary*, since they had to counter a moral outrage that had, even if relatively briefly, borne down on 'the banks'; indeed, hard as it may seem now to remember, for some twelve months or so, from late 2007, academics and public intellectuals, senior economists and the global financial press lined up at least to pose the question: Is this the end of capitalism? Or at the very least in its neo-liberal variants?

If such moral framings were to have effect, they had both relate to and at the same time seek to shape aspects of popular consciousness. Thus these framings are about securing consent, about addressing and negotiating with, publics – and these are processes requiring 'intensive ideological work' (Clarke and Newman, 2012: 300), always fraught with difficulty (Clarke, 2010: 391, Clarke and Newman, 2010). Neo-liberalism 'and its cultural political economy' is always partly about 'sociocultural dynamics, conflicts and struggles' (Wiegratz and Cesnulyte, 2016: 5), and these are particularly intense in times of crisis. Moreover, attempts to emerge from crisis on the basis of new politico-economic settlements always involve utilising elements of existent and past, albeit still somewhere resonant, discourses – and hence the significance of the increased moral capital of capital extending beyond a quarter of a century prior to the crisis.

Identifying blameworthy subjects

One consistent set of discursive responses was a series of morality plays that had their origins in regarding individual bankers as 'villains that brought down the world' (Whittle and Mueller, 2012: 119). Whittle and Mueller's (2012) analysis of the UK Treasury Select Committee hearings of 2009 into the banking crisis and in particular the questioning of four senior bankers therein demonstrates clearly that these were processes of moral condemnation. The conduct and substance of the Select Committee is instructive: within these morality plays, senior individual figures at the head of financial services companies – prime examples being Fred Goodwin, Stephen Hester, Andy Hornby and Tom McKillop[1] – were identified and vilified, often over very long periods of time. Moreover, such processes took place on both sides of the Atlantic (Froud *et al.*, 2012: 44–5). Indeed, these were effectively quasi 'degradation ceremonies' (Garfinkel, 1956; Goffman, 1963) – *quasi* because although they were clearly ceremonial, and certainly involved formal denunciation, not least in moral terms of blame and shame, lacking was any formal calling to account even if, for some who had been vilified, their lives *were* changed, albeit resulting in a lower profile rather than any significant diminution in their material standard of living (Harris, 2012). Moreover, such ceremonial denunciation of specific, named individuals cohered with intermittent, less focused, much broader swipes at the guilty men of the City or Wall Street, which in turn drew upon distinct, but not entirely unrelated and hence utilisable, discourses of *rogue* traders (Pludwin, 2011: 470–2). Such 'rogue traders' – a common discursive mechanism for isolating corporate harms and crimes –

were rarely concretised into identifying specific individuals whose legal responsibility was ever to be tested in court.

In any case, what emerges from this generalised framing of specific or a 'class' of individuals is that, if there were 'lessons to be learned', they were about eliminating bad apples or 'tricksters' (Kelsey, 2014) – and not, therefore, about the necessity of the external restructuring of markets, sectors or fundamental practices within them through re-regulation. Thus, for example, reflecting upon the causes of the global credit crisis and the international recession, Lord Myners, the then financial services secretary in Gordon Brown's Labour government was able to state:

> The failures have not been failures of the market economy. They have been failures of men and women who forgot that market discipline meant that they had to be disciplined in order to get results out of the marketplace. Too many people got complacent and lazy – and the market responded as we should have predicted …
>
> (Myners, 2010)

Here, then, the superior morality of the abstract 'market' is lauded for its ability to discipline aberrant individuals who had not worked hard or creatively enough, and who had been taught a Randian-type lesson.

However, it is worth noting that such was the level of this outrage directed at a broad sweep of leading financiers that this discourse was never easily nor wholly contained simply at the level of specific bad apples; as indicated, popular sentiment extended to 'the bankers', bankers' pay and bonuses, sporadically if briefly widening out to both executive pay and, possibly more significantly, to 'crony capitalism' – to which I return below.

That this was a protracted process of blaming is indicated by the fact that 'banker bashing' entered the popular lexicon. Indeed, some sought to call it to a halt. In January 2011, within days of taking over as chief executive officer (CEO) of Barclays, Bob Diamond told a parliamentary committee that he thought 'There was a period of remorse and apology for banks and I think that period needs to be over' (Treanor, 2011). As Werdigier (2011) put it, he argued that it was time 'to move on from criticizing and to let banks and the private sector create jobs and economic growth'. For Diamond, the question was 'how do we put some of the blame game behind' (cited in Werdigier, 2011). This has become a common refrain by the sector and its apologists. Fraser Nelson, editor of *The Spectator*, lamented in 2013 that 'It has been almost five years since the crash and still the guilty men are being tracked down and subjected to what seems like a never-ending trial for financial war crimes' (cited in Cohen, 2013), while Anthony Browne, chief executive of the British Bankers' Association, pleaded, 'We need to put banker bashing behind us' (ibid.). The message here is simple: if individual men and women had erred, this should not prevent the key engines of neo-liberal capitalism from doing what they do best: finance the only means of recovery from recession, private capitalist investment and wealth creation, already established as the one best way for economic and social progress for over thirty years.

As intimated, this generalised opprobrium took some dangerous turns – dangerous, at least, from the point of view of capital. At a most general level, there was a long-term popular and political outrage at 'executive pay' – an issue that has certainly erupted from time to time in the UK, not least under conditions of neo-liberalism in which the UK has experienced widening levels of income and wealth inequalities, trends exacerbated under conditions of post-crisis austerity that the government was attempting to impose under the rubric 'we're all in this together'. Government responses to such outrage both sought to acknowledge, even to claim at times to share, the popular discomfort but to represent such levels of remuneration as unavoidable in a globalised market – Britain Plc had to attract and retain the best people at the head of their largest companies in order to continue to compete effectively in globalised market places, and thus to facilitate recovery from recession. This latter claim appears to hold considerable sway – perhaps through repetition and a simplistic understanding of labour markets – despite there being absolutely no evidence for it (Bolchover, 2013; Gigliotti, 2013; High Pay Commission, 2011a, 2011b). Were this actually to be the case, then it might be noted that, compared to its European counterparts, the City of London must have some exceptionally talented people: a 2013 report by the European Bankers' Association found that there were 2,400 bankers in the City paid over €1m in 2011 – a total that was more than three times as many as in the rest of the EU put together (Treanor, 2013). Such facts need not, of course, get in the way of the individualistic self-serving justifications at the heart of a neoliberal moral economy.

A second general way in which blame has been apportioned is via the construction and use of a series of moralistic dichotomies. One such dichotomy that circulated in the UK was that between retail (good) versus investment (bad) forms of banking, a discourse that gained such power that it is the basis for the one 'major' reform to the sector that has resulted from the crisis, the so-called ring fence to be erected within banks to protect the former from the risks of the latter. This rather conveniently obscures the fact that the three major waves of consumer victimisation that have occurred in the sector in the past three decades – private pensions, endowment mortgages and payment protection insurance 'mis-selling' – all occurred within the retail sector (Tombs, 2015a).

Further moral dichotomies have distinguished between 'good' and 'bad' borrowers (the latter being the sub-prime borrowers in particular) and predatory as opposed to responsible lenders (Brasset and Vaughan-Williams, 2012: 35). Such divisions have class-based and, in the US, racialised and gendered dimensions – and, while pernicious, these also have resonance as they bear an (albeit distorted) relationship to reality, since saturated markets for mortgages saw less financially able groups exploited as a new, untapped source of super-profit for business (see, for example, on the distribution by ethnicity of sub-prime lending in the US, Sassen, 2013: 31–2, and Dymski *et al.*, 2013).

Such resort to endless victim-blaming discourses (Weissman and Donahue, 2009: 9; see also Ellis, this volume) in turn creates the basis for a wider encompassing of 'suspect citizens' and their 'culture of debt' (Pludwin, 2011: 472). In some ways this used the suspect lending practices of financial services firms and turned responsibility on its head. As Dymski *et al.* have noted of the post-2007 exposes of sub-prime lending in the US, 'The defining aspect of the crisis was not that subprime loans and other forms of predatory lending disproportionately victimized minorities and women, but that borrowers were myopic, overly greedy, or both' (2013: 125). This also created the basis for a further, useful slippage, one that then allowed moral blame to be attached to many of us, logically related to the more audacious claim that 'we' were all somehow responsible for borrowing too much, enjoying easy credit, living beyond our means, and so on (Brasset and Vaughan-Williams, 2012). Thus, in general:

> The relationship between individuals, their houses/homes and their investment and saving habits was suddenly produced as a category of moral analysis in the public sphere. Fear, guilt, shame and anger were mobilised and sovereign responses, typically couched in the humanitarian vocabularies of salvation and helping victims … were not only justified but seen to be necessitated.
>
> (Brasset and Vaughan-Williams, 2012: 41)

There is a double moral-movement at work here. First, the claim that we are all somehow to blame in effect neutralises attempts to target blame more specifically; second, this generally ascribed moral lassitude opens up a space for extraordinary measures – a state of emergency – to be justified on the moral grounds that we need rescuing from a situation that we have all helped to create – and, further, that our legitimate opposition to the nature of any such measures is thereby also undermined. In such ways, the politics and economics of austerity appear as a necessary, albeit bitter, pill that we all have to swallow.

Thus the emphasis upon bad borrow*ing* as opposed merely to bad borrow*ers* also opened up discursive space to invoke the credit card analogy (Broome *et al.*, 2012: 5). This analogy was to prove crucial in the institution of the idea that nation-states had overspent. In 2008, whilst in opposition, Cameron used the *News of the World* to claim that the Labour government 'has maxed out our nation's credit card – and they want to keep on spending by getting another. We believe we need to get a grip, be responsible and help families now in a way that doesn't cost us our future' (Conservative Home, 2008). Thus, although such an analogy is empirically (Reed, 2012) and conceptually (Pettifor, 2012) ludicrous, it had power since it resonated with the relatively successful balanced household budget analogy deployed over thirty-five years ago by both Thatcher and Reagan as they ideologically softened up their respective populations for monetarist experiments. Indeed, Konzelmann charts 300 years of key themes within narratives designed to justify austerity – within which 'appeals to ethics and morality', which in turn are 'reinforced by misleading analogies drawn between government budgets and the accounts of … households', have been central (Konzelmann, 2014: 701). In fact, such claims proved pivotal in the very quick shift from the construction of the crisis as one of private, capitalist institutions to one of national debt, especially debt incurred through public sector and welfare spending, and thus a more general, public lassitude (Robinson, 2012). More generally, then, this renewed attention to a diet of good monetary and fiscal governance via belt tightening on behalf of a gorged population helped to make austerity not just palatable but necessary, both economically and indeed morally (Blyth, 2013b: 1–15).

Such discourses support the claim that everyone and everything was to blame for the crisis (McLean and Nocera, 2011). Thus, 'Who's not to blame? The mortgage brokers were out of control. Regulators were asleep. Home buyers thought they were entitled to Corian counters and a two story great room … This was an episode of mass idiocy' (Pludwin, 2011: 472). If there was idiocy, claiming that this was ubiquitous is important: *if* we were all to blame, then no-one or nothing in particular was to blame; and *if* we were all to blame, then it follows we should all share the pain of 'recovery' – hence, again, the UK government's easy refrain that we are all in this together, albeit a claim always somewhat vulnerable in the context of clear empirical evidence as to the distribution and effects of austerity measures. The ubiquity of blame coupled with the facile credit card analogy are double movements underpinning the representation of private as public debt and ideologically fuelling the legitimation of austerity.

These indications are enough to highlight the prevalence of blaming strategies, albeit this discussion is not exhaustive – blame also extended at specific times to specific institutions (such as ratings agencies; Sinclair, 2010), or to some of their specific practices (such as 'short-selling', limited forms of which were banned in the UK for six months from September 2008; see BBC, 2009). But enough has been said to emphasise that what ties these discursive responses together is that such processes of actively naming and producing blameworthy subjects served:

> a political and ideological function by focusing attention on individuals and groups and away from a confrontation with the normative and systemic violence of capitalism itself. In a moment of economic crisis one cannot merely say, "This is simply the natural force of the market at work," since such a statement would certainly raise questions as to the soundness of the broader system. The restaging of responsibility to the active "discovery" of guilty parties helps maintain the integrity of capital and sustain the mythology that the market is rational, objective, and natural, but had been undermined and polluted by a few bad apples.
>
> (Pludwin, 2011: 475)

Blaming capitalism?

This is not to say that there were no discursive responses to the crisis that had greater potential for placing some of the more individualised accounts into a wider context. Thus the individualised moral critiques of personal greed have intermittently extended, or threatened to extend, beyond purely individual levels – through widespread vilification of 'the bankers' to a general critique of the relationship between pay, bonuses and poor performance, and into wider critical considerations of banking culture and 'crony' capitalism.

One strain here has been to invoke critically a wider, albeit meso-level, immoral banking *culture*, with echoes of what Will – following others – has called, in the context of the US, a Ponzi culture (Will, 2013), one characterised by the valorisation of 'debt, speculation or gambling, and the belief in rapid "investment" growth' (ibid.: 48), and 'a product of the symbiotic relationship between government and financial institutions' (ibid.: 60). Problematic elements of "banking culture" revolved around greed, short termism, 'excessive' risk-taking; but all such 'accounts', if not specifically individualised, were abstracted from their structural and institutional contexts. This decontextualising was further bolstered, in the UK, by the establishment of the 2013 Parliamentary Commission on Banking Standards, the terms of reference of which were to:

> consider and report on: professional standards and culture of the UK banking sector, taking account of regulatory and competition investigations into the LIBOR rate-setting process; lessons to be learned about corporate governance, transparency and conflicts of interest, and their implications for regulation and for Government policy; and to make recommendations for legislative and other action.[2]

What is of interest here is how in the litany of offences in which the financial services sector has been clearly implicated in recent years – from waves of 'mis-selling' to consumers of pensions, endowment mortgages and payment protection insurance, to money laundering, LIBOR and FOREX manipulation, sanctions busting and tax evasion (Tombs, 2015a) – *one* specific issue, the 'problem' of culture, is addressed through only *one* of these offences, the fixing of LIBOR, the inter-bank lending rate. It is unsurprising, then, that the report of the Commission (House of Lords and House of Commons, 2013) did nothing to address the destructive, systemic features of the sector (*Economist*, 2013).

In its formal, political treatment in the UK, then, this focus on culture provided a mechanism through which the crisis was reduced and confined at best to second order phenomena, via which it was also subjected to 'de-democratisation' through 'efforts to refuse social and political dimensions of the financial system, its purposes and its governance' (Clarke and Newman, 2010: 713).

A second, but this time *macro*-level, moral critique has surfaced and resurfaced periodically and briefly – one that has actually spoken the word capitalism, albeit in the context of a series of simplistic moral dichotomies, between 'good' and 'bad', 'moral' and 'immoral', and 'crony' and 'responsible' capitalism. Indeed, in invoking 'crony capitalism, we are seeing the resurrection of a term that last circulated widely in the context of an earlier financial crisis, which afflicted Japan and neighbouring Asian states at the end of the 1990s' (Sinclair, 2010: 91). At times in the UK, the term 'crony capitalism' has been subject to high-level, political rhetoric. Notably, in the space of a few weeks at the start of 2012, all three main party leaders made major political interventions on this issue (Tombs,

2015b). As one might expect, however, the level of political 'debate' was anodyne.

Now, these latter discourses, regarding the 'need' for a renewed moral capitalism that by definition involve a critique of some form of immoral capitalism, are not insignificant. They create specific political risk, perhaps even crises of legitimacy, for governments, and these are typically political contexts in which albeit limited regulatory reform can be pushed through (Bittle, 2012). That said, and at the very same time, they are in themselves not of great significance – at least, not yet – since they have failed, at least in the UK, to assume discursive dominance, partly due to the contemporary balance of social forces, partly an effect of generalised political scepticism and demoralisation, and partly because they in fact have nowhere meaningful to go except that place which all state, institutional and organisational power will be deployed to prevent them going. The only place they can go is a place where they *cannot* go – that is, a more or less adequately conceived 'post'-capitalism. And one of the key effects of forty years of neoliberalism, and indeed the elevated moral capital of capital during much of this period, is to render a world beyond capitalism and a world without the corporation each even less imaginable than had hitherto been the case.

Conclusion

When introducing his budget to the Commons shortly after the formation of the 2010 Coalition government, Chancellor Osborne could quite confidently lay bare the shift from private to public debt, by then already a *fait accompli* that generated measures of urgent fiat, denoted by the naming of the budget as an 'Emergency' budget:

> Questions that were asked about the liquidity and solvency of banking systems are now being asked of the liquidity and solvency of some of the governments that stand behind those banks … This Budget is needed to deal with our country's debts … This is the unavoidable Budget.
>
> (Osborne, 2010)

Thus within what was quickly to become known as the 'Age of Austerity', the price of 'recovery' was to reduce significantly the social wage across the western world. Government debt, recast as state overspending rather than the socialisation of the effects of reckless, capitalist profit-taking, means that unemployment insurance, the deferred wages that are pensions, public services and the often-still minimal protections offered by regulation are luxuries that can now be barely afforded.

What has emerged from the material and discursive responses to the crisis, then, is a crucial meta-narrative – that the conditions for, and nature of, recovery places governments and populations as even more dependent upon private capital. This in turn immediately and necessarily – *for all our sakes* – reduces the scope for reinvigorated regulatory regimes. *Increasing* 'freedom' for capital is prescribed as the solution to the problems created in the first place by the excessive freedoms of capital.

Thus it can now clearly be seen how the morality plays discussed above were *effective* and *neutralising*, as well as *reaffirming* the moral code of neo-liberalism. They were *effective*, had a social and cultural power with some momentum, because they reflected realities: bankers *had* demonstrated greed, recklessness and at best a moral indifference; economies *had* boomed on consumption based on ever-easier access to credit; access to risky credit *was* disproportionately distributed to class fractions and ethnic minorities who were sold lifestyles that could not be supported by low-paying, under – or precarious employment; and the popularised myths of the end of boom and bust really *had* meant that, in some senses and for some, the crash did come unexpectedly, as if of no-one's making but also of everyone's making. But these discourses were also effective precisely because individually, and in their combination, they individualised, isolated and pulverised the crisis, thereby *neutralising* the systematic nature of the financial and broader economic system from the critical, perhaps fatal, popular scrutiny that the events from 2007 onwards merited. At the same time, key elements of the moral code of neo-liberalism – the social valorisation of private wealth-making and profit-taking, of entrepreneurialism even where this necessitates evading 'red tape', of a seething mass of individualised, naked self-interest, all free from the intervention of state, law and regulation, as the necessary means for economic and social good – are *reaffirmed*.

Thus, a series of post-crisis 'mystifications', which shuttled 'between a market-centered responsibility and an agentic-centered blame model of responsibility', served to 'sustain the supposed sanctity of the market' (Pludwin, 2011: 476) and, crucially, the dominant actors within it. None of this was any simple trick nor straightforward process. There is no sense in which the narratives that were eventually to be more successfully attached to the crisis and its aftermath were *necessarily* to be successful, albeit at least two issues were crucial in determining which would be: first, what power and interests could be mobilised *around* which narratives – and, here, the long-term mobilisation and consolidation of interests around the claims of free market economics was crucial (Blyth, 2013a); and, second, to what extent did specific narratives *possess* power: which were authoritative (Stanley, 2012), plausible and cohered with an already existing moral narrative (Whittle and Mueller, 2012). And it is in this latter context that the previously constructed moral capital of capital was crucial. The power of this common-sense served not simply to insulate private capital as a whole from any effective, thoroughgoing critique, but in fact served to restore rather more than business as usual. This settlement is far from wholly secure of course, but a challenge to it must involve a challenge to its claims to a superior morality.

Acknowledgement

This chapter draws upon work funded and made possible by the Leverhulme Trust, via Research Fellowship, RF-2001-173.

Notes

1 The appearance of bankers before the Select Committee prompted a stream of vitriolic press headlines, most infamously in *The Sun*, which ran the front-page headline 'Scumbag Millionaires' alongside images of Sir Tom McKillop, former chairman, and Sir Fred Goodwin, former chief executive of RBS Group (Hawkes and Pascoe-Watson, 2009; see Stanley, 2012).

2 www.parliament.uk/bankingstandards.

References

Albo, G. and Fanelli, C. (2014) *Austerity Against Democracy. An Authoritarian Phase of Neoliberalism?,* Toronto: Socialist Project.

Amable, B. (2011) Morals and politics in the ideology of neo-liberalism, *Socio-Economic Review* 9(1), 3–30.

BBC (2009) UK ban on short-selling expires, *BBC News Online*, 16 January, http://news.bbc.co.uk/1/hi/business/7832486.stm.

Bittle, S. (2012) *Still Dying for a Living: Corporate Criminal Liability after the Westray Mining Disaster*, Vancouver: UBC Press.

Blyth, M. (2013a) Paradigms and Paradox: The Politics of Economic Ideas in Two Moments of Crisis, *Governance: An International Journal of Policy, Administration, and Institutions*, 26(2), April, 197–215.

Blyth, M. (2013b) *Austerity. The History of a Dangerous Idea*, Oxford: Oxford University Press.

Bolchover, D. (2013) *The Myth of Global High Pay Talent Market*, London: High Pay Centre, http://highpaycentre.org/files/CEO_mobility_final.pdf.

Brassett, J. and Vaughan-Williams, N. (2012) Crisis is Governance: Subprime, the Traumatic Event, and Bare Life, *Global Society*, 26(1), 19–42.

Broome, A., Clegg, L. and Rethel, L. (2012) Global Governance and the Politics of Crisis, *Global Society*, 26(1), 3–17.

Clarke, J. (2010) After Neo-Liberalism?, *Cultural Studies*, 24(3), 375–394.

Clarke, J. and Newman, J. (2010) Summoning Spectres: crises and their construction, *Journal of Education Policy*, 25(6), 709–715.

Clarke, J. and Newman, J. (2012) The Alchemy of Austerity, *Critical Social Policy*, 32(3), 299–319.

Cohen, N. (2013) Bankers Carry on Unabashed, Unscathed and Unashamed, *The Observer*, 7 April, www.guardian.co.uk/commentisfree/2013/apr/07/brtish-bankers-unpunished-unashamed.

Conservative Home (2008) Labour has Maxed Out Britain's Credit Card, Says Cameron, 9 November, http://conservativehome.blogs.com/torydiary/2008/11/labour-has-maxe.html.

Dymski, G., Hernandez, J. and Mohanty, L. (2013) Race, Gender, Power, and the US Subprime Mortgage and Foreclosure Crisis: A Meso Analysis, *Feminist Economics*, 19(3), 124–151.

Economist, The (2013) Reforming Britain's Banks, June 22, www.economist.com/news/britain/21579834-parliamentary-commission-attempts-nothing-less-fundamental-change-bankings.

Froud, J., Nilsson, A., Moran, M. and Williams, K. (2012) Stories and Interests in Finance: Agendas of Governance before and after the Financial Crisis, *Governance: An International Journal of Policy, Administration and Institutions*, 25(1), January, 35–59.

Garfinkel, H. (1956) Conditions of Successful Degradation Ceremonies. *American Journal of Sociology*, 61, 420–424.

Gigliotti, M. (2013) The Compensation of Top Managers and the Performance of Italian Firms, *The International Journal of Human Resource Management*, 24(4), 889–903.

Gill S., and Law, D. (1993) Global Hegemony and the Structural Power of Capital, in S. Gill (ed.) *Gramsci, Historical Materialism and International Relations*. Cambridge: Cambridge University Press, 93–124.

Giroux, H. (2008) *Against the Terror of Neoliberalism. Politics Beyond the Age of Greed*, Boulder, CO: Paradigm Publishers.

Goffman, E. (1963) *Stigma*. New York: Simon & Schuster.

Hansen, P. (2014) From Finance Capitalism to Financialization: A Cultural and Narrative Perspective on 150 Years of Financial History, *Enterprise and Society*, 15(4), 605–642.

Harris, J. (2012) Credit Crunch: elusive ghosts of the financial feast lurk in the shadows, *The Guardian*, 7 August, www.guardian.co.uk/business/2012/aug/06/credit-crunch-elusive-ghosts-shadows.

Hawkes, S. and Pascoe-Watson, G. (2009). Scumbag Millionaires: as 2,300 RBS staff lose their jobs, shamed bank bosses 'sorry' for crisis, *The Sun*, 11 February.

High Pay Commission (2011a) *More for Less: what has happened to pay at the top and does it matter?*, May, http://highpaycommission.co.uk/wp-content/uploads/2011/09/HPC-IR.pdf.

High Pay Commission (2011b) *Cheques With Balances: why tackling high pay is in the national interest. Final report of the High Pay Commission*, November, http://highpaycentre.org/files/Cheques_with_Balances.pdf.

House of Lords and House of Commons (2013) *Changing Banking for Good. Report of the Parliamentary Commission on Banking Standards. Volume I: Summary, and Conclusions and Recommendations. HL Paper 27-I, HC 175-I*, London: The Stationery Office Limited.

Kelsey, D. (2014) The Myth of the City Trickster: storytelling, bankers and ideology in the Mail Online, *Journal of Political Ideologies*, 19(3), 307–330.

Konzelmann, S. (2014) The Political Economics of Austerity, *Cambridge Journal of Economics*, 38, 701–741.

McLean, B. and Nocera, J. (2011) *All the Devils Are Here: The Hidden History of the Financial Crisis*, New York: Portfolio/Penguin.

Myners, P. (2010) The Bankers' Moral Hazard, *The Guardian*, 9 March, www.theguardian.com/commentisfree/2010/mar/08/bankers-moral-hazard-discipline-punish.

Osborne, G. (2010) Budget 2010: Full text of George Osborne's statement. *The Telegraph*, 22 June, www.telegraph.co.uk/finance/budget/7846849/Budget-2010-Full-text-of-George-Osbornes-statement.html.

Pettifor, A. (2012) Delusional Economics and the Economic Consequences of Mr Osborne. Mis-measurement of health and wealth. Radical Statistics Annual Conference, London, 24 February.

Pludwin, S. (2011) Rogue Traders, Suspect Citizens and the Invisible Hand: Crisis in the Theater of Responsibility, *New Political Science*, 33(4), 465–477.

Reed, H. (2012) Credit Card Maxed Out? How UK debt statistics have been misrepresented, Mis-measurement of health and wealth. Radical Statistics Annual Conference, London, 24 February.

Robinson, M. (2012) Austerity Blues, *The Guardian. Saturday Review*, 17 March, www.guardian.co.uk/books/2012/mar/16/culture-credit-crunch-marilynne-robinson.

Sassen, S. (2013) The Logics of Finance. Abuse of power and systemic crisis, in Will, S., Handelman, S. and Brotherton, D.C. (eds) *How They Got Away With It. White Collar Criminals and the Financial Meltdown*, New York: Columbia University Press, 26–44.

Shorthose, J. (2011) Economic Conscience and Public Discourse, *Capital & Class*, 35(1), 107–124.

Sinclair, T. (2010) Round Up the Usual Suspects: Blame and the Subprime Crisis, New Political Economy, 15(1), 91–107.

Snider, L. (2000) The Sociology of Corporate Crime: An Obituary: (Or: Whose Knowledge Claims have Legs?), *Theoretical Criminology*, 4(2), 169–206.

Stanley, E. (2012) Scumbag Millionaires: the rhetorical construction and resistance of stigma during the financial crisis. PhD thesis, Birkbeck, University of London.

Tombs, S. (2001) Thinking About 'White-Collar' Crime, in Lindgren, S-Å. (ed.) *White-Collar Crime Research. Old Views and Future Potentials. Lectures and Papers from a Scandinavian Seminar. BRÅ-Rapport 2001:1*, Stockholm: Brottsförebyggande rådet/Fritzes, 13–34.

Tombs, S. (2015a) Corporate Theft and Fraud: crime and impunity in the retail financial services sector, in Whyte, D. (ed.) *How Corrupt is Britain?*, London: Pluto, 168–176.

Tombs, S. (2015b) *Social Protection After the Crisis? Regulation without Enforcement*, Bristol: Policy.

Treanor, J. (2011) Bob Diamond Stands Firm against MPs' Calls He Forgo His Bonus, *The Guardian*, 11 January, www.guardian.co.uk/business/2011/jan/11/bob-diamond-stands-firm-mp-bonus.

Treanor, J. (2013) More Than 2,400 UK Bankers Paid €1m-plus, EU Regulator Says, *The Guardian*, 15 July, www.guardian.co.uk/business/2013/jul/15/uk-bankers-pay-european-banking-authority.

Weissman, R. and Donahue, J. (2009) *Sold Out: How Wall Street and Washington Betrayed America*, Essential Information/Consumer Education Foundation.

Werdigier, J. (2011) It's Time to Stop Criticizing Bankers, Barclays Chief Says Dealbook. *New York Times*, 11 January, http://dealbook.nytimes.com/2011/01/11/time-to-stop-bashing-bankers-diamond-says/.

Whittle, A. and Mueller, F. (2012) Bankers in the Dock: moral storytelling in action, *Human Relations*, 65(1), 111–139.

Wiegratz, J. and Cesnulyte, E. (2016) Money Talks: Moral Economies of Earning a Living in Neoliberal East Africa, *New Political Economy*, 21(1), 1–25.

Will, S. (2013) America's Ponzi Culture, in Will, S., Handelman, S. and Brotherton, D.C. (eds) *How They Got Away With It. White Collar Criminals and the Financial Meltdown*, New York: Columbia University Press, 45–67.

Wintour, P. (2012) David Cameron condemns rhetoric of anti-business snobbery, *The Guardian*, 22 February, www.guardian.co.uk/politics/2012/feb/22/david-cameron-condemns-anti-business-snobbery.

4 Moral economy, unearned income, and legalized corruption

Andrew Sayer

> When plunder becomes a way of life for a group of men living in society, they create for themselves, in the course of time, a legal system that authorizes it and a moral code that glorifies it.
>
> (Frédéric Bastiat)

Introduction: moral economy

As French political economist Frédéric Bastiat appreciated, the origins of our contemporary economy had little to do with deliberations on what might be fair and morally justified and a lot to do with power. Yet our basic economic institutions are generally portrayed as legitimate and as accepted as such, though more as 'facts of life' than as rationally justified, and this acceptance is important for their continued existence. It would be a mistake to assume that because our political economic architecture is largely a product of power that there is no point in considering it in terms of moral and ethical questions of justice, fairness, and human well-being. Unless we consider these things, we have little basis for criticizing anything.

Amartya Sen once drew a distinction between the 'engineering' and the 'ethical' approaches to economics (Sen, 1991). The former treats economies as machines that work in various ways that need to be described and explained, and which economists can fix if they work badly. The ethical approach treats economies as sets of social relations and practices that may be good or bad on moral and ethical grounds and need to be assessed in those terms. In the days of classical political economy, the two were seamlessly merged. But since that time, the emergence of separate disciplines in the social sciences has led to an unhappy divorce of positive (i.e. descriptive and explanatory) thought from normative or evaluative thought. While most social sciences have tried to expel the latter, it has become ghettoized in political theory, which has returned the compliment by discussing ideal models of distribution that ignore the injustices of actually existing economic practices and situations (Sayer, 2007). This approach tends to reduce the social relations through which economies work to transactions between free-standing individuals pursuing their self-interest and encountering others in markets. Hence the work of the likes of Rawls or Dworkin or Sandel poses little or no threat to the established political economic order. (Capitalism or exploitation and parasitism are rarely mentioned in such literature.) The social relations through which economic activities are organized – employer and employee, landlord and tenant, creditor and debtor, tax-payer and recipient of tax-funded goods, carer and cared-for – are ignored or absorbed into generic market relations, allowing any injustices constituted by these social relations to be passed over.

'Moral economy' attempts to correct this. Like 'history', the term 'moral economy' can refer either to an approach or to an object. As an approach, moral economy is most importantly about assessing the moral justifications of basic features of actually existing economic organization, in particular property relations and what institutions and individuals are allowed and required to do. Here questions of justice are to the fore. It also examines and assesses the moral influences on, and implications of, economic activities, and how economic practices and relations are evaluated as fair or unfair, good or bad, by those involved in them. Moral economy treats the economy not merely as a machine that sometimes breaks down, but as a complex set of relationships between people, and between people and nature, increasingly stretched around the world, in which they act as producers of goods and services, investors, recipients of various kinds of income, lenders and borrowers, and as taxpayers and consumers.

As social beings we are dependent on others, most basically for care during those substantial periods of our lives when we cannot provide for ourselves. Dependence can take good or bad forms – life enhancing (for example, good care) or oppressive (for example, usury). As a critical approach, moral economy goes beyond the usual focus on irrationality and systemic breakdown, to focus on injustice and the moral justifications of taken-for-granted rights and practices. For instance, it's not only about how much people in different positions in the economy should get paid for what they do, but whether those positions are legitimate in the first place. Is it right that they're allowed to do what they're doing? An engineering critique of twenty-first-century capitalism might explain the role of the growth of shareholder power in the crisis of 2008 and the preceding boom, but without in any way challenging the legitimacy of the basic property relation involved. Politics without ethics is directionless, while ethics without politics is ineffectual. Moral economy seeks to combine them.

Once economic institutions and practices have become established, these normative questions tend to be forgotten, and a shift takes place from the normative to the normalized or naturalized (de Goede, 2005). Indeed, legitimations of the arrangements may scarcely be needed. Few economic institutions result simply from democratic deliberation about what is fair. Most are products of power. Thus it is not questioned why employees should have no ownership rights over the goods they make, or why absentee shareholders should be entitled to a share of profits. Unless, we challenge such arrangements, they are likely to remain. As Habermas commented, through such normalisation, *questions of validity are turned into questions of behaviour* (Habermas, 1979, p.6). While the powerful may be careful to ensure that their economic activities are described in ways that legitimize them, this is not the only major factor in their acceptance. As Bourdieu argued, acquiescence is often less a product of ideology or dominant discourses, than the facticity of the social world in which people act. It is primarily a product of habituation to subordinate positions and lack of experience of alternatives that produces a bodily attunement to them (2000, p.181): "of all the forms of 'hidden persuasion', the most implacable is the one exerted, quite simply, by the *order of things*" (Bourdieu and Wacquant, 1992, p.168, emphasis in original).

As an object of study, some have defined moral economies in opposition to market economies, as Edward Thompson famously did, but unlike him, though like many more recent users of the term, I regard all economies as moral economies in some respects (Arnold, 2001; Booth, 1994; Keat, 2012; Murphy, 1994; Sayer, 2007; Thompson, 1971), for all invoke some sort of moral/ethical justifications for their key institutions – even, as we shall see, neoliberalism. Again, this is not to imagine that these justifications have much to do with the formation of economic institutions, for this typically depends on power: they primarily serve as rationalizations of the already established. Hence the need to subject them to critical assessment.

To illustrate the kind of ethical critique that moral economy can provide, I next discuss three crucial but often overlooked distinctions that reveal much of what is ethically questionable about our most familiar economic institutions and practices. These are the distinction between earned and unearned income, and the related distinction between property and 'improperty', and thirdly 'investment' in the senses of wealth creation and of wealth extraction. While these have been noted in critiques of capitalism, they are now rarely made even though they have become more relevant.

Vital distinctions

One of the most powerful ways of exposing what is unjust about our economic system is through the old distinction between earned and unearned income. This has fallen out of use in the last 40 years, just when unearned income has expanded enormously.

Earned income is what waged and salaried employees and self-employed people get for producing goods and services. I don't mean to suggest that the size of their pay reflects what they deserve but that their pay is at least conditional on contributing to the provision of goods and services that others can use. The relation between what we might think people deserve for their work – however we might want to measure that – and the amount of pay they actually get is pretty loose. Nevertheless, their income is earned in the sense that it's work-based, and the goods or services they help to produce and deliver have 'use-value', such as the nutritious and tasty quality of a meal, or the educational benefits of a maths lesson, or the warmth provided by a heating system. So there are two criteria here: earned income is dependent not just on working, but on work that contributes directly or indirectly to producing use-values. This is important, because as we'll see shortly, it's possible to work without producing any useful goods or services, and indeed in a way that merely extracts money from others without creating anything in return.

Unearned income is very different. It is not conditional on contributing to the production of new goods and services but can be *extracted* by those who control an already-existing asset, such as land or a building or equipment, that others lack but need or want, and who can therefore be charged for its use. The recipients of this unearned income can get it regardless of whether they are capable of working and hence of *earning* an income, and regardless of whether those who have to pay consider it fair. If the asset, say a house, already exists, then there are no costs of production apart from maintenance costs. Those who receive unearned income from existing assets do so not because they are in any sense 'deserving' or because they are judged by others as needy and unable to provide for themselves, but *because they can*. It's power based on unequal ownership and control of key assets. In most cases they have this power of control by virtue of property rights that legally entitle them to control an existing asset and dispose of it as they wish. This unearned income is *asset-based*. The recipient is a rentier. As John Stuart Mill said of landlords, they "grow rich in their sleep without working, risking or economising" (Mill, 2015 [1848]). Mere ownership, whether it is of land, buildings, money, or technology produces nothing, but can be used for extracting value from others. As we shall see, neoliberalism has promoted unearned income, producing what we might reasonably call a something-for-nothing economy for the asset-rich.

J.A. Hobson, writing in the 1930s, coined the term 'improperty' to refer to the ownership of assets not for direct use but for extracting income from others. For example, whereas a house that someone owns and uses as their home is an example of *property*, a house that is owned just to provide a source of unearned income in the form of rent and capital gains is *improperty* (Hobson, 1937). Similarly for Tawney, property was for direct use or as an aid to work, not as a source of income irrespective of this (Tawney, 2004 [1920]). Hence one can, without contradiction, be against improperty and yet be in favour of private, as well as collective forms of property.

There's a further question about unearned income that unfortunately is all too often overlooked: How can it be possible for someone to live without producing anything? If they're consuming goods and services – in the case of the rich, in vast quantities – but not contributing to their production, then who is producing them? The answer can only be this: *for it to be possible for some to consume without producing, others who are producing goods and services must be producing more than they themselves consume. In other words, others must be producing a surplus.* Even though those workers may be getting a wage or salary, *part of their work must be unpaid*. And it was not only Marx who realized this: it is implicit in Adam Smith's charge that landlords "love to reap where they have not sowed" (Smith, 1976 [1776], Bk 1, Ch. V, p.56) and, again, in John Stuart Mill's challenge: "If some of us grow rich in our sleep, where do we think this wealth is coming from? It doesn't materialize out of thin air. It doesn't come without costing someone, another human being. It comes from the fruits of others' labours, which they don't receive" (Mill, 2015 [1848], Bk. v, Ch. II). Or as, later, Tawney put it, "The man who lives by owning without working is necessarily supported by the industry of someone else, and is, therefore, too expensive a luxury to be encouraged" (Tawney, 2004 [1920], p.80). The unearned income is not extracted through any deceit or fraud, yet for most people, its dependence on the unpaid labour of others – a hidden subsidy – goes unnoticed. To echo Bastiat, improperty is authorized by the legal system, and supported by a common-sense moral code, which presents it as a reasonable payment to a provider of a service.[1]

Rent is the clearest example of unearned income based on improperty. Interest, as money's rent, is another, albeit less-recognized case, today, though historically, as usury, it has been known and reviled for millennia, and often prohibited (Graeber, 2011). There has been a wide range of critiques of usury, both religious and secular, but their strongest argument against it is that it allows the strong to take advantage of the weak. We can see this phenomenon in cases as different as payday loans and the Greek debt crisis. In everyday life we apply double standards to interest. If we felt it necessary to borrow from a well-off friend we would not expect them to charge us interest or have the right to seize our property if we couldn't repay them, and if they did we would object strongly because it would be clear that they were using their relative strength to take advantage of our weakness. But where impersonal economic relations are concerned, we tend to accept interest as normal and legitimate. Obviously, the seriousness of the injustice of usury is relative to the size of the debt charges and the inequalities between lender and borrower, and the equivalent goes for other kinds of unearned income. Even though payment of interest means that there is a net flow of money from the debtor to the creditor, and often the weak to the strong, it is typically the lender who is seen as the benefactor and the debtor who is seen as dependent and morally inferior. Interest charges are often defended as a way of protecting lenders from risk, but the greater the inequality between the lender and the debtor, the easier it is for the lender to refuse to reduce debt charges and hence avoid risk, as we currently see in the relations between Greece, Germany, and the International Monetary Fund (IMF). Rates of interest and their enforcement reflect power, not merely risk. As a debtor unable to repay debts, creditors demand of Greece that it sell off assets like ports, regional airports, marinas, golf courses, water supply, and government buildings.[2]

Money creation itself has now largely been privatized, as private banks are allowed to create 97 percent of money as credit. Further, since they lend very little to business (c. 10 percent of bank lending in the UK) and instead mostly lend against existing property, little of their income in interest derives from productive investment (Turner, 2009). They are effectively allowed to charge a private tax on borrowers. Excessive lending against property inflates its value and facilitates wealth extraction as interest (for lenders) and capital gains for owners, not wealth creation. In the last two years, house prices have inflated by up to £200,000 in one London borough (*Guardian*, 2015). Now, in the UK, 20 percent of households – mainly young, single and living in the south-east – are having to spend over half their income on housing (Gardiner, 2014), and this of course means taking on more debt and paying more interest to lenders.

The enormous increase in private debt during the neoliberal era has been accompanied by a concerted effort on the part of lenders to rid debt of its traditional associations of dependence and burdens, and to present it more appealingly as 'credit', and in the case of mortgages and perhaps student loans, as aids to 'investment' in appreciating assets. In effect, the borrower is invited to see credit as liberating, and as a vote of confidence in their economic prospects. Yet of course, debt burdens have increased, and with that the net flow of payments from debtors to lenders. In Britain and Germany, only the top 10 percent of households in the income distribution receive more in interest payments than they pay out, so interest or usury creates an escalator transferring money from the bottom and the middle to the top (Hodgson, 2013; Creutz, cited in Kennedy, 2012).

In classical political economy, profit is the third member of this trio of sources of unearned income, after rent and interest. The profits of private (productive) employers derive from their ownership of the means of production and the product, and the dependency of non-owners of means of production on them for employment. Pure capitalists – that is ones who just own their firms and delegate management to others – are not contributing to wealth creation, but merely using their power relative to those of propertyless workers to appropriate the difference between costs and the value of what the workers (and managers) produce. Since mere ownership produces nothing, their income is unearned. For working capitalists, those who are not only owners but managers, their income is a mixture of both earned and unearned.

Relatedly, shares provide another gateway to this unearned income. Since the vast majority of share transactions are in the secondary market, the money paid for such purchases goes to the previous owner, not the company, and thus cannot be claimed to be a payment that contributes to any objective productive investment. The extraordinary feature of share ownership is not so much limited liability (for losses made by the company), but that it provides a potentially indefinite source of unearned income – an unlimited asset. Both dividends and gains from trading shares are unearned income. Since growth of demand for shares has exceeded the growth of supply in recent decades, average prices have tended to rise too, creating bubbles, so this source has proved lucrative (Engelen *et al.*, 2011). The development over the last 30 years of the shareholder value movement – a highly successful rentier campaign driven by the rise of major institutional shareholders such as pension funds – coupled with the weakening of trade unions, has made share prices the primary concern of the management of companies. Firms that fail to deliver rising share prices – for example, by ploughing most of their profits into productive investment instead of distributing them as dividends – are disciplined by the market for companies as they become vulnerable to takeover by managements that will deliver shareholder value.

The most glaring but rarely asked questions here are: Why are absentee, uncommitted shareholders the prime stakeholders in firms? Why are workers/employees (present, committed, and dependent), who produce the goods and services on which the firm depends, *not* stakeholders? Why is it you can work for a firm for years and have no say in what happens to the revenue that your work helps to raise, while a rich outsider who has never contributed anything to it can buy up the firm and do what they like with it, including making you redundant if it suits them? The answer is because they can, and they can because that is what the rules allow and they have the power to take advantage of them.

As recipients of unearned income based on improperty, rentiers are often seen as passive, as in Mill's portrayal. Yet many of the rich dissociate themselves from this image of passive free-riding by calling themselves 'the working rich'. Some may indeed get most of their income in the form of salary rather than rent or interest or dividends or capital gains. But many of these are working for rentier organizations, whose revenue comes from rent, interest, and speculation, so their salary is actually paid out of such unearned income. Some may work hard to compete for new and bigger sources of unearned income, and this is effectively what many involved in the financial and property sectors do. In addition, chief executive officers (CEOs) – whether inside or outside the rentier sectors – can use their power – to pay themselves extraordinary salaries, provided they keep the shareholders – the 'functionless investors' as Keynes called them – happy with generous dividends and rising share prices. In the post-war boom, CEOs in the US were paid 24 times as much as the average worker. There are now eight US CEOs who are paid more than a 1,000 times average pay.[3] The immediate cause of this extraordinary change is not a miraculous increase in their managerial skills but the self-interested excesses of remuneration committees (the 'Ratchet, Ratchet and Bingo' compensation consultants, as billionaire Warren Buffett called them).[4] But enabling this growth of legalized extortion is the weakening of organized labour and the strengthening of rentier power in the form of the shareholder value movement and financial deregulation.

One of the most common justifications of many sources of unearned income[5] is that they are 'investments'. This trades on a slippage in the use of the word that is central to the legitimation of the rich, and their symbolic domination. Investment is invariably understood to be a good thing, and can provide an appealing cover for a vast range of activities, yet the term is used in two radically different senses: (1) *use-value/object-oriented definitions* focus on what it is that is invested *in* (e.g. infrastructure, equipment, training), i.e. on *wealth creation* – creating new ways of producing goods and services; and (2) *exchange-value/'investor'-oriented definitions* focus on the financial gains from any kind of lending, saving, purchase of financial assets, or speculation – regardless of whether they contribute to any objective investment (1), or benefit others. Here the focus is *wealth extraction*. This is not just an academic distinction: the difference between the two activities is of enormous practical importance for both economic growth and wealth distribution.

This distinction is almost always elided, allowing the second to be passed off as based on the first. Sometimes the two may indeed go together. But it is also perfectly possible for successful investments in the first sense to fail to provide financial benefits to 'investors' in the second sense. The use of my taxes for investing in infrastructure on the other side of the country may benefit others but not me. Conversely, it is equally possible for lucrative 'investments' in the second sense to have neutral or negative effects on productive capacity – through, asset-stripping, value-skimming, and rent-seeking. The slippage between the two meanings has become common not so much through a desire to deceive than through ignorance, coupled with the fact that under capitalism individuals have little or no interest in checking whether their 'investments' (2) have positive, neutral, or negative effects on the production of goods and services; to the rentier-'investor', £1 million from rent is no different from £1 million from new productive capacity. Further, for particular 'investors', though not for whole economies, purely extractive kinds of 'investment' such as speculating on asset bubbles can be less risky than objective, wealth-creating investment. Given the huge difference between these two meanings of the same word, and the contingent relation between the practices to which they refer, we must be on our guard when rich or super-rich individuals – or indeed small-time rentiers – justify their wealth by claiming to be 'investors'.

Arguments from the standpoint of individual liberty focus on the freedom of formally equal individuals to contract with one another, whether lending or borrowing, or renting, or agreeing to an employment contract, as if these were like buying and selling of goods and services. Allowing individuals to contract freely seems reasonable in the abstract, but when one thinks in more concrete terms about situations in which the contracting parties are unequal in power and improperty is extensive – the dominant situation in many societies – then the implications are very different. The individualistic model of the economy helps draw attention away from the domination of economies by powerful multinationals with annual turnovers in excess of many countries' gross domestic product (GDP). Thus, speculation is passed off by appealing to people as naturally inclined to make 'investments', as a matter of prudence, and indeed responsibility, when improperty is inevitably concentrated in the hands of a wealthy minority.

It is common also to pass off improperty as property by appealing to the rights of the property owner to use and dispose of her property as she wishes. Given that what is at one time property can become improperty at another, then where the rules concerning the former do not debar the latter they can be used to legitimize it – for example, when a farmer decides to switch from growing crops on his land to using it as a source of rent. Exploitative practices may have innocent, clean origins. And extensive improperty of course produces inequality, transferring wealth from those who have limited income based on work, to asset owners, and the greater this inequality the greater the dependence of the former on the latter, though of course the asset-rich are dependent on workers for producing the goods that gives their money value. The more unequal a society, the easier it is for the asset rich to free-ride on the asset poor.

Where moral justifications of economic practices are hard to find, apologists often appeal to a utilitarian argument, attributed to Adam Smith in his famous example of the butcher, the baker and the brewer, who, in competing with others find it in their self-interest to give customers what they want. I say 'attributed' to Smith firstly because he was writing when capitalism ('commercial society') was in its infancy and the baker and co were clearly tiny businesses, not the likes of Microsoft or Monsanto (Smith, 1976 [1776]). (Smith also warned of the dangers to the public of monopoly, which was always capable of arising spontaneously out of competition.) Second, because he was well aware that market relations were entangled with other social relations in which moral considerations were always important, he certainly did not believe the pursuit of self-interest should be unlimited, and he was not a utilitarian. As he put it: "The wise and virtuous man is at all times willing that his own private interest should be sacrificed to the public interest of his own particular order or society" (Smith, 1984 [1759] Pt VI, Sec ii, Ch 3.1, p.235).[6] And as we have already seen, he certainly didn't see the landlords' self-interest in 'reaping where they have not sowed' in a favorable light.

Finally, unearned income based on improperty is not only unjust but dysfunctional – a deadweight cost – since it diverts resources away from the productive economy. We need either to block or heavily tax it, in fact I suggest we tax earned income less and unearned income more. Is it not bizarre that we think it's OK to tax the income of those who work to provide goods and services for others, so they share in the burdens of supporting society, but think it's wrong to tax those who just get a windfall without doing anything?

Neoliberalism and the promotion of improperty

A central but often overlooked feature of neoliberal policies is that they enlarge the sphere of improperty, while presenting this as wealth creation rather than wealth extraction. In the UK, the enforced sale of public housing and housing association properties and the subsidization of buy-to-let housing are among the clearest examples. Housing becomes about private gain, not providing homes, improperty not property. Far from enabling people to become more independent they lead to dependence on rentiers, whether banks for mortgages or landlords for property to rent, so having a home becomes conditional upon supplying them with unearned income. Consequently rents are now higher in Britain than anywhere in Europe, both in absolute terms and relative to income, while the value of buy-to-let properties now nears £1 trillion. While this conversion of property into improperty has enlarged wealth extraction, real investment in new housing – wealth creation – has suffered, falling to just 3 percent of UK GDP between 1996 and 2011, compared to 6 percent in Germany and 5 percent in France.[7]

Privatization of public utilities such as water and energy obliges consumers to provide companies with what James Meek (2012) calls 'a human revenue stream' that has to satisfy shareholders' considerable short-term demands, and these in turn sharply constrain long-term investment. Although, the companies are supposed to compete, they avoid price competition by 'confusion marketing', that is offering complex deals that combine high margin and low margin elements in ways that defy comparison, and by securitizing their revenue from consumers into the future (Allen and Pryke, 2013; Bowman *et al.*, 2014). Water bills have nearly doubled since privatisation (Giles, 2012), but this is no longer the government's responsibility.

Cutbacks to transfer payments via the welfare state have been complemented by the expansion of sources of rentier income, sometimes referred to as 'asset-based welfare'. According to neoliberal moral economy, the prudent, 'financially literate' individual is supposed to buy assets like shares or buy-to-let housing in order to provide themselves with a pension. New Labour moralized it in terms of the duty of everyone to "to accept responsibility to take care of one's own future consumption needs within the context of increasing state retreat from the arena of welfare provision" (Watson, 2009, p.43). Asset-based welfare is of course an oxymoron, for the income is not democratically approved on criteria of need, but is acquired simply on the basis of private ownership and 'investment' in the second, wealth-extraction sense, and at the expense of others, without their knowledge let alone their consent. Without any official acknowledgement, this construction of supposedly free-market forces has the effect of obliging the asset-poor to further subsidize the asset-rich. As Matthew Watson comments, this also "changed the role of the state from direct securing of distinct patterns of housing tenure to securing a macroeconomic environment in which mortgage lending conditions produce continual upward pressure on house prices" (Watson, 2009, p.48). Improperty is both a cause and effect of inequality; the larger economic inequalities are, the greater the opportunities for asset-based wealth extraction. Extraordinarily, this has not yet proved an electoral liability. This is presumably because (1) the media and politics are dominated by the upper reaches of the top 1 percent; (2) many of the merely well-off have stakes in improperty; and (3) the argument is simply not known in popular culture as the social relations of improperty have become thoroughly normalized.

At a larger scale, structural adjustment policies imposed by the IMF and World Bank make loans conditional upon selling off public property to corporations where it can serve as improperty. As Susan George put it, "Debt is an efficient tool. It ensures access to other peoples' raw materials and infrastructure on the cheapest possible terms" (George, 1990, p.143). Usury is not only a means to unearned income in the form of debt charges but a way of dispossessing debtors of their assets. The expansion of improperty and rent-seeking loom large in trade deals such as the Transatlantic Trade and Investment Partnership and the Trans Pacific Pact currently under construction. These are undemocratic in conception and anti-democratic in intent, being designed in secret by corporate lawyers to enable big companies to pursue rent-seeking, unhampered by policies of elected governments, for example, for safeguarding employment protection, health, or the environment. Precedents of these treaties are already allowing companies to sue governments that impede them for millions (Sayer, 2014). Typically, the treaties are defended as expanding free trade, cutting 'red tape', and increasing economic growth.

But again, legitimation depends not only on rhetoric but on how things superficially appear. Thus, it is of crucial importance for the legitimation of capitalist economies that they operate 'without regard for persons', as Weber put it: anyone, in principle, can be a capitalist or rentier or receive an inheritance. This allows those who are critical of them to be dismissed as failures – 'if you're so clever, why aren't you rich?' as the American saying goes – or merely envious. It's also important that it's possible for many to benefit in very small ways from the arrangements that allow a tiny minority to benefit hugely. Thus, those who Engelen *et al.* (2011) call 'the fortunate 40 per cent' in the UK may make receive modest amounts of unearned income, for example, through capital gains in the housing market and indirectly through their pension funds where these are 'invested' in securities. Significantly, the small-time recipients of unearned income are usually dependent on major rentiers such as pension funds and banks for mortgages for access to their capital gains. More generally, neoliberal discourse invites people to see themselves as free and equal choosers, rather than acting under duress within unequal economic relationships such as those of employment, rent, or debt.

In conclusion

Improperty allows huge concentrations of economic power in private hands, so much so that the wealth of the richest thousand people in the UK now stands at £547 billion, over four times the size of the National Health Service budget. With this goes political power. As we have seen in the financial crisis, it allows those who have benefitted most from improperty to hold their countries to ransom when their attempts to expand their take from the rest of the economy precipitate crises. And the combined wealth of the 85 richest people on the planet now equals the total wealth of the poorest half of the world's population. Bastiat's insight might be rephrased: 'Always remember the golden rule: those with the gold make the rules'.

Notes

1 In a piece condemning landlordism, the young Winston Churchill described rent as a payment for a 'disservice' (Churchill, 1909).
2 www.wsj.com/articles/greece-open-to-selling-all-its-major-ports-1402070040.
3 Sanford University Centre on Poverty and Inequality, www.stanford.edu/group/scspi/cgi-bin/facts.php; see also Smith and Kunt (2013).
4 http://seekingalpha.com/article/7395-warren-buffett-on-excessive-ceo-compensation.
5 As I argue in *Why We Can't Afford the Rich*, other sources of unearned income include 'value-skimming' (fees charged for arranging financial deals such as mergers and takeovers and for rent-seeking and arranging tax dodging), many forms of speculation, and of course, inheritance (Sayer, 2014, Ch 7 and 9).
6 Smith (1984 [1759]) (the sixth and final edition was published in 1790, a year after the fifth and final edition of *The Wealth of Nations*). Smith also theorized self-interest in ways that included prudence and consideration of others.
7 www.housing.org.uk/media/press-releases/worst-deal-in-europe-uk-rents-double-the-continental-average/.

References

Allen, J., and Pryke, M. (2013) 'Financializing Household Water: Thames Water, MEIF, and 'ring-fenced' politics', *Cambridge Journal of Regions, Economy and Society*, 6 (3), pp. 419–439.

Arnold, T.C. (2001) 'Rethinking Moral Economy', *American Political Science Review*, 95 (1), pp. 85–95.

Booth, W. (1994) 'On the Idea of the Moral Economy', *American Political Science Review*, 88 (3), pp. 653–667.

Bourdieu, P. (2000) *Pascalian Meditations*, Cambridge: Polity.

Bourdieu, P. and Wacquant, L. (1992) *Towards a Reflexive Sociology*, Chicago: University of Chicago Press.

Bowman, A., Froud, J., Johal, S., Law, J., Leaver, A., Moran, M., and Williams (2014) *The End of the Experiment: From Competition to the Foundational Economy*, Manchester: Manchester University Press.

Churchill, W. (1909) *The People's Rights*, www.wealthandwant.com/docs/Churchill_TPL.html.

de Goede, M. (2005) *Virtue, Fortune, and Faith: A Genealogy of Finance*, Minnesota: Minnesota University Press.

Engelen, E. (2012) *After the Great Complacence*, Oxford: Oxford University Press.

Gardiner, L. (2014) 'Housing pinched: Understanding which households spend the most on housing costs', Resolution Foundation, 14 August, www.resolutionfoundation.org/publications/housing-pinched-understanding-households-spend-housing-costs/.

George, S. (1990) *A Fate Worse Than Debt*, New York: Grove Weidenfeld.

Giles, C. (2012) 'All that money growing on trees', *Financial Times*, 19 March, http://blogs.ft.com/money-supply/2012/03/19/all-that-money-growing-on-trees/#axzz1peBhsxr6.

Graeber, D. (2011) *Debt: The First 5000 Years*, Brooklyn, NY: Melville House Publishing.

Guardian, The (2015) 'Explosion in house prices greatest in the south east', *The Guardian*, 18 March.

Habermas, J. (1979) *Communication and the Evolution of Society*, New York: Beacon Press.

Hobson, J.A. (1937) *Property and Impropriety*, London: Gollancz.

Hodgson, G. (2013) 'Banking, finance and income inequality, Positive Money', https://positivemoney.org/wp-content/uploads/2013/10/Banking-Finance-and-Income-Inequality.pdf.

Keat, R. (2012) 'Market economies as moral economies: the ethical character of market institutions', www.russellkeat.net/admin/papers/74.pdf.

Kennedy, M. (2012) *Occupy Money*, Gabriola Island, BC: New Society Publishers.

Meek, J. (2012) 'Human Revenue Stream', *London Review of Books*, 20 March.

Mill, J.S. (2015 [1848]) *Principles of Political Economy*, Seattle: CreateSpace Independent Publishing Platform.

Murphy, J.B. (1993) *The Moral Economy of Labor*, New Haven: Yale University Press.

O'Neill, J. (1998) *The Market: Ethics, Knowledge and Politics*, London: Routledge.

Pettifor, A. (2006) *The Coming First World Debt Crisis*, Basingstoke: Palgrave.

Sayer, A. (2007) 'Moral Economy as Critique', *New Political Economy*, 12 (2), pp. 261–270.

Sayer, A. (2014) *Why We Can't Afford the Rich,* Bristol: Policy Press.

Sen, A. (1991) *On Ethics and Economics*, London: Wiley.

Smith, A. (1984 [1759] *The Theory of Moral Sentiments*, Indianapolis: Liberty Fund.

Smith, A. (1976 [1776]), *An Inquiry into the Nature and Causes of the Wealth of Nations*, ed. by E.Cannan, Chicago: University of Chicago Press.

Smith, E.B. and Kunt, P. (2013) 'CEO pay 1,795-to-1 multiple of wages skirts US law', *Bloomberg News*, 30 April, http://go.bloomberg.com/multimedia/ceo-pay-ratio/.

Tawney, R.H. (2004 [1920]) *The Acquisitive Society*, The Acquisitive Society, Mineola, NY: Harcourt, Brace and Howe.

Thompson, E.P. (1971) 'The Moral Economy of the English Crowd in the 18th Century', *Past & Present*, 50, pp. 76–136.

Turner, A. (2009) *The Turner Review: A Regulatory Response to the Global Banking Crisis*, London: Financial Services Authority.

Watson, M. (2009) 'Planning for a future of asset-based welfare?', *Planning Practice and Research*, 24 (1), pp. 41–56.

5 The moral economy of post-socialist capitalism

Professionals, rentiers and fraud

Balihar Sanghera

Introduction

This chapter examines the fraudulent nature of professional and financial elites' practices in post-Soviet Kyrgyzstan, focusing on a range of actors from doctors and lecturers to bankers and property developers. It explains how neoliberalism can shape their moral judgements about what are legitimate and illegitimate economic practices, and discusses how their practices can produce negative social consequences. The marketisation and financialisation of the economy can normalise economic practices (such as usury and economic rent) that were previously deemed to be illegitimate, fraudulent and harmful (Hudson, 2014: 185–201; Sayer, 2015: 49–57). At the start of the transition to a market economy in the 1990s, people were promised choice, liberation, autonomy and accountability, but instead concentrated economic power, plutocracy, wealth extraction, household indebtedness and corruption have emerged. Under socialism, economic resources were valued for their productive capacity, property rights functioned to serve society, enterprises had social obligations, workers enjoyed the fruits of their labour, and the state prohibited idle and speculative economic activities (Hann, 1993; see Ledeneva, 1998 on informal dealings). So whereas before there were different types of economic activity and different sources of wealth – ranging from productive and unproductive investment, wealth creation and extraction, just enjoyment of fruits of labour and idle parasitism of privilege and fortune – now neoliberalism treats all economic activities the same, valuing them according to their capacity to make money, and subordinating the production of things to the production of profit (Clarke, 2007; see Tawney, 1921 on the acquisitive society). The neoliberal moral economy has freed people from social obligations to pursue their own self-interest. Economic and social problems are presumed to be corrected automatically by market forces, requiring no social will.

There are two ways in which the neoliberal moral economy can create opportunities and incentives for fraudulent practices, and can alter financial and professional elites' evaluations about moral worth and desert. First, the marketisation of the public sector can generate a competitive environment in which income, social status and power are seen to be more valuable than professionals' excellence of practice, integrity and worthiness (Keat, 2000). Second, the financialisation of the economy can shape laws and policies that entitle financial and political elites to engage in unproductive investments and unearned income (such as property speculation, bank lending, rent and capital gains), extracting wealth produced by others without deserving it with damaging economic and social consequences (see Sayer's chapter in this book). It is a form of legal corruption, or as Tawney (1921: 80) notes of wealth extraction, 'Property is not theft, but a good deal of theft becomes property'.

The chapter addresses a couple of shortfalls in existing studies to offer a critical perspective on social change in Kyrgyzstan. In post-Soviet studies, understanding the illicit, informal and corrupt nature of post-Soviet economies has been a recurring theme in the literature, which usually contrasts the post-Soviet lawlessness, chaos and suppression with the presumed orderly economic and political system in the West (Cooley and Heathershaw, 2015). Three key points are worth noting about fraud in the post-Soviet space. First, transnational financial networks, which include international banks and corporate lawyers, play a major role in channelling illicit capital flows from authoritarian political regimes to legal 'shell' companies and offshore tax havens, whose status and operations are condoned, if not approved, by Western governments (Cooley and Sharman, 2015). Second, informal and illicit economic practices are not marginal, transitional or threatening to people's daily lives, but are part of their repertoire of strategies and tactics for economic survival that engage at some level with the formal economy (Morris and Polese, 2014: 8). Third, unable to secure basic goods and services through the neoliberalising welfare state or imperfect markets, poor people either develop client–patron relationships with local elites, promising political support in exchange for resources, or resort to bribing state officials and using personal connections to acquire state resources and services, such as housing (Radnitz, 2010: 26–33; McMann, 2014: 1–4). While these ideas provide useful insights into the multiple ways in which fraud can occur in the region, some significant forms of corruption are overlooked. As Sayer argues in his chapter, property owners, bankers, monopolies and financial brokers extract wealth from the real economy in ways that are unproductive, unearned and undeserved, yet in international and national dealings, their practices are rarely questioned or challenged, becoming part of the normal economic and moral fabric of society. Modern usury, rent and capital gains are forms of symbolic dominance that normalise unequal social relationships in favour of the property and financial sector.

The moral economy literature contains many accounts of how lay people's ideas of fairness and justice embed local economies (e.g., Scott, 1985). But while everyday forms of politics and resistance and sporadic acts of rebellion offer important insights into the moral lives of peasants, traders and the working class, and to a lesser extent of the middle class, the moral economy of the upper class and the rich is hardly recognised and studied. Reasons for this neglect include elites are harder to access and research on, the need to articulate accounts of poor and disadvantaged groups, and the belief that working class are the key agents of social change. But critical studies on professional and financial elites are required more than ever given their increased power and influence in today's global financial capitalism.

The first section will discuss how the marketisation of professions can undermine professional integrity and competence. The second section will describe the financialisation of the economy and the negative effects of wealth extraction of key industries, including microfinance and private monopolies. Finally, I will make some concluding remarks.

Fraudulent practices in the professions

This section will briefly explain the theoretical framework for understanding professional practices, and then drawing upon my research on professions in Kyrgyzstan will discuss how neoliberalisation can influence professionals' values and practices.

Professional practices are an outcome of a dialectical relationship between professionals and institutions (Keat, 2000: 22–28, 111–115). The latter provides the former with resources and opportunities (i.e., organisational capabilities) to achieve professional excellence and recognition, and to nurture certain moral sentiments and dispositions (including compassion, self-interest, justice, integrity and courage) necessary to make good professional judgements (Oakley and Cocking, 2001: 90-93). Professionals (such as doctors, university lecturers and journalists) can embody pro-social moral qualities as a result of professional education, mentoring, practical training, exposure to professional ethos and having good role models (Blackburn and McGhee, 2004). In addition, professionals use their reflexivity to shape practices in relation to multiple moral concerns (including family well-being, practical worldly achievements and social justice), navigating their way through the world, adapting, circumventing or resisting social and cultural constraints in pursuit of their ultimate concerns (Archer, 2007: 5–22).

But there are two major impediments to good professional practices, as understood by the professional community. First, externally imposed goals and institutional norms (e.g., political pressure, income generation and administrative procedures) can deflect professionals from their primary responsibilities. While professionals can be committed and motivated to achieve good practices and to ensure fairness and justice, they are also governed by organisational rules and discourses, including performance targets. In addition, they seek extra-professional values, such as wealth, social standing and political power (Keat, 2000: 22–28). Professionals can be alert to the dangers of trading professional virtues for extra-professional values, and of the institutional logic superseding professional ethos. Second, social inequalities can shape professionals' moral sentiments and judgements to produce lack of sympathy and unjust treatment towards working class and marginalised groups (Smith, 1976, I.iii.3.1–8). For instance, professional elites can be contemptuous and condescending towards poor groups, and can belittle their worth, depicting them as lazy and deviant, and responding with little compassion to their misfortunes.

In addition, professional elites have implicit moral values and beliefs disguised under a veil of impartiality, rationality and integrity. For instance, the juridical language creates a universalising attitude, designed to express the generality of the rule of law (Bourdieu, 1987: 820). It is committed to facts and objectivity, presupposes an ethical consensus, and has little room for idiosyncratic judgements or personal discretion. But in general the rhetoric of neutrality and universality masks the ideological neoliberal bias towards moral individualism, private property and the market economy.

My study on Kyrgyzstani professions (Sanghera and Iliasov, 2008) reveals how the neoliberalisation of the economy has created opportunities and pressures for fraudulent and harmful professional practices. First, faced with cuts to public subsidies, directors of hospitals, universities and other public organisations have become entrepreneurial in marketing their services and recovering costs. Organisational capabilities have not only become weaker, but also more business orientated. In higher education, Musabaeva (2008) notes that state universities are only nominally so, since state funding does not exceed 10–15 per cent of their budget, and most students pay for their education. In her research paper, Romanchuk (2002: 6) reports how Bakyt, a university director, has no option but to 'sell' diplomas because of reduced public funding:

> The state, which committed itself to financing the universities, has not been doing this for a long time, even at a minimal level. So the universities have to show miracles of commercial inventiveness. The government is to be blamed for failing to fund universities, and we are forced to seek money elsewhere. At our university, almost 90 per cent of the students pay for their studies. With little support from the government, universities largely depend on this money, and also we cannot refuse to 'sell' diplomas to some students.

Not only do university directors acquire business acumen to make their institutions financially viable, but there is a tendency for both students and the university administration to harass lecturers to alter grades to satisfy their 'customers' (Reeves, 2005). Not surprisingly, the marketisation of higher education has also reorganised some universities into personal business enterprises for powerful directors and academics, who extort more money and favours from students and their families for increasingly poor education, with the result that extra-professional values trump professional ethos (Amsler, 2013).

Second, as public organisations become more business orientated, some professionals demand 'gifts' (a euphemism for bribes) for a higher level of 'customer care'. In my study, Damira, a state-employed doctor, is shocked that her colleagues in state hospitals have little compassion for patients, viewing them as customers, whose medical treatment depends on informal payments. On one occasion, her friend died because she did not give enough 'gifts' to receive a proper radiotherapy:

> I told my colleague [the doctor], 'Please do [the treatment] properly, please be careful.' The doctor received my sick friend very rudely and did a bad radiotherapy. My friend brought the doctor some gifts, chocolate and cognac. But still the doctor was impolite and did a poor job, which resulted in her death. You see, doctors are more interested to get money from their patients and if patients bring them only a box of chocolate, doctors feel that it is not enough.

What appals Damira is the doctor's lack of sympathy, care and justice. Although the doctor was reminded of his professional code, he still failed to give adequate attention and care to the patient. As Smith (1976: I.iii.3.1–8) notes, excessive concern for material and symbolic goods can corrupt moral sentiments, resulting in distorted professional judgements.

On the face of it, lack of commitment to professional ethos can be condemned as moral corruption, but some professionals are reflexive about their situation, recognising the difficulty of satisfying multiple moral concerns because of economic hardship. Natalya, a police officer, suggests that corruption can be morally permissible to ensure family well-being:

> *Natalya*: The militia work mostly for money now. Offenders may pay the militia and be released. It works very successfully. You can bribe anyone. There are very few honest people. I wish these people would think about the area of their activities and their obligations. The militia should protect people from offenders, and not promote an increase in their number.
>
> *Interviewer*: Why do you think those who work in the militia changed?
>
> *Natalya*: They have their own families that they need to feed. That's why they take bribes. Maybe, if their salary were bigger, they would be taking fewer bribes.

Poorly paid professionals often justify corruption as necessary for household survival. In trying to dovetail different moral concerns, family well-being can occasionally be incompatible with professional virtues. Janysh, a police officer, describes the context in which traffic police judge it morally acceptable to fine drivers:

> My salary is ridiculous – I get only 2500 soms [US$63], 3000 at maximum. And I have to pay my rent, buy clothes for my kids, myself, feed my children. It is impossible to live like that. Moreover, my children always ask money to buy something for school … When I was working for the GAI [traffic police] officers could somehow find money by extortion … There are some guys in the GAI who do that.

Olivier de Sardan (1999) notes that in developing countries corruption is complex in part because professional practices are deeply embedded in everyday life, so that it is difficult for individuals to abstract and evaluate professional practices. In situations where work, family and social spheres are not clearly demarcated, it is difficult for professionals to see their responsibilities to clients separate from their responsibilities to family members and political patrons. The criteria for what are acceptable professional actions widen to include extra-professional goals. Furthermore, where there are inadequate options, corrupt practices can become firmly established as part of the order of things, and normative questions of legitimacy are forgotten as extortion becomes naturalised. As Sayer notes in his chapter, those in power can institute corruption because they can, without undertaking normative or democratic deliberations.

Third, austerity cuts to welfare and public programmes and the free-market ideology have undermined labour solidarity. Professional associations and trade unions lack the resources and power to counter the erosion of their members' identity and rights, leaving them vulnerable to external actors (such as political elites) shaping their goals and activities. Post-Soviet states are particularly hostile towards independent organisations, in part because they pose a threat to their authority. Beisekul, a university lecturer, suggests that the Kyrgyzstani government fears political competition, and regards professional associations as a platform for political opposition:

> One of the serious reasons of the absence of such a [teaching] association is the lack of development of the whole society and its social structures. Let say, there is an association of teachers here and it is intended to defend professional interests … The Ministry of Education would consider the association as a 'rival'.

The government's distrust of independent associations means that professionals lack adequate labour power to challenge attempts by employers and the state to undermine their autonomy and integrity. After incumbent political regimes were toppled in 'colour' revolutions in Georgia, Ukraine and Kyrgyzstan in 2003–05, all international non-governmental organisations (NGOs) were required to reregister in Uzbekistan, and Kazakhstan closed down most of the NGOs associated with Soros Foundations, which are liberal philanthropic organisations.

Fourth, international and private aid have become part of a neoliberal strategy to reduce state responsibility for the provision of public goods, and to devolve power to non-state actors (such as international development agencies and philanthropists), who are believed to be more effective than the state in delivering services to those in need, because they are free from political machinations, state bureaucracy and government corruption (Morvaridi, 2013). But the dependence on the international donor community to finance educational and professional programmes has created opportunities for unscrupulous directors of NGOs to siphon off funds for themselves, rather than to assist professional members. Zamirbek, a journalist, believes that many mass media associations have become commercial enterprises:

> Many donors give grants for the education of journalists, for their professional skills improvement, for strengthening their material-technical base, for the development of mass media and free press … And those organisations that appear and disappear very fast, I consider those organisations one-minute organisations. They take money, arrange one-time activities and disappear.

Zamirbek notes that some associations are primarily interested in taking income from international donors, and cease to exist once the funding ends. As a consequence, NGOs serve donors' short-term interests, rather than develop professionals' organisational capabilities. International agencies and NGOs have an arm's length relationship with local communities, operating on a low-trust, weak dialogue and quick exit strategy that fosters opportunism and malfeasance on both sides.

Charitable provisions of public goods attempt to depoliticise neoliberalisation by redefining civil society on the basis of religious and moral duties (Morvaridi, 2013; McMann, 2014: 103–111). But charity and philanthropy often co-exist with power to reshape social relationships in the interests of the donors. For instance, Radnitz (2010: 26–29) notes that local rich elites (such as opposition politicians and criminal business leaders) in Kyrgyzstan tend to donate to infrastructure and welfare programmes in local communities with the aim to establish client–patron relationships. Rich elites, who face state persecution, give local communities much needed social and physical investment in exchange for their loyalty and support against the state. Dependent on rich benefactors for resources, professionals (in particular village teachers) are committed to ensure their power and success. They are politically mobilised, and sometimes paid, to protest and vote in support of their benefactors, whose links to drugs, crime or political opposition have caused the state to take action against them. Lay people view charity and politics as self-serving, and feel that the local administration is corrupt.

Fifth, in post-Soviet countries, the privatisation of public goods is often justified in terms of professional autonomy, product innovations, market choice, customer care and freedom from state control. The privatisation of higher education seemingly offers individualised opportunities to study at prestigious universities, to participate in exclusive professional development projects, and to join global intellectual conversations (Amsler, 2013). Privately funded universities can be desirable alternatives to state universities, which usually have poor working conditions, inadequate learning resources and political controls on educational curricula. But most private universities are dependent on philanthropic funding, which is problematic because, in part, donations are derived from financial investments and unearned income, such as capital gains (Sanghera and Bradley, 2015: 183–187). Consider, George Soros, a hedge fund billionaire and philanthropist, who helped to establish the American University – Central Asia (AUCA) as one of the most prestigious universities in the region. Soros Foundations also donated to several other universities, supporting liberal arts teaching, critical social research and professional network development in

Central Asia. But Soros's philanthropy is problematic, partly because his money comes primarily from financial assets that contribute little to the growth of the real economy. Nevertheless, as Sayer (2015: 34–36) notes, Soros and other rentiers obtain moral legitimacy by exploiting the ambiguity of the word 'investment', slipping between two meanings and functions: a) investment in infrastructure, equipment and people that are productive and useful to society; and b) investment in property and financial assets, which yield money to 'investors', irrespective of their social benefits. Although the word is identical, it varies in economic character, social effect and moral justification. In calling himself an 'investor', Soros conceals the difference, and mystifies others (and probably himself) of his work, thereby shoring up his moral power of money and philanthropy. While the few lucky universities, hospitals and schools are glad to receive philanthropic funding, the process is undemocratic, unaccountable and based upon donors' desires, rather than recipients' needs.

Legal corruption in the rentier class

This section examines some key aspects of the rentier class, and then discusses how their activities in Kyrgyzstan can have negative social effects. An important aspect of neoliberalisation is the financialisation of the economy, which occurs because of a shift of power within the economic elite class from capitalists to rentiers, who make money primarily from controlling existing assets, such as land, money and equipment that yield rent, interest and capital gains (Sayer, 2015: 16–18). The rentier class, which includes landowners, moneylenders and property and financial speculators, contribute very little to the production of useful goods and services, but nevertheless enrich themselves by siphoning off wealth that others produce. Although rentier relationships are parasitic and unfair, they are legal by virtue of property rights entitling rentiers to dispose of their assets as they wish. Property rights, laws and policies are not impartial, but are shaped to favour the interests of global financial institutions and the rentier class, resulting in financial liberalisation, privatisation of utilities, mines and quasi-monopolies and tax havens (Hudson, 2014: 333–345). Financial elites decriminalise financial fraud by weakening oversight and regulation, and create legal corruption by capturing the state.

Legal corruption can also refer to economic practices (such as usury and trade speculation) that were previously deemed to be unproductive, harmful and immoral, but now have become normalised and legitimised by a neoliberal theory that makes no distinction between different sources of wealth (Hudson, 2014: 181–183; Watts, 2002: 64–70). Although economic thought during the industrial revolution and the Soviet period distinguished between different types of property, neoliberalism rejects this, claiming that making a profit is the main goal, irrespective of social costs (Hudson, 2014: 116–127). Neoliberalism elides the differences, in part because of the slippage in the two meanings of the word 'investment'.

Another fraudulent aspect of financialisation is how opportunities to hide illegal or illicit capital assets have multiplied as legitimate transnational capital movements have increased (Moore, 2012: 461–463). Tax havens and offshore financial centres reward and motivate illicit movements of money and the illicit activities (such as bribery and drug trafficking) that often underpin these money transfers. Given the economic and political uncertainties (e.g., non-judicial confiscation of private property and usurpation of public office), elites in weak states have significant incentives to secretly expatriate capital, especially as the process is relatively quick and inexpensive (Moore, 2012: 473–474).

Deceptive practices in microfinance

International financial institutions and donor organisations advocate widening access to finance as one of the effective ways to combat poverty and to stimulate entrepreneurial activity, following the model of the Grameen Bank in Bangladesh (Bateman, 2010: 6–27). Microfinance trumpets the values of a neoliberal moral economy: personal responsibility, making money, competition and individual creativity. It helps to legitimise and promote capitalism in developing countries by closing off alternative economic arrangements. Poor groups are taught to see microfinance as their best chance of obtaining a better life and a way to become a micro-capitalist. By advocating self-help, poor groups are discouraged from relying on state resources and collective capabilities (such as the welfare state, trade unions and social movements), which were historically important for reducing poverty in the West. Political elites are relieved of the pressure to introduce structural reforms to redistribute income and wealth, as poor groups are left to escape poverty through their own individual creativity (Bateman, 2013: 4).

In Kyrgyzstan, microfinance institutions (MFIs) have mushroomed since 1990s: their total loan portfolio is about 7.5 per cent of gross domestic product (GDP), and over 441,500 people are credited by MFIs (Asian Development Bank, 2013: 19; National Bank of the Kyrgyz Republic, 2014: 50). The MFI loan portfolio consists mainly of short- and medium-term loans up to three years. Typically, borrowers are families in dire economic situations who want to smooth out consumption, borrowing on average $4,425 (Microfinance Centre, 2011: 14).

MFIs attract funds from international financial institutions. In lending funds to MFIs, development banks and agencies expect a return on their equity, and in turn MFIs charge high interest rates to their borrowers to cover their operating costs and more. Although MFIs are guided by social missions to tackle poverty, to foster social and economic development and to empower women, their priority is always to have financial sustainability, which means to make a profit on their operations (Bateman, 2010: 28–59). The average interest rate on MFIs' loans is about 34 per cent, of which 6.3 per cent is their profit margin (National Bank of the Kyrgyz Republic, 2014: 56).

MFIs have come under severe criticisms. First, by charging high interest rates to vulnerable and needy members of society, MFIs enrich themselves by exploiting the misery of others. MFIs are a contemporary form of traditional usury, which in the past was attacked for being parasitic (Sayer, 2015: 61–76). In an effort to increase their coverage and to have a greater share in the microcredit market, MFIs have lowered loan standards and employed aggressive tactics to push loans on to poor families. Local communities accuse MFIs of 'control fraud' and malpractice, such as a weak vetting process and social shaming techniques to extract payments, causing many poor families to over-borrow and some borrowers to commit suicide (Kabar Ordo, 2013: 6). But MFI field staff, who are paid much lower than MFI executives and managers, have few incentives to be cautious when their salary depends on meeting targets of new borrowers and recovering debt. They need to keep hold of their jobs to provide for their family, so normative questions about microfinance are sidelined as fraudulent and deceptive practices become justified, established and naturalised.

Second, it is a myth that MFI loans enable poor families to escape poverty or to develop innovative microenterprises. The exploitative and restrictive terms and conditions on which they borrow mean that it is unlikely that borrowers can use the loans for an innovative enterprise. Instead MFI loans enable unemployed individuals to set up an 'enterprise', joining the ranks of a burgeoning class of petty traders and producers, who operate on very small margins in highly competitive markets. MFIs do not create a culture of enterprise, but rather a Hobbesian social world, pitting individuals against each other, largely eroding their sense of social solidarity and collective action (Bateman, 2010: 108–110). MFIs, as rentier organisations, not only undertake unproductive and harmful investments, they also extract a significant surplus of what borrowers produce.

Corrupting effects of banking and real estate

The banking sector in Kyrgyzstan underwent a rapid growth with total banking assets increasing from 7.9 billion soms in 2002 to 111.1 billion soms in 2013 ($175.56 million to $2.47 billion[1]) (National Bank of the Kyrgyz Republic, 2014: 20). Many banks have significant foreign ownership, in particular from Kazakhstan. Initially, international financial institutions lent capital to Kazakhstani banks, which in turn lent to their domestic customers and then invested in Kyrgyzstani banks to expand their loan portfolio. The Central Asian banks' leverage and profitability depend on a global supply of cheap credit, which is used to charge 20–25 per cent interest rates to domestic borrowers. In 2013, the net profit of the banking sector in Kyrgyzstan increased by 11.6 per cent, and in 2013 net interest income increased by 18.2 per cent (National Bank of the Kyrgyz Republic, 2014: 24). Despite the 2008–09 global credit crunch, the growth of loans remains resilient: domestic credit grew by 28.5 per cent in 2012; mortgage loans increased by 81.2 per cent in 2013; and loans for mortgage and construction accounted for 16 per cent of total bank loans in 2013 (Asian Development Bank, 2013: 20, 38; National Bank of the Kyrgyz Republic, 2014: 17). In capitalising the real estate market and levying interest rates in excess of what is socially necessary cost-value, bankers and developers obtain unearned income from property (Hudson, 2014: 215–227).

The financialisation of the housing market has had divisive, harmful and corrupting consequences. First, the credit-induced housing construction has inflated apartment prices, and has reproduced social inequalities. Banks and construction companies largely serve the desires of upper middle-class and rich families, but high prices have resulted in many luxury apartments being unoccupied (Toralieva, 2006). For property developers, a high apartment occupancy rate is secondary to making capital gains from rising property prices. Equally for wealthy criminals, purchasing a luxury apartment is not about habitation, but a way to launder money from drug trafficking. In the neoliberal moral economy of real estate, apartments are financial investments, designed to make money for financers and property developers and to cater to affluent families' wants. Many units are more valuable left unoccupied, rather than sold to satisfy working class and poor families' housing needs.

Second, since public investment into social housing has ceased and high apartment prices are beyond the reach of most families' budget, new families have little option but to either rent or illegally build their own homes. Most build adobe houses, providing an easy and affordable way for them to improve their housing situation. Over the last two decades, 53 illegal settlements (with an estimated population of between 200,000 and 300,000) developed on the outskirts of the capital Bishkek, most of them later became legalised as a result of political pressure and bargaining. Many houses lack adequate sanitation, running water, electricity and gas (Sanghera and Satybaldieva, 2012). Some settlements are built near to hazardous and dangerous sites, further endangering residents' health. In condemning many people to substandard accommodation, the government's neoliberal housing policy prioritises financial elites' wealth over poor people's lives. The free-market economy liberates powerful elites from worrying about social obligations, free to make money irrespective of the damaging social consequences.

Third, in the process of acquiring land in prime locations, financiers and property developers bargain with and corrupt city authorities to relax planning permissions. In 2014, a public inquiry into planning applications in Bishkek found that there were 235 illegal building projects (Eurasianet.org, 2014). The connection between finance, property and politics is also evident in Parliament, where many of the deputies have links to the construction industry. Prosecutions of top officials (e.g., city mayors) for fraud do occur, though often motivated by political rivalry, or because they are out of favour with the government. The nexus between rich developers and officials adds to the prevailing political distrust of ordinary people, who feel that they are not well served by the political class.

Fraudulent privatisation and politics

Kyrgyzstan's first two presidential families of Akayev (1991–2005) and Bakiyev (2005–10) were notorious for privatising and controlling the country's prime rent-yielding assets, such as utility companies, gold mines, supermarkets, resort hotels and the international airport. Their activities fuelled allegations of nepotism and embezzlement, leading to political unrest and uprisings in March 2005 and April 2010. Maxim Bakiyev, the eldest son of President Bakiyev, exercised blatant rent-seeking power. In 2009–10, newly privatised electricity and mobile companies hiked their prices, thereby increasing economic rent for the new owners, who were connected to Maxim Bakiyev (Gullette, 2010). Furthermore, MGN, an asset management company that was headed by a close associate of Maksim Bakiyev, was appointed to manage the country's development fund, which had received a $300 million loan from the Russian government. Investigations revealed that MGN had secretly embezzled the fund (Global Witness, 2012: 46). MGN officials also sat on several boards of companies, which were controversially privatised later in 2009–10. These companies, including a major bank, had been managed through an elaborate accounting system designed to conceal Maxim Bakiyev's involvement and to siphon off wealth into secret bank accounts in the UK, Belize and New Zealand (Global Witness, 2012: 56–57).

Corruption has been an integral feature of the privatisation programme. First, the privatisation of natural and artificial monopolies is an example of legal corruption, in that politicians and rentiers shaped laws and property rights in their favour (Sayer, 2015: 267–268). Second, given their economic and geographical dominance in the market, the privatised companies generated economic rent and enriched the ruling elites, who occupying insecure political and economic positions in a weak state had powerful incentives to convert their unearned income into illicit flows to tax havens and offshore financial centres (Moore, 2012: 474–475). Greed and a sense of entitlement were key motivations for the ruling elites to hide their wealth abroad. Third, economic rent is a leakage from the national income flow (Hudson, 2014: 393–401). Some economic rent leaves the country as licit or illicit capital flight into bank accounts overseas. Often, economic rent is invested, or rather speculated, into more rent-yielding assets to get further unearned income. When real goods and services are purchased, they are more likely to be expensive luxury imports that siphon off wealth from the country.

What has emerged since the collapse of the Soviet Union is thus a particular moral economy of wealth extraction. The sphere of unearned income has been enlarged through neoliberal policies and fraud, resulting in a greater concentration of economic and political power. Political and financial elites have radically transformed the character and function of property, from being valued for its social benefits to income-yielding assets irrespective of their social use (see also Tawney, 1921: 87–89). Elites fraudulently acquire income rights without having social obligations. Neoliberal property is functionless because it does not generate sustainable economic development. Lack of productive investment in the country has meant that almost 1 million people have migrated to Russia and Kazakhstan, working in low-paid sectors to send money home, in part to pay off family debts. Despite the economic divide, professionals have more in common with working-class people than with financial and political elites, because they tend to engage in useful and creative work. In the neoliberal economy, the real social cleavage is not between the bourgeoisie and the proletariat, but between those who do useful work and those who profit from their assets irrespective of their social contribution. The growth of the functionless property is parasitic and destructive.

Conclusion

This chapter has argued that neoliberalisation can produce fraud and harm in society. External goods (e.g., income, status and power) can trump internal goods (such as integrity, worthiness and competence) in shaping professional practices. In the context of unsuitable alternatives, professional and financial fraud and deception can become firmly established as part of the order of things, as people shift from normative questions of legitimacy to getting things done. The social legitimation of market values, moral individualism and donor-sponsored activities can also have a negative influence on professional practices. Although corruption is often seen to be illegal and illicit, it can be authorised and normalised as a result of deregulation and reregulation of industries that favour the interests of financial and political elites. Furthermore, rentier activities have become depoliticised and legitimate forms of making money, resulting in an enlarged sphere of wealth extraction with negative social consequences.

The chapter also explored the nature of the moral economy of professional and financial elites, explaining how pro-social moral sentiments and norms can co-exist with self-interest and power. Professional–client relationships tend to be based upon care, fairness and integrity, but they can be exploited and become corrupted for professional interests and personal gains. Professionals can also be exploited by local and global rich elites, who expect political loyalty for their philanthropic funding of public institutions, like schools and clinics. In contrast, rentiers extract wealth without justice and desert from their clients because they own and control vital assets. Arguably, rentiers are motivated by greed and contempt for working-class and poor people, exploiting their vulnerability and need, and belittling their suffering. The neoliberal theory does not distinguish between different types of economic activity and different sources of wealth, so mystifying people's understanding of property, work and morality. The ambiguity over the meaning of the word 'investment' helps to legitimise rentiers' unearned and undeserved income.

The post-Soviet transition is often represented as moving from authoritarian and centralised economies towards democratic liberal market economies, but this is misleading, as this chapter has argued. First, the economic transition can be better characterised as a shift from industrialisation to financialisation, from wealth creation to extraction. The emergence of the moral economy of wealth extraction reflects the growth of functionless property, which entitles income-yielding rights to financial and political elites without social obligations and contribution to foster a flourishing society. Second, transfer payments between social groups have shifted from warranted income (e.g., social support benefits) to vulnerable and needy groups to unearned income to the rich, producing an unfair and unjust distribution of income and wealth. Third, economies are increasingly controlled by international financial institutions without a democratic mandate. Fourth, as debt has become a source of entrapment, there are calls for increased regulation of financial services. While the economy is arguably becoming dystopic, there are some signs of resistance against the rentier class, as people demand another form of moral economy based upon fair prices and adequate provisions for human well-being, rather than one that treats people and objects as exchange values.

Note

1 US$1 = 45 Kyrgyzstani soms.

References

Amsler, S. (2013) 'The politics of privatisation: insights from the Central Asian university', in Seddon, T. and Levin, J. (eds) *Educators, Professionalism and Politics: Global Transitions, National Spaces and Professional Projects.* London: Routledge, pp.255–274.

Archer, M. (2007) *Making our Way through the World.* Cambridge: Cambridge University Press.

Asian Development Bank (2013) *Private Sector Assessment Update: The Kyrgyz Republic.* Manila: Asian Development Bank.

Bateman, M. (2010) *Why Doesn't Microfinance Work?* London: Zed Books.

Bateman, M. (2013) *The Age of Microfinance.* Working Paper 39, Vienna: Austrian Foundation for Development Research.

Blackburn, M. and McGhee, P. (2004) 'Talking Virtue: Professionalism in Business and Virtue Ethics', *Global Virtue Ethics Review*, 5(4), pp.90–122.

Bourdieu, P. (1987) 'The Force of Law: Toward a Sociology of the Juridical Field', *The Hastings Law Journal*, 38(5), pp.805–853.

Clarke, S. (2007) *The Development of Capitalism in Russia.* Abingdon: Routledge.

Cooley, A. and Heathershaw, J. (2015) 'Offshore Central Asia: an introduction', *Central Asian Survey*, 34(1), pp.1–10.

Cooley, A. and Sharman, J.C. (2015) 'Blurring the line between licit and illicit: transnational corruption networks in Central Asia and beyond', *Central Asian Survey*, 34(1), pp.11–28.

Eurasianet.org (2014) 'Kyrgyzstan: After the Revolution Came the Cranes', 22 July. Available at: www.eurasianet.org/node/69141 (accessed: 10 November 2014).

Global Witness (2012) *Grave Secrecy.* Available at: www.globalwitness.org/sites/default/files/GraveSecrecy.pdf (accessed: 15 November 2014).

Gullette, D. (2010) 'Institutionalized instability: Factors leading to the April 2010 uprising in Kyrgyzstan', *Eurasian Review*, 3 (November), pp.89–105.

Hann, C. (ed.) (1993) *Socialism.* London: Routledge.

Hudson, M. (2014) *The Bubble and Beyond.* 2nd edn. Dresden: ISLET.

Kabar Ordo (2013) *On Origin and Nature of Credit Conflicts in Kyrgyz Republic.* Available at: www.sfcg.org/wp-content/uploads/2014/07/KabarOrdo_report_eng_9-report.pdf (accessed: 15 November 2014).

Keat, R. (2000) *Cultural Goods and the Limits of the Market.* Basingstoke: Macmillan.

Ledeneva, A. (1998) *Russia's Economy of Favours.* Cambridge: Cambridge University Press.

McMann, K. (2014) *Corruption as a Last Resort.* Ithaca, NY: Cornell University Press.

Microfinance Centre (2011) *Research on the Level of Indebtedness and Repayment Performance of Individual Borrowers in Kyrgyzstan.* Available at: www.mfc.org.pl/

sites/mfc.org.pl/files/Indebtedness%20report%20Kyrgyzstan_ENG.pdf (accessed: 15 November 2014).

Moore, M. (2012) 'The practical political economy of illicit flows', in Reuter, P. (ed.) *Draining Development*. Washington, DC: The World Bank, pp.457–482.

Morris, J. and Polese, A. (2014) 'Informality – enduring practices, entwined livelihoods', in Morris, J. and Polese, A. (eds) *The Informal Post-Socialist Economy*. London: Routledge, pp.1–18.

Morvaridi, B. (2013) 'The Politics of Philanthropy and Welfare Governance: The Case of Turkey', *European Journal of Development Research*, 25(2), pp.305–321.

Musabaeva, A. (2008) 'Higher Education in Kyrgyzstan: Is it a public good or a private good?', *Institute for Public Policy*, 2(1), pp.77–83.

National Bank of the Kyrgyz Republic (2014) *The Financial Sector Stability Report of the Kyrgyz Republic*. Available at: www.nbkr.kg/DOC/24072014/000000000027976.pdf (accessed: 10 November 2014).

Oakley, J. and Cocking, D. (2001) *Virtue Ethics and Professional Roles*. Cambridge: Cambridge University Press.

Olivier de Sardan, J. P. (1999) 'A Moral Economy of Corruption in Africa?', *The Journal of Modern African Studies*, 37(1), pp.25–52.

Radnitz, S. (2010) *Weapons of the Wealthy*. Ithaca, NY: Cornell University Press.

Reeves, M. (2005) 'Of Credits, *Kontrakty* and Critical Thinking: Encountering "Market Reforms" in Kyrgyzstani Higher Education', *European Educational Research Journal*, 4(1), pp.5–21.

Romanchuk, N. (2002) 'Bribery in Kyrgyz State Universities: Is there anything to worry about?', American University – Central Asia, Bishkek, unpublished research paper.

Sanghera, B. and Bradley, K. (2015) 'Social justice, liberalism and philanthropy', in Morvardi, B. (ed.) *New Philanthropy and Social Justice*. Bristol: Policy Press, pp.175–190.

Sanghera, B. and Iliasov, A. (2008) 'Moral Sentiments and Professionalism in Post-Soviet Kyrgyzstan', *International Sociology*, 23(3), pp.447–467.

Sanghera, B. and Satybaldieva, E. (2012) 'Ethics of Property, Illegal Settlements and the Right to Subsistence', *International Journal of Sociology and Social Policy*, 32(1/2), pp.96–114.

Sayer, A. (2015) *Why We Can't Afford the Rich*. Bristol: Policy Press.

Scott, J. (1985) *Weapons of the Weak*. Yale: Yale University Press.

Smith, A. (1976) *The Theory of Moral Sentiments*. Indianapolis: Liberty Fund.

Tawney, R.H. (1921) *The Acquisitive Society*. London: G. Bell and Sons.

Toralieva, G. (2006) 'The Real Estate Market: Is It Possible to Overcome Chaos?', *Institute of Public Policy*. Available at: www.ipp.kg/en/news/263/ (accessed: 10 November 2014).

Watts, J. (2002) 'Heritage and enterprise culture in Archangel, northern Russia', in Mandel, R. and Humphrey, C. (eds) *Markets and Moralities*. Oxford: Berg, pp.53–74.

6 Do they do evil?

The moral economy of tax professionals

John Christensen

> Taxes are the price we pay for a civilized society.
> (Inscription above the door of the IRS building, Washington DC)

> Rules are rules, but rules are meant to be broken.
> (Guy Smith, tax partner, Moore Stephens, 2004)

Introduction: 'A tricky career for a decent man'

Taxes are the life-blood of the social contract. Without adequate tax revenues states cannot fulfil their obligations to provide healthcare, education, improved water, security, pensions and other public goods, many of which are enshrined in human rights commitments to which most governments are signatories. Across the world national tax regimes are under sustained attack by a globalised industry of tax professionals, including lawyers, bankers, accountants, trust and company administrators and other financial intermediaries (hereafter called tax professionals) who encourage and enable their clients to engage in illicit cross-border financial movements, profit-shifting, tax evasion and avoidance, and who concoct devious and opaque schemes to achieve these goals.

This chapter explores how the behaviour of tax professionals has been influenced by neoliberal thinking, and has in turn contributed to neoliberalism's rise and advancement. It draws on material from face-to-face and online interviews with twenty practising tax professionals (all UK-based) conducted by me between September 2014 and May 2015. Most interviewees preferred to be cited anonymously.

Since the advent of the 'shareholder value revolution' in the 1980s, when the relatively paternalistic corporate model of capitalism prevailing in some countries of the Global North was replaced by a model that emphasises sustained increases in short-term earnings per share, company directors have been incentivised by performance-related pay and stock option packages that prioritise profit-maximisation over other factors. One outcome of this drive to profit-maximisation is that tax has been treated as a cost of production rather than a profit distribution, and companies have adopted artificial measures, frequently involving offshore tax havens, to shift profits away from locations where they are genuinely created. Hiding behind the deliberately misleading term 'tax efficiency', tax professionals have transformed the tax cultures of transnational companies (TNCs) by devising and marketing tax avoidance schemes that are frequently proven to break both the spirit and the letter of national laws. Every interviewee in my sample assessed that since the 1980s, i.e. since the advent of the neoliberal era, tax professionals have become increasingly aggressive in offering advice to boards of directors on how to use sophisticated tax avoidance techniques as a means of boosting short-term dividend distributions and their own stock options.

Many tax professionals are employed by the Big Four transnational accounting firms (known as 'the Big Four'),[1] which are truly global in their operational reach. In addition to marketing tax avoidance schemes to their clients, the Big Four also actively engage in shaping tax policies in many countries through lobbying, funding academic research, donating to political parties, seconding senior employees to revenue authorities, hiring former politicians and civil servants as advisers, and commenting extensively in national and international media on tax policy matters (Mitchell and Sikka, 2011). They seldom, if ever, declare potential conflicts between their clients' interests and public interest when engaging in political processes, working on the assumption that the benefits derived from boosting the post-tax profitability of their clients will automatically trickle-down to wider society. The Big Four, as discussed below, play an influential role in shaping the ethical norms and wider culture of the tax advisory industry.

Note that opinion polls in the UK show a significant lack of public trust in the tax compliance of large companies and their tax professionals. Poll results published in June 2015 showed that only 34 per cent of the British public trust large companies to pay their fair share of tax and, worse from the perspective of tax professionals, only 6 per cent trust companies to report accurately on tax.[2]

The behaviour of many tax professionals has been shaped by the calculation that the potential penalties from a successful legal challenge by revenue authorities against a tax avoidance scheme will almost invariably be significantly lower than the fees earned from selling the schemes (Mitchell and Sikka, 2011: 11–50]. Some of the tax professionals interviewed felt that this purely profit-based calculation, linked to the low likelihood of a legal challenge due to the inadequate resourcing of tax authorities throughout the world, has transformed the culture of tax professionals. As one lawyer remarked: 'Tax advice is a tricky career for a decent man'.

Despite repeated fines, and political appeals to codes of corporate social responsibility, tax professionals persist with devising and marketing highly contrived tax avoidance schemes because the profitability of such schemes is far greater than that of hum-drum audit work. While tax professionals during the era of paternalist capitalism were trained to mediate a professional balance between commercial and public-service interests, in the current era of neoliberalism they continue to enjoy the status of holding public licence and the right to self-regulate but regard profit maximisation, both for their clients and themselves, as their over-riding duty. As one interviewee commented:

> The rampant growth in commercialism of the profession is a key part of [the] change of values, and tax simply becomes an element of making large profits. There are rumours that some tax deals are not even priced on a time basis but on a tax saved basis – so they can be very lucrative. Also the mass marketing of tax avoidance can be hugely profitable, as the cost of the scheme is now spread over a much larger base.

Through their activities, tax professionals have played a significant role in increasing wealth and income inequality and dismantling state welfare provision. This was the context of the remark made by the chair of the UK Parliament's Committee of Public Accounts when in 2013 she said to the director of Google's European subsidiary: 'You are a company that says you "do no evil". And I think that you do do evil'.[3]

Capitalism's freedom fighters

Financial and legal professionals enjoy status and privilege throughout the world. In most countries accounting firms benefit from a state guaranteed monopoly over the external audit and insolvency markets. Empowered to create accounting rules, regulate their own professional behaviour, and advise and publicly comment on public policy matters, they have been described as the 'private police force of capitalism'.[4]

The tax advisory industry is large and multifaceted. It extends from sole practitioners, who might or might not be professionally qualified, through small 'boutique' firms, to large transnational banks, law practices and accounting firms. Designing and promoting tax avoidance schemes has become common practice throughout the industry, and the global presence of the Big Four firms puts them in an advantageous position to market these schemes to their TNC clients.

As the forces of globalisation have increased the market dominance of TNCs, the tax advisory industry has also concentrated into a few dominant law practices and accounting firms whose global span provides them with detailed knowledge of national tax regimes, international guidelines for taxing TNCs, and the treaty networks between countries that can be used to exploit every possible avenue for tax avoidance. In addition to their knowledge and resources, the major players in the tax advisory industry are also go-to experts for governments, enjoying close access to decision-makers at national and international levels. They maintain active and well-resourced presences at relevant international policy fora, for example, the Organisation for Economic Co-operation and Development (OECD) and the European Commission. This access to policy-making processes provides tax professionals with opportunities to both shape tax policies that fulfil the tax minimising objectives of their clients, while also maximising the fee incomes earned from devising and implementing complex tax-avoidance schemes.

Accountants are awarded professional status in the expectation that they will serve the public interest in addition to performing fee-earning services for their clients. Because their clients are largely wealthy individuals and large corporations, tax professionals are in principle well placed to protect public interest by reducing the incidence of tax dodging. However, as Atul Shah comments, the drive to maximise profitability has won out over public interest considerations:

> They [professionals] are faced with a fundamental and cultural dilemma: do they serve the dollar or their professional codes of ethics and responsibility? Past scandals point to instances where this tension has unravelled in spectacular fashion, such as the demise of Arthur Andersen after its unethical and highly conflicted auditing of Enron.
>
> (Shah, 2014: 4)

A significant proportion of my interviewees distinguished between the norms and behaviour of the Big Four and those of smaller, local professional practices. While the former dominate the market for audit services for TNCs, and are consequently well-positioned to sell sophisticated tax avoidance schemes to their clients, the latter's clients typically cannot afford to throw large sums at defending schemes in the courts. One former Big Four employee commented:

> Using arbitrage techniques to avoid paying tax is written into the cultural DNA of the Big Four accounting firms. Their systems and processes have been shaped in ways that bypass or ignore ethical concerns and individual conscience. Any action that increases client profitability or their own fee income is regarded as legitimate, regardless of how negative the impact might be on public interest.

The Big Four dominate the major professional associations, enabling them to take the lead in setting and policing professional guidelines and codes of conduct on tax advisory services. These guidelines are considered by most of my interviewees to be weak or non-existent on matters relating to the ethics of tax avoidance. As one interviewee commented:

> Most professional associations are dominated by the big firms – who will usually act in their own fee-earning interests … My personal view is that the majority of firms are cautious, not adventurous, and advise within the relevant laws. The Big Four may imagine they are above such constraints.

One explanatory cause of this sense of detachment from the constraints of national laws and tax systems is the fact that the Big Four firms' client bases (and the Big Four firms themselves) consist largely of TNCs and ultra-high net worth individuals who inhabit a largely borderless global economy without significant links to nationality. Freed to a large extent from societal attachments, rich people and company directors have little inclination to contribute to the common weal or accept responsibility for their actions. In the era of neoliberalism, company directors are taught that their only duties are to their shareholders and themselves. As former US Labor Secretary Robert Reich commented, globalisation has created a class of 'world citizens' who have rejected 'any of the obligations that citizenship in a polity normally implies' (Reich, 1992). American essayist Christopher Lasch calls this rejection of the constraints of civil society 'the revolt of the elites':

> Instead of supporting public services, the new elites put their money into the improvement of their own self-enclosed enclaves. They gladly pay for the private and suburban schools, and private systems of garbage collection; but they have managed to relieve themselves, to a remarkable extent, of the obligation to contribute to the national treasury.
>
> (Lasch, 1995: 47)

Tax professionals emphasise the distinction between evasion and avoidance, arguing that while the former is always illegal, the latter isn't. They often get this wrong: tax avoidance schemes generally fall into a grey area where legality is unknown until such time as a court ruling clarifies the situation. The absence of legal clarity has created a profitable niche for senior tax lawyers who issue the legal Opinions used by Big Four and other tax professionals to market avoidance schemes to their clients. These Opinions can be cited in law courts as supporting evidence for a particular scheme, even though the legality of the scheme might be questionable. In 2014 London-based tax barrister Jolyon Maugham QC blogged:

> I have on my desk an Opinion – a piece of formal tax advice – from a prominent QC at the tax bar. In it, he expresses a view on the law that is so far removed from legal reality that I do not believe he can genuinely hold the view he says he has. At best he is incompetent. But at worst he is criminally fraudulent: he is obtaining his fee by deception. And this is not the first such Opinion I have seen. Such pass my desk All The Time.[5]

Maugham's blog is supported by comments from some of my interviewees, who agreed that the extraordinary fees lawyers earn from providing legal Opinions can tempt them into behaviour that is neither professional nor ethical.

Investigative journalists have revealed the global scale of tax dodging and the extraordinary schemes that tax professionals concoct to enable clients' nefarious activities. In one instance, the US prosecution of a senior employee of Swiss banking giant UBS revealed how that bank routinely helped its clients evade taxes, even to the extent of senior bank staff smuggling works of art, diamonds hidden in toothpaste tubes and other valuables on their behalf.[6] At the time of writing (April 2015), HSBC is enmeshed in enquiries into its enabling of money-laundering and tax evasion.[7] Tax professionals seldom go on record to discuss such matters, though in one rare instance of openness, a senior Swiss banker, a former president of the Swiss private bankers' association, was quoted in the *Financial Times* saying: 'The large majority of foreign investors with money placed in Switzerland evade taxes … I admit it is undemocratic, but I have a feeling that the democratic system went way beyond their legitimate role against the taxpayer'.[8]

Driven by the profit motive, tax professionals frequently take the lead in designing tax avoidance schemes and mass-marketing them to their clients. A 2005 inquiry by the US Senate Permanent Sub-Committee on Investigations revealed that:

> [A]ccounting firms … have been major participants in the development, mass marketing, and implementation of generic tax products sold to multiple clients … dubious tax shelter sales were no longer the province of shady, fly-by-night companies with limited resources. They had become big business, assigned to talented professionals at the top of their fields, and able to draw on the resources and reputations of the country's largest accounting firms, law firms, investment advisory firms, and banks.
>
> (US Senate Permanent Sub-Committee on Investigations, 2005: 6–9)

Most tax professionals in my interview sample agreed that the commercial pressure to increase profits combined with personal income expectations generally overrides other professional considerations. One interviewee, a member of the Chartered Institute of Tax, admitted that he 'loathed' his work, but was unwilling to change career because he wanted to 'earn his fortune and retire' while still relatively young. Other interviewees cited the challenges of 'helping clients grow their business', identifying 'efficiency gains' and 'reducing client costs', i.e. serving capital rather than broader social interests, as top of their priority list. Such attitudes reflect the neoliberal position that tax avoidance is a legitimate form of 'competition' between companies, which from the right-wing libertarian perspective has the added benefit of 'starving the beast', i.e. the state, of money. As tax barrister David Quentin observes: 'There is a wide spectrum of ideological positioning which protects tax advisers from confronting their role in the predation of the public purse by wealthy individuals and companies' (Quentin, 2014: 8).

Tax professionals refer to their duty to help clients comply with national or international tax laws, but this begs the question: What do they understand by compliance? Does compliance address both the spirit and letter of existing laws, or merely the latter? They typically claim that opportunities for cross-border tax arbitrage allow them to concoct schemes that are not illegal, in many cases because of the permissive tax regimes of tax havens. Such schemes are often described in promotional literature and in financial media as 'innovative', or 'efficient' or similar warm terms, without attempt to address whether they are either legal or ethical. As one tax professional commented in an online interview with me: 'There is a fine line between being regarded as "clever" or "crooked". Major tax advisors can get away with intellectually bullying the tax-officers, particularly if a complex case might be tried in court'.

This situation is made worse by the imbalance between the resources available to tax authorities and those available to the tax industry. An enquiry by the British Parliament's Committee of Public Accounts revealed that while the Big Four employ around 250 UK-based transfer pricing specialists between them, Her Majesty's Revenue and Customs employs only 65, many of whom don't have the knowledge and specialised expertise of practitioners in the private sector. The upshot of this power imbalance is that '[i]t has become practically infeasible, on a literalist interpretation of the law, for tax authorities to stem the enormous loss of revenue brought about by highly contrived tax avoidance arrangements' (Brock and Russell, 2015: 5).

Tax professionals have frequently sought to justify tax avoidance on the grounds that company directors are bound by an overriding fiduciary duty to maximise returns to shareholders (a matter to which I return to below), while others, as Quentin observes, clearly relish their role as developers of tax avoidance schemes that undermine the power of democratically elected states to tax capital: 'Some tax practitioners are positively motivated by their self-image as freedom fighters, liberating wealth (which they view as inherently private) from the clutches of the over-mighty state' (Quentin, 2014: 8).

The supply-side dynamics of the tax avoidance industry

Tax professionals work closely with the governments of offshore tax havens to enable their clients' tax avoidance. In November 2014 an investigation by the International Consortium of Investigative Journalists revealed a vast dataset of special tax deals negotiated between the Luxembourg tax authority and Big Four firm PricewaterhouseCoopers (PwC) on behalf of the latter's TNC clients. The deals allowed these TNCs to avoid taxes in many countries.

The data were leaked to French journalist Edouard Perrin by Antoine Deltour, a PwC employee, and I became involved when Perrin asked chartered accountant Richard Murphy and me to verify the information in November 2011. Even a cursory examination convinced us that the data had public interest importance, not least since the deals it revealed could harm market competition within the European Union and potentially constituted illegal state aid.

When I discussed this with a PwC tax partner in London in early 2015, he displayed cold fury at Deltour's actions, labelling him a 'thief', and rejecting outright any suggestion that his whistleblowing served public interest. From his perspective, tax avoidance is a legitimate area for companies to engage in tax 'competition' with their rivals. He also dismissed concerns that PwC, like other Big Four firms, has multiple conflicts of interest arising from its close working relations with national governments and supra-national agencies. In practice, this has involved Big Four staff being seconded to advise politicians and finance ministries on detailed tax policies, subsequently returning via the revolving door to their former jobs where they can advise clients on potential loopholes in those policies. As the Corporate Europe Observatory has noted:

> LuxLeaks documents recently revealed that the consultancy PricewaterhouseCoopers (PwC) has created questionable strategies enabling big businesses to avoid tax payments. Our research now shows: PwC is represented in numerous EU-Expert Groups advising the commission on tax policy issues. Moreover, the Expert Groups for tax policies are biased.

> Consultancies and corporate lobbyist are dominating, while other civil society interest groups are under-represented.[9]

Recent investigations have revealed the systematic way in which tax professionals devise and market tax avoidance schemes. For example, a US Senate enquiry into the operations of KPMG (a Big Four firm) found that KPMG created a 'Tax Innovation Center' to concoct 'tax enhanced' products that it marketed to clients through its in-house 'Sales Opportunity Center'. Mitchell and Sikka (2011) describe how KPMG operated:

> a telemarketing centre staffed with people trained to make cold calls and find buyers. Staff were coached in sales pattern? Thousands of corporations and individuals were contacted to sell the products. Enormous pressure was put on accountants and lawyers working in the firm's tax unit to sell avoidance products and meet revenue generating targets.
>
> (Mitchell and Sikka, 2011: 19)

The Senate enquiry also revealed internal communications from one senior KPMG tax professional stating that, were the company to comply with the legal requirements of the Internal Revenue Service relating to the registration of tax shelters, the company would place itself at a competitive disadvantage and would 'not be able to compete in the tax advantaged products market'. Despite this stark warning about the legality of its actions, KPMG went ahead with: 'knowingly, purposefully and willfully violating the federal tax shelter law' (US Senate Permanent Sub-Committee on Investigations, 2003: 13). Another US Senate enquiry found that PwC: 'Sold general tax products to multiple clients despite evidence that some, such as FLIP, CDS, and BOSS, were abusive or potentially illegal tax shelters' (US Senate Permanent Sub-Committee on Investigations, 2005).

In 2013, the UK Parliament's Public Accounts Committee received evidence from a former senior PwC employee who disclosed that PwC secretly operated a policy of marketing tax avoidance schemes to its clients that had only a 25 per cent chance of withstanding a legal challenge. As the committee chair stated when taking testimony from PwC: 'you are offering schemes to your clients – knowingly marketing these schemes – where you have judged there is a 75 per cent risk of it then being deemed unlawful' (Committee of Public Accounts, 2013: 24). This statistic starkly illustrates the extent to which a globally prominent professional services firm placed the profit motive ahead of public-service considerations.

Legalised secrecy is key to the successful marketing of tax avoidance services to clients. Mainstream newspapers such as *The Economist* carry advertisements promoting offshore secrecy structures and 'tax efficient' wealth-management schemes. These advertisements reveal a major fault line in the financial liberalisation process: while capital has become almost entirely mobile, the ability to police cross-border financial flows remains largely nationally based. The vast majority of illicit financial flows are laundered via complex ladders involving apparently unrelated legal entities spread across several offshore tax havens.[10] Huge wealth is involved, particularly for oil- and mineral-exporting countries prone to capital flight: Africa is estimated to have suffered a net accumulated illicit outflow, including loss of interest earnings, amounting to US$944 billion since 1975 (Ndikumana and Boyce, 2011).

In order to strengthen their ability to create 'innovative' tax avoidance schemes, the Big Four and many major international law firms have embedded themselves in tax havens, and carefully involved themselves with local politics. One international law firm, a member of the self-styled 'Offshore Magic Circle', even advertises its close working relations with tax haven governments without apparent concern about potential conflicts of interest:

> Appleby Partners have been members of the elected legislatures, and ministers in governments in a number of offshore financial centres. Members of the firm have gone on to not only political office but also in a number of centres (Bermuda, Jersey, the Isle of Man and Cayman) to senior judicial office.[11]

In 1986, when I began my research into how offshore tax havens have integrated themselves into the globalised financial markets, I took up employment with what is now Big Four firm Deloitte at its offices in the British Channel Island of Jersey. My work involved direct contact with tax lawyers, accountants, bankers, trust and company administrators, insurance professionals, estate agents and, of course, clients from around the world. With my professional training as an economist, I was often involved in internal discussions about the tax policies of different countries. What was noticeable about these discussions was the intense effort directed at attacking or subverting tax regimes. On budget days, for example, specialised teams would be deployed to analyse every proposal with a view to pinpointing possible tax loopholes. Within hours of a budget being delivered to parliament, clients around the world would receive detailed advice on how to exploit every conceivable tax avoidance opportunity (Christensen, 2007: 51). At no stage in this process was thought given to any consideration other than the potential fee incomes that could be earned from increasing the clients' post-tax profits. The idea that tax avoidance schemes might infringe the human rights of citizens of poorer countries deprived of much needed tax revenues was simply dismissed as naïve idealism.

As part of their 'theatre of probity', representatives of the tax professions in Europe and elsewhere claim that their standards have improved since the 1980s, but not one of my interviewees felt the situation has changed in any substantive way for the better, if anything some felt that standards have deteriorated and public trust in tax professionals has diminished accordingly. In a comment that reflects how successfully neoliberal thinking has colonised the tax professions, one interviewee noted: 'Tax rules are meant to be broken and undermined, that seems to be the core philosophy and ethic. There is no reflexivity about how this hurts society and the state in the medium to long term'.

Every tax professional in my sample felt that their professional association provides little or no guidance on professional conduct regarding tax avoidance and the use of tax havens, the unspoken assumption being that their primary duty is to support clients with tax minimisation. At best public-interest issues are relegated to being a second-tier consideration, at worst entirely ignored. As one accountant commented:

> It can be reasonably concluded that the tax profession's approach is wholly commercial: that which is within the law may be undertaken by a tax practitioner without ethical concerns being considered so long as 'that will not bring him or his professional body into disrepute' i.e. if confidentiality can be maintained no other issue need be considered beyond bare legality. This means that in effect professional associations provide no useful guidelines to their members on how to balance their duty to the public against their duty to their clients.

The consensus among my interviewees was that professional associations have influenced the transformation of the tax profession by downgrading the public-service role and pushing neoliberal thinking to the fore. A chartered accountant (also an economist) observed that:

> Adam Smith's maxim of self-interest happening, by fortunate coincidence, to maximise general well-being would appear to have been adopted by (the professional associations) as the guiding principle of the public interest, which these bodies seem to think might only be over-ridden when required by statute in the form of anti-money laundering regulations.

Given the extent to which TNC directors and their tax advisers are detached or semi-detached from the societies where their commercial operations take place, this reliance by professional associations on Smith's Invisible Hand (i.e. the argument that maximising self-interest automatically advances social welfare) to guide their member's decisions depends heavily on tax professionals' sense of how public well-being is maximised in practice, which for most of my interviewees means relying on wealth trickle-down. When questioned, however, they acknowledged that in sectors such as the extractive industries, pharmaceuticals, telecommunications and online sales, the possibilities for trickle-down are limited since job creation, knowledge transfer and local procurement are low, while the opportunities for profits shifting to subsidiaries in offshore tax havens are high. Overall, my impression is that tax professionals have accepted neoliberal arguments without giving much critical thought to the possibility that their actions might cause harm to social well-being. As the chartered accountant cited above concluded: 'It is reasonable to assume … that most accountants have an underformed or absent sense of what the public interest may be'.

In 2014 KPMG wrote in its annual report that 'the professional services world has become a buyer's market … In this much more fluid world it's not the quality of our technical skills that sets us apart … it is the experience our clients have of working with us'. This statement raises a number of questions about how KPMG perceives its professional role. Who is the client? Is it solely the fee-paying client who has an interest in their work, or can other stakeholders, including members of the public, reasonably expect that professionals will take account of a wider public interest? How would KPMG react, asks Atul Shah, 'if the client requires a service which stretches the boundaries of the law and its interpretation? What if the client … hates "professional scepticism and challenge"' (Shah, 2015: 25).

In discussion with me, tax professionals working for TNCs have described their relations with revenue officials as a confrontation between their clients' interests and public interest; and almost invariably they side with the fee-paying client. Many tax professionals seem to regard the revenue authorities as 'the enemy' from whom their client needs protection. One interviewee described the attitude as follows:

> In over thirty years of day to day engagement with tax professionals I can safely say that any feeling of obligation to serve the public interest has never been verbalised. This contrasts with pervading day-to-day drivers such as 'the client always comes first', HMRC are the enemy and allegiance to the Duke of Westminster doctrine about a taxpayer's rights to order their tax affairs to pay the least amount of tax.

This sense of antagonism between taxpayer and public interest pervades the tax profession, and is used to justify the aggressive tax avoidance schemes of ultra-rich people, who frequently perceive themselves as a minority group facing persecution by democratically elected governments. As tax barrister David Quentin observed above, some of the more politically militant tax professionals cast themselves as freedom fighters using tax-dodging tactics to 'starve the beast' of Big Brother state. Their attitudes were accurately reflected in the following remark made by a senior tax professional and quoted in a leading international newspaper: 'No matter what legislation is in place, the accountants and lawyers will find a way around it. Rules are rules, but rules are meant to be broken'.[12]

While many tax professionals would probably feel uncomfortable about this sentiment being articulated so openly in the international media, they would recognise it as an accurate reflection of widely held views. This illustrates how tax professionals contribute to facilitating what Brock and Russell term 'institutional corruption': 'the taxation services provided by professionals are morally problematic insofar as they contribute to institutional corruption rather than integrity' (Brock and Russell, 2015: 10).

In my discussions with tax professionals, they have frequently invoked the notion of 'tax efficiency' as a justification for avoidance. After all, which politician would dare argue the case against being 'tax efficient'? Efficiency is a particularly slippery term in this context since the ease with which TNCs can shift profits to tax havens provides them with a significant market advantage over rival small and medium enterprises. Far from promoting productive efficiency, this creates an entirely harmful market distortion that reinforces trends towards concentration of market power into monopolistic or oligopolistic structures, reduces innovation, lowers job creation and exacerbates inequality. Tax professionals' use of the term 'efficiency' therefore begs the question: Efficient for whom?

I have also regularly heard tax professionals claim they have a duty to assist company directors with minimising costs. A senior tax partner of E&Y, writing in the *Irish Times*, explains the reasoning: 'Tax is a cost of doing business so, naturally, a good manager will try to manage this cost and the risks associated with it. This is an essential part of good corporate governance'.[13] This statement is a masterclass in professional obfuscation. First, the corporate income tax is not a business cost but is correctly described on a profit and loss account as a distribution of profits. Second, what risks arise from tax other than those involving a legal challenge to an avoidance scheme or a democratically elected government changing the tax regime? Third, the pursuit of profit maximisation is not a value-free activity. Directors who state they are not mandated to pursue specific values, and who therefore by default pursue profit maximisation at any cost, are imposing one set of values over others, which often conflict with the values of their owners/shareholders. Finally, there is no requirement under company law for company directors to minimise tax payments. The notion that company directors are obliged by their legal duties to shareholders to avoid tax has been widely propagated by tax professionals, but a legal Opinion on this matter from a leading tax barrister confirms that no such obligation exists (see legal Opinion provided to TJN in 2013).[14]

And finally, another frequently heard justification for tax avoidance is that tax policies are overly complex and burdensome for business. In practice, tax rules in most countries have become complex partly in response to the increasingly elaborate strategies used to dodge taxes. In reality, tax professionals welcome complexity since this increases the available options for concocting tax avoidance schemes. This is a chicken-and-egg situation that has added costs to both tax planning and tax collection. A blanket anti-avoidance principle enshrined in law and accompanied by purposive statements in tax laws would cut through this particular Gordian knot.

Conclusion

This chapter has explored the attitudes, norms and assumptions that inform how the here-analysed tax professionals behave. In pursuit of extraordinary fees they devise and operate sophisticated tax avoidance and evasion structures, lobby on their clients' behalf for special treatments and tax breaks, fund political parties and second staff to policy advisory roles in which they promote their clients' special interests, and obstruct investigations of their clients' activities. Granted a privileged position in society, many tax professionals have detached themselves from any sense of loyalty to local or national interests and don't hesitate to take actions that undermine societies' attempts to protect themselves from predatory behaviour.

As with other groups of economic actors, visions of what tax professionals think constitutes a moral economy vary. Some of my interviewees have chosen to refrain from advising clients on how to avoid tax. The majority, however, have not. Most interviewees undertook their training during the neoliberal heyday and their attitudes reflect a worldview based on the notion that the rational calculations of individuals pursuing self-interest in a free, competitive market are both economically 'efficient' and morally right. Seven years after the Great Financial Crisis pulled the rug from under the Efficient Market Hypothesis, tax professionals still seem to work on the assumption that the private sector will invariably allocate capital more efficiently than the public sector, from which line of reasoning they argue that tax avoidance will increase the overall efficiency of market economies.

In a post-financial crisis article, *Financial Times* columnist John Plender suggested that moral capital in the financial sector is in secular decline. 'As long as incentives are at odds with ethical requirements', he said, 'common decency will be a minority pursuit. Scandals are inevitable' (Plender, 2014: 12). Changed incentives are not sufficient, however, to instil a different set of ethics. While neoliberal attitudes remain in ascendance within the tax profession nothing short of a radical overhaul of international cooperation on tax matters, for example to share tax information effectively between tax authorities or require TNCs to provide accounting information on a country-by-country basis, will reduce the supply of tax avoidance services to capital.

Like their clients, some tax professionals describe themselves in heroic terms as 'wealth-creators'. In conversation with me some interviewees appeared genuinely baffled (and enraged!) by the widespread public and political condemnation of tax avoidance since 2010 when the anti-avoidance activists of UK Uncut took to the streets of London to protest against government-imposed austerity measures. This disconnect between public opinion and professional norms stands as testimony to the hegemonic grip that neoliberalism continues to exert over tax professionals.

Notes

1 The Big 4 firms are Ernst & Young (E&Y), Deliotte, KPMG and PwC.
2 http://sse.com/newsandviews/allarticles/2015/06/just-a-third-of-british-adults-believe-big-companies-pay-their-fair-share-of-tax-finds-yougov-research-from-sse-and-icas/ (accessed 13 June 2015).
3 CPA chair Margaret Hodge was referring to Google's corporate motto, 'Don't be evil', which originated from its US stock market flotation prospectus in 2004.
4 www.theaccountant-online.com/features/he-shot-the-sheriff-4430682/ (accessed 8 June 2015).
5 http://waitingfortax.com/2014/08/07/weak-transmission-mechanisms-and-boys-who-wont-say-no/ (accessed 8 June 2015).
6 www.nytimes.com/2008/06/20/business/20tax.html?_r=0&adxnnl=1&adxnnlx=1398616776-a0RXZP5ZgcoOQBnyBZBMcw (accessed 26 April 2014).
7 www.thisismoney.co.uk/money/news/article-2516729/Fresh-money-laundering-inquiry-HSBC-amid-fears-bankers-using-gem-traders-evade-tax.html (accessed 26 April 2014).

8 Konrad Hummler, quoted in *The Guardian*, 5 February 2009.
9 http://corporateeurope.org/expert-groups/2014/11/commission-gets-advice-tax-policies-luxleaks-tax-dodgers.
10 One structure investigated by me involved over fifty special purpose vehicles created in eleven different secrecy jurisdictions for the purpose of laundering embezzled funds from former-Soviet Union countries. The structure was created by a British lawyer based in Brussels.
11 www.applebyglobal.com/about-us/our-history.aspx (accessed 31 May 2015).
12 Guy Smith, tax adviser, Moore Stephens, quoted in *The Guardian*, 18 March 2004.
13 P.J. Henehan, senior tax partner of E&Y, in an article published in the *Irish Times* on 7 May 2004.
14 www.taxjustice.net/cms/upload/pdf/Farrer_and_Co_Opinion_on_Fiduciary_Duties_and_Tax_Avoidance.pdf.

References

Brock, G. and Russell, H. (2015) *Abusive Tax Avoidance and Institutional Corruption: The Responsibilities of Tax Professionals*, Edmond J. Safra Working Paper No.56, Harvard University, Cambridge, MA.

Christensen, J. (2007) Dirty Money: Inside the Secret World of Offshore Banking. In S. Hiatt (ed.) *A Game As Old As Empire*, Berrett-Koehler Publishers, San Francisco.

House of Commons Committee of Public Accounts (2013). *Tax Avoidance: The Role of Large Accountancy Firms*, UK House of Commons Stationery Office, London.

Lasch, C. (1995) *The Revolt of the Elites*, W.W. Norton & Co., New York.

Mitchell, A. and Sikka, P. (2011) *The Pin-stripe Mafia: How Accountancy Firms Destroy Societies*, Association for Accountancy & Business Affairs, Basildon, Essex, UK.

Ndikumana, L. and Boyce, J.K. (2005) Africa's Debt: Who Owes Whom? In G.A. Epstein (ed.) *Capital Flight and Capital Controls in Developing Countries*, Edward Elgar, Cheltenham.

Ndikumana, L. and Boyce, J.K. (2011) *Africa's Odious Debts: How Foreign Loans and Capital Flight Bled a Continent*, Zed Books, London.

Plender, J. (2014) The crisis shows moral capital is in secular decline. *Financial Times*, 10 June.

Quentin, D. (2014) Tax Avoidance as Law-making Rather Than Law-breaking. *Tax Justice Focus*, volume 9, number 3.

Reich, R.B. (1992) *The Work of Nations: Preparing Ourselves for 21st-Century Capitalism*, Vintage Books, New York.

Shah, A.K. (2014) Public Duty, Private Gain: Professional Ethics and Tax, *Tax Justice Focus*, volume 9, number 3.

Shah, A.K. (2015) Systemic Regulatory Arbitrage: A case study of KPMG. Paper given at a research workshop 'Should Nation States Compete?' at City University, London, 25 June.

US Senate Permanent Sub-Committee on Investigations (2003) *The Tax Shelter Industry: The Role of Accountants, Lawyers and Financial Professionals*, Washington DC, US Senate.

US Senate Permanent Sub-Committee on Investigations (2005) *The Role of Professional Firms in the US Tax Shelter Industry*, Washington DC, US Senate.

7 Genealogy, parasitism and moral economy

The case of UK supermarket growth

Paul Jones and Michael Mair

Introduction

In this chapter we examine supermarket growth in the UK. This phenomenon provides a particularly useful case, we argue, because developing an understanding of what has given it shape and direction underscores the point made in different ways by all contributors to this volume, namely that economic activities do not stand alone but are, simultaneously and significantly, social, cultural, political, governmental and, crucially, moral in character – something the concept of moral economy is designed to bring to the fore (e.g. Sayer 2000, 2007). If that concept is to have any analytical purchase, however, the practices – of justification, of representation, of judgement, of valuation, of organisation, of distribution and exchange, and so on – of which moral economies are composed have to be linked to a material ground, to the wider forms of social, cultural and political life which they are intertwined with and help sustain (Tully 2008). This cannot be a matter of opposing one set of generalised and totalising claims (on, for example, the moral virtues or vices of competition) with another. Rather, it is a matter of treating those claims as themselves embedded features of complex contemporary social, economic and governmental landscapes. The question we want to pose in what follows is, therefore, where, when and in relation to what do moral economies acquire their concrete form? What, that is, are the practical conditions of their possibility?

One of the striking features of the forms of economic practice grouped together under the label of 'neoliberalism'[1] is precisely the limited nature of any internal interrogation of the social, political and economic conditions of their own possibility. These forms of practice are presented as outside morality and politics – as amoral and apolitical – and their presentation as such reinforces the idea that they exist in a world in which there are, for instance, clear lines of demarcation between the public and the private (Harvey 2007, Sayer 2007). Economic 'success' and 'failure' stories in the private sector are framed as just that, i.e. private, and do not implicate either the public or the state. Insofar as malpractice is identified, it is as regrettable slips on the part of those involved rather than structural matters. Such narratives are not merely mythological, they are fraudulent – serving to obscure the nature of the hybrid arrangements that link government to business, and in ways that benefit those advancing them. UK supermarket growth, an emergent moral economic form with a particular spatial distribution that is parasitic on patterns of low-paid, insecure work and tithed consumption, is a case-in-point. As we shall show, the parameters and profitability of the contemporary supermarket chain's fields of activity are the product of direct and ongoing state intervention and public subsidy.

The process of recovering what is actually taking place in such hybrid spaces is, however, difficult and requires a shift of analytical focus. If we want to explore the material grounds of contemporary moral economies, we will have to grapple with the fact that their elaboration takes place across many different sites and settings and in many different ways – the practices in question are highly localised/localising, fragmented and heterogeneous, both here-and-now *and* over time. Capturing this requires a genealogical approach, enabling us to identify the multiple points of origin out of which contemporary moral economic formations have arisen as part of a 'history of the present' (Foucault 1977, Tully 2008). We will use the example of supermarkets in order to make this methodological case, focusing specifically on how the growth of supermarket chains has fed into and fed off a remodelling of the built environment, the labour market and the tax and benefit system in the UK to become a constitutive element of a new strain of post-crash (bio)politics organised around harnessing and exploiting poor populations for private gain but at public expense.

The end of the affair?

2014 and 2015 have been bad years for the UK's supermarket giants, Asda-Walmart, Morrisons, Sainsbury's and Tesco, with record losses among the so-called 'Big Four' in the face of growing competition from the 'discounters' Lidl and Aldi, revolt among suppliers (particularly dairy farmers) and increasing levels of scrutiny of their business and employment practices by the public and politicians. Tesco has arguably experienced the greatest fall from grace. One of the largest corporate retailers in the world, from 2013 it began slipping behind its global competitors and down the UK's FTSE 100 share index. On 22 September 2014 Tesco was forced to admit, following the release of the third of three profit warnings in a row, that it had overstated its profits by £250 million in an alleged effort to minimise what were eventually disclosed as losses totalling £6.4 billion (Butler & Kollewe 2015). In the months that followed, alongside a Financial Conduct Authority investigation, the Serious Fraud Office announced a criminal investigation into Tesco's accounting practices and supplier relations (Butler & Kollewe 2015), the latest in a series of investigations focused on practices of allegedly dubious legality within the sector (Simms 2007).

Allegations of criminality and fraud aside, a range of other charges have since been levelled at the supermarket chains. In the wake of the Conservative Party's 2015 general election victory, focus has turned to supermarkets' reliance on state subsidies to shore up profits. As Boris Johnson put it in much-quoted comments on social media:

> It cannot be sensible that we still have companies whose chief executives are given eye-watering salaries and private jets and chauffeured limos, and yet who receive more in subsidies for their lowest paid workers – in the form of in-work benefits – than they pay in taxation. Our five leading supermarkets, for instance, are effectively receiving £1 billion a year in taxpayer-funded subsidies for their wages bill.
>
> (Johnson on Facebook 9 June 2015)

Johnson actually underplayed the extent of those subsidies by a factor of 11 (the Citizen's UK (2015) report Johnson was drawing on put the level of subsidy at £11 billion), but the specific charge being levelled at the supermarkets from the political left and right alike was that they had knowingly framed their employment policies to hire staff on insecure, part-time contracts in order to exploit the UK's tax credit system (which uses the tax system to bring those in work to a specified minimum income threshold) to make up their workers' wages. What the supermarkets had been revealed to be doing, in effect, was securing a workforce without having to pay its reproduction costs – leaving that instead to UK taxpayers, a group to which their workers also belong.

It is interesting to note how the political mood music has changed. In April 2014, in the course of a carefully stage-managed visit to a new Asda store, David Cameron had a quite different message to convey:

> Supporting business, creating jobs and cutting taxes are all part of our long-term economic plan. Yesterday, our tax reforms cut income tax for 26 million people and will help businesses to create jobs. I am delighted that Asda is continuing to invest heavily in the UK, creating another 12,000 jobs.
>
> (Prime Minister's Office, 10 Downing Street 2014)

Cameron had earlier hosted Doug McMillon, president and chief executive officer (CEO) of Walmart, who reaffirmed 'Walmart's commitment to investing in the UK' as a 'great place to do business', continuing:

> [S]ince Walmart acquired Asda 15 years ago we have been able to invest £8 billion in the UK economy – creating over 100,000 jobs, opening 342 new Asda stores and bringing lower prices to millions of customers … Asda [has] … develop[ed] and implement[ed] a strategy that will see it grow – creating more new jobs and bringing real value to more customers in the UK.
>
> (Prime Minister's Office, 10 Downing Street 2014)

We could be forgiven for thinking that something fundamental had changed between 2014 and 2015, but the supermarkets were not behaving any differently: nothing in their practices had altered in the period between Cameron and Johnson's remarks. What we see, however, is a shift in emphasis: with Cameron, on the one hand, praising private sector investment and job creation but Johnson, on the other, condemning public sector subsidy. We thus have two sets of claims articulating seemingly very different orientations to key elements of supermarket growth. Johnson's comments, as part of a wave of supermarket-hostile critique following the troubles of late 2014 and beyond, do at least hint at the tangled relationships between business and government but instead of getting into the substance of the claims themselves (or the purposes behind making them) at this stage, we believe it is crucial to step back and situate them vis-à-vis their object. The more interesting question is what Cameron was attempting to identify the Conservative Party with and what Johnson was attempting to distance it from, namely the supermarket growth machine. As we shall ultimately go on to argue, rather than marking a political break with that machine, the new 'tougher' approach to supermarket growth is itself best seen as an expression of the moral economic logics that have seen the supermarkets rise to a position of spatial and commercial dominance.

Growth without limits? Supermarket expansion in historical perspective

Despite startling losses in recent years, the scale and scope of supermarket growth remains astounding. Recent figures suggest the major supermarkets chains account for 72.8 per cent of the total grocery spend in the UK, with supermarket trading amounting to over £107 billion in the last financial year (IGD 2015). Spending in supermarkets accounts for approximately 53.1 pence in every £1 spent in retail in UK and, despite their recent troubles, sales at Tesco alone accounted for 12.5 pence in every £1 as part of wider operations generating £62 billion in revenue in 2015 (IGD 2015, KWP 2015). Overall, the agri-food sector, which the 'Big Four' dominate, contributed £96.3 billion or 7.4 per cent to national gross value added in 2013 (Department for Environment, Food and Rural Affairs 2013: 8).

Supermarket dominance of the grocery market traces back to the 1960s when they began their inexorable rise, crowding out independents and cooperatives over time (Fair Pay Network 2012). The historical trend has thus been away from smaller retailers to larger corporations with tremendous reach due to extensive distribution networks and economies of scale. Similar stories could be told for a range of countries, but supermarkets have followed very different trajectories in,

Table 7.1 Size, scale and reach of the 'Big Four'

Company	*UK Employees*	*Stores*	*Revenue*	*Market share*
Tesco	500,000	3,561	£62 billon	28.4%
Asda Walmart	180,000	600	£485.5 billon (Walmart total)	17.1%
Sainsbury's	161,000	1,312	£23.9 billion	16.4%
Morrisons	125,000	555	£17.7 billonn	10.9%

Source: Derived from IGD (2015) and KWP (2015)

e.g., France, Germany and the US. Supermarkets have never operated in a vacuum and it is the specific nature of the links forged in different national contexts with wider fields of political, economic and governmental activity that have proved crucial to the shape they have come to assume. Supermarkets in the UK, the US, France and Germany are everywhere but they are not everywhere in the same way. Their differential spatial distribution and configuration is one of their distinguishing features and it is to that we now turn.

From big box to little box: supermarkets, the state and the local

> Imagine living in a Tesco house [with conveyancing done by a Tesco lawyer], sending your child to a Tesco school, swimming in a Tesco pool and, of course, shopping at the local Tesco superstore … this collective monopoly is not an imaginary dystopia.
>
> (Minton 2010)

Supermarkets and their operations – distribution hubs and networks, and producer and supplier linkages – occupy a huge footprint of land in the UK. It is estimated that supermarkets' in-store floorspace alone will rise to 240 million square feet (ft^2) or 22.3 million square metres (m^2) by 2018, equivalent to 17,840 Olympic-size swimming pools (OSPs). However, this figure does not adequately capture the supermarket chains' physical extension. For instance, the largest Tesco in the UK, and the fourth largest supermarket in Europe, is the Tesco Extra in Walkden, Salford which opened in 2010 with 185,500 ft^2/17,230 m^2 (13 OSPs) of floorspace. However, it is not a single development but 'anchors' a wider development (Imrie & Dolton 2014), in this case Derwent Holdings' Ellesmere Centre, with some 2,000 parking spaces. Similarly, the largest Sainsbury's in the UK, Crayford in East London, which opened in 2010, has 100,000 ft^2/9,300 m^2 (7 OSPs) and 510 parking spaces. As with supermarket stores more generally, these stores 'leak' out into the built environment in many ways. Alongside more visible signs like car parks, we might also point to the less visible but nonetheless substantial utility infrastructures – gas, electricity, water, telecommunications (Tonkiss 2013) – that supermarkets require.

We also have to look beyond the physical footprints of the stores and their surrounding infrastructures; we also have to take into account the increasingly large distribution networks that enable these stores to function. Sainsbury's depot in Waltham Abbey is its largest distribution centre in UK at 750,000 ft^2/69,670 m^2 (56 OSPs) and a key relay in a wider supply chain comprised of 18 large-scale distribution centres. Tesco's Daventry Distribution Centre is 840,000 ft^2/78,039 m^2 (62 OSPs) and is a key relay in its wider supply chain of 32 large-scale distribution centres. Finally, there is Asda's Lutterworth Distribution Centre in Leicestershire, at 1 million ft^2/92,903 m^2 (74 OSPs), which is linked into its wider supply chain of 19 large-scale distribution centres. This massive physical presence increases still further when we add in the rail and road links these distribution hubs connect directly into. Such is the scale of these operations that they double up as distribution networks for other businesses too, with the supermarkets utilising underexploited space to provide other corporations logistics support, a major feature of the supermarket's contemporary domain of commercial activity (although who owns what can be difficult to resolve given the complex tax arrangements and spin-off companies in play).

The picture these figures imply – one of 'big boxes' linked to even 'bigger boxes' – only captures one dimension of UK supermarket growth. While the exact nature of the arrangements in place differ, the picture of large stores linked to larger distribution networks is not one that would vary substantially between the UK, the US or continental European markets. What has come to differentiate the UK is a trend that moves in a quite different direction. In the UK, there has been a move to smaller developments in the form of 'community' and 'convenience' store formats across towns and cities, with the creation of 1,867 Tesco Metro and Express stores, 523 Sainsbury Local stores, 180 Asda Supermarket stores and 70 Morrisons M Local stores – taking us from 'big boxes' to 'little boxes'.

The rapid expansion of these 'little boxes' highlights the increased capacity of the large supermarket chains to penetrate urban areas, with supermarket trading no longer simply about 'out-of-town' developments around the urban fringe. This move into urban spaces has led to a remodelling of the urban built environment, with local authorities negotiating planning permissions in return for investment via 'community infrastructure levies' (CILs). A much-needed source of income during the economic downturn, local authorities have worked with supermarkets through the planning system to leverage funds for development projects they could not undertake themselves. The *quid pro quo* is consenting to additional supermarkets, something that further entrenches their business models and employment practices via increased physical presence and its local political significance. This means the spatial reach of supermarkets extends well beyond the stores and their immediate environs into more and more of the local built environment (street and road design, etc.) and their socio-political reach into town halls and local planning committees (see also Imrie & Dolton 2014, Wrigley *et al.* 2002).

Spatial entrepreneurialism and the regulatory environment

While supermarkets no longer just sell grocery items – and a situation that sees supermarkets building houses and schools, while also renovating high streets, supplying prescription medicines, including methadone, and healthcare services, filling in potholes, hosting yoga classes and baby gyms, providing financial loans and issuing credit cards, redirecting roads and other transport links, installing coffee shops and restaurants, and selling funeral packages, certainly warrants analysis – focusing on the spatially situated operations they are engaged in can take us a long way to understanding the nature of the moral economies involved and how and why they have come to assume the form they have. It might appear that the spatial entrepreneurialism of the supermarket chains is simply an extension of market logics, but these market logics, and their valorisation, are also firmly in place in the US where the shape of the supermarkets' presence in the lives of people is different – the big box and the strip mall continue to be the dominant spatial forms (see e.g. Gereffi & Christian 2009). The course on which UK supermarkets have found themselves was not predetermined but contingent on many factors, including political interventions. The move from big to small, and from out-of-town to centre-of-town – which has seen supermarkets become more and more embedded in UK social life, and, hence, more and more central to the remodelling of employment, social security and governance arrangements over time – is itself a response to competition authority scrutiny through the 1990s and 2000s designed to curtail cartelism in the sector. As Burt *et al.* (2010: 4) put it, 'continuing increases in concentration and corporate scale, and the ability of some retailers to continue to expand floorspace, have brought retailing, and especially food retailing, much closer attention from regulatory authorities', particularly the Competition Commission and the (now-defunct) Office for Fair Trading (OFT).

In 1999 the OFT referred the major supermarket chains to the Competition Commission as a result of its concerns about supply chain cost setting and a report, based on the subsequent inquiry, led to the development of a Code of Practice that was intended to regulate the relationship between major supermarkets and their suppliers (Department for Business, Innovation and Skills 2009). In 2006 the OFT and the Competition Commission reported again, this time explicitly addressing anti-competitive practice in local markets with the aim of strengthening the earlier Code of Practice (now enforced by an independent Ombudsman). The inquiry this led to found that the powerful position of supermarkets – who still enjoyed significant leverage over suppliers despite the implementation of the new regulations – had led to a poorer retail offer in terms of prices, quality and service than would otherwise have been the case (OFT 2006). It also found that the retailers, based on their dominant positions in local markets, were able to generate additional profits not only due to weak competition in those markets but also due to relatively low land values, allowing the supermarkets to 'bank' land, i.e. acquire but not use it. This inquiry ruled that, with respect to land banks, supermarkets should divest themselves of the land or develop it (OFT 2006). From initial concerns about competition, then, regulators came to focus on the supermarkets' exploitation of their control over land, and this set of largely uncoordinated interventions, by diluting that control, channelled and directed supermarkets' activities in a new direction, one that would lead supermarkets to concentrate much more on another of Polanyi's fictitious commodities, labour (Polanyi 1944). That change in orientation was not entirely straightforward, however.

In the wake of the 2006 ruling, and as supermarkets began to 'use' their banked land, the implementation of new planning policy frameworks saw in-town developments given priority over the large store formats that were predominantly out-of-town. The interpretation and enactment of these planning policies – including the Conservative-instigated Section 106 (Minton 2010), the Coalition Government's CIL in the 2010 Localism Act (Lord *et al.* 2015), and the older

Planning Policy Statement 6 (Friends of the Earth 2006) – actually increased the reach of supermarkets into urban areas and intensified highly localised disparities created by supermarket development.

This was not something the regulators had foreseen. Where land is cheap and local government political will and capacity to explore alternative sources of (what on the surface looks like) 'private sector investment' and 'job creation' may be weaker, supermarkets flourish. Negotiations around planning applications reflect the relative power of supermarkets vis-à-vis local authorities. While supermarkets and local authorities alike may point to the infrastructure delivered by bartering around planning, it is evident that CIL produces outcomes dependent on local authorities' strength and will to leverage concessions from developers who are – at least in their own self-representations – 'footloose' (Harvey 1989). As a spokesperson for Tesco, asked to comment on the growth of mixed-use urban development in which supermarkets are now so heavily implicated, put it: 'these are urban areas which have not received investment for a number of years. We are willing to invest, and that kind of investment has to be applauded and welcomed … Councils are very welcoming because we are bringing in jobs and investment' (cited in Minton 2010).

In this changing regulatory and governmental context, UK supermarkets gradually adopted politically adept, 'agile' spatially entrepreneurial approaches. However, while the supermarkets were capitalising on the opportunities that emerged out of a reformed planning system and the financial crisis to begin building a new kind of business approach in which land assumed a different valence as a conduit for accessing urban populations, it cannot be assumed that this was long-anticipated or desired by them. Instead, this adapted spatial model was born as a response to regulatory scrutiny from central government and the drive to reconfigure opportunities for investment in urban centres by local government. As Anna Minton (2010) has suggested:

> The irony is that there is little evidence that the superstores themselves want to create entire communities. Instead, policy is pushing them in that direction, with local authorities prepared to grant permission for superstores they may have previously refused, as long as they are accompanied by the sweetener of housing, schools and sports facilities, which the councils don't have the funds to provide.

Among other things, in seeking to diversify their operations so as not to be reliant on exclusionary control of land and to circumvent regulatory objections, supermarkets had to increasingly take on what we might call a more overtly bio-political role with much more active involvement in population management in conjunction with central and local government (Foucault 1977). This has meant their operations have become more woven into the fabric of social life than the supermarkets themselves might otherwise have liked them to be, a process in which supermarkets and political arrangements have adapted in new ways to each other. However, that social life increasingly revolves around the supermarket is not just an issue for supermarkets – it affects those who rely on them for paid work too.

Labour for whom? The paradox of state-supported private employment

As small 'local' supermarkets have proliferated in urban areas, those who shop in them are increasingly also those employed by them, and it is in this trend we see the most troubling aspects of the particular growth trajectory supermarkets have followed since the 2000s. As Table 7.1 shows, supermarkets are major employers, with their increased spatial presence in urban areas swelling the ranks of their employees in recent years. Grocery retail in general and the Big Four in particular represent a massive employer bloc, second only to the National Health Service in the UK. Together they employ almost 1 million people directly (approx. 1 in 30 of the UK workforce), with around 3.3 million involved in the wider agri-food sector (approx. 1 in 10 of the UK workforce) (Department for Environment, Food and Rural Affairs 2013). Taking the sector as a whole, this is likely to be higher still, due to links with logistic and distribution firms, joint ventures and the use of 'independent contractors' and 'freelancers' in many areas of their operation. The supermarkets' turn to urban areas has coincided with their growth as employers and their approach to managing this growing workforce has contributed to the reshaping of the UK labour market in conjunction with a reconfiguration of its tax and benefit system, the latter a change they have taken particular advantage of.

In the UK in-work poverty is now at the same level as out-of-work poverty (Joseph Rowntree Foundation 2014) and supermarket employment is a major factor in this. The UK currently has 31.12 million people in work, the highest ever, but that includes 8.35 million part-time jobs (6.15 million of them undertaken by women), 4.5 million self-employed workers and 744,000 zero-hour contract positions, with the last two often held by 'independent contractors' who have had to accept indeterminate employment status in order to secure supermarket and supermarket supply chain jobs (Office of National Statistics 2015). As the Fair Pay Network showed in a landmark 2012 report on the supermarket sector, although they account for 1 in 30 of the workforce, 29 per cent of all low-paid employees in the UK work in retail (Fair Pay Network 2012). Among supermarket workers, 56 per cent did not have full-time contracted hours and relied on overtime, a second job or state benefits to survive; 51 per cent of employees were taking regular overtime hours, outside of the hours they were contracted to work; of those that were doing so, 42 per cent stated the reason for taking overtime was that they 'did not earn enough with basic pay and contracted hours'. Only 18 per cent of employees were covered by an employer pension scheme and only 18 per cent of employees hold membership of a trade union (Fair Pay Network 2012). Women, who constitute 57 per cent of employees in food retailing, are particularly badly affected. With 50 per cent of food sector jobs part time, women are more likely to be concentrated in low-paying, less-protected and less-secure work

(Department for Environment, Food and Rural Affairs 2013). Supermarket employment is, for the majority, then, a poorly paid, insecure form of underemployment connected to in-work poverty, with the supermarkets' remodelled business practices directly contributing to economic insecurity in a major sector of the UK's economy.

In-work poverty is not restricted to supermarkets; it is a growing feature of the UK's labour market as a whole. Nonetheless, supermarkets' 'successes', lauded by Labour and Conservative governments alike, demonstrated the commercial viability as well as the political attractiveness of the model. In the UK, because a great deal of available work, especially supermarket-related retail and food sector work, is almost a guarantee of poverty, in order to reach even minimum income levels, workers' wages have to be supplemented by state benefits. In the UK, 3.23 million working households receive tax credits, and 930,000 working households receive housing benefit (Department for Work and Pensions 2013). These comprise sizeable fractions of the £29.6 billion spent on tax credit and £16.9 billion spent on housing benefit in 2012–13 (Department for Work and Pensions 2013). Post-2008, this regressive system has become more entrenched. As the supermarket chains have grown, tax credits and housing benefit have become a multi-billion pound annual subsidy channelled to these highly profitable businesses (Citizens UK 2015). Effectively, the taxpayer now underwrites supermarket employment/employment practices and so profits, with poverty wages topped up through the tax and benefit system. Under these arrangements, the workforce of the UK is paying for its own underemployment locally and nationally – the system is increasingly predicated upon it.

If this situation was merely exploitative along the employment dimension alone, it would be much easier to disentangle. However, those increasingly forced into under-employment in conjunction with workfare and the benefits system are also those the supermarket chains rely upon in order to generate sales, with many shopping in the same places where they work, taking 'advantage' of the store cards they are issued with. Although it may initially seem a trivial detail, 58 per cent of supermarket workers have received a discount store card (Fair Pay Network 2012). This is telling and points to the fact that the model directly exploits people and their marginal labour. Recent growth, put most simply, relies upon those who staff supermarkets to access goods and services through them. In the absence of sustainable wages, store cards, tax credits and commercial credit plug the gap and ensure income streams in areas that, until a few years ago, were regarded as untouchable by the major supermarkets – poor, inner-city areas characterised by high scores on the indices of multiple deprivation. Indeed, it is the proliferation of supermarket sites in such communities that is one of the most remarkable developments in the history of UK supermarket growth, one reinforced by local authorities' desire to anchor regeneration schemes with supermarkets whose building and running relies on the diversion of local council tax funds to them. These are, then, as investigative journalist Joanna Blythman (2010) has put it 'companies which feed off the communities' they are embedded within and the workers they employ, making this a parasitic moral economic form. This is a system in which the state is directly implicated, which it has encouraged and which it helps keep in place.

Conclusion

We have looked at two effects of supermarket expansion, the remodelling of the built environment and employment relations/the tax and benefit system (which form two sides of the same low-denomination coin). We could have looked at others: the displacement of jobs, supply chain issues domestically and internationally, the problematic nature of the goods sold, environmental damage, etc. But what we have covered is sufficient to provide an understanding of the imbroglio we are dealing with.

Supermarkets' parasitism is not accidental and it did not take place behind decision-makers' backs. They have known exactly how supermarket growth – which has moved from the exploitation of land, primarily, to the exploitation of marginal labour and its metabolic 'twin', the consumption expenditures of the marginalised (Arendt 1958) – has functioned for some time and they have been complicit in it. This is not, however, just a straightforward example of capitalist super-exploitation. The rise of supermarkets cannot be explained solely with reference to the dominance of capital and the corporate capture of the state. For one thing, supermarkets in the UK have been forced into playing 'community building' roles that, in other national contexts, they do not. We need a moral economic analysis to tease out 'elective affinities' between contemporary politics and the differential omnipresence of the supermarket and, as part of that, we have to acknowledge the room that was created and the encouragement and direction given by governments for supermarkets to assume these roles. The state has played and is playing a critical role in supporting them. Crucially, this is not something for nothing, and we have to think about what supermarket expansion, of the kind we have witnessed over the last five years in particular, does for government too.

If, to adapt Ferguson, supermarket growth ends up forming any kind of strategically coherent or intelligible whole it is because it constitutes a particularly effective anti-politics and anti-morality machine. The supermarket complex is not 'incidentally involved with the state bureaucracy' (Ferguson 1994: 180) but central to many of its contemporary fields of operation. What supermarket growth has done, like other aspects of the remaking of the political economy of the local, is work effectively to 'submerge' political decisions and priorities, obscuring their status as moral and political matters that could be open to collective deliberation (Mair & Jones 2015, Mettler 2011, Tully 2008). Government priorities are still delivered, and delivered by large-scale bureaucracies entrusted with their delivery, just not by the state. Thus it is less and less possible to hold anyone to account for these consequential transformations in social life, something that works to the advantage of successive governments: change is effected, but without the messy business of direct scrutiny. The colonisation of urban space, labour markets and the tax and benefit system by supermarkets is one troubling consequence of this approach to the management of governmental affairs but not in ways it is easy to unpick. It is in arrangements of this sort that claims relating to the apolitical and amoral forces of market economies lie, i.e. in their shielding from collective oversight by the state and the market through the telling of a distorting and fraudulent species of narrative that it is increasingly important to challenge. However, in order to challenge it, we have to be able to link moral economies to their material grounds. If we ask, for instance, where the moral economy of supermarket growth resides or on what bases it rests, the answer is in multiple ongoing negotiations spread across geographical locations and political boundaries, at the centre and the periphery, in government regulatory activities and the tax code, in political programmes that redraw state–market–society relationships, in public offices, trading floors and boardrooms, and more. Our analyses have to be equal to that complexity.

The need for analyses of the material grounds of moral economies is particularly acute in areas where the target is constantly moving. Genealogical investigations are useful here as they enable us to make sense of the changing character of the moral claims made in relation to contemporary economic affairs, as with supermarket growth and the trajectories it has followed. For instance, current political criticisms of the supermarkets' employment policies, as set out by the Conservatives, notably Cameron (implicitly) and Johnson (explicitly), are best understood, we suggest, by treating them as the extension of governmental logics already in play. Having insinuated welfare with work, and particularly supermarket work, the tax credit regime succeeded in partially privatising welfare functions – no longer a collective matter it was individualised and linked to employment, albeit in the context of a regime held up by public monies. That the proposed scrapping of the tax credit regime is a logical extension of this can be seen when set out as follows: if welfare is not a collective but private and individually negotiable matter, then the welfare of employees is employers' moral responsibility, not governments. Via this double step – first link welfare to employment, then detach government from welfare – a new moral economy emerges linked to concerted governmental action over a span of time. Within that moral economic form, workers are not to be guaranteed protection against exploitation. Instead, their employment has been successively *re*-moralised – it ought to be paid at a fair rate but whether it is or not can only be a matter for individuals and their employers. We are individually free to judge, even condemn those employment practices but we cannot, indeed *should* not look to government to intervene. It is by studying the specificities of such things as supermarket growth that we thus gain insights into how new moral economic forms come to take hold.

Note

1 We agree entirely with the thrust of critiques of neoliberalism but do have concerns that the label suggests a degree of programmatic coherence and stability that actually existing arrangements often demonstrably lack.

References

Arendt, H. (1958) *The Human Condition*, London: University of Chicago Press.

Blythman, J. (2010) 'Saviours or Killers of Community? Big Society should not involve helping Supermarkets to Clear up their Mess', *The Grocer*, 13 November.

Burt, S., Sparks, L. and Teller, C. (2010) 'Retailing in the United Kingdom – A Synopsis', in Schnedlitz, P., Morschett, D., Rudolph, T., Schramm-Klein, H. and Swoboda, B. (eds) (2010) *European Retail Research*, Wiesbaden GmbH, Wiesbaden: Gabler Verlag.

Butler, S. and Kollewe, J. (2015) 'Tesco Timeline – The Highs and Lows of the UK's Biggest Retailer', *The Guardian*, 15 January.

Citizens UK (2015) *The Public Subsidy to Low Wage Employers*, London: Citizens UK.

Department for Business, Innovation and Skills (2009) *Groceries Supply Code of Practice,* London: The Stationery Office.

Department of Environment, Food and Rural Affairs (2013) *Food Statistics Pocketbook 2013*, London: The Stationery Office.

Department for Work and Pensions (2013) *Benefit and Tax Credit Expenditure in Great Britain*, London: The Stationery Office.

Fair Pay Network (2012) *Face the Difference: The Impact of Low Pay in Supermarket Chains*, London: Fair Pay Network.

Ferguson, J. (1994) 'The Anti-Politics Machine: "Development" and Bureaucratic Power in Lesotho', *The Ecologist*, 24(5): 176–181.

Friends of the Earth (2006) *Calling the Shots: How Supermarkets Get Their Way in Planning Decisions*, London: Friends of the Earth.

Foucault, M. (1977) *Discipline and Punish: The Birth of the Prison*, New York, NY: Pantheon.

Gereffi, G. and Christian, M. (2009) 'The Impacts of Wal-Mart: The Rise and Consequences of the World's Dominant Retailer', *Annual Review of Sociology*, 35: 573–591.

Harvey, D. (1989) 'From Managerialism to Entrepreneurialism: The Transformation in Urban Governance in Late Capitalism', *Geografiska Annaler*, 71(1): 3–17.

Harvey, D. (2007) *A Brief History of Neo-Liberalism*, Oxford: Oxford University Press.

Imrie, R. and Dolton, M. (2014) 'From Supermarkets to Community Building: Tesco Plc, Sustainable Place Making and Urban Regeneration', in Imrie, R. and Lees, L. (eds) *Sustainable London? The Future of a Global City*, Bristol: Policy Press.

IGD (Institute of Grocery Distribution) (2015) *UK Grocery Retailing Report*, London: IGD.

Joseph Rowntree Foundation (2014) *Monitoring Poverty and Social Exclusion*, York: Joseph Rowntree Foundation.

KWP (Kantar Worldpanel) (2015) *UK Grocery Market Share Report*, London: KWP.

Lord, A., Jones, P., Mair, M. and Sturzaker, J. (2015) 'A Planner's Dream? Studying the Localism Act', unpublished manuscript.

Mair, M. and Jones, P. (2015) 'Politics, Government and Corruption: The Case of the Private Finance Initiative', in Whyte, D. (ed.) *How Corrupt is Britain?* London: Pluto Press.

Mettler, S. (2011) *The Submerged State: How Invisible Government Policies Undermine American Democracy*, Chicago, IL: University of Chicago Press.

Minton, A. (2010) 'This Town Has Been Sold to Tesco', *The Guardian*, Wednesday, 5 May.

OFT (Office for Fair Trading) (2006) 'OFT to Refer Grocery Market to Competition Commission', Press Release, London: Office for Fair Trading

Office of National Statistics (2015) *UK Labour Market, October 2015*, London: Office of National Statistics.

Polanyi, K. (1944) *The Great Transformation: The Political and Economic Origins of Our Time*, Boston, MA: Beacon Press.

Prime Minister's Office, 10 Downing Street (2014) 'David Cameron welcomes Asda's Creation of 12,000 Jobs', Press Release, www.gov.uk/government/news/david-cameron-welcomes-asdas-creation-of-12000-jobs.

Sayer, A. (2000) 'Moral Economy and Political Economy', *Studies in Political Economy*, 61: 79–103.

Sayer, A. (2007) 'Moral Economy as Critique', *New Political Economy*, 12(2): 261–270.

Simms, A. (2007) *Tescopoly: How One Shop Came Out on Top and Why it Matters*. London: Constable.

Tonkiss, F. (2013) *Cities by Design: The Social Life of Urban Form*, Cambridge: Polity Press.

Tully, J. (2008) *Public Philosophy in a New Key: Volume I, Democracy and Civic Freedom,* Cambridge: Cambridge University Press.

Wrigley, N., Guy, C. and Lowe, M. (2002) 'Urban Regeneration, Social Inclusion and Large Store Development: The Seacroft Development in Context', *Urban Studies*, 39(11): 2101–2114.

8 Transnational tobacco companies and the moral economy of cigarette smuggling

Chris Holden

Introduction

Smuggling of tobacco products, most commonly cigarettes, is a major problem for both revenue and health reasons. The extent of cigarette smuggling is difficult to estimate because smuggling routes are so complex and accurate data are consequently hard to collect (Yurekli and Sayginsoy, 2010). Joosens and Raw (1998) estimate that up to a third of all exports (300–400 billion cigarettes) were smuggled in the 1990s. Recent estimates of smuggling as a proportion of total global cigarette consumption vary between 3.4 percent (Yurekli and Sayginsoy, 2010) and 11.6 percent (Joossens *et al.*, 2010). Joossens *et al.* (2010) put the total loss to state revenues at US$40.5 billion a year.

Smuggling of tobacco products not only reduces government income from taxation, it also leads to increased tobacco consumption as a result of cheaper cigarette prices. Raising the price of cigarettes through taxation has been shown to be one of the most effective means of reducing tobacco consumption and, therefore, the harms that such consumption causes (Chaloupka *et al.*, 2000). Such price-based policies form a key part of the World Health Organization's (WHO) Framework Convention on Tobacco Control (FCTC), which at the time of writing had 180 States Parties (WHO, 2015). The adoption of the Protocol to Eliminate Illicit Trade in Tobacco Products (WHO, 2013) as the first protocol to the FCTC in 2012 signaled the importance of the global effort to combat smuggling in tobacco products. Smuggling is the illegal trading of a product across borders (Joossens and Raw, 2012). It can range from small-scale opportunistic activity by individuals to large-scale smuggling of whole containers by organized criminal networks. During the 1990s, the latter constituted by far the greatest form of illicit trade in tobacco products (Joossens *et al.*, 2000). This form of smuggling usually exploits regulations that allow genuine products to be exported tax free from any given jurisdiction, since the products are due to be taxed in the market of final sale. Products are often sold on to distributors many times via a series of transactions that make it difficult to track them (Joosens *et al.*, 2000). At some point, a portion of the product will be diverted into the illicit market, i.e. sold tax free, sometimes within the country from which the exports originated. Smuggling of this kind can be differentiated from the sale of counterfeit or other illegally manufactured products.

This chapter focuses on the complicity of transnational tobacco companies (TTCs) in large-scale organised smuggling in the 1990s. The chapter focuses on the 1990s for two reasons. First, we know about the complicity of TTCs in smuggling primarily as a result of analyses of internal industry documents made public as a result of litigation in the US (discussed further below), and there are very few of these documents covering the period subsequent to the 1990s. Second, the pattern of illicit trade in tobacco products has changed in recent years. As TTCs have come under greater scrutiny in relation to smuggling, the available evidence suggests that the nature of the illicit trade has begun to change, with a greater extent of it now composed of cigarettes that have been manufactured for the primary purpose of illegal trade rather than the genuine brands produced by the TTCs. Cigarettes manufactured intentionally for illicit trade include counterfeits of TTCs' brands and the production of 'illicit whites' – cigarettes that are produced mainly or solely for illegal sale in other countries (Joossens and Raw, 2012; Walker Guevara, 2009).

First, the chapter discusses the rationales for TTC complicity in smuggling. It then moves on to discuss the ways in which TTCs have attempted to rationalize their behavior, both internally and for external audiences, and how they have attempted to manage external criticism. Finally, it discusses the moral economy of large-scale cigarette smuggling and its possible relationship to the corporate form. It is argued that, whilst in some ways TTCs' products are unique – in that they are the only legal products that cause their users substantial harm when used exactly as the manufacturer intends – the behavior of TTCs is consistent with the broader moral economy of the corporation in market society, which values profit maximization over social impacts.

Transnational tobacco companies and smuggling

Much of the evidence which points to the complicity of TTCs in smuggling comes from analysis of internal tobacco industry documents which were released to the public as a result of litigation in the USA. Action by US states to recover the costs of ill health caused by tobacco use, during a period when tobacco companies were still denying that nicotine is addictive, resulted in the release of approximately 70 million pages of internal company documents (Hurt *et al.*, 2009). These documents are now publicly available online via the Legacy Tobacco Documents Library of the University of California, San Francisco (UCSF, 2015). The documents have allowed researchers to analyze how tobacco companies have behaved in relation to a number of important public health questions. Summarizing some of these, Bero (2003: 271) states that: 'Deception has been the *modus operandi* of the industry. The tobacco industry has deceived the public and policy makers by controlling information about addiction, product design and chemistry, adverse health effects of tobacco, and marketing'. It has also influenced policy-makers globally via a variety of political tactics designed to secure and promote its interests (Holden and Lee, 2009). This section sets out the different ways in which TTCs appear to have utilized smuggling as a part of their economic and political strategies, namely: (1) tax evasion and increasing consumption; (2) maintaining market share; (3) entering new markets; and (4) lobbying for reduced taxation. In practice, many of these rationales for smuggling may coexist simultaneously, although they are discussed separately below.

Tax evasion and increasing consumption

Taxation of tobacco products is a widely used strategy by governments to raise their price and thereby reduce consumption. The magnitude of tobacco taxes thus creates the potential for tax evasion by manufacturers, smokers, and organized crime groups (Guindon *et al.*, 2013). Cigarettes are particularly attractive to smugglers because of the ease with which they can be handled and concealed. As Joossens and Raw (1998) indicate, one container load of cigarettes may have a tax value of millions of dollars. Joossens and Raw (1998: 68) argue that tobacco companies are the largest gainers from the evasion of excise tax on tobacco products, since they gain their normal profit from cigarettes that are diverted into the illicit market, whilst consumption is likely to increase as smuggled cigarettes are sold substantially below their official price.

Smuggling routes usually involve transit sites where large numbers of cigarettes are imported solely to be re-exported (Joossens and Raw, 1998; Yurekli and Sayginsoy, 2010). TTCs appear to have been complicit in these forms of smuggling and to have knowingly produced and exported large numbers of their products to various locations that are far in excess of what could be consumed in those locations (Lavrov, 2009; Marsden, 2009a; Sullivan and Radu, 2009). However, evidence suggests that TTCs gain in ways other than simply the evasion of tax.

Maintaining market share

Evidence relating to a number of countries and regions has demonstrated how an involvement with the illicit market appears to have been a routine part of the operations of some TTCs, in an apparent attempt to maintain or increase market share. This can be seen in Andean Pact countries in the 1990s, for example, where British American Tobacco (BAT) and Philip Morris competed intensely with each other for market share. The apparent complicity of TTCs in smuggling in this region has been well documented (ASH, 2000; Gillespie, 2003; Holden *et al.*, 2010). Particularly relevant for this chapter is the degree to which the licit and illicit markets sometimes appear to have been treated by TTCs as simply two segments of one overall market (Holden *et al.*, 2010). Evidence of this is provided by internal documents of BAT. The following quote from Keith Dunt, BAT's regional director for Latin America in 1992, explains how BAT would export their products from Venezuela to the island of Aruba, only for them apparently to be shipped back for illegal distribution in Venezuela:

> Because of relatively high excise in Venezuela (50%) considerable DNP [duty not paid] re-enters the Venezuelan domestic market (currently 27.6%)

> from Colombia (ex Aruba and Ecuador). Our share of DNP was 44.4% in 1991 compared to our share of DP [duty paid] at 77% … Likewise our S.O.M. [share of market] of total market at around 68%.
>
> (Dunt, 1992a: 502637509)

'DP' is a term used in internal industry documents to refer to 'duty paid' cigarettes (i.e. legally traded cigarettes on which duty has been paid), whereas 'DNP' stands for 'duty not paid' and in this context is used to refer to cigarettes sold in the illicit market (BAT, 1992; Collin *et al.*, 2004).

Internal documents also suggest that BAT executives considered whether this routine involvement in the illicit market might reflect negatively on its 'ethical' image. In April 1992, Dunt asked of a colleague:

> Can we pursue the approach noted in your last strategy submission, i.e. continuing with D.P. and D.N.P in parallel *and* be seen as a clean and ethical company at the same time… This "ethical correctness" would be achieved via letters to Government, presentations to them, papers prepared for excise departments, etc, etc – can we really do all this *AND* continue D.N.P.
>
> (Dunt, 1992b: 500025875, emphasis in original)

The importance that the company attached to the maintenance of its share of the illicit market, and the extent to which it regarded this activity as a normal part of its overall operations, is suggested by Dunt's letter to a colleague in June 1992, when he stated that: 'We will be consulting here on the ethical side of whether we should encourage or ignore the DNP segment. You know my view is that it is part of *your* market and to have it exploited by others is just not acceptable' (Dunt, 1992c: 301674939, emphasis in original). Writing later in *The Guardian* newspaper in response to allegations of the company's involvement in smuggling, Kenneth Clarke, BAT's deputy chairman and formerly both UK minister of health and chancellor of the exchequer, admitted that: 'Where any government is unwilling to act or their efforts are unsuccessful, we act, completely within the law, on the basis that our brands will be available alongside those of our competitors in the smuggled as well as the legitimate market' (Clarke, 2000). Overall, the evidence suggests that BAT saw the availability of its products in the illicit market as necessary to maintain its market share, since if its products were not present there it would lose ground to its competitors. Orientation to the illicit market thus became a routine part of its operations, with the illicit 'segment' regarded as just another part of the overall market.

Entering new markets

The encouragement of smuggling appears to have been utilized by some TTCs as part of a broader strategy to break into new markets. A number of countries have historically had domestic monopolies in tobacco products and/or protectionist bans on the import of foreign cigarettes. Smuggling can be a means of gaining sales and brand awareness before a company's products have obtained legal entry and to exert pressure on targeted governments to lift protection. Shepherd (1985), for example, suggests that smuggling was frequently used by TTCs to 'soften up' target markets in Latin America in the 1960s and 1970s, prior to the subsequent acquisition of domestic firms by the TTCs. According to Shepherd (1985), increases in smuggling have been highly correlated with TTC expansion, often reaching their peak shortly prior to, during, and after TTC entry into a particular target market.

Similar tactics appear to have been used in Asia. Collin *et al.* (2004: ii106) describe how BAT brands were widely available in countries such as Vietnam in the early 1990s, despite the operation of an import ban on foreign cigarettes. Similarly, smuggled cigarettes were shipped to Thailand at the same time that the US trade representative was pressuring the Thai government to remove its import ban (Collin *et al.*, 2004: ii106). Sometimes, concerted advertising campaigns were conducted by TTCs for brands that were only available via the illicit market (Collin *et al.*, 2004: ii106). In China, where the cigarette market remains highly protected, smuggling has been a key means of ensuring that TTCs' brands are available (Lee and Collin, 2006). Smuggling has also been a key means of establishing imports into and gaining market share in a number of other countries, including those of the former Soviet Union (Gilmore and McKee, 2004), Africa (LeGresley *et al.*, 2008), and the Middle East (Nakkash and Lee, 2008).

Lobbying for reduced taxation

The involvement of tobacco companies in cigarette smuggling in Canada, and the policy responses of the Canadian government, offer an illustration of the ways in which tobacco company complicity in smuggling can be used simultaneously as a means of tax evasion and as a focus of lobbying for tax reductions. During the 1980s, tobacco companies were involved in a scheme whereby cigarettes were exported to the US and then smuggled back into Canada to be sold tax free in the illicit market (Marsden, 1999). At its peak, this illicit trade is estimated to have reached up to 40 percent of the overall Canadian cigarette market (Kelton and Givel, 2008: 472). Free trade zones in the US were a crucial conduit for the cigarettes during their journey back to Canada. It is estimated that from 1980 to the mid-1990s, 80 percent of the tobacco products exported to US free trade zones were smuggled back into Canada (Kelton and Givel, 2008: 478). In 2008, Imperial Tobacco Canada Limited and Rothmans Benson & Hedges agreed to negotiated settlements whereby they would pay a combined total of C$1.15 billion over 15 years in criminal fines and civil restitution (RCMP, 2013: 5–6; Marsden, 2009b). In 2010, guilty pleas by JTI-Macdonald Corp (formerly RJR-Macdonald) and the RJ Reynolds subsidiary Northern Brands International resulted in C$550 million in criminal fines and civil restitution (RCMP, 2013: 5–6).

Tobacco company involvement in smuggling was in part an attempt to evade substantial increases in Canadian tobacco taxes during the 1980s, which by 1994 were more than five times the US average (Joossens *et al.*, 2000: 400). Despite high rates of smuggling, however, the tax rises were effective in contributing to a reduction in tobacco consumption, with a 43 percent decline in per capita cigarette consumption between 1979 and 1993, even after factoring in the consumption of smuggled cigarettes (Joossens *et al.*, 2000: 400). Despite this, and even whilst some of them were involved in the illicit trade, the tobacco companies launched a concerted campaign to convince the Canadian government that the tax raises were the cause of the smuggling and therefore needed to be cut back. In 1994, the Canadian federal government and a number of provinces relented, leading to a substantial roll back of cigarette taxes. Cigarette consumption duly increased, with average per capita consumption in provinces where taxes were significantly reduced climbing 27 percent higher in 1998 than they had been in 1993 (Joossens *et al.*, 2000: 401). Tax revenues from cigarette sales also fell (Joossens *et al.*, 2000: 401), contradicting industry claims that cutting taxes would lead to a rise in revenues as smuggling fell. Collin *et al.* (2004: ii106) present evidence that similar coordination of smuggling with political pressure for reduced taxation took place in Bangladesh, Burma, and Thailand.

Denying responsibility and framing the debate

Evidence suggests that senior personnel in BAT were aware of their company's involvement in smuggling and that it was a key part of the company's overall strategy (Collin *et al.*, 2004: ii107; Holden *et al.*, 2010). The evidence revealed by the release of internal industry documents about the complicity of TTCs in smuggling, as well as their activities in influencing policy to impede effective tobacco control and their attempts to conceal the harmfulness and addictiveness of their products, has led in many countries to a considerable reduction in the extent to which they are regarded as legitimate actors in the policy process. One positive outcome of this increased understanding of TTCs' behaviour has been the entry into force of the WHO's FCTC in 2005 and the adoption of its Protocol to Eliminate Illicit Trade in Tobacco Products in 2012. TTCs' efforts to impede effective tobacco control policy have been so serious that Article 5.3 of the FCTC states that: 'In setting and implementing their public health policies with respect to tobacco control, Parties shall act to protect these policies from commercial and other vested interests of the tobacco industry in accordance with national law' (WHO, 2005). Despite uneven implementation of this clause on the part of governments, TTCs have sometimes found it more difficult to gain access to policy makers than in the past.

However, rather than acknowledge the validity of external criticism, the work of Fooks *et al.* (2011, 2013) suggests that TTC executives have instead internally rationalized their behavior and sought to reshape external perceptions of them via 'corporate social responsibility' (CSR) programmes. Drawing on the work of Sykes and Matza (1957), Fooks *et al.* (2013) conclude that BAT executives utilized 'techniques of neutralization' in order to rationalize firm behavior, in a similar way to the way that individuals may use cognitive devices to justify, excuse, or rationalize behavior that flouts social norms. This takes place via a three-stage process in which, when confronted with social censure and increased regulatory risk, corporate decision-makers first reject and then contest the arguments of policy reformers. In the first stage, declining political authority is seen as arising from weaknesses in the design and coordination of the firm's political and communication strategies, rather than from public awareness of the company's conduct and its social impacts. In the second stage, external social actors such as public health advocates are blamed for the company's declining authority and corporate decision-makers attempt to counteract the impact of these other actors by designing alternative methods of political management in the form of CSR. In the third stage, an attempt is made to ward off regulatory change by altering perceptions of the company and framing opposition to regulatory change as consistent with the public interest. This is done partly by making a distinction between 'sensible' and 'unreasonable' forms of regulation, with the company itself cast as a responsible and reasonable actor.

In relation to smuggling, TTCs' public relations strategies display a number of characteristics. Fooks *et al.* (2013: 293) highlight how BAT's Framework for CSR identifies responsibility for the problem of smuggling as lying with governments and multilateral organizations, which must 'establish workable fiscal regimes and economic policies that do not create the conditions for illicit trade'. However, BAT also claims to 'fully support regulators, governments and international organisations … in seeking to eliminate all forms of illicit tobacco trade' (BAT, 2015). Ironically, TTCs appear to be using the issue of illicit trade as a means of forging partnerships with a number of governments (Malone and Bialous, 2014). Particularly relevant in this regard are the agreements that the four main TTCs have signed with the European Union (EU) since 2004. At least three of these were signed to settle or avoid legal disputes with the EU concerning the companies' alleged involvement in smuggling (Joossens *et al.*, 2015). The agreements involve annual payments by TTCs to EU member states totalling $1.9 billion over 20 years and additional payments when TTCs' branded products are seized by customs authorities. However, although the seizure payments constitute 100 percent of the evaded taxes in the event of seizures of TTCs' products above 50,000 cigarettes, they comprise only a small fraction of the revenue lost from cigarette smuggling (Joossens *et al.*, 2015). This is partly because only large seizures qualify for payments and partly because payments apply only to genuine TTC cigarettes, not counterfeits. The EU relies on the TTCs to determine whether seized cigarettes are counterfeit, thus providing an incentive for the misclassification of genuine products as counterfeit (Joossens *et al.*, 2015).

The relative shift towards counterfeiting and the production of illicit cigarettes is damaging to both governments and to the TTCs. It deprives governments of substantial amounts of tax revenue and undermines public health through the sale of cheap cigarettes, which may be even more harmful to health than genuine brands. However, it also conflicts with the interests of TTCs, since it competes with their legally produced and sold products. TTCs have therefore sought to reframe the problem of smuggling as one primarily of counterfeiting and illicit production. Ironically, however, these new smaller producers of illicitly traded cigarettes are often simply utilizing practices and smuggling routes formerly used by distributors working with TTCs and now vacated by them (Marsden, 2009b; Candea *et al.*, 2009; Walker Guevara *et al.*, 2009). Furthermore, there is evidence that TTCs have failed to adequately secure their supply chains since the signing of their agreements with the EU (Joossens *et al.*, 2015: 4).

Joossens *et al.* (2015) conclude that the EU agreements conflict with Article 5.3 of the FCTC and are in fact part of a strategy by TTCs to position themselves as part of the solution to the problem of illicit trade: 'Illicit tobacco provided a perfect opportunity for the TTCs, despite their inauspicious history, to signal shared concerns with policy makers and convince authorities that they were acceptable partners in addressing a trade in which they had previously been complicit' (Joossens *et al.*, 2015: 4). Furthermore, the TTCs appear to have used the agreements to establish partnerships with other authorities at the national and international level. In 2011, for example, Philip Morris International agreed a deal with INTERPOL in which they donated EU€15 million to fund a global initiative against trafficking in illicit goods (INTERPOL, 2012; Joossens *et al.*, 2015: 4).

Cigarette smuggling and the moral economy of the corporation

A question that commonly arises when discussing the involvement of corporations in illicit activity is the extent to which senior executives in the organization were aware of this activity, or whether it can be explained as the result of rogue employees. In the case of TTCs and cigarette smuggling, the evidence suggests that smuggling has often been a core component of corporate strategies (Collin *et al.*, 2004; LeGresley *et al.*, 2008; Holden *et al.*, 2010). Is there then a moral 'subsystem' in the tobacco industry, or is it reflective of a broader moral economy of capitalism/corporations? The tobacco industry appears exceptional because of the unique harm that its products do to their consumers, and it might be argued that the regulatory response this calls forth from governments in the form of high taxation and other tobacco control measures elicits an unusually strong counter-response from TTCs, in the form of both attempts to influence policy (Holden and Lee, 2009) and in some cases to evade taxation. Yet other industries produce products that are harmful, and policy influence, tax evasion, and corporate fraud are not unique to the tobacco industry. Perhaps what is unusual about the tobacco industry is the access to internal documents, made public as a result of litigation in the US, which give us an unparalleled look inside the 'black box' of the relevant corporations. A research resource such as this is seldom available for other industries.

Therefore, we cannot be sure that the tobacco sector is indeed exceptional or whether what we know about TTCs can tell us anything about transnational corporations (TNCs) more generally. Central to our understanding of the moral economy of the corporation is its relationship to the law in capitalist, and particularly in neoliberal, societies. As Bakan (2005) notes, corporations are legally constructed such that they must pursue the maximization of profit. The corporation is the exemplar of the neoliberal construction of 'rational economic man', according to Bakan 'a legally designated "person" designed to valorise self-interest and invalidate moral concern' (2005: 28). The people within the corporation are, of course, moral beings, but the overriding moral responsibility of the corporate executive is to the corporation's shareholders, necessitating a 'compartmentalization' whereby the relentless pursuit of profit at work can and must be separated from relationships in one's personal life. The corporation thus becomes an 'externalizing machine' (Bakan, 2005), whereby all social costs are passed on to someone else where possible. CSR is permitted only where it serves the interests of the corporation, not where it is in the interests of society.

The constraint upon the actions of the corporation in its pursuit of profit is, of course, the law, which determines what it can, what it must, and what it cannot do. For economic actors in a market society, it is the law that sets the parameters of acceptability, not personal relationships; all relationships are predominantly market transactions and everything not defined as illegal is acceptable. However, as McBarnet (2006: 1091) notes, the role of the law as the only arbiter of what is permitted tends to lead to 'creative compliance' on the part of corporations, whereby 'technical legal work' is used to:

> manage the legal packaging, structuring and definition of practices and transactions, such that they can claim to fall on the right side of the boundary between lawfulness and illegality. It is essentially the practice of using the letter of the law to defeat its spirit, and to do so with impunity.

Once creative compliance becomes the norm – 'a matter for business congratulations and professional pride ... routine practice deemed absolutely legitimate' (McBarnet, 2006: 1092) – then it also becomes commonplace for corporations to go beyond this and actually break the law, but to pass this off as creative compliance. McBarnet (2006: 1102) shows how it has become routine to incorporate 'hidden deals and illegalities in what might on the surface appear to be simply complex legal structures'.

In the case of the TTCs, it is not so much complex legal and financial structures that have made it difficult to check compliance, but complex distribution chains that make it difficult to track tobacco products in their journey from factory to final point of sale. The claim that smuggling arises from the failure of governments to act (Clarke, 2000) distracts from the company's responsibility to ensure due diligence in selecting its distributors and monitoring the links in the chain to market. A similar refusal to accept responsibility, even within the firm itself, seems to be present in the utilization of 'techniques of neutralization' (Fooks *et al.*, 2013). It is easy to see how, from within the moral perspective of the profit-maximizing corporation, external criticism and attempts to regulate corporate behaviour are seen as either the failure of the firm to explain itself properly or as the fault of hostile outsiders such as public health advocates.

Ultimately, as Bakan (2005) argues, whether a corporation actually complies with the law or not may rest on a simple cost/benefit analysis. Since the corporation's owners have no legal liability for its conduct and managers are seldom prosecuted, a cost/benefit analysis needs primarily to take account of the risks of getting caught and the potential fines and weigh these against the costs of complying (Bakan, 2005: 80). In other words, the profit-maximizing mandate of the corporation produces a moral economy that evaluates decisions on infringing the law on a narrow financial basis, rather than intrinsically valuing the goods and harms that may result for others.

In the case of the TTCs, despite substantial evidence of complicity in smuggling, the companies and their senior executives have for the most part 'remained unaccountable via litigation or public enquiry' (LeGresley *et al.*, 2008: 344). Whilst there have been a small number of successful prosecutions of tobacco company employees, most notably in Canada (Marsden, 1999; RCMP, 2013: 5–6), governments have been reticent to take legal action. Even in Canada, where the two largest tobacco companies pleaded guilty to aiding and abetting tobacco smuggling, the government's settlement with the two companies released all former and present executives, employees, directors, and officers from civil or criminal prosecution (Marsden, 2009b). The companies' foreign owners and affiliates were also released and they were able to divest themselves of key assets or move them offshore before they could be seized or frozen by the government (Marsden, 2009b). In the UK in 2004, the Department of Trade and Industry abandoned plans for an official enquiry into tobacco companies' complicity in smuggling, which would have included the publication of its results, following private meetings between the chairman of BAT, Martin Broughton, and Trade Secretary Stephen Byers (Evans *et al.*, 2004). Instead, an enquiry held in secret concluded that there was insufficient evidence to support a prosecution and no report was published (Fooks *et al.*, 2011).

TTCs' behavior might thus be seen as entirely consistent with the broader moral economy of the corporation, especially in a period of neoliberalism. Tobacco products are in some ways unique in the harm that they cause, in that they are the only legal products that can be expected to kill many of their long-term users (about 5 million people each year globally) when used as directed by manufacturers (WHO, 2012: 4). Yet the TTCs' rationalization of this as acceptable on the basis that the product is legal is entirely in keeping with the broader moral construction of corporations in general within market society. This moral economy determines that corporations' overriding moral responsibility is to their shareholders, as long as the law is obeyed. Yet the unremitting drive for profit leads to a compliance with the law that is often at best 'creative', and at worst actually contravenes the law because it is profitable to do so. The tendency for public authorities to accept partnership arrangements with corporations that have apparently violated the law, rather than to take more robust action, may contribute to the perception that such violations are normal and unlikely to be punished. Nevertheless, these issues require much more research in order to establish the extent to which the behaviors of particular industries and corporations are determined by the broad moral economy of the corporate form within neoliberal capitalism, and conversely, the extent to which they are determined by the distinct moral subsystem operating within the particular sector or corporation. Such research is needed especially for those sectors, like tobacco, that have a direct impact on human health and wellbeing.

Acknowledgements

This research was funded in part by the National Cancer Institute, US National Institutes of Health, under award number R01-CA091021. The contents of the chapter do not necessarily represent the official views of the funder.

References

ASH (Action on Smoking and Health) (2000) *British American Tobacco*, www.ash.org.uk/ash_y4c7hti5.htm. (accessed 19.2.15).

Bakan, J. (2005) *The Corporation: The Pathological Pursuit of Profit and Power*. London: Constable.

BAT (British American Tobacco) (1992) *Venezuelan Market Definitions and Assumptions*, Bates 500025647-500025648, http://legacy.library.ucsf.edu/tid/rqm87a99. (accessed 19.2.15).

BAT (2015) *Tobacco Trafficking: A Growing Black Market*, www.bat.com/group/sites/UK__9D9KCY.nsf/vwPagesWebLive/DO6TNKVW?opendocument (accessed 19.3.15).

Bero, L. (2003) 'Implications of the Tobacco Industry Documents for Public Health and Policy', *Annual Review of Public Health*, 24: 267–88.

Candea, S., Campbell, D., Lavrov, V., and Shleynov, R. (2009) 'Made to be Smuggled: Russian Contraband Cigarettes "Flooding" EU', in *Tobacco Underground: The Global Trade in Smuggled Cigarettes*, International Consortium of Investigative Journalists Digital Newsbook. Available at: www.icij.org/project/tobacco-underground/ebook-tobacco-underground. (accessed 15.6.15).

Chaloupka, F.J., Hu, T., Warner, K.E., Jacobs, R., and Yurekli, A. (2000) 'The Taxation of Tobacco Products', in P. Jha and F. Chaloupka (eds) *Tobacco Control in Developing Countries* (pp. 237–72). Washington DC: World Bank.

Chen, T. (2009) 'China's Marlboro Country: A Massive Underground Industry makes China the World Leader in Counterfeit Cigarettes', in *Tobacco Underground: The Global Trade in Smuggled Cigarettes*, International Consortium of Investigative Journalists Digital Newsbook. Available at: www.icij.org/project/tobacco-underground/ebook-tobacco-underground. (accessed 15.6.15).

Clarke, K. (2000). Dilemma of a Cigarette Exporter. *The Guardian*, 3 February. Available at: www.theguardian.com/bat/article/0,,191288,00.html. (accessed 5.6.15).

Collin, J., LeGresley, E., MacKenzie, R., Lawrence, S., and Lee, K. (2004) 'Complicity in Contraband: British American Tobacco and Cigarette Smuggling in Asia', *Tobacco Control*, 13 (Supplement II): ii104–ii111.

Dunt, K.S. (1992a) *KSD Talk at Staff Presentation (30 Mins): Royal Berkshire Hotel: 17 February 1992*, Bates 502637499-502637537, http://legacy.library.ucsf.edu/tid/ioo08a99. (accessed 19.2.15).

Dunt, K.S. (1992b) *Letter from Keith S Dunt to DO Laux Regarding Project Lean Strategy*, Bates 500025874-500025875, http://legacy.library.ucsf.edu/tid/bum87a99. (accessed 19.2.15).

Dunt, K.S. (1992c) *Letter from Keith S Dunt to EG Grant Regarding DNP Market*, Bates

301674939-301674940, http://legacy.library.ucsf.edu/tid/bgd21a99;jsessionid=8AA82359EFFD3F8FEBCBC669BE075FB3. (accessed 19.2.15).

Evans, R., Leigh, D., and Maguire, K. (2004) 'Tobacco Firm Gained Secret Access to Blair', *The Guardian*, 27 October, Available at: www.theguardian.com/uk/2004/oct/27/freedomofinformation.politics. (accessed 13.3.15).

Fooks, G.J., Gilmore, A.B., Smith, K.E., Collin, J., Holden, C., and Lee, K. (2011) 'Corporate Social Responsibility and Access to Policy Elites: An Analysis of Tobacco Industry Documents', *PLoS Medicine*, 8(8): e1001076.

Fooks, G., Gilmore, A., Collin, J., Holden, C., and Lee, K. (2013) 'The Limits of Corporate Social Responsibility: Techniques of Neutralisation, Stakeholder Management and Political CSR', *Journal of Business Ethics*, 112(2): 283–99.

Gillespie, K. (2003) 'Smuggling and the Global Firm', *Journal of International Management*, 9: 317–33.

Gilmore, A. and McKee, M. (2004) 'Moving East: How the Transnational Tobacco Industry Gained Entry to the Emerging Markets of the Former Soviet Union – Part 1: Establishing Cigarette Imports', *Tobacco Control*, 13: 143–50.

Guindon, G.E., Driezen, P., Chaloupka, F.J., and Fong, G.T. (2013) 'Cigarette Tax Avoidance and Evasion: Findings from the International Tobacco Control Policy Evaluation Project', *Tobacco Control*, published online first, DOI: 10.1136/tobacco-control-2013-051074.

Holden, C. and Lee, K. (2009) 'Corporate Power and Social Policy: The Political Economy of the Transnational Tobacco Companies', *Global Social Policy*, 9(3): 328–54.

Holden, C., Lee, K., Fooks, G., and Wander, N. (2010) 'The Impact of Regional Trade Integration on Firm Organization and Strategy: British American Tobacco in the Andean Pact', *Business and Politics*, 12(4): Article 3.

Hurt, R.D., Ebbert, J.O., Muggli, M.E., Lockhart, N.J., and Robertson, C.R. (2009) 'Open Doorway to Truth: Legacy of the Minnesota Tobacco Trial', *Mayo Clinic Proceedings*, 84(5): 446–56.

INTERPOL (2012) *INTERPOL Targets Organized Crime with Global Initiative Against Trafficking in Illicit Goods*, Media release, 22 June, www.interpol.int/News-and-media/News/2012/PR050. (accessed 10.6.15).

Joossens, L. and Raw, M. (1998) 'Cigarette Smuggling in Europe: Who Really Benefits?', *Tobacco Control*, 7: 66–71.

Joossens, L. and Raw, M. (2012) 'From Cigarette Smuggling to Illicit Tobacco trade', *Tobacco Control*, 21: 230–34.

Joossens, L., Chaloupka, F.J., Merriman, D., and Yurekli, A. (2000) 'Issues in the Smuggling of Tobacco Products', in P. Jha and F. Chaloupka (eds) *Tobacco Control in Developing Countries* (pp. 393–406). Washington DC: World Bank.

Joossens, L., Merriman, D., Ross, H., and Raw, M. (2010) 'The Impact of Eliminating the Global Illicit Cigarette Trade on Health and Revenue', *Addiction*, 105: 1640–49.

Joossens, L., Gilmore, A.B., Stoklosa, M., and Ross, H. (2015) 'Assessment of the European Union's Illicit Trade Agreements with the Four Major Transnational Tobacco Companies', *Tobacco Control*, doi: 10.1136/tobaccocontrol-2014-052218.

Kelton, M.H. and Givel, M.S. (2008) 'Public Policy Implications of Tobacco Industry Smuggling through Native American Reservations into Canada', *International Journal of Health Services*, 38(3): 471–87.

Lavrov, V. (2009) 'Ukraine's "Lost" Cigarettes Flood Europe: Big Tobacco's Overproduction Fuels $2 Billion Black Market', in *Tobacco Underground: The Global*

Trade in Smuggled Cigarettes, International Consortium of Investigative Journalists Digital Newsbook. Available at: www.icij.org/project/tobacco-underground/ebook-tobacco-underground. (accessed 15.6.15).

Lee, K. and Collin, J. (2006) '"Key to the Future": British American Tobacco and Cigarette Smuggling in China', *PLOS Medicine*, 3(7): e228.

LeGresley, E., Lee, K., Muggli, M.E., Patel, P., Collin, J., and Hurt, R.D. (2008) 'British American Tobacco and the "Insidious Impact of Illicit Trade" in Cigarettes across Africa', *Tobacco Control*, 17: 339–46.

Malone, R.E. and Bialous, S.A. (2014) 'WHO FCTC Article 5.3: Promise but Little Progress', *Tobacco Control*, 23(4): 279–80.

Marsden, W. (1999) 'Tobacco Insider Talks: Major Firms were Deeply Involved in Cross-border Smuggling, Former Executive says', *The Gazette*, Montreal, Quebec, 18 December.

Marsden, W. (2009a) 'Tobacco Companies Linked to Criminal Organizations in Lucrative Cigarette Smuggling', in *Tobacco Underground: The Global Trade in Smuggled Cigarettes*, International Consortium of Investigative Journalists Digital Newsbook. Available at: www.icij.org/project/tobacco-underground/ebook-tobacco-underground. (accessed 15.6.15).

Marsden, W. (2009b) 'How to Get Away with Smuggling', in *Tobacco Underground: The Global Trade in Smuggled Cigarettes*, International Consortium of Investigative Journalists Digital Newsbook. Available at: www.icij.org/project/tobacco-underground/ebook-tobacco-underground. (accessed 15.6.15).

McBarnet, D. (2006) 'After Enron Will "Whiter than White Collar Crime" Still Wash?', *British Journal of Criminology*, 46: 1091–109.

Nakkash, R. and Lee, K. (2008) 'Smuggling as the "Key to a Combined Market": British American Tobacco in Lebanon', *Tobacco Control*, 17: 324–31.

RCMP (Royal Canadian Mounted Police) (2013) *Contraband Tobacco Enforcement Strategy: Third Progress report (2010–2011)*, Royal Canadian Mounted Police. Available at: www.rcmp-grc.gc.ca/pubs/tobac-tabac/2012-contr-strat/2012-eng.pdf. (accessed 15.6.15).

Shepherd, P. (1985) 'Transnational Corporations and the International Cigarette Industry', in R.S. Newfarmer (ed.) *Profits, Progress and Poverty: Case Studies of International Industries in Latin America*. Notre Dame: University of Notre Dame Press.

Sullivan, D. and Radu, P. (2009) 'Blame the Distributor: How Gallaher Stayed in the Smuggling Game', in *Tobacco Underground: The Global Trade in Smuggled Cigarettes*, International Consortium of Investigative Journalists Digital Newsbook. Available at: www.icij.org/project/tobacco-underground/ebook-tobacco-underground. (accessed 15.6.15).

Sykes, G.M. and Matza, D. (1957) 'Techniques of Neutralisation: A Theory of Delinquency', *American Sociological Review*, 22(6): 667–70.

UCSF (University of California, San Francisco) (2015) 'Legacy Tobacco Documents Library', University of California, San Francisco: https://industrydocuments.library.ucsf.edu/tobacco/ (accessed 15.6.15).

Walker Guevara, M. (2009) 'The World's Most Widely Smuggled Legal Substance', in *Tobacco Underground: The Global Trade in Smuggled Cigarettes*, International Consortium of Investigative Journalists Digital Newsbook. Available at: www.icij.org/project/tobacco-underground/ebook-tobacco-underground. (accessed 15.6.15).

Walker Guevara, M., Rehnfeldt, M., and Soares, M. (2009) 'Smuggling Made Easy: Landlocked Paraguay Emerges as a Top Producer of Contraband Tobacco', in *Tobacco*

Underground: The Global Trade in Smuggled Cigarettes, International Consortium of Investigative Journalists Digital Newsbook. Available at: www.icij.org/project/tobacco-underground/ebook-tobacco-underground. (accessed 15.6.15).

WHO (World Health Organization) (2005) *Framework Convention on Tobacco Control*. Geneva: World Health Organization.

WHO (2012) *Mortality Attributable to Tobacco*. Geneva: World Health Organization.

WHO (2013) *Protocol to Eliminate Illicit Trade in Tobacco Products*. Geneva: World Health Organization.

WHO (2015) *Parties to the WHO Framework Convention on Tobacco Control*, Available at: www.who.int/fctc/signatories_parties/en/ (accessed 17.2.15).

Yurekli, A. and Sayginsoy, O. (2010) 'Worldwide Organized Cigarette Smuggling: An Empirical Analysis', *Applied Economics*, 42, 545–61.

9 Troika, austerity and the reluctant resort to criminality in Greece

Steve Hall and Georgios A. Antonopoulos

Introduction

This chapter is part of an on-going and broader research project on illegal markets and the informal economy in Greece and beyond. The aim here is to draw attention to a specific type of 'illegal marketer' – the entrepreneur operating in the legal market economy who has become involved in illegal markets related to the legitimate business solely to sustain its viability. One case has been selected from a larger sample of thirteen case studies that we analysed during the collapse of the Greek economy. In an effort to sustain his legal businesses under the financial pressure that has recently built up in Greece, particularly since late 2009, the owner of a confectionary shop entered an illegal market in dark chocolate. We have published data and analyses of some of the other case studies elsewhere (Antonopoulos and Hall, 2014). In line with colleagues who have used a limited number of case studies (e.g. Gadd and Farrall, 2004), we have chosen this case because it clearly expresses the characteristics of the whole sample.

In the first section we present the empirical case study contextualised by a brief synopsis of the recent financial situation in Greece from late 2009 until the signing of the memorandum with the International Monetary Fund (IMF), the European Central Bank and the European Commission – henceforth 'the Troika' – in 2010. Hopefully our synopsis will give a flavour of how difficult that environment has become. In the second section we outline some of the philosophical and theoretical problems associated with the thesis that underpins this collection – that in its current neoliberal phase the capitalist socioeconomic system is reproduced by a dominant 'moral economy' understood as a set of normalised and rather brutal 'values'. A brief examination of these problems suggests that some points of departure and reformulation might be possible.

The case study: Nick the confectioner

What follows here is the account of the owner of a small–medium size enterprise, a confectionary shop. This business had been doing quite well but suffered significant loss of custom as the Greek economic crisis deepened. In the period 2001–2007 the Greek economy's average annual growth rate of 4.2 per cent was one of most rapid in Europe, but this was sustained by high domestic demand, which was in turn artificially sustained by credit and a large public sector. Despite the 'safeguard' of quantitative easing, the economic convulsion of 2007–2008 had a significant negative effect on Greece. This was the start of the most severe financial crisis since the restoration of democracy in the country in 1974. The crisis was precipitated by a neoliberal investment regime imposed by the government and key lenders, and was exacerbated by irresponsible bank lending and a combination of political and institutional weaknesses. Together, these problems have plagued the economy, contributing to Greece's poor productivity, foreign investment and competitiveness.

Yet more pathogenic politico-economic factors included an expensive bureaucratic apparatus, a large informal labour market, the proliferation of cartels, speculation in important commodity markets, the state's inadequate attempts to protect small/medium-size entrepreneurship, a complex and unfair tax system that consistently disadvantaged those with smaller incomes, and what appeared to be a remarkable disconnection between research and the national economy (OECD, 2012). Outdated modes of government intervention, poor investment and resource allocation in crucial industries, excessively lax quality standards, low early-stage entrepreneurial activity and the failure of the Greek state to promote products and services effectively in the international arena have all contributed to the current parlous condition of the Greek economy (see OECD, 2007).

In October 2009, the newly elected government of Greece announced that the country's deficit was exceeding the national income by 12 per cent. By early 2010 it was more than obvious in international financial circles that to avoid default Greece would have to resort to external assistance. After two harsh austerity packages implemented in early 2010 failed to alleviate the situation, the Troika prepared a harsh programme of economic policies that would impose upon the nation the conditions of austerity required to secure a larger loan. On 1 May 2010, the Greek government announced a series of austerity measures to persuade primarily Germany to sign a larger EU and IMF loan package: a three-year EU€110 billion loan with a 5.5 per cent interest rate that, according to Varoufakis (2011: 207), was 'high enough to make it very unlikely that the Greek public purse would be able to repay this new loan as well as the existing ones'. An important condition was attached to this loan; that the Greek government would implement an additional series of austerity measures:

- Cuts in pay, pensions and jobs;
- Revenue increases through direct and indirect taxation;
- Increase in the average retirement age for public sector workers from 61 to 65.

This memorandum was 'revised' twice in August and November of 2010 to include cuts in public investment and public utilities and the erosion of employment rights. Despite these interventions, banks have still been reluctant to lend because of their fear of bad loans, which has led to a liquidity crisis. Moreover, as our ethnographic data below will confirm, this cocktail of a global recession, pessimism and severe austerity measures has had abrupt traumatising effects on the economy and the everyday lives of Greek citizens.

First, this neoliberal restructuring impacted on the country's economic activity and gross domestic product (GDP) growth. From 2008 onwards the economy has been continuously shrinking, from -0.1 per cent in 2008 to -6.9 per cent in 2011 (IMF, 2012). Second, the effect has been reflected in unemployment and plummeting living standards. Third, additional tax measures and high inflation led to a further drop in consumption. The estimated negative or zero growth rates in income in many employee categories led to a significant reduction in the buying power of the Greek public in late 2009 and early 2010, causing 'negative psychology' and a steep reduction in the consumer confidence of the Greek public (European Commission, 2012). According to a report published by the Greek Foundation for Economic and Industrial Research in November 2010, Greek consumers have been in a state of constant depression because 'they see no light at the end of the tunnel' (Georgas, 2010).

This rapid reduction in consumption was unprecedented in post-war Greek history. It affected not only the vast majority of small–medium enterprises but also the traditionally 'healthy' big transnational enterprises. The Greek government has been unable or perhaps unwilling to understand that the reduction in consumption as a result of high taxation increased the cost of production and transportation of commodities as well as inflation, which further depressed consumer confidence. In such an environment, a number of entrepreneurs were 'obliged' to become financially less diligent, which significantly affected intra-market trust and led to business introversion in a sociocultural climate of increasing suspicion and cynicism. Others were simply forced to close their businesses (NCGC, 2012). This overall economic climate of austerity, economic instability and consumer depression sets the scene for our case study of a small businessman struggling on the edge of solvency.

Nick is 24 years old and lives with his parents in a town on a large island in southern Greece. His father is a retired confectioner who in the late 1980s established a confectioner's shop in the town's biggest, busiest and most-central street. According to local people the shop is 'the best shop of its kind in the town if not the whole island'. The reason for the success of the shop was that Nick's father ran the place with a particular business philosophy that was valued by customers:

> My father was the best confectioner ... The most important reason for his success was that he always used good quality raw materials ... And this is what he always used to say to me: 'If you want to succeed in this business, always use the best materials'... Dark chocolate. That's very important. What others do is that they mix small quantities of dark chocolate with vegetable oil and make it look thicker. In this way they can make many more small chocolate bars ... But the customers know when they taste them ... This is why the others have always been second to my father...

After immense pressure from his father, Nick rather reluctantly enrolled in a private confectionery school. As the only child, he was expected to continue the family business. Towards the end of his studies his father fell seriously ill and could not continue running the shop. Nick's cousin, George, also a confectioner who was working in the same workshop, assumed responsibility for producing the bulk of the merchandise until Nick's graduation. When Nick completed the theoretical part of his studies in May 2010, he immediately joined the business. From the beginning the pair encountered many practical and financial problems. The biggest challenge was not for Nick to live up to his parents' quality-related expectations but the already rapidly declining sales:

> Generally, with George's help, I did not have any significant problems in making the stuff … But people nowadays do not buy as much as they used to. Two years ago [meaning 2008] those who came into the shop used to say 'I want a kilo of this, a kilo of that … Nowadays [late summer 2010], the whole environment has changed … Small chocolate bars … they [customers] say 'a piece of this small chocolate bar, a piece of the other small chocolate bar, one small piece of this cake' … stuff we previously used to give as tasters! And others may come in to buy one cup of ice-cream while before they'd buy a kilo, maybe more … People do not consume as much anymore, even the richer of our customers who used to buy stuff for their houses … Some come and ask 'can you "write them" [meaning to get the merchandise on credit] and I will pay you at the end of the month?'.

The significant reduction of sales and profits made Nick decide to reduce the functional expenses of the business. Evading even more tax was almost impossible and he already owned the property his shop was located in. Expenses were reduced in stages. The initial move was to reduce the days his shop assistant attended work before eventually sacking her, and immediately after that to keep merchandise longer on the shelf:

> In the beginning I told to the Albanian girl working in the shop to come at the weekends, maybe big name days when there are more customers. Then I told her 'we are not doing anything, we can't collaborate anymore …'. Then we started keeping stuff for longer. For example, we started keeping two–three-day old cakes, which are not as fresh anymore, in the refrigerator so that they last longer. We are even more conscious of losses now that the sales are low. If something bad happens you have a serious problem. A few years ago another girl we had working in the shop left the door of the refrigerator open, the ice-cream melted and we had a loss of €1,500. Five years ago we'd say 'these things happen, it's part of the business'. If something like this happened now, we'd probably have to close the shop.

Given the significant reduction in consumption, these steps could not maintain profitability. Having no employees other than the indispensably productive and supportive George and no intention of compromising further the quality of his merchandise and jeopardising the business's reputation, Nick approached a representative of the island's legal wholesaler who had a personal relationship with his cousin. Nick asked him to provide significantly cheaper dark chocolate, which, as it is considered a luxury product, is subjected to numerous layers of taxation in Greece:

> I thought we needed to make some more reductions in the expenses of the shop. George is too important until I can fully stand on my feet. You cannot cut down on electricity, of course … 50 per cent of the shop, if not more, is its refrigerators and freezers … So the next thing you can cut down on is raw materials. But I did not want to ruin the 'name' of the family by making low-quality products. The last thing I wanted was people to say '[name of shop] is not as good as it used to be'. Once your customers get used to a level of quality, you can't offer them anything less. So, I went to this friend of my cousin who is representative of [name of company] in [name of island], they are confectionery material wholesalers in Athens, and asked where I could find 'cheaper' but good dark chocolate. Do you know what I mean? He said 'give me a few days and I will get it for you. How much do you want?'

Nick initially ordered 1 tonne of raw dark chocolate, which was transported by boat from Piraeus to the island and a few days later delivered large barrels (as opposed to the 'normal', wrapped 10 kilo plaques of dark chocolate) to his grandmother's small warehouse at the back of her house in a village a few kilometres from the town. Nick is not aware of the origin of this dark chocolate, although he suspects it might be stolen from a known specialist company's warehouse in mainland Greece. However, not only is the quality of the merchandise excellent but the illegal transaction was very convenient because, under the current financial and entrepreneurial conditions in Greece, legal intra-trade exchanges between wholesalers and procurers on one hand, and shop owners on the other, have become inflexible because a loss of the commercial trust that has traditionally been so vital to long-term collaborators in the trade:

> The quality is excellent and it is cheap … why should I care where it comes from? … I can buy it in that price. Listen [name of interviewer], we have a battle every day here. When you do business normally with invoices etc., the wholesalers, even those who know you for years, now ask for cash up front only; there are no cheques, no credit, as it happened previously, nothing … just cash. There are so many bounced cheques in the market that no one trusts anyone else any more … And who has this much cash to give upfront now?

Nick keeps only a few days' supply of raw dark chocolate in the shop in order to avoid an unpleasant situation should the financial police pay him a visit for an inspection. His mother transports small quantities of chocolate during her numerous visits to Nick's grandmother. He was not willing to disclose the exact amount of money saved by buying dark chocolate in the illegal market, although, as he suggested, it was big enough to alleviate some financial burdens:

> We are not talking about big profit here. Enough to 'cover some holes' in the business and survive in these times … The times when the shop made a lot of money enough for my parents to live very well, pay for my school, go on holiday, buy stuff, and even have savings, are long gone … A few years ago my father, my mother and I even considered expanding the business to [name of nearby town]. Back then we could get a loan from the bank and that was it. But this is not going to happen now … Now we are marginal. We pay bills, standard expenses, the accountant, and there is hardly any profit … We just survive now.

What's virtue got to do with it?

As we noted in the introduction, Nick's case was selected because his situation, response and sentiments are typical of the larger sample. All the respondents are small business owners, not corporate executives or the 'masters of the universe' who inhabit the stratosphere of global finance. However, although the former group is far less powerful and influential than the latter two, its members are far more numerous and represent the majority in the world of business. Our analysis is limited to the former group, but the characteristics shared by its members regarding their current drift into illegality – which revolve around the anxious resignation, compulsory pragmatism and quiet subterfuge that constitute the culture of 'capitalist realism' (see Fisher, 2009) – pose some questions for both mainstream and critical approaches to the issue of corruption.

Some criminologists working in the mainstream of the discipline still regard corruption in the business world as an aberration, a temporary diversion from a life normally guided by good values and relatively autonomous social agency. For instance, Karstedt and Farrall argue that crimes committed by otherwise 'respectable' individuals '[s]how that a syndrome of market anomie comprising distrust, fear and cynical attitudes towards law increases the willingness of respectable citizens to engage in illegal and unfair practices in the marketplace' (2006: 1011). They describe 'market anomie' in terms of the 'normative orientations that lead to illegal, unfair and unethical behaviour endemic in the core, not in the margins of society' (ibid.: 1029). This argument, drawing implicitly upon selected aspects of Durkheim and Weber, posits the primary cause of corruption and economic crime as the temporary disorientation of a moral system that normally affirms socioeconomic actors' orientation towards fair interactions in a potentially harmonious system. There is significant agreement here with liberal philosophers such as Sandel (2012), who suggests that specific individuals in important institutional positions can temporarily lose their values – a notion that echoes Matza's (1964) criminological concept of 'moral holiday' – and thus disorientate their 'moral compass'. The solution is to revive and institutionalise good values that can subsequently be practiced by these pivotal individuals.

However, precisely how individual actors operating in today's condition of unforgiving competition and extreme precariousness – some on the very edge of solvency – are to withstand the pressures exerted by the system's internal logic and rediscover their 'moral compass' in the crisis-ridden context of neoliberal capitalism is not discussed, which leaves a gaping hole in this standard moral constructivist argument. A more convincing critical perspective that takes into account neoliberalism's broader cultural and political context is offered as the theme of this collection. The basic thesis suggests that corruption is not an aberration creating a temporary anomic condition affecting specific individual actors in core institutions but the 'new normal' across the globe. It is an important aspect of a 'moral project', an attempt by the ideological forces of neoliberalism to establish a new 'moral economy' – constituted by brutally competitive anti-social values that inform, encourage and justify economic practice – as the prevailing norm.

We certainly agree that acts of corruption are present at all levels of socioeconomic life and under-researched by social scientists. However, can our beleaguered small business owners in Greece be seen as either willingly or unwillingly incorporated subjects of neoliberalism's brutal and corrupt moral economy? For us, establishing such subjective incorporation into a moral order is problematic, which suggests that some fundamental conceptual problems need to be overcome before this critical perspective can move forward.

First, the term 'corruption' itself, whether used by mainstream criminologists or critical criminologists, is, like 'normlessness', an essentially *negative* concept with its metaphorical root in the corrosive processes of moral debasement and degeneration – the rotting away of something that was once substantial. Using this term places the radical edge in partial agreement with the mainstream centre – something that was once good, or at least was capable of being better, has turned bad and eventually disappeared. The main substantive difference between the two positions is that mainstream criminologists see acts of corruption as mere aberrations temporarily despoiling specific institutions whilst critical criminologists see corruption as a normalised reproductive characteristic of the neoliberal capitalist system. Of course the term has gathered some substance in its everyday denotative meaning of 'corrupt practices' – fraud, bribery and so on – but it lacks substance at the deeper ontological and zemiological levels: what it actually is and what harms it might inflict upon ourselves and our multiple environments. Any ethical judgement we make on forms of corruption is dependent on such substantive conceptualisation, without which our critical analysis is unable to escape the mainstream and move into new and more fertile intellectual territory. We need more distance between ourselves and the mainstream before we can get the problem into clear focus and offer something substantive about the psychological forces that drive human action towards 'corrupt' practices, how they are connected to culture and social relations, and how they are systematically applied in specific everyday economic practices such as those outlined in our case study above.

Emerging philosophical and theoretical perspectives are beginning to question the relation between the 'mainstream' and 'critical' perspectives in criminological theory. The relation as it currently stands perhaps sets the debate's parameters a little too narrowly and prevents the latter fully escaping the former to forge its own unique position (see Hall and Winlow, 2015). These new perspectives are based on the fundamental claim that it is impossible to detect any values or indeed the corruption of such values performing an active role at the core of capitalism's market-driven system. Indeed, neither Nick nor any of the other respondents in our sample seemed aware of the possibility that their business life has a moral foundation. They were aware of the distinction between legality and illegality, but these perceptions seemed to be detached from moral issues. What came across constantly was their awareness of the insecurity and anxiety associated with business life, balanced with the rewards of autonomy and modest wealth, and the unforgiving logic of the market – it was simply the way things worked, and, to some extent depending on the broader economic climate, 'things' are either working well for them or not. To risk stating the blindingly obvious, our brief description of Greece's current economic condition in the first section would suggest that at the moment 'things' are not working very well for them at all.

Do 'things' have a moral basis? Our respondents' perceptions tend to support the ideas of contemporary philosophers such as Dews (2008), Žižek (2010) and Stiegler (2010), who argue that at its psychosocial core capitalism is little more than institutionalised insecurity, anxiety and envy in the service of a cold, abstract accountant's logic (see also Hall, 2012a; Winlow and Hall, 2013). Of course, broadly speaking, this sort of conceptualisation of the core's ontological constitution is not new. It is quite remarkable that the ideologists of classical liberalism, neoliberalism's eighteenth-century predecessor, never posited intrinsic values at the core of their developing economic system. Using utilitarianism's consequentialist ethics and logic, they portrayed the individual as at root a natural amoral hedonist. All economic systems are driven by solicited *private vices*, 'sinful' pre-moral drives such as greed and envy that could, as Mandeville (1970) noted, be miraculously turned into *public benefits* – later expressed by utilitarianism as the 'greater good' – by the magic 'invisible hand' of the market. Economists from Smith (1986) through Keynes (1935) to current thinkers (see Akerlof and Shiller, 2009) were untroubled by this concept. Keynes named these active, circulating, systematised vices 'animal spirits' and cautioned against their volatility and the subsequent unreliability of any system founded upon them. Žižek (2010), in an instructive passage on Chinese history, reminds us that pre-modern imperial regimes were also quite untroubled by the harnessing and brutal practicing of vices should their consequences be security, economic progress and geopolitical expansion.

We can approach this problem philosophically by emphasising the distinction between *intrinsicalist* and *consequentialist* modes of understanding values. Whereas intrinsicalists demand that the means and ends of human life must be governed by the same moral order – expressed most clearly by Kant's *categorical imperative* or with more naturalism and flamboyance by Nietzsche's *eternal recurrence* – consequentialists see a more pragmatic, distinct, temporal and causal relation between the two, and thus give the means significantly more leeway. Unless the 'moral economy' position can deal with the functional complexity of the means/ends distinction – which has existed practically and ideologically at the core of capitalist politics and economics at least since the eighteenth century and can be detected in a nascent form much earlier (see Hall, 2014) – it will be vulnerable to attack. Whereas the left has tended to present intrinsicalist moral arguments, the right, as classical liberalism gradually ousted traditional conservatism as its main philosophical platform, has adopted a consequentialist stance expressed as utilitarian pragmatism. As the institutionalised left faced powerful right-wing hegemony it often compromised and shifted towards this consequentialist stance for the sake of electability, a position adopted in stark relief by Blair's New Labour project, which moved the left beyond compromise to full incorporation. If we attempt to compare Blairism to neoliberalism, the ends of life and the means towards them appear too similar to make a clear distinction.

Put simply, greed, envy, power-seeking, self-interest and so on have for a long time been posited by the classical liberal right in a consequentialist and utilitarian-pragmatic mode as *natural human vices* that can be tempered and harnessed to the achievement of beneficial social ends. Capitalism was never an intrinsicalist moral project. Even what it tends to posit as beneficial ends have in moral terms an air of least-worst incremental pragmatism and relativist naturalism about them – wealth and individual freedom will bring with them their own problems but at least they are 'better' than the poverty and authoritarianism that pre-existed them. There is no need to posit any virtues at the heart of the system, as Nick and our other respondents showed. In the capitalist ideology's moral universe 'greed is good' not because it is *intrinsically* good in itself but because, when 'things' are working reasonably well, it *consequentially* produces relatively good results. Right-wing ideology operates effectively by emphasising the relatively good results rather than the vices that right-wing ideologues believe – or at least want others to believe – to be a timeless and unavoidable aspect of human nature. However, our conception of human vices, which we will outline very briefly later, is that they are not natural and permanently active but latent and systematically incited (see Hall, 2012a, 2014; Hall *et al.*, 2008).

We can approach the philosophical problems concerning the location and function of values by introducing the concept of *the pseudo-pacification process* (see Hall, 2012a, 2014). The fundamental claim in this thesis is that capitalism has never been a civilising process – an attempt to constitute the core of subjectivity, cultural values, social institutions or political economy in a mode orientated towards the Virtues – and neither has the working class or any other subordinate group stood in coherent and enduring moral opposition to the system. From its roots in late Mediaeval Europe, and initially in England (Macfarlane, 1978), the psycho-cultural and economic dimensions of capitalism's co-evolutionary system (see Harvey, 2010) were founded and integrated on the principle of organised competitive individualism. By initially removing entitlements to material subsistence and legally dissolving the family, the community and the distributivist local economy as the principal social units, the nascent capitalist system subsequently cast out insecure and anxious individuals into a competitive marketplace (Hall, 2012a, 2014). The removal of substantive security and protection left these individuals with little choice but to compete. This basic situation has not changed for Nick and his fellow travellers in business, and now appears to be in its most precarious condition to date. The Christian-centred attempt to extend the values and institutional practices of *agape* into the broader socioeconomic system was abandoned (Eagleton, 2009), as Nick's inability to find substantive support suggests, and, in a process of reversal, it was replaced by a culture of private desires informing personal life-projects (Thomas, 2009). The system's remaining ethical principles, agents and institutions, reluctant to question this core move and possibly jeopardise the economic dynamism it seemed to generate, were relocated to the periphery to administer the regulation of the system's operational consequences.

In the later period of Western capitalist consolidation and early industrialism from the eighteenth century, the vices that drove socioeconomic interaction in what had become an unforgivingly insecure and competitive economy were regarded as necessary evils. Vices they might be, but they could be ushered away from the manifest form of brute violence and harnessed for the 'greater good' as they were organised by the market, sublimated by consumer culture's gradually proliferated and democratised opportunities to acquire wealth and status, and ultimately converted into the economically dynamic form of aggressive yet non-violent sociosymbolic competition. The potentially destructive effects of this aggressive competition were restrained by developing systems of cultural norms in formal regulatory institutions – law, parliamentary politics, education, welfare and so on. These norms, gradually disseminated from formal institutions to everyday culture, were informed but not constituted by relocated values that had been evacuated from the core of human life. This new dynamic structure furnished individuals with a set of flexible 'strategic normative practices' (Hall *et al.*, 2008: 62) to regulate competitive moves, partially appeasing insecurity and anxiety and the unconscious drives they activated. Thus incited and harnessed vices were prevented from plunging the system into a vortex of chaotic aggression and violence (Hall, 2014). Nick's quiet and clandestine shift into illegality represents the flexibility of strategic normative practices and their ability to maintain at least a semblance of normative conduct even in the most stressful conditions – although of course there are occasions of extreme duress when this structure can simply collapse into violence. However, a system such as capitalism, founded on cold logic and pre-moral drives, cannot understand or react to either positive or negative aspects of any moral order that exists at any point on the spectrum from the benign to the brutal: it exists simply to continue onwards. Such a system cannot be reformed in any substantive way. It can be regulated, but should regulation be relaxed the system will immediately revert to its original form. All we can say is that the system's numerous regulatory institutions can be informed by the values that exist in a condition of constant revision on various points on that spectrum. Put very simply, in basic terms neoliberal capitalism is the most advanced and complex example of an unconscious, libidinal drive-based economy controlled by a set of relocated values and norms.

Because it appears to convert dangerous drives into functional and more manageable practices – creating pacification as prosperity increases to satiate drives whilst control institutions become more expansive and efficient as they learn how to regulate drives – the sublimation process can from a distance look like some sort of morally driven civilizing process. But it is not. It is predicated on the stimulation of aggressive drives by means of induced insecurity and anxiety, followed by their controlled release in a rule-bound competition. Thus the pseudo-pacification process is pre-moral, unstable and fragile because the strength and durability of its quasi-ethical normative insulation is over-reliant on expanding opportunities for prosperity and maintaining systems of external control (Crogan, 2010; Hall, 2014).

However, recently, the pseudo-pacification process has taken a new and rather disturbing turn. As the current marketisation of formal institutions takes the process a step further it is evacuating values from even their regulatory roles (Whitehead, 2015). A globalising consumer culture is simultaneously eroding informal regulatory norms and any oppositional culturally based politics that might still exist (Hall *et al.*, 2008; Winlow *et al.*, 2015). Underneath the pseudo-pacification process lies the individual's potent unconscious urge to escape insecurity and anxiety into a comprehensible order of symbols: for Lacan the birth of the subject is this movement from primal unconscious nature to symbolic culture (see Hall, 2012b). Today, however, this movement into subjectivity takes on a different form. As Žižek's (2010) Super-Ego injunction to enjoy has been brought into play, we have seen popular culture and formal regulatory institutions simultaneously apply themselves to the loosening of symbolic restraints and the subsequent coarsening of strategic normative practices. Whereas the traditional Super-Ego restrained the Id's impulses by making us feel guilty about some of the enjoyments we desired, the new consumer-based Super-Ego makes us feel guilty when we fail to take opportunities to enjoy ourselves.

However, we now enjoy wealth, success, enjoyment, power, autonomy, consumer sensations and so on not as the fulfilment of basic human needs or intrinsic values but as the temporarily successful instrumental means of appeasing the anxiety constantly provoked in the individual by the competitive and unstable capitalist system, as the accounts of Nick and the other respondents suggest. There is something at once tragic and heroic about the way these small business owners 'enjoy' their minor victories by pushing the strategic normative order beyond its limits in their constant independent struggle to maintain a consumer lifestyle in the face of insolvency and humiliation. These 'victories' and 'enjoyments' can be perceived as virtuous because they are presented by neoliberal ideology as least-worst relative values, the consequential end-products of the system's ability of arrange on our behalf the necessary flight from insecurity and anxiety that the subject craves, the 'escape from evil' (Becker, 1975). What we have witnessed during the neoliberal era is not a shift in the moral order but a significant shift in the strategic normative order that controls the functioning of the pseudo-pacification process and allows the majority what meagre comforts are possible.

The data gathered from Nick and the others support the proposition that the ideological strengthening and reproduction of neoliberalism's hegemon does not require a shift in core values but simply an increased acceptance of the systemic logic and pre-moral drives that constitute the core. Since the fall of socialism and the ascendancy of neoliberalism on a global scale, mainstream ideology has taken advantage of what Fisher (2009) calls 'capitalist realism', the prevailing 'end of history' mentality in which visions of a genuinely alternative morally driven and politically organised socioeconomic system no longer seem credible. Put simply, most people have swallowed the negative 'there is no alternative' doctrine and no longer believe an alternative is possible. Acceptance has been normalised and the daily acting out of the system's core drives and logic is 'fetishistically disavowed' (Žižek, 1989) – which means that most people know they are doing it but don't want to know and therefore, effectively, don't know. With attention permanently diverted, all eyes are on the peripheral normative structure where relocated values attempt to perform regulatory functions. Therefore this is where we perceive the changes that seem to suggest a new 'moral economy', but they are not substantive because positive core values no longer exist where they should or act as they should, and thus no longer order or drive forward our everyday socioeconomic lives.

We can see this whole drama being played out to the full in today's Greece. Syriza's capitulation to the Troika's demands in early 2015, despite a heartening election victory, has once again revealed the gridlocked institutional power behind 'capitalist realism'. This primary power has a global reach and has nothing to do with moral authority or discursive disciplinary control – it is rooted firmly in the entitlement to debt-generate investment capital and legally demand repayment. Isolated in a neoliberal Europe and laden with debt, Syriza has not been able to disturb the overall ideological climate of 'capitalist realism', the resignation and cynicism in which Greece's distressed small businessmen can see only one real choice – to participate in illegal activities or close their businesses and face the likelihood of material poverty, humiliation, loss of social status and the terrifying return to insecurity. Their degree of commitment to 'values' new or old is barely relevant. Individuals must simply compete to return profits and repay debts.

Commercial competition is one of capitalism's fundamental logical and functional principles. Other confectioners may have been put out of business by the success of Nick's father but now Nick is dying by the same sword that killed his father's former competitors, albeit in a situation where alternative commercial ventures or employment are far more difficult to come by. As our discussion of Nick's situation suggests, *agape* was never established in the broad socioeconomic milieu and there is little love or trust amongst actors in the marketplace in the current economic reality. Customers will not buy more ice-cream, fellow shopkeepers will not club together to save his business, there will be no surprise gift from a wealthy benefactor and, in the grip of the Troika, no immediate or substantive help from the government. Not only are there are no values at the heart of markets, merely subjects resigned to the unsentimental economic logic and personal insecurity induced by the rule of 'compete or die', but Nick can also detect the diminution of values in the formal and informal dimensions of the regulatory framework. Markets give the false impression of being able to accommodate moral regulation only when times are sufficiently prosperous for the majority of traders to be profitably selling things to each other, where the displaced values operating in the normative structure can be brought to bear a little heavier on everyday socioeconomic life. In times of slump, however, all this evaporates (Cross, 2000; Winlow and Hall, 2013), exposing the notion of the system's moral core as a myth. What has never existed in this context can neither be reinstated nor ideologically reworked into a more brutal form.

Neoliberalism represents a hitherto unexperienced intensification of a pseudo-pacification process that has spanned the capitalist project, an intensification that has currently brought its main dynamics of anxiety, competition, sublimation and displacement into stark relief. The precariousness of the individual's position in the economy is ubiquitous – even the top 10 per cent could see their money or assets evaporate virtually overnight in vortices of inflation or deflation, with only an intense competition for assets in the resulting fire-sale as the way back to riches for the very wealthiest and most opportunistic. The prospects of imminent poverty and insignificance loom large in the imagination of all involved with business or waged work, no matter where they are in the social hierarchy, but of course Nick exists on the very edge of the precipice. In the absence of strong social ties, substantive ethical codes and political solidarity born of the recognition of social antagonism, the illegal activities outlined in our data are the most likely pragmatic outcomes of austerity. Earlier we outlined the economic conditions currently afflicting Greece in enough detail to convey the extreme difficulty and political intractability the nation faces. In this climate the anxious, beleaguered yet driven and politically cynical entrepreneur facing the unforgiving logic of a global capitalist economy administered by unsympathetic neoliberal governance will reluctantly resort to unethical acts in order to ensure the survival of the business and, ultimately, the self as a social subject of its times. The new and relatively more brutal norms that seem to prevail in the neoliberal era can indeed loosen the regulatory structure and ideologically justify certain harmful actions, but the initial drives and encouragement towards such actions are located in a different and more fundamental order of being.

References

Adorno, T. (1973) *Negative Dialectics*. New York: Seabury.

Akerlof, G. and Shiller, R. (2009) *Animal Spirits*. Princeton: Princeton University Press.

Antonopoulos, G. and Hall, S. (2014) 'The Death of the Legitimate Merchant?'. In van Duyne, P.C., Harvey, J., Antonopoulos, G.A., von Lampe, K., Maljevic, A. and Markovska, A. (eds) *Corruption, Greed and Crime Money*. (pp. 313–336) Nijmegen: WLP.

Badiou, A. (2002) *Ethics: An Essay on the Understanding of Evil*. London: Verso.

Becker, E. (1975) *Escape from Evil*. New York: Free Press.

Crogan, P. (2010) 'Knowledge, Care and Transindividuation: An interview with Bernard Stiegler', *Cultural Politics*, 6(2): 157–170.

Cross, G. (2000) *An All-Consuming Century*. New York: Columbia University Press.

Dews, P. (2008) *The Idea of Evil.* London: Blackwell.

Eagleton, T. (2009) *Trouble with Strangers.* Chichester: Wiley-Blackwell.

European Commission (2012) 'Greece Consumer Confidence Indicator'. http://ycharts.com/indicators/reports/european_economic_sentiment_indicator.

Fisher, M. (2009) *Capitalist Realism.* Winchester: Zero.

Gadd, D. and Farrall, S. (2004) 'Criminal Careers, Desistance and Subjectivity', *Theoretical Criminology*, 8: 123–156.

Georgas, V. (2010) 'IOBE: 3 sta 4 Noikokyria Sfiggoun ki Allo to Zonari', *Eleftherotypia*, 4 November: 53.

Hall, S. (2012a) *Theorising Crime and Deviance.* London: Sage.

Hall, S. (2012b) 'The Solicitation of the Trap: On transcendence and transcendental materialism in advanced consumer-capitalism', *Human Studies: Special Issue on Transcendence and Transgression*, 35(3): 365–381.

Hall, S. (2014) 'The Socioeconomic Function of Evil'. In Ray. L. and Kilby, J. (eds) *Sociological Review Monograph*: *Violence and Society.* (pp. 13–31) Chichester: Wiley.

Hall, S. and Winlow, S. (2015) *Revitalizing Criminological Theory: Towards a New Ultra-Realism*. London: Routledge.

Hall, S., Winlow, S. and Ancrum, C. (2008) *Criminal Identities and Consumer Culture.* Cullompton: Willan.

Harvey, D. (2010) *The Enigma of Capital.* London: Profile.

Hobbs, D. (2013) *Lush Life.* Oxford: Oxford University Press

Horsley, M., Kotze, J. and Hall, S. (2015) 'The Maintenance of Orderly Disorder: Law, markets and the pseudo-pacification process', *Journal on European History of Law*, 6(1): 18–29.

IMF (International Monetary Fund) (2012) *World Economic Outlook.* Washington, DC: IMF.

Jameson, F. (2010) *The Valences of the Dialectic.* London: Verso.

Karstedt, S. and Farrall, S. (2006) 'The Moral Economy of Everyday Crime', *British Journal of Criminology*, 46: 1011–1036.

Keynes, J.M. (1935) *The General Theory of Employment, Interest and Money*. New York: Harcourt and Co.

Macfarlane, A. (1978) *The Origins of English Individualism.* Oxford: Blackwell.

Mandeville, B. (1970) *Fable of the Bees*. London: Penguin.

Matza, D. (1964) *Delinquency and Drift*. New York: Wiley.

NCGC (2012) 'I Troika Vlaptei Sovara tin Ygeia'. www.esee.gr/page.asp?id=3903.

OECD (Organisation for Economic Co-operation and Development) (2007) *Greece.* Paris: OECD.

OECD (2012) 'Greece 2012'. www.oecd.org/greece/sti-outlook-2012-greece.pdf.

Rousseau, J.-J. (1990) *Rousseau, Judge of Jean-Jacques.* Hanover, NH: Dartmouth College Press.

Sandel, M. (2012) *What Money Can't Buy*. London: Allen Lane.

Smith, A. (1986) *The Wealth of Nations*. London: Penguin.

Stiegler, B. (2010) *For a New Critique of Political Economy.* Cambridge: Polity.

Thomas, K. (2009) *The Ends of Life: Roads to Fulfilment in Early Modern England.* Oxford: OUP.

Thompson, E.P. (1971) 'The Moral Economy of the English Crowd in the Eighteenth Century', *Past and Present*, 50: 76–136.

Varoufakis, Y. (2011) *The Global Minotaur.* London: Zed.

Ward-Perkins, B. (2005) *The Fall of Rome and the End of Civilization.* Oxford: OUP.

Whitehead, P. (2015) *Reconceptualising the Moral Economy of Criminal Justice*. Basingstoke: Palgrave-Macmillan.
Winlow, S. and Hall, S. (2013) *Rethinking Social Exclusion*. London: Sage.
Winlow, S., Hall, S., Treadwell, J. and Briggs, D. (2015) *Riots and Political Protest: Notes from the Post-Political Present*. London: Routledge.
Žižek, S. (1989) *The Sublime Object of Ideology*. London: Verso.
Žižek, S. (2008) *Violence*. London: Profile.
Žižek, S. (2010) *Living in the End Times*. London: Verso.

10 Entrepreneurialism, corruption and moral order in the criminal justice system of the Democratic Republic of Congo

Maritza Felices-Luna

Corruption discourses and the production of moral order

As a rhetorical figure, corruption provides a new angle through which we can analyse work, everyday life, human relations and practices of power (Drackle, 2005). For instance, the attribution of practices or actors as corrupt or otherwise serves to selectively confer morality to some and stigmatise others (Mitchell, 2007). Furthermore, underpinning discourses of corruption are (self)representations of (im)moral behaviours and attitudes towards a wide variety of moral issues (justice, legality, trust, solidarity, generosity, altruism, reciprocity and accountability) (Zerilli, 2005, p. 84). Consequently, the premise of this chapter is that when social actors[1] speak about corruption they are participating in the discursive production of a moral order. The Democratic Republic of Congo (DRC), currently ranked 186 out of 187 countries in the United Nations development index[2] and 154 out of 175 countries in the Transparency International corruption index,[3] is the object of extensive anticorruption discourses and reforms. Drawing on empirical material produced during two different fieldworks carried out in Lubumbashi, this chapter explores the production of a moral order in the DRC by examining the coexistence of multiple discourses on corruption.

In 2007 I conducted 12 semi-structured interviews with practitioners working in the area of justice in the DRC. The second fieldwork took place in 2010 and the semi-structured interviews focused on the experiences and practices of 11 members of the military or the police who worked during the three political periods that have characterised the DRC since its independence (dictatorship, civil war and democratic transition).[4] Whereas in 2007 the goal was to discover and support forms of resistance to the justice system, in particular the criminal justice system, in 2010 the goal was to explore the role of the police and the military as protectors of the political regime and economic order by controlling, discouraging and breaking down dissent.[5] Although corruption was not the object of either research, participants discussed this topic extensively. In both instances corruption was used to provide context to life in the DRC, to frame the work culture embedded in their institutions, to denounce the working conditions they were subjected to and to justify their own questionable practices. The centrality of corruption in the interviews steered me towards a research area I was unfamiliar with. As I turned to the scientific literature it became apparent that a large number of publications appeared to be part of an anticorruption discourse that upholds neoliberal political and economic agendas.

This chapter contrasts the discourses on corruption produced by the anticorruption complex in the North to the rhetoric of corruption crafted by those directly involved in petty corruption[6] within the police, the military and the justice system in the DRC. I attempt to expose the moral orders produced through these discourses by looking at corruption as a category of thought and an organising principle with political and cultural implications (Shore and Haller, 2005). In the first section I describe how anticorruption discourses construe corruption as a problem of the South caused by its own deficiencies that can only be remedied through the implementation of neoliberal policies. In the second section I present three conflicting but concomitant moral orders that appear through locally produced discourses on corruption. The first moral order supports the discourses from the North condemning corruption and explaining it through Africa's deficiencies, insufficiencies and absences. The second is a moral order that challenges the immorality attributed to specific practices and provide us with alternative lenses through which to interpret those actions. The third moral order supports predation and accumulation by dispossession as a legitimate enterprise based on the reproduction of a hierarchical social order. In the conclusion I attempt to show how the moral orders produced through discourses on corruption within the criminal justice system can be connected to a general neoliberal morality and the implications this 'shared morality' has for neoliberal projects.

Crafting the immoral other: denouncing corruption and (re)producing the African vassal

Despite the fact that massive and systemic corruption is common in the North, grand corruption continues to be portrayed as something that belongs to the non-Western 'other' or to defective state bureaucracies (Shore and Haller, 2005). Corruption has become the standard cause of what is considered to be the economic and democratic failure of the developing world (Bukovansky, 2006). A symbiosis has thus been constituted between underdevelopment and corruption: underdeveloped countries are corrupted and corrupted countries are underdeveloped (Assiyi, 2008). Meanwhile, given that most of what is considered valid knowledge is still produced by the North, ex-colonial powers continue to deem themselves legitimately entitled to determine what is best for the rest of the world (Stiglitz, 2005). As a result, a corruption industry has emerged where networks of academics, policy makers and practitioners determine proper and improper forms of political-economic development (Swain *et al.*, 2010). This means that scientific discourses continue to normalise the right of the North to dictate, adapt and reshape the structures, practices and ways of life of the South according to Northern standards (Abrahamsen, 2003).

The rhetoric produced by Northern anticorruption discourses is one based on the idea of deficiency (Zerilli, 2005). Discourses emphasising presumed absences, delinquencies or distinctiveness exclusive to Africa support the image of Africa as being marginal to or standing on the outskirts of global processes of development (Harrison, 2010). According to Sender (1999, p. 89) journalists, social scientists and economists portray a tragic view of development in sub-Saharan Africa through medical/biological language[7] (blood, rot, scars, mutilation, plagues) to convey 'disappointment, moralistic outrage, repugnance and a barely concealed, if not overt contempt for African barbarism'. The image produced is one of 'backward societies' trapped within 'their' culture where endemic corruption results from a combination of social pathology, third world instability, a lack of social discipline as well as society's partial bureaucratisation and incomplete penetration by the State (Shore and Haller, 2005).

Since the end of the cold war, the corrupt African state has been identified as the culprit of all African problems. It has been demonised and 'vilified for its weaknesses, its over-extension, its interference with the smooth functioning of markets, its repressive character, its dependence on foreign powers, its ubiquity, its absence, etc.' (Mkandawire, 2001, p. 293). This characterisation of the African State serves to make claims on the need for good governance, efficiency, accountability and transparency (Shore and Haller, 2005). Furthermore, the World Bank and the IMF use portrayals of endemic corruption (caused by the State's inefficiency) as prime justification for the liberalisation of international markets and structural reforms in developing and transitional economies (Swain *et al.*, 2010). Under the guise of avoiding clientelism and rent seeking, the state is squeezed fiscally and hampered politically rendering it incapable of carrying out its basic functions, which in turn is used to justify further implementation of policies that erode its economic and political capacity (Mkandawire, 2001).

Neoliberalism represents the most recent example in a long tradition of imperialist imposition of practices, policies and reforms seeking to benefit Europe (Harrison, 2010). By conditioning aid to the implementation of neoliberal policies (Renton *et al.*, 2007) international organisations facilitate the continued looting of Africa by the West (Bond, 2006). Consequently, the real challenge to the (re)construction of African states is neoliberalism (Botchway and Moudud, 2012). Although neoliberalism is not a fixed programme or ideology (Shamir, 2008) it does have at its core the premise that society must be organised on the basis of individual competition, freedom, liberty and an ethic of self-reliance (Amable, 2011; Harvey, 2005). For neoliberalism, there is no common good, social problems are depoliticised and must be dealt with by citizens construed as entrepreneurs and consumers (Brown, 2006). In this regard, neoliberalism considers that welfare at the collective or societal level can only be achieved through self-interest, acquisitiveness and ruthlessness of individuals (Wiegratz, 2010) responsible for their own existence and integration into the market (Amable, 2011). In doing so, neoliberalism glorifies the callous entrepreneur, disconnects economic activity from its wider social consequences (Bone, 2012) and inverts humane values such as social responsibility, care and altruism (Cowling, 2012). Economic orders, relations and practices have moral dimensions, preconditions and implications that, once established, become naturalised (Sayer, 2007). Neoliberalism is therefore a cultural programme (Wiegratz, 2010) precisely because its policies and reforms undermine, delegitimise, overwrite and displace pre-existing neoliberal norms, values, orientations and practices while promoting those intrinsic to neoliberalism (Harrison, 2005).

Discourses on corruption produce a social order where the South is constructed as inferior and constituted as corrupt, poor, ignorant and irrational (Shore and Haller, 2005). These discourses also produce and reproduce a moral order where certain forms of accumulation in certain places are considered legitimate whereas others are not. For instance, Northern capitalism's extirpation and exploitation in Africa and the Americas (Glassman, 2006) as well as modern forms of accumulation by dispossession[8] (Harvey, 2004) are considered legitimate when conducted by the state or corporations but illegitimate when conducted by those opposing the state or those attempting to act outside the current economic order. Furthermore, the moral order produced by neoliberalism fosters a predatory economy where rules are set to indicate the limits of unpunished conduct and where predators compete by going over the limits because they are not enforced (Galbraith, 2006). As a result, more subtle versions of corruption are nowadays acceptable in the North as much as in the South precisely because corruption is intrinsically connected to market values (MacLennan, 2005).

By defining corruption as 'the abuse of public office for private gain', the World Bank ensures that the focus is directed solely to the public sector while ignoring the private sector, free to act in similar ways without any moral condemnation (Adebanwi and Obadare, 2011). As a result the state and its agents are morally dubious whereas the private sector is endowed with a certain level of moral probity. The state is construed as potentially deviant and intrinsically feckless, whereas the private sector is lauded for being able to work effectively within the limitations imposed by the corrupt or incompetent state. It is this assumed intrinsic morality of the private sector that is used to justify the imposition of neoliberal reforms. Although these reforms are presented as neutral, objective and acultural, they actually serve to maintain Northern hegemony by reifying a particular set of neoliberal values and morals as being natural, good and universal (Heidenheimer, 2004; Shore and Haller, 2005). These values enshrine the self-interested individual entrepreneur as morally superior to any indolent collectivity that lets its interests be (badly) represented by the State.

Crafting a moral self: framing practices and (re)producing moral orders

The moral order promoted by the anticorruption complex of the North is in some instances reinforced and in others challenged by those who are actively involved in petty corruption in the South. Through reframing practices of corruption, the interviewees produced discourses whose underlying premises, values and morals have concrete productive effects: they constitute moral orders that, then, are used to justify the continuation of questionable practices.

Justice workers, police and the military in the DRC recited effortlessly discourses of corruption produced by the North: corruption is bad, corruption is the source of all the problems in the DRC and the only solution is neoliberal good governance (Felices-Luna, 2012). Interviewees in both research projects reproduced the moral order of the anticorruption complex by using the same rhetorical devices. Furthermore, interviewees drew on medical analogies: 'corruption is the fundamental illness ailing the DRC',[9] 'everything is connected, the political, economic and social because the system is gangrenous'; 'corruption is the biggest problem gnawing at the justice system'. Framing corruption this way implies on one hand that the problem is intrinsic to the (social) body that is morally tarnished or impure and on the other hand that we are dealing with a life threatening situation that needs immediate, drastic and external intervention. The moral order produced therefore reinforces the idea that problems of corruption are due to the internal immoral workings of a society and not due to systemic problems caused by the international economic and political order. Neoliberalism and its attacks on the social body are not the problem but the solution, the means to fixing the problem. To continue the analogy, neoliberalism becomes the antibiotic used to cure society and restore its moral health.

Another rhetorical device deployed by the interviewees was to reiterate that the root causes of corruption are the DRC's own deficiencies, insufficiencies and idiosyncrasies. In fact, every interview mentioned at least one but usually a combination of the following causes: lack of education and training, lack of intelligence, lack of money, lack of adequate laws, lack of moral guidance by politicians and people in power, lack of public service ethic as well as lack of independence from ethnic or tribal lines.[10] It would appear as if, in order to be recognised as moral beings,[11] interviewees participated in a self-deprecating ritual that acknowledges their inferiority and the need to repair their immoral condition. By contributing to a discourse that constitutes them as barbaric, backwards and uncivilised, interviewees demeaned themselves while simultaneously reifying Northerners as moral beings whose lead must be followed. Although these discourses signal to hegemony (the worldview imparted by the North has been integrated by the South) and contribute to its reproduction, they can also be read as an attempt to gain something at the individual level.

The following quote exemplifies how the majority of the interviewees were able to use Northern discourses in a strategic way to accomplish different things: make claims to being moral individuals; denounce the immorality of others; demand economic aid, technical support and political backing from the North; legitimise their institution (police, military or justice system) and render it a central piece in the reconstruction of the DRC as a democratic society:

> The real problem of the DRC, is a problem of justice. Justice does not work, therefore nothing else works … Our justice system is completely dysfunctional but we are convinced that in order for this new democracy to grow, we

> need justice to be strong and independent. Good governance, the rule of law and anything else we might be attempting to put in place will not work without a strong justice system. We keep telling the international community that we need funds and training to be directed toward justice. If there is a strong justice, then people who embezzle funds and who abuse power will think twice before doing it. But right now, you kill and you are named general, you embezzle and you get promoted.
>
> (Judge interviewed in 2007)

Through this quote, the interviewee actively attempted to highlight the centrality of justice for good governance and democracy. In fact, it is in the best interest of justice workers to keep justice at the core of the social structure to ensure that they remain at the crossroads of power (Felices-Luna, 2012). This is an instance where hegemony and self-interest come together to reinforce the moral order produced by anticorruption discourses.

Alternative moral order: illegal practices, blunders and entrepreneurialism

Condemning corruption does not always mean accepting, implementing or embracing policy changes and anticorruption initiatives. Despite describing instances where they had to bear the brunt of practices of corruption by others as well as situations where their career was hindered by these deeds, all interviewees admitted having also been actively involved in such practices. Not only is it almost impossible to avoid taking part of corruption when it is embedded in the activities of everyday life, but police officers, members of the military and people working with the justice system do benefit economically, socially or politically from practices of corruption. As a result, interviewees needed to reframe these practices to be able to present themselves as moral beings. They needed to challenge the moral order produced by anticorruption discourses and offer an alternative moral order where their practices of corruption are no longer morally reprehensible or are thought of as something other than corruption.[12] Through this reframing, interviewees can then denounce, accept, embrace and even participate in practices of corruption whilst portraying the self-image of a moral person. To this effect, interviewees used four distinct strategies: first humour and irony; second, euphemisms; third, transmutation; and fourth, valorisation.

Irony is commonly used to refer to 'social practices widely judged as pathological but still recognised as normal in a specific context. It serves the purpose of relativizing without minimising and, more importantly, to keep distance without assuming moralistic attitudes' (Zerilli, 2005, p. 86). Humour[13] and irony were evident when interviewees presented justice in the DRC as either a commercial or criminal enterprise. Through the commercial analogy the majority of the interviewees presented justice as a 'good for sale': people 'buy justice' and sometimes get into 'bidding wars' to win a case to the point where 'in the morning you might be the plaintiff but by the end of the day you're the accused'. As a result, workers fight for 'juicy cases' from which they will be able to 'make a profit'. The commercial analogy continues when interviewees described that those with influence, power or money get 'justice at a discount rate' while everyone else has to 'pay full price'. Civilians avoid the justice system as much as possible: if there is a car accident they'll say 'quick, quick let's fix this before they get here and it ends up costing us both more'. Justice then is 'a luxury that most people can no longer afford'. Those who do not (or no longer) have money end up, at best, losing the case and, at worse, going to prison. So when the population has to go to court they say they are going the 'court of injustice' from where they 'don't know if they'll come out alive'. By using a commercial language interviewees ascribed these practices to the 'economy' and the issue thus becomes whether they are legitimate or illegitimate transactions depending on whether one considers that justice should be thought of as a commodity or not.

The criminal analogy is apparent in the interviewees' discourses when they described how justice workers 'hold cases hostage' until civilians 'pay a ransom', while the police and the military are said to be 'agents of disorder' who should be avoided or risk being 'pillaged'. When victims have to deal with the justice system, they say that 'disaster has struck twice' as now they are also the 'victims of justice'. By producing a criminal analogy that refuses to name these practices as corruption, the interviewees acknowledged them as illegal but drown out precisely what makes it different from other criminal activities. Whether this is to prevent civil servants from being identified as criminals or on the contrary to highlight that civil servants are all common criminals is unclear but it is precisely through these ambiguities that multiple framings and re-framings of corruption practices that concomitant moral orders can be produced. These ambiguities also create the interviewees as moral beings given that they are acknowledging some of those practices as crimes.

Euphemisms were commonly used in an effort to decriminalise, at least rhetorically, certain practices of corruption by reframing them in three different ways. The first one is that of hassle or aggravation for civilians. In this instance '*tracassérie*' (red tape) is used to describe asking money for doing their job, charging inexistent fees or requiring payment for fines that do not exist or that they should not be collecting. The second frame is one of a civilian's obligations toward a state worker given that the state is no longer assuming its responsibilities vis-à-vis its employees. '*Subventionner*' (subsidise) is used when someone, of their own initiative, offers money for their services, whereas '*désapprovisionner*' (which literally translates as un-supply) refers to practices where civilians are stopped or their property is inspected and all material possessions are confiscated (even the clothes from their backs and the shoes from their feet). The third frame is that of a misstep or regrettable mistake. Interviewees described situations where someone died or was seriously injured as a result of their actions (i.e. from being beaten up to extort money from him or his family) as '*événements malheureux*' (unfortunate events), '*bévues*' (blunders) or '*égarements*' (go astray). The first frame renders these practices more acceptable by attributing to it an almost bureaucratic connotation and appeals to the neoliberal criticisms of the state. The second reframing aims at legitimising these practices by appealing to their need to earn a living and be compensated for their work. This reframing only applies to those who are 'honest and don't overdo it' whereas those who 'exaggerate' must be considered immoral.[14] Finally the third reframing seeks to produce those who engage in questionable practices as moral but fallible beings.

The third strategy was that of transmutation. There are two different ways through which the interviewees went from being the guilty party to being the victims. First of all, interviewees presented themselves as being the victims of the state who has relinquished its economic responsibilities towards its employees. They need to find ways to survive and the only option available to them is to 'rely' or 'fall back' on civilians. Their actions are therefore simply part of the '*economie de survie*' (economy of survival) to which they are subjected. The second way was by justifying their improper actions (charging or not charging someone for instance) as being done under duress. Lower-ranked workers need to do as they are told or they risk retaliation: being mutated to a 'depot' where they won't be able access the economy of survival, getting fired or being sent to prison. They described themselves as being the 'mailbox' through which others get things done. As such, they are no longer actors but instruments and therefore should not be held morally responsible for their actions. Furthermore, despite refusing to use the term corruption to refer to their own actions and practices, the interviewees were not hesitant to describe and denounce similar practices of those in a higher up position as corruption. This allowed them to create a moral distinction between what they do and what others do: survival instead of corruption, necessity instead of greed.

The last strategy was to valorise or reframe these practices using positive terms: '*se débrouiller*' (find a way, fend for yourself), '*se résponsabiliser*' (take care of yourself and your family, take your fate in your own hands), '*faire des accrobaties*' (doing acrobatic feats) or '*bricoler*' (knock together a solution to a problem). These terms bring to mind the values associated with a neoliberal moral order: individualism,[15] entrepreneurialism, responsibilisation, self-interest and not relying on the state. Furthermore, interviewees described practices of corruption as having positive consequences.[16] In this regard, although it was rare, interviewees described themselves as providing a service, as getting things done instead of 'simply' extorting money from the public. This reframing highlights the positive effect of questionable practices and serves to reconceptualise what they do as providing a service (even if it is outside their mandate) and being compensated for it. Through the implicit premises of this positive reframing, the logic of the market is integrated to practices of corruption. The first implied premise is that the role played within the system, their expertise and networks are resources that can be contracted out, sold or used as an economic opportunity.[17] The second implied premise is that justice and security are commodities that can be bought and sold within a market. As a result, on the one hand interviewees described some of their colleague as 'savvy businessmen' who have become 'successful' by investing their 'corruption earnings' into legitimate commercial enterprises. On the other hand interviewees complained that they face 'unfair competition' when workers do not respect the boundaries of their role and attempt to steal potential 'clients'. For instance when judges offer their services as counsel to one of the parties in a 'juicy' case, lawyers decry an unfair competition given that as judges they are in a better position to influence the decision of the court. Another instance is when constables take matters in their own hands and instead of referring a case to the prosecutor, negotiate between the victim and the accuser. The moral order produced is one that enshrines the commodification of justice and security, placing them within the grasps of the market.

The interviewees reproduced a moral order of Northern superiority and Congolese inferiority while, at the same, time providing alternative ways of interpreting practices of corruption therefore producing alternative moral orders to those of the anticorruption literature. Yet, interviewees produced a further type of moral order that reinforces a hierarchical social structure and exploitative social relations. Interviewees presented a negative, derogatory or condescending view of civilians as 'uneducated', 'blind', 'stupid', 'in need of guidance' but also as 'trouble makers', 'violent' in need of 'domestication' and, in some instances, even as the 'enemy'. Civilians or service seekers are therefore construed not as citizens to be served but as a source of income, as someone who can be exploited and whose commodities can be expropriated. They are 'prey to be hunted', who can be 'pressed like limes' and 'plucked like chickens'. By setting the ground for localised relations of domination and exploitation, they create structural conditions for the production of a moral order that legitimises appropriation by dispossession. This predatory moral order is only possible through previous reframing that removed corruption practices from the purview of the criminal in order to insert it within the purview of the market.

When justice is up for sale: neoliberalism against entrepreneurism, self-reliance and commodification

Following Boltanski and Chiappello's (2006) description of the responsibilised employee as a creative and innovative person who uses his or her networking and entrepreneurial skills to foster their own employability, we might think of justice workers in the DRC as ideal employees. They are driven by self-interest; they use their networks to find ways to resolve situations brought before them; and they actively seek ways to provide for themselves and their families without relying on the state to do so. If we were willing to close our eyes to the specific context in which it takes place (the realm of justice), we might be able to praise the ingenuity, resourcefulness and entrepreneurialism of these individuals. We might even claim that they represent the ideal neoliberal citizen.

Practices of corruption in the DRC are not the result of the implementation of neoliberal policies (they were in place long before the 1990s) but the values and reasoning that underpins these practices are compatible with those attributed to neoliberalism. In fact the three moral orders produced through the discourses on corruption by those practicing it seem to be congruent with or even support neoliberalism: the first moral order favours and justifies the implementation of neoliberal policies; the second produces the self-reliant, responsible, entrepreneurial, financial subject and reframes justice and security as commodities or potential new markets; and the third legitimises a predatory economy based on appropriation through dispossession. These moral orders attempt to resist anti-corruption discourse yet they remain within the material and discursive realities imposed by neoliberal good governance and policy reform and therefore cannot fully resist it. Furthermore, it actually aids neoliberalism as it encourages appropriation by dispossession through more privatisation and further structural adjustment.

Notes

1 By social actors I mean: local and state government; national and international organisations; 'experts'; those who practice corruption; those who live with the consequences of corruption; as well as those who 'battle' corruption.
2 www.Hdr.undp.org (visited June 14, 2015).
3 www.transparency.org/cpi2014/results (visited June 17, 2015).
4 During both fieldworks I identified the interviewees by snowball sampling using multiple lines of referral in order to obtain a contrasted sample in terms of their areas of work. For the first fieldwork I interviewed three lawyers working for human rights non-government organisations, three activists, two police officers, two judges (one civilian and one military), one prison warden and one lawyer representing the bar. All the interviewees were males between the ages of 33 and 46 and ten of them had obtained a law degree. For the second fieldwork I contrasted in terms of the entry point into the military or the police and the different institutions they had worked for. Due to individual and institutional changes the sample contained experiences from the military as well as from the colonial police, provincial police, national police, republican guard, gendarmerie, military police, border police, mining police and the new national police. All the interviewees were male; their age ranged from 40 to 75 and their level of education varied from high school to university. Both fieldworks were possible thanks to the CEFOCRIM (Research and training Centre on Criminology and Human Rights) as well as the ECOCRIM (School of Criminology, University of Lubumbashi).
5 In the first project the interviews explored: the workings of the justice system implemented by the Belgians; the coexistence of the system with alternative ways of thinking and practicing justice; the possibility and willingness to produce a different justice system. In the second project, the interviews explored the role of the police and the military in society by contrasting their practices (what members of these institutions actually did) during the three political periods the RDC has experienced since its independence (dictatorship, war and democracy).
6 Macro-political level of corruption involves high government and other states, corporations or the national elite; micro-political level or petty corruption involves interactions between a superior and a subordinate (Ayissi, 2008).
7 Johnson's (2009) book is a prime example of this rhetoric. Throughout 518 pages he describes the problems and solutions to Africa's problems using medical terms: 'The DRC: A Diarrheatic State', 'Kenya: Cancerous Corruption & Poisonous Politics', 'Education: the Cardiovascular System' and 'Auto-immune Systems: the Military and Police'.
8 Accumulation based upon predation, fraud and violence (Harvey, 2004).
9 All quotes have been translated from French by me.
10 I have described these discourses in-depth elsewhere (Felices-Luna, 2010). See also Lovell (2005).

11 The interview is a social situation that can be taken by stigmatised individuals to present themselves as worthy and valuable beings (Felices-Luna, 2015).
12 It is interesting to note that the use of these strategies is not limited to those working within the system in the context of the interview. They were repeatedly used by everyone I met during my four visits to Lubumbashi.
13 The reader might not find the following descriptions humorous but it is the tone of voice, the facial expressions, the body language and the accompanied laughter that renders it a humorous account instead of a tragic one.
14 However, the line is easily blurred when it is no longer about earning a living in a precarious context but in a neoliberal one where 'individual material aspiration, success, status, and security' (Weigratz and Cesnulyte, 2016, p. 21) are important.
15 Although in many instances these practices are conducted with others and require the collaboration of others, they are not collective actions given that they are driven by individual self-interest. Prentice (2006) found a similar logic in Trinidadian factory workers.
16 Corruption practices by the police do solve problematic situations for the parties involved (Bady Kabuya, 2009). The military also resolves issues outside their mandate: commercial disagreements, conflict surrounding family affairs and grievances related to personal rivalries, grudges, revenge and retribution (Baaz and Verweijen, 2014).
17 For instance, police officers set up roadblocks in high traffic areas off their own initiative to make money out of drivers. In 'hot spots' it is possible to find five roadblocks in a row.

References

Abrahamsen, R. (2003) 'African Studies and the Postcolonial Challenge', *African Affairs*, 102, pp. 189–210.

Adebanwi, W. and Obadare, E. (2011) 'When Corruption Fights Back: Democracy and Elite Interest in Nigeria's Anti-corruption Aar', *Journal of Modern African Studies*, 49(2), pp. 185–213.

Amable, B. (2011) 'Morals and Politics in the Ideology of Neo-liberalism', *Socio-Economic Review*, 9(3), pp. 3–30.

Ayissi, L. (2008) *Corruption et gouvernance*. Paris: L'Harmattan.

Baaz, M.E. and Verweijen, J. (2014) 'Arbiters with Guns: The Ambiguity of Military Involvement in Civilian Disputes in the DR Congo', *Third World Quarterly*, 35(5), pp. 803–820.

Bady Kabuya, G. (2009) 'Une approche criminologique pour un autre regard sur le travail d'un magistrat du parquet à Lubumbashi'. Thèse de doctorat, Bruxelles: ULB.

Boltanski, L. and Chiapello, E. (2006) *The New Spirit of Capitalism*. London: Verso.

Bond, P. (2006) *Looting Africa: The Economics of Exploitation*. London: Zed Books.

Bone, J. (2012) 'The Deregulation Ethic and the Conscience of Capitalism: How the Neoliberal "Free Market" Model Undermines Rationality and Moral Conduct', *Globalization*, 9(5), pp. 651–665.

Botchway, K. and Moudud, J. (2012) 'Neo-Liberalism and the Developmental State: Consideration for the New Partnership for Africa's Development', in Bobo, B. and Sintim-Aboagye, H. (eds) *Neoliberalism, Interventions and the Developmental State*. New Jersey: Africa World Press, pp. 13–54.

Brown, W. (2006) 'American Nightmare: Neoliberalism, Neoconservatism, and De-Democratization', *Political Theory*, 34(6), pp. 690–714.

Bukovansky, M. (2006) 'The Hollowness of Anti-corruption Discourse', *Review of International Political Economy*, 13(2), pp. 181–209.

Cowling, M. (2012) 'Neoliberalism and Crime in the United States and the United Kingdom' in Whitehead, P. and Crawshaw, P. (eds) *Organising Neoliberalism: Markets Privatisation and Justice*. London: Anthem Press, pp. 23–43.

Dracklé, D. (2005) 'Where the Jeeps Come From: Narratives of Corruption in the Alentejo (Southern Portugal)', in Haller, D. and Shore, C. (eds) *Corruption: Anthropological Perspectives*, London: Pluto Press, pp. 194–228.

Felices-Luna, M. (2010) 'La Justice en République Démocratique du Congo: transformation ou continuité?', *Champ Pénal* 7, http://champpenal.revues.org/7827#text.

Felices-Luna, M. (2012) 'Justice in the Democratic Republic of Congo: Practicing Corruption, Practicing Resistance?', *Critical Criminology*, 20(2), pp. 197–209.

Felices-Luna, M., (2015) 'Appelez-moi Papa Seya : production identitaire des policiers et militaires en République Démocratique du Congo', *Recherches Qualitatives*, 34(1), pp. 74–96.

Galbraith, J. (2006) 'Predator state: Enron, Tyco, Worldcom … and the US government', *Mother Jones*, 31(3), pp. 30–32.

Glassman, J. (2006) 'Primitive Accumulation, Accumulation by Dispossession, Accumulation by 'Extra-economic' Means', *Progress in Human Geography*, 30(5), pp. 608–625.

Harrison, G. (2005) 'Economic Faith, Social project, and a Misreading of African Society: The Travails of Neoliberalism in Africa', *Third World Quarterly*, 26(8), pp. 1303–1320.

Harrison, G. (2010) *Neoliberal Africa: The Impact of Global Social Engineering*. New York: Zed Books.

Harvey, D. (2004) 'The "New Imperialism": Accumulation by Disposession', *Socialist Register*, pp. 63–87.

Harvey, D. (2005) *A Brief History of Neoliberalism*. Oxford: Oxford University Press.

Heidenheimer, A. (2004) 'Disjunctions Between Corruption and Democracy? A Qualitative Exploration', *Crime Law and Social Change*, 42, pp. 99–109.

Johnson, S. (2009) *Suffering and Smiling: A Diagonosis of African Impovrishment*. Toronto: University Press of America.

Lovell, D. (2005) 'Corruption as a Transnational Phenomenon: Understanding Endemic Corruption in Postcommunist States', in Haller, D. and Shore, C. (eds) *Corruption: Anthropological Perspectives*, London: Pluto Press, pp. 65–82.

MacLennan, C. (2005) 'Corruption in Corporate America: Enron – Before and after' in Haller, D. and Shore, C. (eds) *Corruption: Anthropological Perspectives*, London: Pluto Press, pp. 156–170.

Mitchell, T. (2007) 'The Properties of Markets' in Mackenzie, D., Muniesa, F. and Siu, L. (eds) *Do Economists Make Markets? On the Performativity of Economics*, Princeton: Princeton University Press, pp. 244–275.

Mkandawire, T. (2001) 'Thinking about Developmental States in Africa', *Cambridge Journal of Economics*, 25(3), pp. 289–313.

Prentice, R. (2006) '"Thiefing a Chance": Moral Meanings of Theft in a Trinidadian Garment Factory' in Browne, K. and Milgram, L. (eds) *Economics and Morality: Anthropological Approaches*, Toronto: Altamira, pp. 123–141.

Renton, D., Seddon, D. and Zeilig, L. (2007) *The Congo: Plunder and Resistance*. London: Zed books.

Sandel, M.J. (2012) *What Money Can't Buy*. New York: Farrar, Straus and Giroux.

Sayer, A. (2007) 'Moral Economy as Critique', *New Political Economy*, 12(2), pp. 261–270.

Sender, J. (1999) 'Africa's Economic Performance: Limitations of the Current Consensus', *Journal of Economic Perspectives*, 13(3), pp. 89–114.

Shamir, R. (2008) 'The Age of Responsibilization: on Market-embedded Morality', *Economy and Society*, 37(1), pp. 1–19.

Shore, C. and Haller, D. (2005) 'Introduction – Sharp Practice: Anthropology and the Study of Corruption' in Haller, D. and Shore, C. (eds) *Corruption: Anthropological Perspectives*, London: Pluto Press, pp. 1–26.

Stiglitz, J. E. (2005) 'FMI, la preuve par l'Éthiopie', *Manière de Voir*, 79, pp. 37–41.

Swain, A., Mykhnenko, V. and French, S. (2010) 'The Corruption Industry and Transition: Neoliberalizing Post-Soviet Space?' in Birch, K. and Mykhnenko, V. (eds) *The Rise and Fall of Neo-liberalism: The Collapse of an Economic Order?*, London: Zed Books, pp. 112–132.

Wiegratz, J. (2010) 'Fake Capitalism? The Dynamics of Neoliberal Moral Restructuring and Pseudo-development: the Case of Uganda', *Review of African Political Economy*, 37(124), pp. 123–137.

Wiegratz, J. and Cesnulyte, E. (2016) 'Money Talks: Moral Economies of Earning a Living in Neoliberal East Africa', *New Political Economy*, 21(1), pp. 1–25.

Zerilli, F. (2005) 'Corruption, Property Restitution and Romaniannes', in Haller, D. and Shore, C. (eds) *Corruption: Anthropological Perspectives*, London: Pluto Press, pp. 83–99.

11 Murder for gain

Commercial insurance and moralities in South Africa

Erik Bähre

Introduction: moralities of finance[1]

South Africa has a well-developed insurance industry with a wide range of South African companies such as Sanlam, Old Mutual, Metropolitan, Hollard, Liberty Life and ABSA. Historically, not least due to apartheid, most of the clients belonged to the wealthier white population and business world. But this started to change after the first democratic elections of 1994. These commercial insurance companies started to sell a wide range of policies, but especially life insurance, to people living in South Africa's townships and rural areas. They started building new offices, sold insurances through voluntary organisations, churches, local retail stores or had sales agents who would go door-to-door (see Bähre 2011, 2012).

The marketing practices of these South African insurance companies led to a host of questions and concerns. In this chapter I clarify how commercial insurance, especially life insurance, became debated in South Africa. I show how segmented these debates were in that different moral concerns were dominant in different parts of society. This segmentation of debates appears to reflect the everyday inequalities, both economic and racial, that still permeate South African society today. While the elite and upper middle classes – predominantly white – were concerned about fraud and the mismanagement of claims, the poor and lower-middle classes – predominantly black – were concerned with the immoral effects that insurance could have on personal relations, especially among kin and neighbours. Commercial life insurance made it possible for poor clients to get a relatively large sum of cash – without anyone knowing about it – after someone they had a policy on died. This fuelled concerns about insurance murder. Although the new, poorer clients too experienced the mismanagement of their claims, these did not enter the public domain.

Insurance is highly technical *and* moral in that it raises questions about legitimate entitlements and responsibilities, the boundaries of solidarity and the collectivisation of risks (see Bähre 2011, Baker 2000, Chan 2012, Golomski 2015, Maurer 2005, Zelizer 1978). This chapter explores these moralities and tries to shed light on how within one country there can be such a variety of moral concerns. The theoretical importance of examining this diversity is that it shows that financialisation and marketisation have moral dynamics but that these moral dynamics are far from ubiquitous. To some extent, South Africa's financial sector and its clients are witnessing a 'neoliberal morality' as the authors of the introduction to this volume point out. At the same time, the moral dynamics are only partly a result of neoliberal ideology. National political transformations and socio-cultural expectations are equally, if not more, important. This chapter explores how clients, particularly the new clients living in Cape Town's townships, navigate the dynamic forces that make up their financial landscape.

The expansion of commercial insurance needs to be set against the complex problems that society is facing, many of which touch upon finance. South Africa is among the countries with the highest level of economic inequality in the world. The World Bank estimates that South Africa had a Gini index of 63.4 in 2011.[2] Since the abolishment of apartheid with the first democratic elections of 1994, a lot has changed but the high level of inequality continues to characterise South African society. Corruption also continues to plague South African society. According to Lodge (2002), corruption was a feature of the apartheid era but then it was less about personal gain and more in light of strengthening patronage and Afrikaner nationalism. Corruption continued after the abolishment of apartheid. There was the 1999 South African Arms Deal. In order to get this military procurement package worth close to US$5 billion, companies had been paying bribes to several high-powered politicians (Liebenberg and Barnard 2005). Another scandal led to the imprisonment of former National Police Commissioner and Interpol President Jackie Selebi in 2010 for accepting money from a crime syndicate (Schwella 2013). The expansion of commercial insurance needs to be seen in the light of these specific complexities.

The data on which this chapter is based were collected between 1995 and 2014 during several research periods ranging from a few weeks to a year in length – about three years of fieldwork in total. I have held interviews with actuaries and others working in the insurance industry in Johannesburg and Cape Town and interviewed people who were otherwise involved in developing insurance policies, selling policies or managing insurance claims. Most of the research was carried out among (potential) clients in the townships of Cape Town. Almost all of the residents are Xhosa who, with the abolition of apartheid in 1994, left the impoverished Bantustans Ciskei and Transkei to try to earn an income in the city (see Ross 1999 for a concise history). In addition to interviews, participant observation and other standard ethnographic research methods, I developed two surveys. One was for the residents of the townships of Cape Town (n=110) and contained questions about the use of financial services, trust in financial institutions and networks, concerns about risks and engagement in social networks. A second online survey was carried out among actuaries (n=79) and contained questions on developments in the sector, political changes and market opportunities (see also Bähre 2011, 2012).

Neoliberalism and democratisation in South Africa

The 'discovery' of new clients with a low income was at the heart of a changing morality on poverty and finance that emerged internationally and might best be summarised as a neoliberal ideology. Neoliberalism profoundly challenged stereotypes and ideologies about poverty and finance. The old stereotype of the poor can be characterised as a reminiscent of what Oscar Lewis (1959) called the 'culture of poverty'. This basically meant that the poor were seen as incapable of handling money in a productive way and that culture was an obstacle to poverty alleviation. With the rise of the neoliberal ideology, particularly since the 1980s, the stereotype changed. The poor were not anymore seen to be helpless and their culture, whatever that was, was not anymore perceived as an obstacle but as a resource. Neoliberal ideology held that the poor were skilled and creative entrepreneurs. It stipulated that if the poor would be presented with a wide range of choices, including choices for financial services, they would rationally choose what was best for them and use these facilities in such a way that they could escape poverty. This new ideology was among others expressed by the business guru Prahalad who argues that the poor offer an important business case *and* that business can eradicate poverty. In *Fortune at the Bottom of the Pyramid: Eradicating Poverty Through Profits* Prahalad (2004) develops a business case that should open up the so-called BOP (bottom of the pyramid) market.[3] This ideology suggested a win-win situation in that financialisation was profitable for the financial sector and made it possible for people to escape poverty.

Financial institutions like banks and insurance companies around the world came to see the poor as relatively trustworthy and rational entrepreneurs. The most widely known and influential case is the Grameen Bank, which Yunus established in Bangladesh in the mid-1970s. The Grameen Bank provided small loans to poor women without requesting conventional collateral such as a job or house. Instead, collateral had to be ensured through group pressure.

The belief was that expanding commercialisation and financialisation to the poor would bring more harmonious societies. The moral impetus of this development became particularly clear when in 2006 Yunus was awarded the Nobel Peace Prize – and not the Nobel Prize in Economic Sciences. The microfinance industry challenged the dominant stereotype that the poor were irresponsible and passive *and* replaced it with a morality that emphasised that financial products can rely on the poor's social relations, and that the poor are creative and trustworthy entrepreneurs. Over the last twenty to thirty years, microfinance became an industry involving billions of dollars, with hundred millions of clients. Studies that highlighted the positive impact of microfinance with encouraging titles such as *The Miracles of Barefoot Capitalism: A Compelling Case for Microcredit* (Klobuchar and Wilkes 2005) and *Money with a Mission: Microfinance and Poverty Reduction* (Copestake *et al.* 2005).

Neoliberal policy had a profound moral dimension, one that has been heavily criticised. Elyachar, based on research in Egypt, concluded that one of the key transformations of neoliberalist ideology was that 'practices once dismissed as "backward" and situations once seen as transitional have become the vanguard of entrepreneurial savvy in the global age' (Elyachar 2002: 496). Neoliberal ideology ignores the structural causes of high levels of inequality in society and defines corporate welfare as public interest (see also Whyte and Wiegratz, introduction to this volume).

Several scholars have argued that neoliberal ideology has deeply permeated South African society, suggesting that today's government policy, society's problems and economic ontologies are caused by or at least amplified by neoliberalism (Bond 2000, Comaroff and Comaroff 2001, Ferguson 2007). There is, however, a tendency to identify neoliberalism too quickly as the cause of immorality in South Africa. In South Africa, the moralities of marketisation and financialisation frequently point to *more* government control, in addition to the rapid development of a welfare state (Bähre 2011, 2014, 2015). There are clear indications that South Africa is not as neoliberal as some would have it, that immoralities (or rather, moralities underpinning practices regarded as 'bad') do not necessarily result from neoliberalism, and that immoralities have additional sources (see Bähre 2011, 2015). In short, prevailing moral economies in many realms of South African society are the result of very mixed and hybrid moral sources of which neoliberalism is only one of many.

One of the key drivers of marketisation of commercial insurance to the poor was political change. Democratisation in South Africa was crucial for the 'discovery' of tens of millions of new clients. After the abolishment of apartheid and the 1994 elections, the South African government emphasised that in order to establish social justice, resources had to be redistributed along racial lines. The state had to ensure that the previously excluded African population has proper jobs, housing, education, be entitled to social grants and gain access to financial companies that previously neglected them. They should become shareholders of financial companies, and part of the higher ranks of employment; thus, financial companies had to develop services for previously excluded Africans. The African National Congress (ANC) government for instance urged banks to expand their business to the previously disadvantaged communities, which meant that they had to establish offices in the townships and former Bantustans and lower the bureaucratic requirements for taking on new clients.[4]

Against this background, the Actuarial Society of South Africa (ASSA) saw the need to change the profession. The political changes that were taking place in South Africa made actuaries realise more than ever that their business had to change as well. For this purpose, ASSA established 'Actuaries On the Move' in 2000. Actuaries on the Move had to increase the profession's diversity, among others by offering mentoring and training programmes that could support black students who wanted to become actuaries. Hillary Murashiki, chairman of the diversity committee of ASSA publically stated: 'Thanks to a R20 million series of initiatives by the Actuarial Society of SA [South Africa] and its sponsors, there are today four black South African actuaries and many more to come'. About 60 per cent of the actuarial students are black, which reveals that a large shift can be expected in the future.[5] The implication is that in this instance it is not that finance creates a particular morality, but that the morality that is part of democratisation is changing the South African financial landscape.

The Financial Sector Charter on Black Economic Empowerment played a pivotal role in the transformation of a sector that many associated with apartheid exploitation and white rule. The charter came into effect in 2004, after the 2002 financial sector summit organised by NEDLAC (National Economic Development and Labour Council), a partnership that represents business, labour and the government.[6] The financial sector committed itself to increase non-whites in senior positions, to support the establishment of black-owned small and medium enterprises, and to make it easier for the poor to access financial services.[7]

Actuaries as well as others working in the predominantly white-staffed insurance industry were worried that if the sector would not transform, government legislation would force them to do so in ways that were threatening to the business. In 2005, for example, there were persistent rumors that the government would establish a national funeral policy and actuaries told me that they feared that the government would waste tax payers' money and take profitable business away from them. In the beginning of 2006, the rumors of a national funeral policy had ceased and the concern was more about the government's plans to establish a National Health Insurance, a scheme that had simmered already since democratisation in 1994 but that became more realistic after 2007 (see Botha and Hendricks 2008). Some were worried that the government would take the most viable part of the market away from them and thus undermine the insurance sector as a whole. They were concerned that a government-run insurance scheme would suffer from mismanagement and some were worried that politicians would use the National Health Insurance to enrich themselves and their family members. Here too, national political dynamics had a profound moralising effect on South Africa's expanding financial sector.

Actuaries that were developing policies for the poor were often fairly young, around forty years of age, male white South Africans, with degrees from South Africa's top universities such as the University of Stellenbosch, University of Cape Town, or University of Witwatersrand. Some of the actuaries that I met felt that they were part of a new era and they wanted to contribute to a new South Africa. As an actuary in his thirties and working for one of South Africa's major insurance companies explained to me: 'it is now our time. We are young and we do not have the burden of history like the older people working here. We have to make something of this country'.

Insurance companies started to establish special branches to develop policies for black clients. Today, it is common to see insurance advertising billboards in the townships, sometimes even in schools, to find insurance adverts in local newspapers that are freely available, and see insurance adverts on television that seem to be aimed at African clients in particular. Supermarkets and other stores sell insurance, and churches have become particularly popular venues for selling policies. My survey in two townships in Cape Town showed that 75 per cent of the residents had an insurance policy and that some had as many as nine policies. Even the poor respondents had policies: 41 per cent of those with incomes under R1000 (about EU€100 at the time of the survey) had at least one insurance product, usually a funeral policy.[8]

In short, in South Africa, there was a successful and one might even say aggressive marketisation of insurance policies to new clients, predominantly the poor and lower-middle classes. This marketisation was due, at least in part, to neoliberal ideologies that reframed the poor as successful entrepreneurs, as well as a result of democratisation where the government increased its grip on the financial sector and enforced racial and economic inclusion.

Multiple moralities

It is possible to distinguish two debates about the immorality of insurance in South Africa. One of these debates focuses on the insurance companies. The debate is about misselling insurance products, immoral investments by insurance companies, poor handling of claims, illegal practices and failing to contribute to a just society.

These concerns have found their way in the South African media. Acclaimed financial journalist Bruce Cameron regularly wrote about insurance policies in *Personal Finance*, a newspaper section and website that was part of Independent Online.[9] Cameron warned his readers about crooked financial advisers, also those selling insurance products.[10] These public debates were about pension and retirement annuities, a type of long-term insurance. Financial journalists reported how pension funds charged inappropriate and undisclosed fees or used other illegal measures. It has been estimated that inappropriate fees are charged for managing pension funds that costs about R3 billion a year (at the time approximately €300 million) (Fisher-French 2010).

In 2009, a national scandal emerged involved Old Mutual, one of South Africa's larger insurance companies. Old Mutual had invested in Zimbabwean's diamond fields, which was at odds with international sanctions against Mugabe's repressive regime (Saunders 2007). The insurance company's breach of international sanctions led to a Zapiro cartoon that presented Old Mutual as a loyal and violent partner of Mugabe's Zanu PF.[11] The company was depicted as sacrificing human rights, freedom of press, as well as the rules of the United Nation's Kimberley Process Certification Scheme that aimed to limit the spread of so called 'blood diamonds'. The cartoon below shows the Zimbabwean military closely cooperating with the insurance company at the expense of human lives.

In 2010, South Africa's newspaper *Mail and Guardian* reported another major scandal that involved SA Quantum, a financial services company that was set up by the financial industry to sell and administer its financial products. According to the newspaper SA Quantum gave R60,000 (approximately €4000) a month to the wife of the general secretary of the Congress of South African Trade Unions (COSATU). It was alleged that in return the general secretary's wife sold financial products – mainly pension annuities – to the nearly 2 million members of COSATU. Once the story was about to become public, SA Quantum's chief executive officer (CEO) offered the journalist a bribe of R120,000 (approximately €8000) if he would not publish the story (Letsoalo 2010, Vavi 2010). The journalist agreed to meet the CEO and accepted part of the bribe at a parking lot but

Figure 11.1 Old Mutual's blood diamonds

Source: © 2009–2015 Zapiro (All Rights Reserved). Printed/used with permission from www.zapiro.com.

did so while filming with a hidden camera. When this became public, allegations of corruption by the insurance sector only became stronger.[12]

This public debate about the immorality of commercial insurance received input from financial journalists, ombudsman organisations, the Financial Services Board, the Pension Fund Adjudicator as well as court rulings. These public debates expressed concerns that resonated with predominantly white and relatively wealthy insurance clients who would read the newspapers that reported these practices and could also mobilise ombudsman organisations, financial journalists or legal institutions to express their concerns.

These new clients could often not find their way to these institutions (see also Bähre 2012). The poor were by-and-large unable to bring their experiences to the media attention; they did not have the knowledge and skills to successfully submit a complaint to ombudsman organisations; they did not have the means to hire a lawyer for judiciary support. This meant that their experiences with misselling, the refusal to honour legitimate claims or concerns about illegal financial deductions did not enter the public domain. The problems that they had with the financial products that they bought from the insurance companies, typically relatively small funeral policies, remained largely out of sight of policy makers, financial sector regulators and others involved in the insurance sector.

The second debate was about the impact that insurance, particular funeral insurance, had on the personal relations of the person that took out the policy or could benefit from the policy. This debate mainly took place among the new clients, predominantly black and relatively poor South Africans. Many of the new and prospective clients that I interviewed in Cape Town's townships were concerned that insurance damaged personal relations, i.e. insurance was seen as an opportunity to profit from someone's misfortune. In the survey that I set up 75 per cent of the respondents agreed or fully agreed with the statement that insurance was a threat to mutual help. In the same survey, one out of six respondents said that they personally knew about people being killed in order to cash in on a life insurance policy. Three out of four respondents said that they saw how someone had registered someone because they knew that the person might die soon. Many were worried that there are people who take out an insurance policy on the life of people who look sick. Especially in a country where AIDS is rampant there are concerns that there are people who you might not even know personally, or with whom you only have a very distant relationship, who could make money on your death. In the survey, a vast majority (70 per cent) of the respondents said that they saw how people took advantage by registering someone who was not a family member. Another 15 per cent said that they saw instances where someone pretended that someone was dead in order to get benefits.

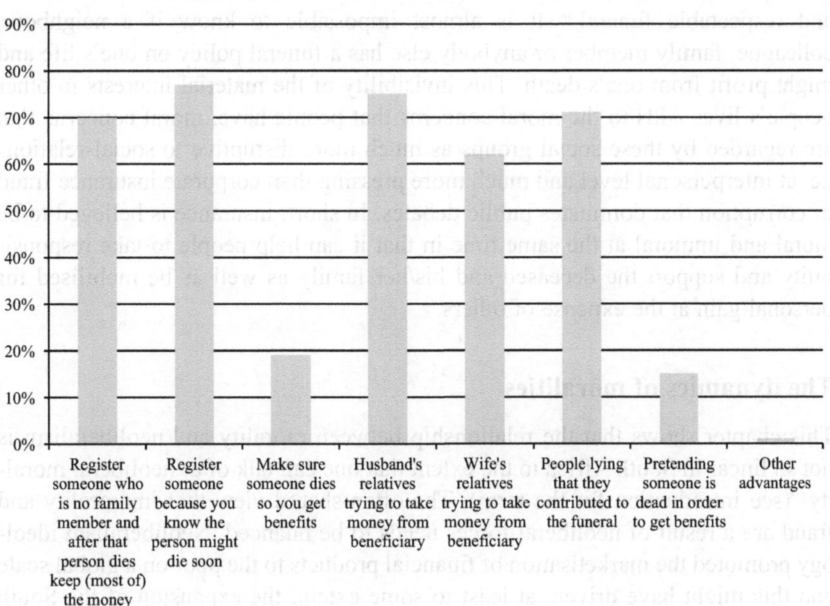

Figure 11.2 Funeral: advantages taken

The fears associated with the marketisation of commercial life insurance need to be set against the high levels of violence in South Africa. South Africa has been in the world's top ten of highest intentional murder rates for all but two years since 2000. The Western Cape Province, which includes Cape Town, is the province with the highest murder rate in the country.[13] Cape Town has recently been ranked as the twentieth most violent city in the world.[14] The townships where the respondents live and where new insurance products are being marketed are part of the 'Cape Flats'. It is where most of the approximately 4 million Capetonians live. Within Cape Town, most crime is concentrated on the Cape Flats, in Khayelitsha, Gugulethu, Nyanga and Mitchells Plain (Manaliyo 2014: 597). CrimeStats South Africa makes an annual top ten of South Africa's police precincts with the highest number of reported crimes. The top ten of worst precincts is based on statistics from the South African police. Here too, the Cape Flats come out very unfavourable. In 2014, six out of ten precincts with the highest murder rate in South Africa were on the Cape Flats. In the same year, of the precinct that made it to the top ten of South Africa's highest number of attempted murders, seven were from the Cape Flats.[15] Such high levels of violence in everyday life make it much more probable that someone is actually killed in order to cash in on insurance money or that rumours on insurance murder circulate widely.

During one of the interviews a woman told me that she felt it was appropriate to hide insurance policies, even from close family, to avoid rumours. She was worried that her family would become suspicious of her when they knew that she would receive money when they would die, even though the only reason for her to have these funeral policies was to ensure that she could contribute to a decent and respectable funeral.[16] It is almost impossible to know if a neighbour, colleague, family member or anybody else has a funeral policy on one's life and might profit from one's death. This invisibility of the material interests in other people's lives adds to the moral concerns that people have, moral concerns that are regarded by these social groups as much more disruptive to social relations i.e. at interpersonal level and much more pressing than corporate insurance fraud or corruption that dominates public debates. In short, insurance is believed to be moral and immoral at the same time in that it can help people to take responsibility and support the deceased and his/her family as well as be mobilised for personal gain at the expense of others.[17]

The dynamics of moralities

This chapter shows that the relationship between morality and neoliberalism is not so linear in South Africa to the extent that one can talk of a 'neoliberal morality' (see introduction for the term). The often-shared view that immorality and fraud are a result of neoliberal forces needs to be nuanced. Neoliberalism ideology promoted the marketisation of financial products to the poor on a global scale and this might have driven, at least to some extent, the expansion of the South African insurance market to predominantly black lower and middle classes. These neoliberal forces, however, should not be overestimated and the definition of neoliberalism should not become so overarching that it becomes a pseudonym for capitalism.

South Africa is a capitalist society with an expanding financial market, but this expansion cannot be narrowed down to neoliberalism. This is particularly salient when examining the politics of post-1994 South Africa. The political ideology centred on democratisation, inclusive citizenship and overcoming racial equality. Over the past twenty years, the South African government has increased its control over consumer finance and has enforced a wide range of policies and laws on the financial sector. Marketisation in South Africa is driven by these political ideologies, which leads to an at-times contradictory moral landscape. This landscape includes ideological reorientations of the poor that are part of neoliberalism, basically the view that the poor are not passive people but energetic entrepreneurs, as well as the political ambition to have more control over the financial sector that has to contribute to a more-equal society. The expansion of the South African insurance market was intimately connected to these two moralities: one moral framework that can be traced to a global neoliberal ideology where business interest were seen to coalesce with a humanitarian agenda and one that was deeply rooted in the establishment of a democratic South Africa.

This diversity is apparent when examining clients, both old and new, white and black, wealthy and poor. Their moral agendas reflect the economic and racial inequalities that still permeate South African society. The predominantly white elites and upper-middle classes are concerned about fraud by insurance companies. They are worried about how insurance companies charge illegal fees, that they break international treaties regarding investments and that they do not have the interests of clients at heart. They are able to voice their criticisms through national media, ombudsman organisations and legal actions against the insurance companies.

The new and predominantly poor and black clients have their own concerns. They too have problems with their insurance but these are different kinds of problems, often from different kinds of policies. Furthermore, the moral debates not only centre on the insurance companies. They pay attention to the ambiguous consequences that insurance policies, especially life insurance, have on kinship and neighbourhood relations. Many recognise that insurance helps to overcome adversities and makes it possible to offer help, but they see also a darker side to insurance. To them, the marketisation of life insurance reveals that mutual support is declining and that it has become possible to make money on the death of others.

The challenge is to gain insight into the multiplicity of moralities. This multiplicity features in two ways. First, moralities are pegged to multiple economic regimes, in this particular case both to neoliberal understandings of poverty, as well as expectations of the financial sector in an emerging democracy. Instead of studying a single financial or economic origin of morality one needs to unravel, through detailed empirical studies of actual financial practices, how moralities emerge when several economic regimes intersect and interact. Second, different groups in society have different concerns and even more so different priorities.

The high levels of inequality that continue to characterise South African society today have resulted in a skewed public discourse about the morality of financial practices. The concerns of people who are wealthier and better educated are heard much easier than those of the poor and uneducated. The ways in which moralities are defined in public debates, economic policies, as well as judiciary measures, are not always inclusive. These inequalities, particularly so in South Africa, mean that some concerns about the financial sector receive more attention than others.

The inequalities that characterise society – which can be economic, racial, gendered and so on – need to be approached reflexively when defining fraud and corruption. If one fails to do so, definitions of fraud and corruption might end up reflecting the interests and world views of specific, usually more powerful, groups in society. Seemingly universal claims about what constitutes fraud, corruption and injustice might actually reflect very particular interest and world views that gloss over the experiences of people living at the fringes of the global capitalist system.

Notes

1 I would like to express my gratitude to Jörg Wiegratz and David Whyte for their very helpful and inspiring feedback on earlier versions of this chapter.

2 The data are presented on the site http://data.worldbank.org/indicator/SI.POV.GINI.

3 Prahalad ranks eighth in the *Financial Times*' Top 50 'Most important living management thinkers'; twelfth in the Thinkers Top 50, 2003; and twenty-third in the Top 50 of Management Gurus.

4 The Zantsi account is an example of a new type of bank account especially made to cater to the needs of the poor. It appears to be relatively successful.

5 Lloyd Coutts, black actuaries are on their way, says Assa, in a business report, 22 January 2006 (www.busrep.co.za/index.php?fArticleId=3076460). See Bähre (2012).

6 The charter can be found on the financial sector council's website www.fscharter.co.za.

7 www.treasury.gov.za/press/other/2003101701.pdf.

8 FinScope 2003 states that almost nobody earning below R1000 a month has a policy. Because the study on which the FinScope data is based is unavailable, even though the study was publicly funded by the UK Department for International Development (DFID), the reason for this vast discrepancy remains unclear. See Bähre (2011).

9 He was awarded a Sanlam Award for Excellence in Financial Journalism 2009, which was the twelfth year that he received this award. See www.sanlam.co.za/wps/wcm/connect/sanlam_en/Sanlam/Sponsorships/Media/Financial+Journalism+Awards/Previous+Winners.

10 See www.roylaw.co.za/home/article/protectyourfamily/pageid/insurance.

11 See www.mg.co.za/zapiro/fullcartoon/2337.

12 At the same time, insurance companies are pointing out that their clients can be fraudulent. According to a Standard Bank report issued in 2011, consumers are submitting fraudulent claims that are estimated to cost about R3 billion a year (at the time about €300 million). See *Mail and Guardian*, http://mg.co.za/article/2011-05-02-insurance-fraud-costs-consumers.

13 Based on statistics provided by the South African Police Service, which can be found online at www.saps.gov.za/resource_centre/publications/statistics/crimestats/2015/crime_stats.php.

14 Ranking compiled by Mexico's Citizens' Council for Public Security and Criminal Justice, see www.seguridadjusticiaypaz.org.mx/biblioteca/view.download/5/177. Violence in South Africa is not limited to murder but murder is the most relevant crime in relation to funeral insurance.

15 www.crimestatssa.com/topten.php. The six precincts with the highest murder rates were Nyanga, Harare, Mitchells Plain, Gugulethu, Khayelitsha and Delft. The seven precincts with the highest number of attempted murders were Mitchells Plain, Elsies River, Nyanga, Bishop Lavis, Manenburg, Khayelitsha and Mfuleni.

16 Similar moral concerns about life insurance were also crucial when life insurance became popular in nineteenth-century America (Zelizer 1978), and insurance murder is still a popular theme for many novels and films.

17 It is important to note that there already existed informal insurance arrangements in the form of burial societies. These societies mainly offered services and sometimes cash to the bereaved. The rules and procedures were regularly discussed at meetings where the members would discuss the legitimacy of claims and entitlements (see Bähre 2007). The benefits from commercial life insurance are much less visible than those from burial societies, which opens up more space for speculations.

References

Bähre, E. (2005). 'How to Ignore Corruption: Reporting the Shortcomings of Development in South Africa', *Current Anthropology*, 46(1): 107–120.

Bähre, E. (2007). *Money and Violence: Financial Self-Help Groups in a South African Township*, Brill Academic Publisher: Leiden.

Bähre, E (2011). 'Liberation and Redistribution: Social Grants, Commercial Insurance, and Religious Riches in South Africa', *Comparative Studies in Society and History*, 53(2): 371–392.

Bähre, E. (2012). 'The Janus Face of Insurance in South Africa: From Costs to Risk, From Networks to Bureaucracies', *Africa*, 82(1): 150–167.

Bähre, E. (2014). 'A Trickle-Up Economy: Mutuality, Freedom and Violence in Cape Town's Taxi Associations', *Africa*, 84(04): 576–594

Bähre, E. (2015). 'Ethnography's Blind Spot: Intimacy, Violence, and Fieldwork Relations in South Africa', *Social Analysis: The International Journal of Social and Cultural Practice* 59(3): 1–16.

Baker, T. (2000). 'Insuring Morality', *Economy and Society*, 29(4): 559–577.

Bond, P. (2000). *The Elite Transition: From Apartheid to Neoliberalism in South Africa*. London: Pluto Press.

Botha, C. and Hendricks, M. (2008). *Financing South Africa's National Health System through National Health Insurance: Possibilities and Challenges (Colloquium Proceedings)*, Pretoria: Human Sciences Research Council.

Chan, C.S.-c. (2012). *Marketing Death: Culture and the Making of a Life Insurance Market in China*, Oxford: Oxford University Press.

Comaroff, J. and Comaroff, J (2001). *Millennial Capitalism and the Culture of Neoliberalism*, Duke University Press: Raleigh.

Copestake, J., M. Greeley and S. Johnson (2005) *Money with a Mission: Microfinance and Poverty Reduction*, Rugby: ITDG Publishing.

Elyachar, J. (2002). 'Empowerment Money: The World Bank, Non-Governmental Organizations, and the Value of Culture in Egypt', *Public Culture*, 14(3): 493–513.

Ferguson, J. (2007). 'Formalities of Poverty: Thinking about Social Assistance in Neoliberal South Africa', *African Studies Review*, 50(2): 71–86.

Fisher-French, M. (2010). 'The growing role of graft and unethical practice', *Mail and Guardian*, 30 April.

Golomski, C. (2015). 'Compassion Technology: Life Insurance and the Remaking of Kinship in Swaziland's Age of HIV', *American Ethnologist*, 42(1): 81–96.

Klobuchar, J. and S. Wilkes (2005). *The Miracles of Barefoot Capitalism: A Compelling Case for Microcredit*, Minneapolis: Kirk House Publisher.

Letsoalo, M. (2010). 'Mrs Vavi, the pension funds and the bribe', *Mail and Guardian*, 1 April.

Lewis, O. (1959). *Five Families: Mexican Case Studies in the Culture of Poverty*, New York: Basic Books.

Liebenberg, I. and Barnard, L. (2005). 'Arms Acquisition and Procurement in South Africa: the Socio-history of Arms Deals with Reference to Attitudes, Strengths and Limitations in Decision-making (1935–1994)', *Journal for Contemporary History*, 30(3): 76–91.

Lodge, T. (2002). 'Political Corruption in South Africa: From Apartheid to Multiracial State', in A.J. Heidenheimer and M. Johnston (eds) *Political Corruption: Concepts and Contexts*, New Brunswick and London: Transaction Publishers, pp. 403–424.

Maurer, B. (2005). *Mutual Life, Limited: Islamic Banking, Alternative Currencies, Lateral Reason*, Princeton and Oxford: Princeton University Press.

Manaliyo, J.-C. (2014). 'Townships as Crime "Hot-Spot" Areas in Cape Town: Perceived Root Causes of Crime in Site B, Khayelitsha', *Mediterranean Journal of Social Sciences* 5(8): 596–603.

Prahalad, C.K. (2004). *Fortune at the Bottom of the Pyramid: Eradicating Poverty Through Profits*, Upper Saddle River, Wharton School Publishing.

Ross, R. (1999). *A Concise History of South Africa*, Cambridge: Cambridge University Press.

Saunders, R. (2007). 'Crisis, Capital, Compromise: Mining and Empowerment in Zimbabwe', *African Sociological Review*, 12(1): 67–89.

Schwella, E. (2013) 'Bad Public Leadership in South Africa: The Jackie Selebi Case', *Scientia Militaria: S.outh African Journal of Military Studies*, 41(1): 65–90.

Vavi, Z. (2010) 'Mrs Vavi and the pension funds: Zwelinzima Vavi responds', *Mail and Guardian*, 1 April.

Zelizer, V.A. (1978). 'Human Values and the Market: The Case of Life Insurance and Death in 19th-Century America', *The American Journal of Sociology*, 84(3): 591–610.

Zierenberg, M. (2008). *Stadt der Schieber: Der Berliner Schwarzmarkt 1939–1950* [City of Sliders: The black market of Berlin 1939–1950], Göttingen: Vandenhoeck & Ruprecht.

12 Economic freedom mis-sold

Neoliberalism and the moral economies of the PPI scandal in the UK

David Ellis

Introduction

In May 2011, the British Bankers Association (BBA) withdrew its appeal to the High Court contesting the regulatory measures taken by the Financial Services Authority (FSA) and the Financial Ombudsman Service (FOS) for the redress of consumers in what was judged to be the inappropriate sales of payment protection insurance (PPI) (Grey 2011). The decision taken by the BBA marked the end of six-year standoff between the banking industry and regulators following a 'super-complaint' made by the Citizens Advice Bureau (CAB) to the Office for Fair Trading (OFT) in 2005. During this period, the FSA repeatedly found that lenders were in breach of regulatory principles in the sales of PPI, resulting in final notices, public censure and fines amounting to £12,619,700 for firms found to have contravened these principles (Ashton and Hudson 2013).

Despite these attempts to curb what was seen as an intractable problem within the industry, PPI complaints to the FOS surged from 1,315 to 104,597 between 2006 and 2011 (Ferran 2012). With the failure of the BBA's attempt to overturn the actions taken by the FSA, the PPI scandal has come at a massive cost to the banking industry, with £20.5 billion being paid out in consumer redress since 2011 as a result of the mis-sold PPI (Financial Conduct Authority 2015). However, despite the industrial scale of financial wrongdoing, the term 'fraud' has been conspicuous by its absence throughout the various regulatory investigations and legal wranglings of the PPI mis-selling saga.

The lack of reference to 'fraud' indicates an unwillingness on the part of regulators to openly submit such conduct to the social censure of either criminal or moral opprobrium. This failure to acknowledgment of PPI 'mis-selling' as wrongdoing raises significant questions about the norms and practices underpinning the provision of PPI. It is the intention of this chapter to explore these questions through an understanding of 'moral economy' (Sayer 2007; Wiegratz 2012). In the first half of the chapter, an examination of the normative practices and values of the PPI scandal will consider the legitimations for these norms within the context of neoliberalism. This will include assessing neoliberal regulatory policies and the rights and responsibilities of both financial institutions and consumers, characterised by the ideals of 'freedom of contract' and 'economic freedom' (Atiyah 1990).

A key task of 'moral economy' also involves relating these legitimations to the everyday life and experiences of individual economic subjects (Sayer 2007). With this in mind, the second half of the chapter offers an account of how neoliberalism, along with the processes of financalisation, have created the opportunity structures for financial fraud in contemporary society. It also reveals how these processes have instituted a moral economy through which subjects are responsibilised to adopt a 'particular financial rationality' in response to neoliberal restructuring (Finlayson 2009; Watson 2010). These norms are primarily played out within the context of the creditor–debtor relationship, wherein the neoliberal legitimation and promise of economic freedom is exposed to reveal significant and unequal power asymmetries similar to those at work during the PPI mis-selling scandal.

Mis-selling or fraud? *'A rose by any other name …'*

PPI policies are intended to provide borrowers with insurance cover if they find themselves unable to make credit repayments on their loans. A borrower may require PPI if they experience unexpected interruptions in their regular income stream that prohibit repayment, such as through sickness, unemployment, accidental injury or even loss of life. Like any other form of insurance, PPI policies specify strict terms and conditions that may limit the coverage of claimants. As such, borrowers could potentially buy policies that are unsuitable for their needs, leaving them ineligible to make claims under the terms of their agreement.

From the 1970s onwards, PPI became widely available in the UK. Though initially only applied to mortgages, it went on to become an increasingly common insurance practice in other forms of unsecured lending, such as credit cards, personal loans, car loans and store cards. By 2005, approximately 20 million PPI policies were in force, with an estimated value of £5.5 billion to the banking and insurance sectors. Of these, unsecured loan PPI made up the bulk (60 per cent), with mortgage PPI (20 per cent), credit card PPI (15 per cent) and car finance PPI (5 per cent) making up the remainder (OFT 2006a). However, this growth in the market for PPI was largely driven by government policies and interventions that removed existing protections for borrowers and encouraged private insurance provision.

Government assistance for mortgage interest payments had been available for owner-occupiers claiming benefits since 1943. By the 1980s, however, the rapid growth of owner-occupation, coupled with equally dramatic increases in the number of people out of work, led to an escalation in those needing assistance with mortgage interest payments. Consequently, throughout the 1980s and 1990s, cutbacks in public spending and interventions by successive governments served to boost the take-up of PPI, particularly in relation to mortgages. In 1995, for instance, the Conservative government introduced a nine-month waiting period for those out of work to receive assistance with their mortgage interest. It was argued at the time that it should be the responsibility of owner-occupiers to cover themselves against risk in the event that they should fail to meet their mortgage payments (Kemp and Pryce 2002). Following on, an agreement was reached, under the Labour government in 1997, for improved standard terms of PPI as part of an initiative to create 'sustainable home ownership' (Wilcox and Williams 2013). These measures represented a concerted and explicit policy strategy that transferred responsibility from the state to individuals, creating new norms and expectations around the provision of private insurance, thereby fuelling the demand for PPI.

As the market for PPI increased rapidly in the early-2000s, so too did the number of complaints from policyholders to the FOS. While these complaints were initially mostly concerned with unsuccessful claims, the overall character of the complaints shifted to how the original sale of the policies had been conducted by PPI distributors. At the same time, closer scrutiny by consumer groups and media investigations began to highlight problems within the PPI market. By the time the FSA assumed regulatory responsibilities for insurance intermediation in 2005, the spectre of misconduct in the possible mis-selling of PPI made it a matter of priority for the regulator. Later on that year, the OFT received a 'super-complaint' from the CAB, prompting an investigation into the PPI market. The findings of the OFT's investigation revealed significant concerns regarding the sale of PPI and the provision of PPI on all credit products was subsequently referred to the Competition Commission (CC) for further review (OFT 2006a).

The concerns emerging from the report by the OFT (2006a) and in further investigations by regulators (CAB 2005; CC 2009; FSA 2006, 2007a) were consistent with one another and can be broadly summarised in three distinct categories (Ashton and Hudson 2013). First, PPI was considered poor value for most consumers due to the limited insurance coverage provided. Ultimately, this meant that there was a considerably low claims ratio, estimated at 13 per cent. Conversely, the sale of PPI policies was an extremely profitable business for distributors, who collected exceptionally high commission fees, averaging 53 per cent across all PPI products. By comparison, commissions paid to motor insurers were estimated to be as low as 10 per cent (OFT 2006a).

Second, the adverse use of market segmentation in PPI markets led to the targeting of groups with lower levels of financial literacy, leading to poor comprehension of the products they were being offered (Ashton and Hudson 2013). On the whole, PPI consumers were more likely to be younger and earn less than the national average, or occupied the lowest socio-economic groups (CC 2009). As such, they were also more likely to have difficulties in comprehending technical and marketing language regarding PPI sales, thereby compounding competitive concerns within the market (Ashton and Hudson 2013). Furthermore, the complexity of PPI policies, particularly in relation to single-premium policies (where the cost of the policy is added to the principal loaned, in some cases without the consumers knowledge), only added to the detrimental effect on consumers' ability to navigate the market (CC 2009).

Third, consumer inertia and the sales techniques of distributors, including high-pressure selling without due consideration of eligibility or suitability, were found to contribute to insufficient competition in the PPI market. Because consumers rarely sought out alternative PPI from that offered by their credit provider, it was estimated that 91 per cent of policies were purchased at the point-of-sale of the credit product (OFT 2006a). This gave credit providers a significant advantage compared to other distributors of PPI and reduced competition pressures on prices. Even where price did play a role in consumers' decision making, the lack of available information from suppliers about the true cost of PPI reduced their ability to make informed choices. Instead, consumers tended to focus on rates of interest, with the majority of lenders including the price of PPI as part of the overall quote for the loan rather than separately (Ashton and Hudson 2013). Moreover, the point-of-sale provision of PPI also led to instances of misleading information being given, with a third of consumers either assuming, being told or given the impression by the distributor that purchasing PPI would assist their credit application (OFT 2006a).

To the extent that these investigations revealed extensive evidence of deceptive and even fraudulent malpractices within the PPI market, the findings must first be qualified within the context of the neoliberal moral economy. A prominent feature here revolves around the promise of economic freedom through the economic and political ideal of 'freedom of contract' enshrined in law (Atiyah 1990). This legal doctrine is framed as a guarantee for individuals to act in the marketplace where they can make their own choices in pursuit of their own self-interests without 'paternalistic' government interference. Although consent and understanding is a prerequisite of any agreement, a neoliberal conception of individual behaviour assumes actors are fully capable of rational decision-making and may therefore reserve the right to choose whether to enter into agreement or not. Because common law starts from principles of '*caveat emptor*' (or buyer beware), the evidence of adverse market segmentation and deceptive practices in the PPI market is somewhat mitigated by the expectations placed on consumers within the transaction process. So, while consumers have the right to economic freedom, they also have responsibilities to 'make a reasonable effort to understand what is on offer and properly evaluate the information provided' (FSA 2008: 10). As a consequence, the lack of effective policing of fraud has been described as a reflection of 'some Victorian conception of prudence whereby everyone who does not take sufficient care of their own property deserves little sympathy' (Levi 2014: 229).

In light of these contextual factors, it was predictable that the most significant regulatory measures taken to address the PPI scandal were concentrated upon a 'primary virtue' of neoliberal doctrine, namely the improvement of market competition (Harvey 2005). Under the 2002 Enterprise Act, the CC exercised powers to order measures in this direction to remove some of the detrimental impacts on consumers (Ferran 2012). These measures included a ban on single-premium PPI and a prohibition on the joint sale of credit and PPI at the point-of-sale. The ban on single-premium PPI was intended to reduce product complexity and improve the way information was presented to consumers to give them more informed choice when comparing PPI policies (CC 2011). More importantly, the point-of-sale prohibition was intended to improve market competition by removing the barriers that limited consumer choice, increasing market access to other standalone providers and eliminating the significant advantages and incentives that credit providers previously had in selling PPI policies. Consumers would therefore be expected to take a more active role in purchasing PPI, which, it was claimed, would reduce inertia and increase competitive pressures in the market (CC 2011).

The UK regulatory bodies involved in addressing the mis-selling of PPI took a two-pronged approach to dealing with the banking industry. First, the CC, as the competition law regulator, treated the scandal as an outcome of restrictive competitive practices by banks and other lenders. As such, the package of remedies ordered by the CC under section 134 of the 2002 Enterprise Act sought to mitigate or prevent 'the adverse effect on competition concerned or the detrimental effect on customers so far as it had resulted from, or may be expected to result from, the adverse effect on competition' (CC 2011: 2). Second, the FSA, as the integrated regulator for financial services, sanctioned transgressing lenders for breaches of the 'Principles for Businesses' put in place by the FSA in 2007. This approach was consistent with the FSA's market-friendly, light-touch regulatory regime. Rather than a system that relied upon prescriptive rules, the FSA instead placed greater emphasis on self-regulation by the finance and banking industry, guided by principles to achieve regulatory aims and outcomes (FSA 2007b). This lack of regulatory oversight was predicated on a central tenet of neoliberal moral economy that 'overbearing' external regulation is inefficient and places a 'burden on business'. As such, by relying on a 'principles-based' approach, financial institutions were, in effect, entrusted with policing fraud within the industry themselves. Of course, the consequences of self-regulation in these circumstances saw the sustained and unhindered long-term perpetration of fraudulent practices before regulatory action was eventually taken.

In the cases involving PPI mis-selling uncovered by regulators, banks and other lenders were repeatedly found to be in breach of the following principles:

> Principle 3: A firm must take reasonable care to organise and control its affairs responsibly and effectively, with adequate risk management systems;
> Principle 6: A firm must pay due regard to the interests of its customers and treat them fairly;
> Principle 7: A firm must pay due regard to the information needs of its clients, and communicate information to them in a way which is clear, fair and not misleading;
> Principle 9: A firm must take reasonable care to ensure the suitability of its advice and discretionary decisions for any customer who is entitled to rely upon its judgement.
>
> (FSA 2007b)

The breaches related mainly to issues of customer interests, such as the inadequate provision of relevant information and the breakdown of trust within the transaction relationship. For example, these cases involved adding the cost of single-premium PPI to the quoted interest on a loan without customers' foreknowledge and the failure to relate the conditions of PPI to assist customers in making informed choices (Ashton and Hudson 2013).

The basis for the BBA's appeal to the High Court was that the principles gave rise to direct obligations by firms to their customers, resulting in compensation. It was claimed this was in direct contravention of statutory rules in the Financial Services and Markets Act 2000 to the contrary and therefore was not actionable. Furthermore, the BBA claimed that because they had acted in compliance with the rules prevailing at the time, they were not liable for compensating customers (Gray and Belcher 2011). In dismissing the BBA's arguments, the presiding High Court judge, Mr Justice Ouseley, stated that:

> The Principles are best understood as the ever-present substrata to which the specific rules are added. The Principles always have to be complied with. The specific rules do not supplant them and cannot be used to contradict them. They are but specific applications of them to the particular requirements they cover. The general notion that the specific rules can exhaust the application of the Principles is inappropriate. It cannot be an error of law for the Principles to augment specific rules.
>
> (*British Bankers Association v Financial Services Authority and Financial Ombudsman Service* [2011] EWHC 999)

The failure of the BBA's appeal paved the way for unprecedented levels of customer redress in cases of PPI mis-selling and was seen as a vindication of the FSA's principles-based approach to regulation in responding to systemic failings in retail finance services (Grey 2011).

The handling of the PPI scandal by the FSA and FOS was seen as a crucial step in increasing trust and confidence in retail financial service provision in the UK (Grey 2011). Nevertheless, their investigations into the mis-selling of PPI uncovered a corporate culture and normalisation of deceptive practices on an unprecedented scale. Indeed, it is only the legal ambiguity of pre-conviction caution that these investigations were characterised as 'scandals' rather than 'crimes' (Levi 2014). The regulatory principles that offending firms were repeatedly found to have been in breach can analogously be interpreted as fraud offences in the criminal justice process, notably in relation to deception through false representation, failure to disclose information and abuse of position.

However, the successful prosecution of fraud in financial misconduct cases is mitigated to some degree by the labour-intensive expense of reconstructing complex financial arrangements and the sparse resources of regulators (Whyte 2004). Furthermore, a successful corporate or individual criminal prosecution relies upon finding that senior executives had sufficient awareness of fraudulent mis-selling practices. The difficulties of proving the mental element of fraud therefore deter costly investigations by regulators where a successful conviction is an unlikely outcome. So, whether or not these abuses are considered a direct consequence of senior management imposed incentive structures, such as employee bonuses and target-setting, they are investigated as regulatory issues rather than prosecuted as criminal matters (Levi 2014).

By pursuing a 'pragmatic approach' then, based on principles-based regulation as opposed to criminal prosecution, the FSA could celebrate a 'successful outcome' in forcing offending firms to compensate victims of PPI mis-selling. However, this ultimately represented a hollow victory akin to shutting the stable door after the horse had bolted. As Tombs (2013: 14) concludes, even though the breaches of regulatory principles were 'referred to euphemistically by the anaesthetising term "mis-selling", these are best viewed as systematic theft and fraud'. The regulatory agencies' approach was therefore less to do with punishing and deterring criminal wrongdoing, than it was an outcome of neoliberal moral norms valorising private enterprise and its ability to regulate itself for the common good. When significant action was finally taken, it was as a response to the threat that the PPI scandal posed to the legitimacy of retail financial service provision in the UK following the financial crisis and other high-profile scandals that had rocked the industry in the public imagination (see Tombs in this volume).

Rather than attempting to control institutional lenders and insurers, the role of regulation, in this sense, can be seen as an aspect of 'social order maintenance' designed to the preserve the existing status quo (Whyte 2004). It does not attempt to challenge the acceptability of the prevailing norms, but instead 'maintains the steady rate and function of the machinery of industry' (Whyte 2004: 144). Within this state of affairs, the exposure of millions of customers to widespread and systematic fraudulent practices is a wider symptom of an increasing reliance on financial services in the UK that must be maintained at all costs (Levi 2014). It is therefore necessary to examine how this reliance was facilitated by successive governments in the UK as part of a neoliberal paradigm to promote the norms and behaviours of 'financialised capitalism', particularly through the provision of credit and debt.

Neoliberalism, asset-ownership and the moral economy of debt

The PPI mis-selling scandal represents just one example of how millions of consumers have been exposed to pervasive fraudulent practices within the finance industry. Other examples include the 1980s' pension mis-selling scandal (Tombs 2013), the investigation into default charges of credit card companies (OFT 2006b) and irresponsible lending practices of the payday loan industry (OFT 2013). Because the pursuit of profit in the finance industry is more rapacious than in any other capitalist enterprise, it therefore lends an inherently 'noxious' characteristic to transactional relations, where the threat of fraud and deception is never far away (Lapavitsas 2003). Over the last three decades, financial services in the UK have grown significantly in relevance and have become a pervasive presence in the everyday lives of the vast majority of the population. However, this exposure is not the outcome of pure market forces, but an outcome of the symbiotic relationship between the financial services industry and the ideological political and economic project known as neoliberalism. The transformations that have led to the financialised economy are intrinsically associated with and have been facilitated by the emergence of neoliberal policies at all levels of society. As a result, the relationship between the state and its citizens has also transformed, with a redistribution of rights and responsibilities. This ongoing embedding of new subjectivities and modes of calculation corresponds with a financialised moral economy based on a fundamental relationship between creditor and debtor, thereby providing the opportunity structures for fraud within the financial services industry.

Over the last 35 years, the political and economic landscape of the UK has transformed irrevocably through the policies and practices of the neoliberal project. Neoliberalism has entailed an ongoing commitment by successive governments to implement market relations at all levels of society to achieve the neoliberal ideal of 'economic freedom' (Dean 2014). What this primarily relates to is the freedom of consumers and businesses alike to participate in what are ostensibly free markets in pursuit of their own self-interests. Because individual actors are considered sovereign, they are seen as the most capable arbiters for discerning their own welfare needs, with government intervention of any kind eschewed as a matter of doctrine. The legitimation for these policies is the claim that the establishment of a free-market economy based on economic freedom and unrestrained voluntary exchange 'has within it the potential to promote both prosperity and human freedom' (Friedman and Friedman 1980: 11).

In terms of specific policies, neoliberalism in the UK took the form of an organised political struggle to implement an ideological approach to the economy based on 'non-inflationary growth policies'. In response to the seemingly intractable economic stagflation and recurring industrial tensions of the 1970s, the Conservative Party in opposition successfully framed the crises as the outcome of 'an overextended, overloaded and ungovernable state' (Hay 1996: 255). The Conservatives' subsequent landslide general election victory in 1979 provided them with the opportunity to establish neoliberalism at the highest policy levels within the British state. This new approach to economic governance was predicated with the promise that it would produce stable inflation rates and minimal direct government intervention in the economy, which would in turn create a favourable environment for private capital investment and therefore economic growth. More specifically, it amounted to an integrated set of policy prescriptions that included: the privatisation of nationalised industries; maintaining price stability; the liberalisation of financial services; involvement in free-trade agreements; deregulation of labour markets; deregulation of interest rates; deregulation of exchange rates; and cuts in public spending (in particular welfare provision) (Montgomerie 2007).

Through the mutual reinforcement of these policies, the whole of UK society transformed politically, economically and socially through the process of 'financialisation'. The concept of financialisation allows us to understand the dynamic processes through which the flows of global finance capital have taken on an increasing prominence in the UK domestic economy. These processes have, in turn, led to far-reaching changes in the moral norms, values and behaviours within the everyday lives of individuals (Watson 2009). This new moral economy requires individuals to conform to a 'particular financial rationality' requiring the inculcation of the market imperatives of risk and reward as behavioural norms within neoliberal society (Finlayson 2009). To embrace these shifts and participate in the financialised economy is to be a 'responsible' citizen, someone capable of taking care of their own welfare needs. Contrastingly, the alternative of not participating is to rely on state assistance, an act of 'irresponsibility' in the financialised moral order (Watson 2009). These understandings of financialisation demonstrate how the expansion of financial markets has relied upon the integration of more and more people into the networks of global finance, a process facilitated and mediated at a domestic level by the state and the retail finance industry.

The most significant of the neoliberal policies to this process was the liberalisation of financial services. This battery of reforms relied on extolling the virtues of self-regulation in the financial sector and the economic and political benefits that were claimed to inherently follow as a consequence (Engelen *et al.*, 2011). As stated previously, the legitimacy of this approach was based on normative assumptions that external regulation was inefficient and an impediment to properly functioning market mechanisms. In these terms, financial liberalisation was seen as a way to insulate markets from the interference of political decision-makers and unleash market forces in pursuit of boundless economic growth (Moran 1991). These measures effectively removed the rules and regulations that had inhibited banks and financial service providers from operating in global finance markets, giving them greater freedom for pursuing 'financial innovation'. The neoliberal legitimation of financial innovation was that it improved the allocation of capital by pooling risks, creating liquidity and 'democratising' access to credit (Engelen *et al.* 2008). Such innovations included the use of securitisation and other forms of securities trading to remove liabilities from financial institutions balance sheets, thereby allowing them more opportunities for profitable investments, most notably through their lending activities (Coakley 1994). Following the 2007/8 financial crises, it was revealed that financial innovation practices were largely responsible for the chaos in global financial markets after widespread evidence was uncovered of fraudulent practices, or 'moral hazards' (Engelen *et al.* 2011).

At a domestic level, financial liberalisation was most evident in the 1980s reforms to retail banking. Whereas previously building societies had held a virtual monopoly over mortgage lending, banks were given greater agency to compete in the provision of housing finance. Building societies, for their part, were also given more freedom to offer a wider range of financial services. As a direct consequence, the competition that this created was seen as a boon for consumers, as banks and building societies embarked on mass-marketing campaigns to offer their financial services, particularly in the provision of mortgage finance and consumer credit (Coakley 1994). Complementing the liberalisation reforms was an extensive programme of privatisation that provided financial institutions with 'an additional pool of collateral' (Coakley 1994: 709). This included the privatisation of nationalised industries, such as British Telecom (in 1984) and British

Gas (in 1986), which were marketed as an opportunity for small-scale investors to become shareholders. More importantly though, it referred to the privatisation of municipal housing, giving council tenants the 'right to buy' their council homes at significantly reduced rates.

With greater opportunities to access mortgage finance following the banking reforms, the privatisation of municipal housing had the effect of stimulating the housing market (Coakley and Harris 1992). By releasing significant quantities of real assets into the economy, the privatisation of housing and the subsequent increases in homeownership rates provided the foundation to establish new layers of credit relationships that ultimately fuelled the long-term expansion of the financial sector (Coakley 1994). This alignment between finance and property markets also established the driving forces that would propel the neoliberal model of economic growth (Crouch 2011; Hutton 1995). For those entering the housing market, the promise of significant capital gains through rising house prices were seen to offset concerns about the high levels of indebtedness that were required to invest. As the expectation of near-constant increases in house prices became the norm, homeowners were encouraged to view these capital gains as permanent, thereby raising consumer confidence as household wealth soared (Mellor 2010). Correspondingly therefore, the growth in house prices also influenced higher levels of debt-financed consumer spending, either through equity withdrawal or the consolidation of unsecured consumer debt against properties (Langley 2008). In this way, housing debt leaked into the domestic economy, fuelling consumer spending and sustaining domestic economic growth (Crouch 2009).

The housing market boom was central to the legitimacy claims of neoliberalism as the dominant economic model. On one level, it provided the motivation for increasing numbers of people to enter into long-term credit relationships with financial institutions. On another level, it demonstrates how more regressive neoliberal policies were legitimised. In particular, the deregulation of labour markets that led to wage stagnation and the cuts to public spending and services. The implications of rising house prices and capital gains mean that households can overcome the limitations of their earned income by investing in capital and property markets (Montgomerie 2013). As such, neoliberal policies have been successful insofar as they have maintained 'economic growth by increasing demand without pushing wage-inflationary pressures into the economy' (Engelen *et al.* 2011: 48).

Likewise, the retrenchment of social provisions and public services, such as housing, pensions and higher education, was predicated on the ability of households to use debt as 'safety-net'. Homeownership is seen here as a key component for meeting households' welfare requirements. In this sense, property is treated as a 'proverbial ATM', whereby households may withdraw equity as needs dictate (Montgomerie 2011). For households without sufficient asset holdings, the only alternative is to access other forms of unsecured borrowing to make ends meet, often at higher levels of interest. Rather than using traditional policy mechanisms, such as redistribution, governments attempt to mobilise these individuals and households within the networks of financial markets, which are seen as panacea for alleviating poverty. This is the rationale behind the neoliberal policy strategy known as 'asset-based welfare' (Finlayson 2008; Watson 2009), which is aimed at encouraging asset-acquisition among those who are defined as being 'excluded'. The intention of asset-based welfare is to remove the 'burden' of recipients dependent on state welfare provision and to 'create the sorts of citizens who will themselves create the conditions for their own inclusion' (Finlayson 2003: 154). However, within these market relations of finance, credit and debt lie fundamental injustices that contradict the 'dominant neoliberal tropes of financial inclusion and democratisation of credit' (Soederberg 2014: 47).

In aiming to institute market relations at all levels of society, the neoliberal project endeavours to secure 'economic freedom' within ostensibly free markets, through which individuals can achieve a more general sense of freedom and security (Friedman and Friedman 1980). With the predominance of financial markets in contemporary society, individuals must therefore become financialised agents exhibiting a 'particular market rationality' to achieve this freedom (Watson 2010). It is no longer enough to be a passive recipient of state welfare. Instead, individuals must be self-disciplined citizens who are prepared to take responsibility for their own welfare needs by participating in the financialised economy. To embrace asset ownership is to adapt to the economic environment and therefore to act in a 'responsible' manner to ensure one's own future needs are provided for. By failing to acquire sufficient assets, the only alternative is to rely on state provision, which is to say, an act of 'irresponsibility'. The failure to adapt to the financialised economy is, in consequence, a failure of the 'moral test of prudent self-management' (Watson 2009: 46). Through the provision of a ready supply of credit and access to free markets, neoliberal policies are legitimated on providing individuals with the opportunity to fulfil the moral imperative of achieving 'independence, freedom and security'. Those who fail to take that opportunity are ultimately destined to be 'dependent, trapped and insecure' (Langley 2008). In this way, a clear moral separation is made between what is considered 'socially acceptable' behaviour and what is 'socially unacceptable'.

For all the claims of neoliberalism about the benefits of economic freedom for individuals in the financialised economy, the benefits to the financial industry itself are seldom foregrounded. The liberalisation of financial services allowed retail banks to move assets off their balance sheet through securitisation, which in turn became the 'feedstock of wholesale markets' (Froud *et al.* 2009). A highly lucrative industry emerged as a result, with profit seeking retail banks using the excess capacity to increase their lending activities across a range of services and products, including credit cards, personal loans and mortgage loans. The proliferation of interest-bearing loans within creditor–debtor relationships inevitably led to a regressive transfer of wealth, from those who are asset-poor to those who are already asset-rich (Pettifor 2006: 137). Furthermore, the increased reliance on financial intermediaries for basic welfare needs exposes individuals and households to the threat of fraud and deceit (Lapavitsas 2007), as has been demonstrated with the case of PPI fraud. As such, neoliberal platitudes about economic freedom and the 'democratisation of finance' disguise the exploitative character and underlying asymmetry in relations of power between creditor and debtor.

Rather than an equal relationship of mutual benefit between two rational individuals, debtors are subjected to secondary forms of class-based exploitation such as interest rates and late fees. Simultaneously, the dependence of low-income groups on consumer credit also distorts primary forms of exploitation in the workplace, where wages have failed to keep up with living standards (Soederberg 2014). The irony of these power relations is that institutional lenders escape external oversight and are for all intents and purposes self-regulating. In contrast, borrowers have been subjected to evermore-pervasive forms of surveillance through the use of credit reporting and scoring by financial institutions backed by the legal violence of the state, which 'ultimately plays the same role as the freelance violence of the "debt-enforcer"' (Lapavitsas 2003: 76). Moreover, by internalising these methods of surveillance, borrowers not only feel compelled to fulfill their debt obligations, but are also disciplined as 'responsible borrowers' in accordance with the supposed 'rationality' of credit scoring techniques (Langley 2014). In this way, the moral dimension of debt becomes an underlying norm to societal relations, both economic and non-economic. Masquerading as economic freedom, these inequalities form the basis of creditor–debtor relationships that are constituent within the 'strategic heart of neoliberal politics' (Lazzarato 2012: 25).

Conclusion

This chapter has demonstrated how the moral economy of fraud present within the PPI mis-selling scandal was reinforced through overlapping moral economies at different sites and scales, connected to one degree or another by the legitimations of neoliberalism. On the one hand, the PPI scandal was addressed at a regulatory level due to the absence of competition in the market, which is marked out as a 'primary virtue' of neoliberalism (Harvey 2005). On the other hand, the lack of sufficient regulatory oversight in the first place, highlighted with the FSA's 'principles-based approach' (FSA 2007b), provided the opportunity structures for the proliferation of sustained and widespread fraudulent practices. The neoliberal eschewal of regulation of financial services rests upon normative assumptions that unregulated markets are the most efficient and therefore provide the most beneficial outcomes for consumers and businesses alike.

These assumptions are underpinned by the neoliberal ideals of 'freedom of contract' and 'economic freedom' (Atiyah 1990), which are claimed to guarantee the rights of individuals to participate in markets for their own benefit. Of course, this claim is qualified with the common law principle of '*caveat emptor*', which posits that, along with rights, individuals also have responsibilities to due diligence within the contract. This is highlighted as problematic when we consider some of the deceptive practices uncovered in the PPI scandal, particularly the market segmentation of those with poor financial literacy (Ashton and Hudson 2013) and the insufficient provision of information in PPI sales techniques (OFT

2006a). It reveals how significant power inequalities exist within the contractual process, notably with knowledge asymmetries and vulnerabilities exposed.

Far from an isolated incident, it has also been shown how these same dynamics exist within the 'strategic heart of neoliberal politics' (Lazzarato 2012: 25), namely in the exploitative creditor–debtor relationship. The institution of this relationship emphasises the role of the neoliberal state in the development of the financialised moral economy that seeks to 'responsibilise' subjects along the lines of a 'particular financial rationality' (Finlayson 2009; Watson 2010) in a shift of rights and responsibilities from the state to the individual. Moreover, this financial rationality is intended play a key role in the legitimation of continuing neoliberal restructuring, through which stagnant wages and cuts to public provisions are presumed to be mitigated by the wealth-generating expectations of asset speculation (Mellor 2010). Such legitimations remain uncertain at best, as the contemporary global economy lurches from calamity to catastrophe. Even so, as the PPI mis-selling scandal so poignantly demonstrates, behind these financial relations, the spectre of fraud is never far away.

References

Ashton, J. K. and Hudson, R. S. (2013) 'The mis-selling of payments protection insurance in mortgage and unsecured lending markets' in J. M. Pastor and J. Fernández de Guevara (eds) *Modern Bank Behaviour*. Hampshire, Palgrave Macmillan, pp. 8–33.

Atiyah, P. S. (1990) 'Freedom of contract and the New Right' in P. S. Atiyah (ed.) *Essays on Contract*. Oxford, Oxford University Press, pp. 356–386.

CAB (Citizens Advice Bureau) (2005) *Protection Racket: CAB Evidence on the Cost and Effectiveness of Payment Protection Insurance*. London, Citizens Advice Bureau.

Coakley, J. (1994) 'The integration of property and financial markets', *Environment and Planning A*, 26 (5), pp. 697–713.

Coakley, J. and Harris, L. (1992) 'Financial globalisation and deregulation' in J. Michie (ed.) *The Economic Legacy 1979–1992*. London, Academic Press Ltd, pp. 37–57.

CC (Competition Commission) (2009) *Market Investigation Into Payment Protection Insurance*. London, Competition Commission.

CC (2011) *Payment Protection Market Investigation Order 2011*. London, Competition Commission.

Crouch, C. (2009) 'Privatised Keynsianism: an unacknowledged policy regime', *The British Journal of Politics and International Relations*, 11 (3), pp. 382–399.

Crouch, C. (2011) *The Strange Non-Death of Neoliberalism*. Cambridge, Polity Press.

Dean, M. (2014) 'Rethinking neoliberalism', *Journal of Sociology*, 50 (2), pp. 150–163.

Engelen, E., Ertürk, I., Froud, J., Leaver, A. and Williams, K. (2008) 'Financial innovation: frame, conjecture and bricolage', CRESC Working Paper Series, 59.

Engelen, E., Ertürk, I., Froud, J., Johal, S., Leaver, A., Moran, M., Nilsson, A. and Williams, K. (2011) *After the Great Complacence: Financial Crisis and the Politics of Reform*. Oxford, Oxford University Press.

Ferran, E. (2012) 'Regulatory lessons from the payment protection mis-selling scandal in the UK', *European Business Organization Law Review*, 13, pp. 247–270.

Financial Conduct Authority (2015) 'Monthly PPI refunds and compensation', www.fca.org.uk/consumers/financial-services-products/insurance/payment-protection-insurance/ppi-compensation-refunds (accessed 8 August 2015).

FSA (Financial Services Authority) (2006) *The Sale of Payment Protection Insurance – Results of Follow-up Thematic Work*, London, FSA.

FSA (2007a) *The Sale of Payment Protection Insurance.* London, FSA.

FSA (2007b) *Principles-based Regulation: Focusing on the Outcomes That Matter.* London, FSA.

FSA (2008) *Consumer Responsibility*, 08/5. London, FSA.

Finlayson, A. (2003) *Making Sense of New Labour.* London, Lawrence and Wishart.

Finlayson, A. (2008) 'Characterizing New Labour: the case of the child trust fund', *Public Administration*, 86 (1), pp. 95–110.

Finlayson, A. (2009) 'Financialisation, financial literacy and asset-based welfare', *The, British Journal of Politics and International Relations*, 11 (3), pp. 400–421.

Friedman, M. and Friedman, R. (1980) *Free to Choose: A Personal Statement.* New York, Harcourt Brace Jovanvich.

Froud, J., Johal, S., Montgomerie, J. and Williams, K. (2009) 'Escaping the tyranny of earned income? The failure of finance as social innovation', CRESC Working Paper Series, 66.

Gray, P. and Belcher, G. (2011) 'When a principle becomes law: why the recent PPI judgment should be heeded by all regulated entities and not just banks', *Banking Law Journal*, 128 (8), pp. 750–754.

Grey, J. (2011) 'Legality of payment protection insurance compensation arrangements examined on judicial review', *Journal of Financial Regulation and Compliance*, 19 (4), pp. 396–406.

Harvey, D. (2005) *A Brief History of Neoliberalism.* Oxford, Oxford University Press.

Hay, C. (1996) 'Narrating crisis: the discursive construction of the winter of discontent', *Sociology*, 30 (2), pp. 253–277.

Hutton, W. (1995) *The State We're In.* London, Vintage.

Kemp, P. A. and Pryce, G. (2002) *Evaluating the Mortgage Safety Net.* London, Council of Mortgage Lenders.

Langley, P. (2008) *The Everyday Life of Global Finance: Saving and Borrowing in Anglo-America.* Oxford, Oxford University Press.

Langley, P. (2014) 'Equipping entrepreneurs: consuming credit and credit scores', *Consumption, Markets and Culture*, 17 (5), pp. 448–467.

Lapavitsas, C. (2003) *Social Foundations of Market, Money and Credit.* Oxon, Routledge.

Lapavitsas, C. (2007) 'Information and trust as social aspects of credit', *Economy and Society*, 36 (3), pp. 416–436.

Lazzarato, M. (2012) *The Making of the Indebted Man: An Essay on the Neoliberal Condition.* Los Angeles, Semiotext(e).

Levi, M. (2014) 'Regulating fraud revisited' in P. Davies, P. Francis and T. Wyatt (eds) *Invisible Crimes and Social Harms.* Hampshire, Palgrave Macmillan, pp. 221–243.

Mellor, M. (2010) *The Future of Money: From Financial Crisis to Public Resource.* London, Pluto Press.

Montgomerie, J. (2007) 'The logic of neo-liberalism and the political economy of consumer debt-led growth' in S. Lee and S. McBride (eds) *Neo-liberalism, State Power and Global Governance.* Dordrecht, Springer, pp. 157–172.

Montgomerie, J. (2011) 'The age of insecurity: indebtedness and the politics of abandonment', CRESC Working Paper Series, 92.

Montgomerie, J. (2013) 'America's debt safety-net', *Public Administration*, 91 (4), pp. 871–888.

Moran, M. (1991) *The Politics of the Financial Services Revolution: The USA, UK and Japan.* Hampshire, Macmillan.

OFT (Office of Fair Trading) (2006a) *Payment Protection Insurance, OFT869*. London, Office of Fair Trading.

OFT (2006b) *Calculating Fair Default Charges in Credit Card Contracts: A Statement of the OFT's Position, OFT842*. London, Office of Fair Trading.

OFT (2013) *Payday Lending: Compliance Review Final Report, OFT1481*. London, Office of Fair Trading.

Pettifor, A. (2006) *The Coming First World Debt Crisis*. Hampshire, Palgrave Macmillan.

Sayer, A. (2007) 'Moral economy as critique', *New Political Economy*, 12 (2), pp. 261–270.

Soederberg, S. (2014) *Debtfare States and the Poverty Industry: Money, Discipline and the Surplus Population.* Oxon, Routledge.

Tombs, S. (2013) 'Corporate theft and fraud: business as usual', *Criminal Justice Matters*, 94 (1), pp. 14–15.

Watson, M. (2009) 'Planning for a future of asset-based welfare? New Labour, financialized economic agency and the housing market', *Planning Practice and Research*, 24 (1), pp. 41–56.

Watson, M. (2010) 'House price Keynsianism and the contradictions of the modern investor subject', *Housing Studies*, 25 (3), pp. 413–426.

Whyte, D. (2004) 'Regulation and corporate crime' in J. Muncie and D. Wilson (eds) *Student Handbook of Criminal Justice and Criminology*. London, Cavendish Publishing, pp. 133–152.

Whyte, D. (2010) 'An intoxicated politics of regulation' in H. Quirk, T. Seddon and G. Smith (eds) *Regulation and Criminal Justice: Innovations in Policy and Research.* Cambridge, Cambridge University Press, pp. 162–191.

Wiegratz, J. (2012) 'The neoliberal harvest: the proliferation and normalisation of economic fraud in a market society' in S. Winlow and R. Atkinson (eds) *New Directions in Crime and Deviancy*. London, Routledge, pp. 55–70.

Wilcox, S. and Williams, P. (2013) *Building an Effective Safety Net for Home Owners and the Housing Market: Unfinished Business*. York, Joseph Rowntree Foundation.

13 Seeking God's blessings

Pentecostal religious discourses, pyramidal schemes and money scams in the southeast of Benin Republic

Sitna Quiroz

Introduction

In 2010, thousands of people lost their savings in the Benin Republic during the biggest financial scam in the history of this country: the ICC services affair. The money investment agency called ICC services (Investment Consultancy and Computering [sic] Services) was a money investment agency that operated as a pyramidal or Ponzi scheme between 2006 and 2010. After its collapse, it was revealed that high-ranking members of the government and religious organisations, especially the Celestial Church of Christ and some Pentecostal churches, were among those involved in the scam. In recent years, these types of scams have been a common phenomenon in many African countries: a feature of neoliberal capitalism on this continent (cf. Comaroff, 2009: 22; Comaroff and Comaroff, 2001; Krige, 2012).

This chapter explores some of the conditions and relationships that nowadays contribute to placing religious organisations in the Benin Republic – mainly Christian churches – very close to practices of economic 'illegality'. In line with the general argument of this book, I suggest that these scams do not happen in a vacuum. Nor are they due to the lack of 'moral values'. Instead, fraudulent practices are embedded in a set of social norms, values and relationships that are not fraudulent per se (Olivier de Sardan, 1999: 26). These norms and values provide the 'logics' by which fraudulent practices find a way to operate at the intersection of other social dynamics, such as the religious, as this case demonstrates. This chapter illustrates how in the Benin Republic, neoliberal discourses and policies have contributed to creating specific conditions in which fraudulent organisations, such as ICC services, find an easy way to operate outside official legislation. Thus, the moral economy of financial scams is intrinsic to the promotion of neoliberal policies in this country.

To understand the conditions in which this scam took place in the Benin Republic, I argue, we need to pay attention to local ideas of trust, trust-building practices and to the role of money in articulating social relations, across religious and non-religious contexts. These practices and ideas give us a clue to understanding how fraudulent organisations, such as ICC services, acquired social legitimacy and found a way to operate in a context where discourses and aspirations of prosperity abound.

In order to analyse the moral economy of fraud, one needs to take into consideration that West African economies and transactions have been shaped throughout their history at the interface of European forms of exchange and local social dynamics (Guyer, 2004: 5–6). These economies have operated on principles that do not conform to models of financial formalisation as outlined in mainstream economic theories (Guyer, 2004: 6–7). One of the central principles that articulate economic and political relationships in many African contexts is what anthropologists have called 'wealth in people' (cf. Guyer, 1995). This concept refers to the idea that a person's wealth is not necessarily measured by the accumulation of material possessions, instead, wealth is measured by the number and quality of social relationships that a person has access to and can mobilise for specific purposes (Guyer, 1995: 86). In Benin, the principles and values of 'wealth in people' play a central role in articulating social, economic and political relationships and in mobilising resources across different social spheres. These principles manifest in demonstrations of solidarity measured by economic contributions offered to a 'client' or potential 'clients', relatives or friends. They also manifest in the redistribution of resources via gifts of money, the sumptuous distribution of food in public events or social gatherings, and when a person delivers on her promises. Failing to comply with these principles equates with breaking the bases of trust at interpersonal and institutional levels. These breaches of trust account more for what people consider unacceptable, rather than the presumed 'illegality' of certain economic activities. These principles will help us understand the dynamics of the moral economy of fraud that the ICC services case illustrates.

In the first part of this chapter, I present the context in which many Christian churches, particularly Pentecostal, have flourished in Africa. In the Benin Republic, this happened alongside political changes that led to its 'democratic transition' and the implementation of neoliberal policies. Second, I describe the way in which ICC services started operating in Benin, and the events that led to its collapse. Third, I present the role that this and similar money investment agencies played in the everyday life of people (the pastor and fellowship) at a local Pentecostal church: the Assemblies of God (AoG) in a town that I call here Ipese.[1] Finally, I present the parallels between the dynamics that shaped the relationship between ICC services and their clients, and those between the pastor and his fellowship. I provide a general conclusion about how religious discourses were used to legitimise practices of money investment, and the role of trust and the dynamics of 'wealth in people' in this scam.

The material I present here is the product of an ethnographic fieldwork of 19 months, between 2008 and 2010, in the southeast of the Benin Republic. This fieldwork was part of a doctoral research project in anthropology that explored the ways in which conversion to Pentecostalism shapes kinship and gender dynamics, and their implications for the political and economic spheres. In this chapter, I refer to events that happened in the AoG church in Ipese, a semi-rural town situated in the proximities of the border with Nigeria. Ipese is a multi-ethnic town with approximately 5,000 people, characterised by the burgeoning commercial activity of its two weekly markets. Although this area is predominantly Yoruba, Ipese has a large population of migrants from other regions in Benin and Nigeria that belong to different ethnic groups. These groups are the Gun, Fon, Bariba and Fulani from Benin, and Igbo from Nigeria. The AoG church in this town had a membership of approximately 300 people, mostly Gun, followed by Yoruba. The main economic activities of its members fell into the category of the 'informal' sector, combined with occasional agricultural activity for self-consumption. Most of them, especially women, were small-scale traders, followed by service-oriented activities, such as tailors, hairdressers and drivers. Others, a minority, were teachers and low-rank civil servants. The majority did not receive a regular income; they lived day by day and did not have the possibility to access the services provided by banks. I now turn to describe the political and economic context in which Christian churches, especially Pentecostal, have flourished in recent years in the Benin Republic.

Neoliberalism and neo-Pentecostalism in Benin Republic

Several studies have stressed the historical convergence of the growth of neo-Pentecostal churches in Africa with the implementation of neoliberal policies during the post-cold war era (Comaroff, 2001, 2009; Comaroff and Comaroff, 2012; Freeman, 2012; Gifford, 2004; Krige, 2012; Maxwell, 1998). The liberalisation of African economies in the 1980s, the implementation of structural adjustment programmes (SAPs) and a drastic fall in the living standards of many people, opened new avenues for the proliferation of non-government organisations (NGOs) and similar organisations in the continent that operate somewhat independently from the state (cf. Freeman, 2012: 2). These conditions have created opportunities for these organisations to capture foreign 'development aid' through various avenues, including scams (Smith, 2007: 88–111). In this context, the remarkable growth of so-called neo-charismatic churches has taken place. Alongside with NGOs, these churches and other religious organisations have intervened to fill a void left by the state in the provision of social services. They are interpreted as a reaction to a societal environment of fear, deprivation and lack of confidence in the future that the period of structural adjustment has left among people (cf. Marshall, 1991; Freeman, 2012).

In recent years, the study of Christianity in Africa has been dominated by the study of so-called neo-Pentecostal churches, particularly in urban contexts. One of the central features of these churches is the emphasis they place on the prosperity gospel. This is a doctrine that proclaims that every convert, or Born Again, has the right to access to God's blessings in the form of abundant health and wealth (cf. Coleman, 2002: 8; Gifford, 2001). It is considered that these churches promote individualistic ethics and entrepreneurial values that encourage the formation of capitalist attitudes and a moral justification to personal accumulation (cf. Gifford, 2004; Maxwell, 1998: 350–354; Meyer, 1998: 186; Smith, 2001:

608). Sometimes this moral justification is used to cover up dubious forms of enrichment (Smith, 2007: 213). Thus, Pentecostals are often perceived as standing very close to the world of the 'occult' that is used to explain the presence of illegal forms of accumulation and enrichment (cf. Comaroff, 2009; Comaroff and Comaroff, 2001; Newell, 2007).

In the Benin Republic, the growth of neo-Pentecostal churches and their public presence has also happened hand in hand with the implementation of neoliberal reforms. The political transition in 1991 from a communist country, under Mathieu Kerekou's regime (1972–1991), to democracy was accompanied by the declaration of religious freedom, and the consequent proliferation of religious groups. In fact, Catholic religious authorities played a crucial role in enabling this democratic transition (Claffey, 2007; Mayrargue, 2002, 2006; Strandsbjerg, 2008; Tall, 1995).

In 1996, Mathieu Kerekou converted to Pentecostalism and returned to power, but this time, he was democratically elected. During his electoral campaign, he used his Born Again identity to convey his distancing from a sinful past, corruption and 'the forces of evil' (Mayrargue, 2002; Strandsbjerg, 2000, 2008). Strandsbjerg suggests that Kerekou's 'conversion' was part of a political strategy to accommodate to new external sources of power, particularly the American donor community (2008: 305). Since then, Pentecostalism became the predominant political discourse in the country and grounded its influence in state institutions through informal, personal networks of local and transnational character (Strandsbjerg, 2005: 225).

The Pentecostal presence in the political sphere has continued to be predominant. In 2006, former president of the West Africa Development Bank (BOAD) and a member of the AoG church, Thomas Yayi Boni, became president of Benin. In 2011, he was re-elected to remain in power until 2016. Although, in 2006, Yayi Boni did not explicitly exploit a Christian discourse during his campaign, he has always been open about his Christian beliefs and church membership (Mayrargue, 2006: 168–169). During the time of his presidency, several members of his cabinet and government offices were members of the AoG church. In 2010, before the run up to 2011 elections, I witnessed the mobilisation of different Evangelical Christian groups for prayer meetings across the country, in support of Yayi Boni's candidacy. The imbrication of personal relationships in religious and political networks indicates that the moral economy that shapes relationships in one sphere is closely linked to the moral economy of the other.

In recent years, the language of the prosperity gospel popularised by neo-charismatic churches has influenced practices of money offerings and giving across different Christian denominations in the country and outside church settings. I should clarify, however, that although many neo-charismatic churches in the continent proclaim a prosperity gospel, not all Pentecostal churches officially subscribe to this theology. For example, the AoG church in Ipese is closer to the theology of Classical Pentecostalism and the Holiness movement. This theology emphasises the observance of a strict moral conduct among its converts. The pastor and fellowship in this church were suspicious of prosperity gospel pastors, especially from Nigeria, who emphasised the importance of material wealth as a testimony of God's blessings.

One of the reasons for the pervasiveness of the prosperity gospel language outside church settings is that ideas of money and spiritual power in southeast Benin are, to some extent, compatible with it. In the Yoruba, Fon and Gun Cultures of Southeast Benin, health, children and money are considered manifestations of 'good life' (Guyer, 2004: 119). The acquisition and spending of money are forms of self-realisation that articulate social relations. The processes of buying and selling in the market; setting credit arrangements; and interests and profits constitute 'a complex of metaphors by which the spiritual and social worlds are envisaged' (Barber, 1995: 207).

These ideas played a role in the way in which money investment practices in pyramidal schemes, such as ICC services, dovetailed with religious life. In the prosperity gospel, monetary offerings are considered to be vehicles for tapping into God's power to secure blessings of health and wealth. When a person gives money to a church, it becomes a form of personal 'investment' in spiritual power, but also in social relations with members of the same church. However, to give money, a person needs to have access to it. Therefore, ICC services and similar agencies became relevant because they provided the cash that people needed to make these 'investments'. I now turn to describe the conditions in which ICC services and similar agencies started their operations in Benin, and the events that led to ICC services' collapse.

Promises of economic prosperity: money investment practices and pyramidal schemes

At the time of my fieldwork, money investment agencies working as pyramidal schemes were very popular. They attracted customers advertising their commitment to the alleviation of poverty. Most of these agencies promised a return of at least 50 per cent on interests per trimester, and up to 200 per cent per year. Although many people held mixed opinions about these agencies, most regarded them rather positively, or at least legitimate, until the ICC services affair.

I met many people who regularly invested their money in ICC services and similar agencies. One of them was the pastor of the AoG in Ipese. One day, during our conversation, he encouraged me to invest in ICC services. He said that he felt sorry that I was a student spending money in Benin without a salary, this way I could make some money until my departure. He often encouraged other members of the church to do the same, especially those with a regular income, who had the possibility to put some savings aside. I learnt that he also invested money whenever he was going through economic difficulties.

In response to his advice, I expressed scepticism towards ICC services. However, the pastor reassured me saying that this organisation was reliable. He had seen on national television that the agency invested people's savings in agricultural products abroad, and this is how the agency made profits to pay customers' interests. Moreover, ICC services' leaders often appeared on TV doing charitable works and, on many occasions, the president of Benin had talked favourably of this organisation. This information gave him the guarantee and reassurance that their activities could not be crooked. Unfortunately, subsequent events proved the opposite.

ICC services started operating in December 2006, the same year that President Yayi Boni began his mandate. The Ministry of the Interior and National Security registered this organisation as an NGO. During the four years of its operations, ICC services claimed to carry out a wide range of development activities that included agriculture, education, construction building, health, information technology and microfinance. However, their so-called microfinance activities were their pyramidal investment activities that the national media often described as an American tontine[2] or *tontine à l'américaine*.

In a short period, the leaders of ICC services managed to build a reputable image through charitable works advertised in national media. People described them as men of good will, who were doing the work of God. In fact, the founder of this organisation was a reputable member of the Celestial Church of Christ, with very close links to the former leader of this church. Similarly, it had become a very popular agency among Pentecostal circles.

By mid-June 2010 people in Ipese tried to collect their money at the local branch of ICC. However, they were told to return at a later date because there were insufficient funds available. Rumour had it that ICC leaders had been caught transferring the client's funds to their personal accounts abroad. A few days later, it was officially announced that the agency was bankrupt. In Porto Novo's branch, savers gathered angrily at the doors demanding reimbursement for their savings, with no success (Honvoh, 2010).

In response to people's discontent, the minister of the interior declared that the government had never authorised ICC financial activities, or those of similar structures (Kouton, 2010). A couple of days later, ICC leaders were arrested to proceed with interrogations. This declaration and arrest appeared suspicious to the general public. The general opinion of the people I spoke to was that the government could not have been blind to this organisation's activities, which they had endorsed many times on national TV. They also thought that the arrest had been a government move to protect ICC leaders from angry mobs.

Days later, President Yayi Boni organised a meeting with 88 leaders from other money investment agencies. During this meeting, it became evident that the major issue at stake was the lack of official legislation to control these organisations' activities. All these agencies were registered as NGOs and not as financial institutions. However, in its defence, the government declared that these agencies had been allowed to operate in the country with little or no supervision with the intention of promoting a free-market economy (*Quotidien Le Matinal*, 29 June 2010), which presumably, would lead to economic growth and social prosperity. With this argument, authorities were avoiding taking responsibility for the lack of legislation and adequate enforcement of the law.

Official investigations revealed that the money missing from ICC's accounts had been spent on three main areas. The first was described as 'public expenditure'. In other words, these were 'gifts' offered to sponsor events that enhanced the image of the head of the state. For example, 3 million CFA (US$5,000 approx.)[3] was offered to sponsor national celebrations for the international women's day (E.G., 2010). The second area was described as 'prestige expenditure' that ICC leaders offered to their 'clientele'. One of them declared having spent up to 20 million CFA ($33,998 approx.) per month on gifts to ministers of the state and judiciary officials, who often approached him asking for economic favours. ICC services also sponsored several public prayer vigils and meetings in support of the president. The third area was 'charitable donations'. These were offered mainly to the Celestial Church of Christ, which received enough money to build a new temple and a hospital (*Quotidien Le Matinal*, 9 July 2010). The total loss was calculated to be around 100 billion CFA. In an attempt to appease the population, the government promised to reimburse victims for their losses by October 2010, but this never happened.

At the beginning of July, the minister of the interior was dismissed and held temporarily under arrest with charges of traffic of influences and complicity with ICC leaders. This event tarnished the political legitimacy of the president because the minister of the interior was one of his closest collaborators. It was also a great humiliation for Pentecostal and evangelical Christians. The minister of the interior was widely known for his Pentecostal affiliation and for having contributed to building a strong political clientele among evangelical and Pentecostal groups in Benin. He often represented the president at public religious events, such as Pentecostal national conventions and public prayers.

ICC services built its popularity and trust among people because it was an agency that seemed to deliver on its promises. It delivered high-interest rates during the initial years of its operations; it displayed public demonstrations of solidarity and generosity through charitable donations; and its leaders engaged in 'gift-giving' activities that 'redistributed' resources. People did not condemn ICC services' activities until the organisation failed to sustain and deliver these principles. Many people were aware that their financial activities were not completely transparent. However, they decided to trust it because they could see that it delivered results.

As this section illustrates, the direct or indirect involvement of religious organisations in these types of money-lending schemes and scams is very common. Very often, the media and general public blame prosperity gospel preachers for setting up these schemes and encouraging people to get rich at any expense. However, this does not mean that all Pentecostals or religious organisations can be labelled as corrupt or held responsible for these scams. Even though some pastors, like the AoG pastor, considered these agencies as legitimate and encouraged their fellowship to invest money in them, it does not make them direct accomplices of their activities. In many cases, these pastors were also victims of those who manipulated religious discourses and their religious credentials to their advantage. Although these pastors follow some principles of the same moral economy as those who commit fraud, this does not mean that they also practice fraud.

I now turn to explore how the activities of ICC services became tightly related to the life and activities of the AoG church in Ipese. This micro-level scenario will make more visible the principles and values that articulate the moral economy of fraud and the church.

The role of economic hardships and social obligations in the moral economy of fraud

One Sunday service, weeks before the ICC services affair happened, members of the AoG church in Ipese were encouraged to collect money to buy a plot of land to build a temple in an annexe town. During fundraising events such as this, the money was collected by encouraging members to give generously as a demonstration of their faith in God. At first, members of the church were hesitant about giving money, until the main pastor stood up and committed himself to give generously. The money collected was handed over to the pastor inside an envelope, so he with other members of the church could finalise the purchase. That day, the pastor said, he went back home and placed the envelope in a plastic box that he kept in a locked compartment under the coffee table in his living room. He normally kept money from the church there. Afterwards, he got busy attending other matters. The next day, when he went to get the envelope, he realised that it was no longer there. He and his wife looked for it everywhere but could not find it. He deduced that he probably forgot to lock the compartment, and concluded that someone must have stolen it while he was busy. They were extremely upset because they could not let people down after the huge sacrifice they had made to collect the money. I knew he was not lying. Over the course of my fieldwork, I developed a close friendship with him and his wife, and I knew that they would not dare to keep the money to themselves.

He decided not to tell the whole assembly about this incident. The reason behind it was that pastors in Benin continuously have to invest themselves in gaining and maintaining trust from their fellowship. In an environment where livelihoods are precarious, distrust is more prevalent than trust (cf. Englund, 2007: 479). Therefore, developing mechanisms of accountability within the church is of crucial importance to building trust between pastors and their fellowship (ibid., 2007: 485–486). Whenever the pastor received donations for specific purposes, members of the church had to see concrete evidence, such as witnessing the purchase of the plot of land in this case. Moreover, the pastor used to write regular reports to give an account of the church's expenses. This way the people entrusted him with money.

However, the pastor confided the incident to a select group of close friends and some of his fellow pastors, whom he asked to pray for the situation. As soon as they heard the news, they immediately offered to lend him money to pay for the plot. Interestingly, some of them did it with explicit instructions to deposit part of the money in ICC services. This way, the pastor could keep the interest earned to repay his debts. In the end, the pastor and his wife managed to save their face with the members of the church. They gathered enough money to pay for the plot on the date agreed and decided to invest the rest of the money in ICC services to pay their debts. It was not the first time I saw something similar happening. The pastor very often went through economic difficulties. However, he and his wife always found ways to stay afloat. They relied on their relationships with other people, who usually lent them money and/or gave them food or other goods. They also invested money on pyramidal agencies, and benefited from the interest received.

Shortly after this incident, the news about ICC services affair broke. Luckily, the pastor was not among the victims of the scam. When he went to ICC services to invest part of the money lent, his application was rejected because he was not allowed to collect the money before the minimum three-month period stipulated by the agency. Since he needed the money before the three-month clause, he decided to invest in another agency. However, many members of the church were among ICC services' victims. Some had invested all their savings with the intention of saving money to build a house or buy a car. Interestingly, they did not blame the pastor for his advice or make him responsible for their situation. After all, the pastor was not the one who had profited from the scam at the expense of others. Moreover, the pastor had a reputation for honesty and accountability that he had earned through his consistent behaviour. In this situation, his reputation helped him to stay away from any ill judgement.

Moreover, everybody knew that the pastor often faced economic hardship because he regularly assisted other members of the church. People expected to receive the pastor's support and he responded accordingly. In every church, the pastor is considered a kind of surrogate father because of his spiritual endowment and, as such, he is regarded as a strong man with certain duties to fulfil. Whenever there were fund-raising activities, he first had to set the example to others by donating generously. If he had failed consistently to do so, he would have been judged as 'eating the money', and this would have meant the loss of church membership.

Many people, including Pentecostals, are very wary and critical of the way in which many pastors use their religious credentials to gather money, only to 'eat it'. In other words, these pastors do not comply with the principles of solidarity and redistribution that people expected from them. Therefore, these kinds of pastors often end up being victims of their ambition: they rarely manage to build a strong or long-lasting fellowship. The type of trust that regulates the relationships between pastors and their memberships, therefore, is based on elements such as redistribution, solidarity and a demonstration of concrete results.

This incident illustrates that in Benin, people like the AoG pastor, who are in social positions that require them to provide for and support others, very often face economic hardship. ICC services and similar agencies capitalised on such people. For them, ICC services became a viable resource to earn some extra money to stay afloat. However, it is worth pointing out that the same pressures that the pastor faced to fulfil social obligations were of the similar kind to those that leaders of ICC services faced towards their clientele. The moral economy of these pyramidal schemes responded to the same logic of social relations and obligations as the church. I now explore these parallels in more detail.

Trust-building mechanisms and religious discourses in the moral economy of fraud

In the last part of this chapter, I want to bring attention to two main issues in the moral economy of practices that this case reveals. The first concerns the parallels between church dynamics and ICC services and the dynamics of 'wealth in people'. The second aspect concerns the 'syncretic' (cf. Olivier de Sardan, 1999) features of money investment agencies, such as ICC services, and their use of religious and non-religious registers to justify and legitimise their fraudulent operations.

As mentioned earlier, in this society the so-called dynamics of 'wealth in people' play a crucial role articulating social relations. The demands of solidarity intrinsic to these dynamics, which are central to building trust between people, are often measured by economic contributions. When a person is in hardship, she asks for and expects to receive support from the members of the same kin group who are senior, considered richer or stronger. The same happens at a broader level. When a member of a political party is economically or politically stronger than her peers, those in lower ranks ask for her economic and social support. The person who is stronger is expected to 'help' those below her and, by doing this, she builds her political platform: patron and clients have a mutually beneficial relationship. However, in a precarious context where people spend more money than they make, maintaining solidarity and building trust through this principle tends to put a strain on people's economic conditions. Many times, the demands of the 'smaller' threaten the collapse of the 'bigger' by causing economic hardship and pushing her to engage in dubious economic activities to fulfil her obligations.

These dynamics mentioned were clear in the way in which ICC services leaders handled their economic resources and their relationships with their clients. Despite the perennial nature of pyramidal schemes, the leaders of ICC services faced additional pressure from the increasing demands for solidarity (i.e. redistribution) from their political and religious clients. These ended up accelerating the fatal effects of this organisation's collapse. Similar dynamics play out in the church, where the pastor who is considered a surrogate father is expected to support his fellowship. Many people who, like the pastor, faced these kinds of social obligations and expectations, also invested in pyramidal schemes. For them, these organisations appeared to be one viable option to earn money and cover their economic needs, even though these agencies operated in dubious ways. These people had a strong and 'legitimate' social motivation to invest their money in these agencies. Therefore, practices of money investment in pyramidal schemes need to be understood in the light of this societal role. One cannot separate the analysis of the economy and the management of economic crises in Benin from their social underpinnings.

The second element I want to bring attention to is the 'syncretic' aspect of these money investment practices. ICC services presented itself as a blend of a reputable and socially accepted 'traditional' institution, such as the tontine, but with a 'modern' facade. It had some qualities of the saving schemes that usually take place between trusted friends. However, it also combined elements that made it look like a thriving global investment agency. In their efforts to promote a 'free-market economy', which is one of the key elements of SAP conditionality, the government allowed this and similar agencies to operate without official legislation. However, the lack of regulation became the means by which certain groups, such as the owners of these schemes, the churches, pastors and government officials that benefited directly from ICC services' donations, took advantage of the status quo. To fill the void left by a lack of legislation, ICC leaders used religious discourses and the endorsement of high-ranking members of the government and religious organisations to earn people's trust and secure clients.

In this sense, religion played a crucial role in two levels: the level of discourse and the level of social relations. I have mentioned that the historical popularity of the prosperity gospel, with its emphasis on health and wealth, is compatible – to some extent – with neoliberal values and aspirations of economic success (cf. Gifford, 2004; Maxwell, 2005). These discourses have permeated those of other churches that do not necessarily subscribe 'officially' to its theology. In the same way that political actors have used religious discourses to launch their political campaigns (cf. Strandsbjerg, 2008), the owners of these schemes have used prosperity gospel discourses to earn investors' trust, and reinforce the idea that large returns on investments are a manifestation of God's blessings. However, religious discourses cannot fully explain why people trusted these organisations. Ultimately, a precarious economic context provided a fertile soil for these discourses to flourish, and pyramidal schemes grounded their success in the social relations that these discourses mobilised, especially in the church.

Friendships and religious networks within churches were the building blocks on which ICC services and similar organisations established their bases of trust. For example, ICC services invested in charitable donations to the Celestial Church of Christ and sponsored Pentecostal prayer vigils and conventions: 'the church' and 'the market' became closely interlinked. When ICC services collapsed, many people expressed their suspicion and criticism towards their religious (and political) leaders. However, they did not necessarily became suspicious of, or rejected, their own religious practices. Shortly after these events, I asked one of my acquaintances, an active member of the Celestial Church of Christ, his opinion about ICC services. He said that people who had invested their money in these agencies were paying the consequences of their ambition. I also asked his opinion about the fact that the founder of ICC services was a member of the Celestial Church of Christ and a close friend of its religious leader. He replied: 'Oh well, I know that not all the members of my church are trustworthy, but that does not have to do anything with God'. Many members of the AoG church had similar opinions. People were often critical of their pastors and were aware that they could potentially let them down. However, this suspicion did not undermine their engagement with their own religious practices. After all, trust in friendships and religious networks can be rebuilt in a different church or setting, if required.

In a neoliberal context characterised by constant uncertainty and change in the economic and political spheres, the religious sphere – as opposed to the other areas of social life – can provide with certain continuity and stability. People's engagement with religion often goes beyond the specific social relationships of one particular church or group. Different religions, particularly world religions, such as Christianity, also proclaim principles, values and norms that go beyond those that prevail in specific social settings. Therefore, the religious sphere allows for some room and flexibility to create alternative spaces of trust and forms of renewing social relations, especially when trust fails in non-religious contexts, such as in politics or 'the market'. Even in politics, when all else fails, politicians tend to draw strategically on different religious groups and discourses to provide themselves with legitimacy and supporters.

Concluding remarks

This chapter has explored the relationship between religious organisations and financial scams in the Benin Republic. It has outlined some aspects of the moral economy of fraud. A focus on trust-building practices and the role of money in articulating social relations in Benin has revealed that the dynamics of 'wealth in people' were crucial in bringing churches and pyramidal schemes very close to each other.

The implementation of neoliberal reforms in the Benin Republic contributed to creating the conditions in which ICC services affair took place. These policies have facilitated a proliferation of organisations that range from NGOs to pyramidal schemes, and a wide variety of churches, in particular, neo-Pentecostal. Some of these organisations, especially churches and NGOs, have increasingly taken over the provision of social services that were in the hands of the state. Churches have gained popularity in a context of uncertainty, fear and deprivation. In particular, neo-Pentecostalism, with its promises of health and wealth, has become influential across Christian denominations and religious groups, with its discourses that speak to people's aspirations for economic prosperity.

The liberalisation of the economy in Benin has opened opportunities for foreign investment and the increase in the flow of money. However, it also has created the conditions in which fraudulent organisations can operate with little or no regulation. Moreover, the majority of the population still does not have access to formal banking systems, and most of them rely on the informal economy. In a context of change and lack of formal regulation, the principles of wealth in people continue to articulate social relations across the political, economic and religious spheres. Thus, pastors, politicians and leaders of fraudulent organisations often participate in the same moral economy. ICC services capitalised on the context outlined above and manipulated religious discourses and personal networks to build its legitimacy and secure clients.

Nevertheless, one should be careful when analysing the role of religion in the moral economy of fraud. Just because neo-Pentecostal discourses are compatible with certain aspects and aspirations of neoliberalism, it does not mean that they follow the same agenda. Christian values are incompatible with an idea of illegal enrichment and the self-seeking accumulation of wealth. As this case has illustrated, what enabled the imbrication of pyramidal schemes and churches was the moral economy that articulates relationships in Beninese society through the principles of 'wealth in people'.

A focus on the moral economy has been useful to understand the imbrication of the economy, politics and religion in relation to fraud. However, this explanation does not exonerate the damage that fraud causes to people who are victims of it. Practices perceived as 'fraudulent' need to be analysed in relation to the context in which they take place.

Notes

1 This name is a pseudonym.
2 Tontine is a popular method of saving money in Benin Republic and other parts of West Africa. It consists of a group of people, usually friends, who agree to pool a fixed amount of money every month that is collected by one member of the group. The recipient of the money is consecutively rotated every month until everyone benefits.
3 Based on an exchange rate of US$1=588.272 XOF (CFA).

References

Barber, K. (1995) 'Money, Self-realization and the Person in Yoruba Texts', in Guyer, J.I. (ed.) *Money Matters. Instability, Values and Social Payments in the Modern History of West African Communities.* London: Heinmann and James Currey, pp. 205–224.

Claffey, P. (2007) *Christian Churches in Dahomey-Benin. A Study of their Socio-Political Role.* Leiden: Brill.

Coleman, S. (2002) 'The Faith Movement: A Global Religious Culture?', *Culture and Religion*, 3(1), pp. 3–19.

Comaroff, J. (2009) 'The Politics of Conviction. Faith on the Neo-liberal Frontier', *Social Analysis*, 53(1), pp. 17–38.

Comaroff, J. (2012) 'Pentecostalism, Populism and the New Politics of Affect', in Freeman, D. (ed.) *Pentecostalism and Development: Churches, NGOs and Social Change in Africa.* Hampshire: Palgrave Macmillan, pp. 41–66.

Comaroff, J. and Comaroff, J. (eds) (2001) 'Millennial Capitalism: First Thoughts on a Second Coming', *Millennial Capitalism and the Culture of Neoliberalism.* Durham: Duke University Press, pp. 1–56.

E.G. (2010) 'Affaire ICC-Services: Boni Yayi fait le ménage au Palais', *Aube Nouvelle*, 9 July, Available at : http://egbade.over-blog.com/tag/politique/172 (accessed 04/02/16).

Englund, H. (2007) 'Pentecostalism Beyond Belief: Trust and Democracy in a Malawian Township', *Africa*, 77(4), pp. 477–499.

Freeman, D. (2012) 'The Pentecostal Ethic and the Spirit of Development' in Freeman, D. (ed.) *Pentecostalism and Development: Churches, NGOs and Social Change in Africa.* Hampshire: Palgrave Macmillan, pp. 1–40.

Gifford, P. (2001) 'The Complex Provenance of Some Elements of African Pentecostal Theology', in Corten A. and R. Marshall-Fratani (eds) *Between Babel and Pentecost. Transnational Pentecostalism in Africa and Latin America.* London: Hurst and Company, pp. 62–79.

Gifford, P. (2004) *Ghana's New Christianity. Pentecostalism in a Globalising African Economy.* London: Hurst and Company.

Guyer, J.I. (1995) 'Wealth in People, Wealth in Things', *Journal of African History*, 36(1), pp. 83–90.

Guyer, J.I. (2004) *Marginal Gains. Monetary Transactions in Transatlantic Africa*. Chicago: University of Chicago Press.

Honvoh, C. (2010) 'Porto-Novo: ICC-services insolvable, les clients fâchés', *Adjinakou*, 16 June, Available at: http://bj.jolome.com/news/article/icc-services-insolvable-les-clients-faches-porto-novo-563?t=similaire (accessed 04/02/16).

Kouton, A. (2010) 'AFFAIRE ICC SERVICES: Le ministre de l'Intérieur appelle les déposants au calme et à la patience', *L'Autre Quotidien*, 22 June, Available at: http://egbade.over-blog.com/article-affaire-icc-services-le-ministre-de-l-interieur-appelle-les-deposants-au-calme-et-a-la-patience-52749840.html (accessed 04/02/16).

Krige, D. (2012) 'Fields of Dreams, Fields of Schemes: Ponzi Finance and Multi-level Marketing in South Africa', *Africa*, 82 (special issue 1), pp. 69–92.

Marshall, R. (1991) 'Power in the Name of Jesus', *Review of African Political Economy*, 52, pp. 21–37.

Maxwell, D. (1998) 'Delivered from the Spirit of Poverty? Pentecostalism, Prosperity and Modernity in Zimbabwe', *Journal of Religion in Africa*, 28(3), pp. 350–373.

Maxwell, D. (2005) 'The Durawall of Faith: Pentecostal Spirituality in Neo-Liberal Zimbabwe', *Journal of Religion in Africa*, 35(1), pp. 4–32.

Mayrargue, C. (2002) Dynamiques Religieuses et Démocratisation au Bénin. Pentecôtisme et Formation d'un Espace Public. PhD Thesis. CEAN, Universite de Bordeaux.

Mayrargue, C. (2006) 'Yayi Boni, un Président Inattendue? Construction de la Figure du Candidat et Dynamiques Électorales au Bénin', *Politique Africaine*, 102, pp. 155–172.

Meyer, B. (1998) '"Make a Complete Break with the Past": Memory and Postcolonial Modernity in Ghanian Pentecostal Discourse', in Werbner, R. (ed.) *Memory and the Post-colony. African Anthropology and the Critique of Power*. New York: Zed Books, pp. 182–208.

Meyer, B. (2004) 'Christianity in Africa: from African Independent to Pentecostal-Charismatic Churches', *Annual Review of Anthropology*, 33, pp. 447–474.

Newell, S. (2007) 'Pentecostal Witchcraft: Neoliberal Possession and Demonic Discourse in Ivorian Pentecostal Churches', *Journal of Religion in Africa*, 37, pp. 461–490.

Olivier de Sardan, J.P. (1999) 'A Moral Economy of Corruption in Africa?', *The Journal of Modern African Studies*, 37, pp. 25–52.

Quotidien Le Matinal (29 June 2010) 'Crise dans les structures de placement d'argent: Intervention musclée du pouvoir', *Quotidien Le Matinal*, 29 June.

Quotidien Le Matinal (9 July 2010) 'Perquisition hier du domicile de Tégbénou: Les premières grandes révélations sur Icc services', *Quotidien Le Matinal*, 9 July.

Smith, D.J. (2007) *A Culture of Corruption. Everyday Deception and Popular Discontent in Nigeria*. Princeton: Princeton University Press.

Strandsbjerg, C. (2000) 'Kérékou, God and the Ancestors: Religion and the Conception of Political Power in Benin', *African Affairs*, 99(396), pp. 395–414.

Strandsbjerg, C. (2005) 'Les Nouveaux Réseaux Évangéliques et l'Etat: le Cas du Bénin' in Fouchard, L., Mary, A. and Otayek, R. (eds) *Entreprises Religieuses Transnationales en Afrique de l'Ouest*. Ibadan, Paris: IFRA, Karthala, pp. 223–241.

Strandsbjerg, C. (2008) Les Sens du Pouvoir: des Forces "Occultes" à la Grâce Divine. Religion et Transformations Politiques dans le Bénin Contemporain. PhD Thesis. EHESS, Paris.

Tall, E.K. (1995) 'De la Démocratie et des Cultes Voduns au Bénin', *Cahiers d'Études Africains*, 35(137), pp. 195–208.

14 Producing moral ambiguity

State illegality, economic growth and norm change in Argentina's sweatshop business

Matias Dewey

The globalisation of markets – the interconnectedness created by new modes of transportation and telecommunication – and the liberalisation of the same have led to a profound transformation in the garment industry in Argentina. Today, after twenty-five years of neoliberal policies followed by more than ten years of protectionism, the garment market has become strongly segmented. The elimination of trade barriers and the influx of Asian garments have forced local textile companies to concentrate their efforts on the premium segment of the market and abandon the mass-market segment in order to survive. Despite making use of sweated labour, these companies produce high-end garments sold in shopping malls and other stores catering to well off Argentines. Meanwhile, the portion of the market orientated towards the lower and middle classes – consumers for whom genuine high-end and branded garments are usually unaffordable – is organised by informal production units; that is, sweatshops and informal marketplaces located all over the country. In other words, the segmentation of the garment market corresponds to a dualisation, or heterogenisation, of consumers.

This chapter deals with the moral transformation triggered by the reaction of governmental agencies to the economic repercussions of the neoliberal policies that were introduced in the Argentine garment sector during the 1990s, and the global economic transformations affecting the local industrial landscape. While the shadow economy described in this chapter emerged as a consequence of neoliberal policies during the 1990s, the last twelve years of protectionism have not reversed the situation. A major part of the garment sector remains in the shadows and serves as a supplier of services to legal enterprises nurtured by protectionist policies. Beneficiaries of such protectionist policies have been legal garment enterprises that meet only a portion of local demand. Meanwhile, the suppliers of the enormous demand remaining have not been the subject of any serious attempt to transformation. On the contrary, authorities reacted to this economy by undertaking actions that violate and/or undermine official laws but that, paradoxically, foster the creation of informal jobs and consumption. The moral transformation analysed here – i.e. the shift from more or less clear expectancies associated with public servants to an increasing dominance of ambiguity – is, then, the result of a double state response: one legal (the policies regulating the garment sector) and one in the shadow (the de facto illegal state interventions). I define these actions as 'shadow policies': state decisions aimed at fostering consumption, economic growth, political control and economic survival by informal or even illegal means. These shadow policies have created and promoted an informal industrial landscape concerned with meeting the garment consumption demands of the lower- and middle-class segments.

The empirical reference to a shadow policy is what I call here a 'money collection', or 'protection racket', structure, which is run by state officials and resembles a taxation system. Along with several informal agreements, this well-established and smooth-functioning structure is the cornerstone of La Salada, an informal and illegal marketplace that has become the most important supplier of low-cost garments in Argentina. Today, La Salada market is the most visible face of this underground economy. The money collection structure regulates 7,822 stalls that are open for business three times per week. Ninety-five per cent of the stalls are garment orientated, operating in conjunction with 31,288 sweatshops located in the immediate vicinity (in 2013).[1] The promotion of this specific economic activity intensified at the same rate as the country's economic recovery after 2002, once purchasing power and domestic consumption had increased. Thus, unlike other black markets emerging after major economic crises, this money collection structure, which promotes unregulated work, counterfeiting and, subsequently, the supply of low-cost clothing, survived the 2001 crisis and still remains in place today as an informal regulatory framework for the market.

Examining these shadow policies helps to explain a specific political and moral configuration of the economy, the most visible outcome of which is twofold. On the one hand, a dramatic growth in informality and illegality was reflected in a remarkable mushrooming of sweatshop numbers and low-cost garment consumption. On the other hand, a moral transformation occurred resulting from the economic actors' personal experience of state authorities behaving ambiguously; that is, contradicting laws and procedures that should guide their actions. By racketeering garments manufactured in sweatshops and sold in La Salada, the state affords the market a valuable advantage when it comes to exchanges outside the law: sweatshop producers and informal workers are able to expect that the law will not be enforced. Overall, the present analysis is intended to contribute to the investigation into the embeddedness of economic action (Beckert 2002; Granovetter 1985; Streeck and Beckert 2007; Wiegratz 2012). In the present case, economic action is embedded in a context characterised by state practices that openly violate the law. The moral transformation consists of a normalisation of illegality or, in other words, a state legitimisation of illegal economic practices. In that social context, moral ambiguity is prevailing; an ambiguity that is based on contradicting expectations: market actors know that their actions are unlawful and, at the same time, they know that the state will not prosecute them. In the long run, contradictory limits of moral behaviour and justifications of moral behaviour are institutionalised, e.g. workers defending unregulated or illegal job conditions.

The chapter is structured as follows: first, drawing on contributions from different strands of research, the notion of 'shadow policy' is discussed from a theoretical perspective. Second, a brief description of the recent history of the garment industry explains the rationale behind shadow policies that leads governmental authorities to facilitate the workings of the shadow garment economy through protection rackets, a situation that generates political gains in return. By preserving the jobs of thousands of informal workers and giving broad sectors of the population access to cheap garments, governmental authorities can maintain political control and gain political support (i.e., votes). The third section of the chapter presents empirical evidence supporting the existence of the collection structure described previously, as well as informal agreements that aim to promote La Salada's economic activities. Fourth, the chapter addresses the aforementioned moral ambiguity present in La Salada market.

Regulating markets through shadow policies

While the informalisation of the garment industry production chain and the associated deterioration of labour conditions have been the subject of much research, studies on how these social constellations are fostered locally are few and far between.[2] The revival of sweatshops in many Asian countries, including Bangladesh, Indonesia, Sri Lanka, Cambodia, China and Thailand, but also in Brazil and the USA, is usually seen as part of a much broader phenomenon termed the restructuring of global capitalism (Adams 2002: 149; Bonacich and Appelbaum 2000; Esbenshade 2004; Sluiter 2009). In the case of Argentina, such a reconfiguration of the global economic order refers to a set of processes, the final outcome of which has been the spread of informal labour relationships reflected in a clear decline in the manufacturing industrial complex after the mid-1970s (Arcos 2013; Busso 2010; Campos 2008; Coatz 2010; Di Bonis 2012; Kestelboim 2012; Kosacoff *et al.* 2004; Lieutier 2009; Tavosnanska 2010). Providers in the garment industry production chain found that they lacked the capacity to remain competitive, resulting in a casualisation of work in small businesses, growing self-employment, homework and sweated labour, and a weakening of national labour frameworks. These consequences are directly connected to global tendencies such as the spread of free trade policies, the outsourcing of production, the introduction of new management technologies and an increase in labour migration (Buechler 2004; Hum 2003; Lieutier 2009; Silva 2008; Waldinger 1984).

The focus of the aforementioned literature is predominantly on the global, far-reaching processes, both economic and technological, that affect local industrial and labour relations. What this strand of literature has not sufficiently considered, however, are the informal arrangements that mediate such major forces and reinforce their tendencies locally. The existence of shadow policies emphasises the importance of such arrangements. Indeed, these policies are defined as local ways of reacting to global structural drivers; at the same time, they are a key element of the local arrangements that enable a dual industrial landscape to persist in which sweatshops proliferate as fast as the measures introduced by the authorities to combat them. However, unlike policies supported by law, shadow policies seek to intervene in the economy by promoting or even creating informal institutions that, once institutionalised, become essential for the smooth functioning of informal or illegal markets. Thus, it would be inaccurate to explain the radical deregulation of labour relationships in La Salada by highlighting only the spread of neoliberal policies. Actually, the consequences of the deregulation brought about by neoliberal policies – for example, the growth of sweatshops – have been exploited by means of informal local regulation (taxation or protection rackets) aimed at stimulating the garment industry.

The introduction of a system of protection rackets run by state officials openly contradicts the idea of an unambiguous, ideal type of the state whose regulatory capacity is assumed to always follow the rule of law. Hence, such a view prevents us from adequately capturing the significant phenomenon of states regulating markets informally. In other words, the case of La Salada shows that the state has a far-from limited regulatory capacity. By means of a protection racket structure, the state reacts to overarching drivers by tolerating the undermining of official work regulations in order to enhance sweatshops' competitiveness.

The transformation of the Argentine garment industry

'It's difficult; it's increasingly difficult to sell these shirts. And I'm one of the few who has a workshop especially set up for doing the sublimation! [a technique for transferring images to fabric]', worries Humberto, a small-business owner who used to print the official Argentine national football shirts. One month later, just 10 kilometres away from Humberto's fully equipped workshop, another workshop owner, Sergio, informed us that he was exhausted due to the heavy workload. His entire stock of fake Adidas jackets (around 1,500 pieces) had been sold in barely four hours. Unlike Humberto with his worried demeanour, Sergio was overjoyed.[3] Replicating the illegal business model of La Salada, one of its managers had opened a new marketplace in another province, Mendoza, and Sergio had managed to set up a stall there to sell his jackets. Sergio and Humberto's contrasting experiences are both replicated frequently and thus the question arises: how can these contradictory landscapes in the same economic sector be explained?

The deep divide in the Argentine garment market (i.e., the structural division between quality-orientated and price-orientated production and consumption) can be traced back to the introduction of radical free market-orientated policies by the military authorities in the mid-1970s. Throughout the 1980s and becoming more pronounced in the 1990s, the structural division between quality-orientated and price-orientated segments progressed in parallel with the implementation of an additional set of new and innovative information and communication technologies. After almost thirty years of radical transformation, a new garment market emerged. Phenomena such as growing unemployment, vertical disintegration of the production chain, a generalised contraction of demand, an informalisation of working conditions and garment companies' 'flight to quality' shaped a second mode of production and consumption.[4] An insight into these elements serves as an introduction to the money collection structure, as well as being necessary in order to gain an understanding both of the emergence of La Salada market and of the moral transformation that took place there.

Collecting money in the shadow

The hundreds of Adidas jackets produced in Sergio's sweatshop and displayed in La Salada are intended for a market segment that has insufficient financial means to access to the original items. This is something Sergio is well aware of. In La Salada, 7,822 stalls are open for business three times per week and 95 per cent of stallholders sell garments including T-shirts, jeans, jackets, shoes, socks, underwear, children's clothing and aprons. Entrepreneurs from several locations around Greater Buenos Aires and to the south of the city attend the market in order to sell their production. These entrepreneurs – many of them sweatshop owners – are responsible for designing patterns, buying and cutting the fabric, and carrying out some of the final sewing work. The remaining tasks, mostly consisting of sewing, are outsourced to other sweatshops. Through this chain all sweatshops in Greater Buenos Aires are linked to the garment business of La Salada.

The informal regulatory mechanism at play in this economy is a robust illegal money collection structure, a good example of what this text refers to as shadow policy. The existence and success of these policies are based on two interwoven elements. First, that the illegalities related to sweatshops and counterfeit activities are not subject to moral rejection by either consumers or authorities in general, and second, that its economic activities generate two positively assessed market externalities: creation of jobs (though informal) and increase in consumption. This absence of moral rejection and the 'positive' consequences of the workings of the markets are key elements in explaining the protection racket structure. The fact that illegally produced garments provoke a type of moral reaction that differs from, for instance, the reaction to child pornography or the organ trade, helps to explain the tolerance shown towards certain types of shadow structures. The suspension of law enforcement enabled by the protection racket structure, therefore, becomes a mechanism that brings economic and political benefits to several actors, but is also a mechanism that brings about a silent and incremental moral change.

The 7,822 market stalls are distributed between five sheds and along the streets nearby, which are permanently occupied by wire-mesh stalls. Besides the infrastructure, the main difference between the sheds and the wire-mesh stalls on the street is the way they are controlled: the sheds have managers who have an extended and efficient network of informants at all levels of the marketplace. Depending on the location, between 40 and 60 per cent of the stalls sell counterfeit clothing branded with Adidas, Puma, Nike and Disney, among others. Around half of the garments sold in La Salada do not violate trademark law, a figure often misrepresented in mass media. Regardless of the quality of the copy, each stall displaying garments with brand logos must pay a fee known as 'brand' (*marca*). Those who do not sell any branded garments do not pay this protection fee. It is interesting from an organisational perspective that the 'brand' fee has to be paid every time a garment with a logo is exhibited on the stall, and if the stallholder should fail to pay, a debt will be recorded. The shed markets, with their centralised administration, also centralise fee collection, and designated collectors walk through the aisles collecting the 'fixed protection fee' sums. Lacking the same structured organisation as the sheds but matching them in terms of effectiveness, fee collection on the streets is carried out by the police (apparently without intermediaries), who illegally collect the 'fees' directly from the street-market vendors.

The collectors justify levying such fees to the stallholders by claiming the need to pay compensation to the authorities or even to the companies who own the copyright of the counterfeited brands. The fact that such justifications are simply lies (official procedures order the immediate confiscation of counterfeit products) shows not only the amount of lacking contextual knowledge and uncertainty at play in these shadowy contexts but also the moral breach opened by state officials: the expansion of the moral limits of what is morally accepted or not constantly opens up space for free-riders. In the shed markets, a high level of organisation and institutionalisation of practices is shown in the non-negotiable nature of the amount of the fee whereas, on the street markets, stallholders have some scope to negotiate a discount. While this may seem advantageous, street-market vendors must contend with the uncertainty of dealing with a number of people collecting money, all identifying themselves as policemen, while stallholders in the sheds must deal with only one collector. Stallholders selling counterfeited garments – usually entrepreneurs who own sweatshops – take this illegal fee into account when calculating their production expenses. According to several interviews, it is accepted that this fee is the price they must pay in order to increase their sales. Equally significant is the widespread acceptance of this kind of 'taxation': protest related to the issue is notably absent. This lack of resistance to fee collection is not only based on the considerable demand for the branded garments (which leads to increased profits and lessens the impact of the imposition of the fee) but, even more importantly, stems from the fear of the consequences of refusing to pay. The latter is particularly true for stallholders in the street markets, who are more exposed to a variety of dangers. The total sum of the fees collected from both the shed and street markets – US$771,955 each month – is distributed between at least eight state agencies at both national and provincial levels, and also in the Municipality of Lomas de Zamora. An ex-employee of a shed market recounted his experience as a fee collector:

> We went and collected inside, going through the aisles, gathering money. [When I asked if there are female collectors] yes, there are a lot, they go and collect for … say, Delitos y Estafas [the Crime and Fraud Agency], la Brigada de Mitre [the Mitre Police Service], Narcotráfico [the Anti-Narcotics Agency], la distrital and the departamental [District and Departmental

> Offices]. Pepe [the manager] went to have lunch with Ordaz [a police chief] every market day. You have no idea! Sometimes we had plastic bags full of money and then the members of the Police Service came to collect the money and I joked with them telling them that we were recording them.

As the quote suggests, the powerful individuals running the markets – the collectors among them – are colluding with different state agencies whose officials regularly pick up the collection. A current manager of one shed market confirmed that this is the way in which the police forces collect protection fees. When I mentioned what other managers had said – namely, that the people collecting money are policemen who are independently demanding money without any connection to the market administration – he offered the following explanation:

> Nobody tells me the true story. Who would? The police come and surround you. On weekends they know you have [the collected] money from the 'brand' tax and they come to pick it up … Well, you [as manager] have to deal with all these things. I know who I have to give it to [the collected tax money]. There are around ten of them [state agencies, police]. The Federal, ehhh, you have to give it to everyone. Because otherwise they stop the vans [of stallholders or buyers] when they enter [La Salada]. They took the vans when they were arriving and they really fucked me up.

Finally, a public servant currently working for the Montañitas municipality who was previously the right-hand man of one of the managers goes further when he describes the final stage of illegal fee collection and the relationship between La Salada and the government:

> In La Salada markets, and I'm not only speaking of the Yellow Market, I also mean in Larroque and Turdera, the guy who has a stall and sells 'brand' has to pay 450 bucks, and those who don't sell 'brand' pay three hundred. The difference is because people go and buy branded clothing … Do you understand how it works? Do you understand what I'm saying to you? Nobody knows that. In this district there are three hundred organisations. All of them received bags with thirty pairs of shoes [from the government]. Brand new. Nike, Adidas, and so forth. Do you know where they came from? From La Salada. It's called 'Ropa para Todos'. I warn you, if you repeat what I'm saying tomorrow, I don't know you.

What the interviewee reveals here is a picture in which state agencies needs cheap products for popular distribution in order to shore up state legitimation. As mentioned before, the suspension of law enforcement by means of a broad system of protection rackets produces not only private benefits to state officials (corruption) but also helps the workings of the state and its capacity to meet social demands. The aforementioned moral change, therefore, is paralleled by a structural change of political organisations and of the state itself.

The second fee is not imposed on stallholders but on the buyers travelling to the markets by long-distance bus. This is collected by a federal security force and is similar to bribes because it is collected at random, does not involve fixed amounts and the amount charged is not registered. However, similar to the 'brand' fee, the function of the payment is to suspend law enforcement. Therefore, the officially illegal economic activity is not abolished but 'taxed' instead. An ex-chief of the National Gendarmerie claims:

> But it isn't in anyone's interest [to prevent buses from getting to La Salada]! Look, it isn't convenient for any authority that buses don't come any more … because they regularly leave an *ovule* [protection fee]. If the business is over, we are fucked. I take you and tell you, 'Stupid! [He imitates a senior police officer speaking with a junior officer who has stopped a bus] What are you doing? I told you, stop the buses from time to time: of twenty [buses] you stop one. If you take one hundred pesos from each passenger … with fifty passengers … you do the math!'. It is not that they don't check; they make arrangements for everything. Do you think that if I see a bus on the highway I don't know it's coming from La Salada? They even have the money ready! The passengers themselves say, 'Guys, we should put the money there'.

With these fees, particularly the 'brand', the state has access to resources that allow political control, strengthen patronage networks and enable it to address issues regarding administration and the state budget. Such fees ensure the functioning of an essential market: the garment market. On the one hand, political control over the population stems from the fact that the state assures a certain level of income by creating jobs, though these are insecure and against official regulations. On the other hand, political stability is achieved by promoting consumption and also assuring access to garments. The results of the political elections in those constituencies close to La Salada market provide clear evidence of this political control: in Lomas de Zamora as well as in the south of the City of Buenos Aires, political candidates from the ruling party have always won. Patronage networks are strengthened, for instance, through the implementation of social programmes like 'Ropa para Todos' (Clothes for Everyone) aimed at providing emergency help to citizens and administered by community-based organisations. The aforementioned 'informal' taxes indirectly enable the state administration to function at the provincial and municipal level. In fact, as already pointed out by the former right-hand man of a manager quoted earlier, the shed markets pay a monthly sum of 4 million pesos in 'formal' taxes (property tax, waste collection tax, street lighting tax, and taxes and fees for other public services); a sum the state budget could not do without. In other words, the performance of local and provincial governments depends on the money gathered through illegal fee collection but also on the market externalities. Here, we face a scenario in which the state capacity to meet social demands is closely linked to of the existence of the illegal market. Political authorities and state agencies benefit from the creation of informal jobs and from the increasing consumption of illegally produced garments. Positive effects of this kind and the perceived harmless nature of the products themselves (the garments) are key elements when it comes to explaining the links between this political economy configuration and the moral change that it brings about.

Moral ambiguity

By now, it should be clear that a sociability characterised by ambiguity is the outcome of the way these state actors intervene in this social space. As many interviewees stated, the informal money collection structure is a form of state intervention: it is the 'releasing of zones' from police enforcement, meaning that authorities suspend law enforcement in cases of counterfeiting, informal employment, sweatshops, robbery, fraud and so forth in exchange for money.[5] This turning a blind eye to certain forms of law-breaking in return for money does not happen at random, and the best example for the systematic application of this policy is the aforementioned protection racket structure.

While the 'released zone' or the space 'protected' through protection rackets, creates a particular social space and provides a general frame for the constant expansion of textile enterprises, the immediate consequence is that all individuals within this social context are left without legal protection. Individuals who are robbed or swindled in commercial transactions, for instance, are left without any chance of receiving legal support, and their expectations regarding state protection remain unfulfilled. Sweatshop producers, distributors and informal workers in general benefit from the lack of law enforcement, but the price they pay for it is absence of protection. This situation is little different from what happens in illegal markets in general; that is, actors are not backed up by the legal system. But what makes this constellation special is that the state deliberately promotes, to paraphrase Giorgio Agamben, a state of exception in which several rights are suspended. In other words, the novelty of this does not lie in the well-known fact that actors cannot protect themselves and their expectations by turning to the justice system, but in the fact that state agencies create a sociability marked by distrust and ambiguity as a result of contradictory signals sent by state representatives. From the actors' perspective, the protection fees coupled with this particular everyday sociability constitute the price they must pay for an economic opportunity. The latter not only means that individuals working in La Salada may adapt to the extreme circumstances by developing their own strategies for self-protection in order to be safe in the market, but also that distrust pervades the kind of sociability present in everyday life. In other words, actors working in La Salada are left without third parties (usually the state) who might intervene during problematic situations.

Alongside the generalised perception of La Salada as a place of opportunity, the perception of interdependence among actors or roles in the market shapes what may be described as hope in the future of the market. However, this by no means implies that we are in the presence of a morale-fostering solidarity. In fact, with the exception of social ties among migrants, the best evidence for this lack of generalised solidarity is the complete absence of sectorial associations, or groups claiming or defending their rights.[6] On the contrary, there is a high degree of atomisation among the actors and opportunities are understood as an isolated, individual, or family enterprise. That market actors are accustomed to the respecting of informal agreements should be understood in light of the acknowledgment that one's own existence depends on others, and that the current opportunity – for many residents probably the only opportunity – should not be missed. The lack of solidarity in terms of labour unions stems not only from informality or illegality (situations that in and of themselves deny actors the access to justice), but also from the ambiguous role played by the governmental authorities.

Interestingly, the presence of ambiguity is a shared feature among illicit markets that emerge after cataclysmic situations (Mörchen 2011; Steege 2007; Zierenberg 2008) and other closely related situations (Auyero 2007). Atomisation and the lack of cooperation in social relationships impose a heavy burden on actors' everyday lives, but this is not enough to change the perception that the possibility of achieving stability or material progress in La Salada still exists. Opportunities are often seen in terms of a personal trajectory. Even when they discourage cooperative strategies and lead to an enormous increase in transaction costs, they are still the expression of possible futures. Paradoxically, what confirms and reinforces the experience of being in a place where opportunity abounds is the well-established protection racket structure promoted by the state. As long as the aforementioned informal taxation or protection racket system provides a frame for action, coordination among producers and the acknowledgement of interdependencies among commercial actors will be possible. Even when it is not the particular kind of morality capable of introducing trust among actors, it is still a frame for reshaping routines and, in doing so, helps to temporarily stabilise expectations. In other words, the illegal structure introduced by governmental authorities stabilises a set of norms necessary for repeated commerce in the long run.

Conclusion

This contribution argues that the mushrooming of sweatshop numbers and informal and illegal exchanges have been fostered by the introduction of what are referred to here as 'shadow policies'. These are domestic political decisions aimed at producing specific economic and political outcomes; for example, the creation of jobs and an increase in clothing consumption, and reproduction of political and bureaucratic power. Such political decisions are *shadow* because they promote both the expansion of means of production that contravene official regulations, and informal or even illegal exchanges. They are *policies* because they seek to generate regular income and increase consumption in poverty-stricken populations. Thus, shadow policies foster a paradoxical type of political economy: whereas the policies 'preserve' and 'protect' jobs and consumption, they also produce a rare and radical deregulation of work relationships. A crucial element in determining the existence and reproduction of shadow policies is the widespread opinion that the economic activities involved are harmless and capable of generating wealth. As a result of this type of neoliberal state intervention, everyday sociability is characterised by high levels ambiguity; provoked by state official's behaviours, the line between 'legal' and 'illegal' becomes blurred. However, such dissolution of moral limits does not mean the absence of norms. In fact, the opposite is true since shadow policies show that states can also regulate markets informally or even illegally by suspending law enforcement and introducing regulations in the shadow.

This analysis also provides strong empirical evidence of the shadow policies promoting the informal and illegal garment market in Argentina and, consequently, moral ambiguity. The evidence is found in the existence of an extended and robust money collection structure, or protection rackets, imposed upon stallholders selling clothing in La Salada marketplace. By illustrating how this illegal system functions, which state agencies are involved at different levels, and the volume of resources that flow around the system, this contribution demonstrates that shadow policies do indeed have the ability to frame expectations and enable a smooth-running and deeply entrenched system of exchange. From a broader perspective, what this case study shows is a parallel transformation: the introduction of abrupt neoliberal policies in the garment industry followed by a period of protectionism that did not reverse the social landscape left behind by the neoliberal policies corresponds to a moral transformation characterised by the acceptance of illegally produced products and the delegitimisation of governmental authorities. In that sense, at the cost of huge moral change, this configuration enables the reproduction of both state power and shadow capitalism.

Notes

1 The author counted the stalls with the help of a manual counter in July 2013. The estimated margin of error is approximately 100 stalls and variations in this number depend on whether new streets are being occupied. The average number of associated sweatshops and seamsters per sweatshop was calculated based on the author's own interviews with entrepreneurs and two reports (INTI 1995; D'Ovidio 2007).
2 With the exception of Fernandez-Kelly and Garcia (1989).
3 Names and places mentioned in the chapter have been anonymised. As the shed markets, their managers and their employees are few in number and therefore easily identifiable, gender and age have also been changed.
4 I take the expression 'flight to quality' from Kosacoff *et al.* (2004). It defines a focus on high-end products as a way of coping with negative economic changes.
5 On corrupt police structures and protection rackets in the Greater Buenos Aires area, see Dewey (2012).
6 The only exception is the group of 145 cart pullers who work in the Urkupiña marketplace within La Salada.

References

Adams, R. J. (2002). Retail profitability and sweatshops: a global dilemma. *Journal of Retailing and Consumer Services*, 9 (3), 147–153.

Anjaria, J. S. (2011). Ordinary states: Everyday corruption and the politics of space in Mumbai. *American Ethnologist*, 38 (1), 58–72.

Arcos, M. A. (2013). 'Talleres clandestinos': el traspatio de las 'Grandes Marcas'. Organización del trabajo dentro de la industria de la indumentaria. [Sweatshops: the backyard of the big brands. Organisation of work within the garment industry]. *VII Jornadas Santiago Wallace de Investigación en Antropología Social.* Sección de Antropología Social. Instituto de Ciencias Antropológicas. Facultad de Filosofía y Letras, UBA, Buenos Aires.

Auyero, J. (2007). *Routine Politics and Violence in Argentina: The Gray Zone of State Power*. Cambridge, U.K.: Cambridge University Press.

Beckert, J. (2002). *Beyond the Market: The Social Foundations of Economic Efficiency* (B. Harshav, Trans.). Princeton: Princeton University Press.

Beckert, J. and Wehinger, F. (2013). In the shadow: illegal markets and economic sociology. *Socio-Economic Review*, 11 (1), 5–30.

Bonacich, E. and Appelbaum, R. P. (2000). *Behind the Label: Inequality in the Los Angeles Apparel Industry*. Berkley and Los Angeles: University of California Press.

Buechler, S. (2004). Sweating it in the Brazilian garment industry: Korean and Bolivian immigrants and global economic forces in São Paulo. *Latin American Perspectives*, 31 (3), 99–119.

Busso, M. (2010). Las ferias comerciales: también un espacio de trabajo y socialización. Aportes para su estudio [The marketplace: also a work and socialisation space. Contributions for its study]. *Trabajo y Sociedad*, 16, 105–123.

Campos, M. (2008). La heterogeneidad del trabajo informal. Los resultados de un estudio cualitativo sobre los sectores del comercio textil, la construcción y el transporte [The heterogeneity of informality. The results of a qualitative study on the textile trade, construction, and transport]. In *Aportes a una nueva visión de la informalidad laboral en la Argentina* [Contributions to a new vision of labour informality in Argentina] (pp. 231–258). Buenos Aires: Ministerio de Trabajo, Empleo y Seguridad Social.

Carr, M. and Chen, M. A. (2002). *Globalization and the Informal Economy: How Global Trade and Investment Impact on the Working Poor*. Geneva: International Labour Office.

Castells, M. and Portes, A. (1989). World underneath: The origins, dynamics, and effects of the informal economy. In A. Portes, M. Castells, and L. A. Benton (eds) *The Informal Economy: Studies in Advanced and Less Developed Countries* (pp. 1–37). Baltimore: Johns Hopkins University Press.

Centeno, M. A. and Portes, A. (2006). The informal economy in the shadow of the state. In P. Fernández-Kelly and J. Shefner (eds) *Out of the Shadows: Political Action and the Informal Economy in Latin America* (pp. 23–48). University Park: The Pennsylvania State University Press..

Coatz, D. (2010). Heterogeneidad productiva e informalidad en la cadena textil-indumentaria [Productive heterogeneity and informality in the textile-clothing chain]. *Buenos Aires: Centro de Estudio UIA*. Special Issue (December): 28.

Cross, J. C. and Peña, S. (2006). Risk and regulation in informal and illegal markets. In P. Fernández-Kelly and J. Shefner (eds) *Out of the Shadows: Political Action and the Informal Economy in Latin America* (pp. 49–80). University Park: The Pennsylvania State University Press.

Dewey, M. (2012). Illegal police protection and the market for stolen vehicles in Buenos Aires. *Journal of Latin American Studies*, 44 (04), 679–702.

Di Bonis, L. C. (2012). *La industria textil argentina en escenario global actual. Un análisis del impacto de China y los países asiáticos en la cadena de valor local* [Argentina's textile industry in today's global scenario. An analysis of the impact of China and the Asian countries on the local value chain]. Buenos Aires: Facultad de Ciencias Económicas de la Universidad de Buenos Aires.

D'Ovidio, M. (2007). *Quién es quién en la cadena de valor del sector de indumentaria textil* [Who's Who in the value chain of the textile garment sector]. Buenos Aires: Fundación El Otro.

Esbenshade, J. (2004). *Monitoring Sweatshops: Workers, Consumers, and the Global Apparel Industry*. Philadelphia: Temple University Press.

Fernandez-Kelly, M. P. and García A. M. (1989). Informalization at the core: Hispanic women, homework, and the advanced capitalist state. In A. Portes, M. Castells, and L. A. Benton (eds) *The Informal Economy: Studies in Advanced and Less Developed Countries* (pp. 247–264). Baltimore: Johns Hopkins University Press.

Granovetter, M. (1985). Economic action and social structure: The problem of embeddedness. *American Journal of Sociology*, 91 (3), 481–510.

Hum, T. (2003). Mapping global production in New York City's garment industry: The role of Sunset Park, Brooklyn's immigrant economy. *Economic Development Quarterly*, 17 (3), 294–309.

INTI (1995). *Caracterización de las empresas de la confección de Quilmes* [Characterisation of the companies making Quilmes]. Buenos Aires: Centro de Investigaciones Textiles.

Kestelboim, M. (2012). *La formación del precio de la ropa* [The formation of the price of clothing]. Buenos Aires: Fundación Pro Tejer.

Kosacoff, B., G. Anlló, C. Bianco, R. Bisang, C. Bonvecchi, F. Porta, A. Ramos, E. Spector, and J.E. Zabala Suárez (2004). *Evaluación de un escenario posible y deseable de reestructuración y fortalecimiento del complejo textil Argentino* [Evaluation of a possible and desirable scenario for the restructuring and strengthening of the Argentine textile complex]. Buenos Aires: CEPAL.

Lieutier, A. (2009). *Esclavos: los trabajadores costureros en la Ciudad de Buenos Aires* [Slaves: the seamsters of the City of Buenos Aires]. Buenos Aires: Retórica Ediciones.

Meagher, K. (1995). Crisis, informalization and the urban informal sector in Sub-Saharan Africa. *Development and Change*, 26 (2), 259–284.

Mörchen, S. (2011). *Schwarzer Markt: Kriminalität, Ordnung Und Moral in Bremen 1939–1949* [Black Market: Criminality, order, and morality in Bremen 1939–1949]. Frankfurt am Main: Campus Verlag.

Portes, A. (2010). *Economic Sociology: A Systematic Inquiry*. Princeton: Princeton University Press.

Silva, C. F. (2008). *Trabalho informal e redes de subcontratação: dinâmicas urbanas da indústria de confecções em São Paulo* [Informal work and subcontracting networks: urban dynamics of the garment industry in São Paulo]. São Paulo: University of São Paulo.

Sluiter, L. (2009). *Clean Clothes: A Global Movement to End Sweatshops*. New York: Pluto Press.

Steege, P. (2007). *Black Market, Cold War: Everyday Life in Berlin, 1946–1949*. Cambridge, UK: Cambridge University Press.

Streeck, W. and Beckert, J. (eds) (2007). Moralische Voraussetzungen und Grenzen Wirtschaftlichen Handelns [Moral preconditions and limits of economic action]. *MPIfG working paper*, 07 (6).

Tavosnanska, A. (ed.) (2010). La industria argentina en el ciclo 2003–2008. Nuevas dinámicas, nuevos actores, perspectivas [The industry cycle in Argentina 2003–2008. New dynamics, new actors, perspectives]. *Universidad de Buenos Aires: Documento de Trabajo 23*.

Venkatesh, S. A. (2006). *Off the Books: The Underground Economy of the Urban Poor*. Cambridge, Mass.: Harvard University Press.

Waldinger, R. (1984). Immigrant enterprise in the New York garment industry. *Social Problems*, 32 (1), 60–71.

Weiss, L. (1987). Explaining the underground economy: State and social structure. *The British Journal of Sociology*, 38 (2), 216–234.

Wiegratz, J. (2012). The neoliberal harvest: The proliferation and normalisation of economic fraud in a market society. In S. Winlow and R. Atkinson (eds) *New Directions in Crime and Deviancy* (pp. 55–70). London: Routledge.

Zierenberg, M. (2008). *Stadt der Schieber: Der Berliner Schwarzmarkt 1939-1950* [City of Sliders: The black market of Berlin 1939–1950]. Göttingen: Vandenhoeck & Ruprecht.

15 Public good for private gain

Public sector reform, bureaucrats, and discourses of moral accountability in post-socialist Central Europe

Nicolette Makovicky

Shortly after the fall of the Berlin Wall, political scientist George Kolankiewicz (1994) published an article pondering the problems of legitimacy faced by Central Europe's first post-Communist governments. Having gained moral authority by virtue of their opposition to state socialism, most post-Communist elites had quickly shelved earlier ideas of 'local and economic self-government' in favour of the neoliberal doctrine of 'shock therapy' (ibid. 1994: 148). Policy-makers in his native Poland immediately set about reforming the country's centralized command economy, withdrawing price controls and subsidies for state-owned industries, liberalizing trade and investment and organizing the privatization of publicly owned assets. And yet, while free-market capitalism and representative democracy had 'at first appeared to possess their own built-in self-legitimating impetus', the realities of this post-socialist reform quickly revealed that liberalization had come at the price of growing social inequality and class conflict (ibid. 1994: 144). Consequently, Polish politicians found themselves saddled with a legitimacy problem. As Kolankiewicz wryly noted, it is 'difficult enough to mobilize society on the promise of greater inequality let alone admit that [reform] will be inherently unjust and will consign one-third of its citizens to social redundancy' (1994: 147). Indeed, the re-election of the national-conservative Law and Justice Party to parliamentary majority in October 2015 illustrates that the neoliberal politics of economic intervention has never quite managed to shed its legitimacy problem.

Neoliberalism is often presented as a morally bankrupt ideology that 'promotes a society in which materialism overwhelms moral commitment' (Stiglitz 2010). Commentators from the political left have condemned it for championing capital at the expense of labour, and self-reliance in place of collective responsibility, characterizing neoliberalism as a form of 'amoral market fundamentalism' that has replaced 'the moral economies of twentieth–century welfarism' (Muehlebach 2012: 5, see Bauman 2000, Harvey 2007). Locating social and moral economies 'outside' the market, others have claimed that (neo)liberal economic culture has led to 'moral breakdown' (Zigon 2010) and the impoverishment of social ties (Swader 2013). Going one step further, still others identify neoliberalism as the source of financial, fiscal, and political malfeasance.

According to Janine Wedel, the rise of neoliberal government, finance, and policy has been accompanied by a development of 'need corruption' into 'greed corruption' (2015: 7). 'Greed corruption', she writes, flourishes at the interstices of the private and public sector. It is perpetrated by elite members of the academic, business, and political worlds that make use of positions of public consultancy to advance their own agendas at the expense of the companies, institutions, and voters they are meant to represent. These individuals promote policies of fiscal and financial (de)regulation that depreciate the public purse, negotiate unfair advantages for select business and industrial sectors, and even take nations to war (Wedel 2009). Yet, because they are engaged in practices that are technically legal, they escape conventional methods of audit and control. Despite violating public trust, Wedel argues, these 'shadow elites' remain literally 'unaccountable'.

In this chapter, I investigate the emergence of such 'new' forms of fraudulent behavior in one particular Polish public–private partnership, the Czech-Polish Euroregion of Těšínské Slezko-Śląsk Cieszyński; a self-governing network of public and private actors that works to foster transnational cooperation in the area and acts as an implementation agency for programs and funding stream programs under the European Union's (EU) Cohesion Policy. This particular Euroregion brings together 56 municipalities from each side of the Czech-Polish border and is managed jointly by two regional associations, one Czech and one Polish.[1] My interest, however, lies less in documenting instances of the partnership's malpractice, and more in understanding how Euroregion administrators account for their choices and practices concerning the allocation of EU funding. Focusing on their struggle to implement 'best practice' for cross-border cooperation, I examine how they make use of neoliberal ideas and practices of audit and 'partnership' in an effort to explain their behavior. Administrators, I argue, do not simply adopt the language and logic of neoliberalism in respect to themselves. Faced with dubious requests from applicants for information on how to '*wyciągnąć pieniądze*' ('pull out the money') from European funds, they take on the role of disciplining agents, advocating an official agenda of 'sustainability' in order to reform individual and organizational citizens from corrupt into morally robust citizens. And yet, their own notions of moral accountability do not always match official criteria for 'best practice'. Rather, a tight fiscal environment and the existence of strong communities of interest in the area mean that institutional relationships built along pre-existing economic, ethno-historical, or personal lines are often simply re-described using a discourse of 'partnership'. In this way, efforts to introduce principles of 'best practice' may lead to a 'black-boxing' (and thus concealment) of key social and economic relationships between Euroregion partners.

In short, I argue that fraudulent behavior in the Euroregion organization can be seen as a consequence of the 'moral restructuring' (Wiegratz 2010) of bureaucratic discourse and practice along to neoliberal lines. As such, I follow my fellow contributors to this volume in challenging some of the orthodoxies of the current literature on the connections between neoliberalism and fraud. The first is the notion that neoliberalism is inherently immoral. The second is the notion that corrupt and fraudulent behavior is the preserve of certain social groups or professions, and is perpetuated by a few 'bad apples' who have embraced the 'higher immorality' of neoliberal ideology (Wright Mills 2000). In contrast, my argument rests on the assumption that the Europeanization of the Polish state has been accompanied by the cross-societal adoption of a certain neoliberal moral economy. This moral economy gives priority to specific values, including economic efficiency, self-government, and self-regulation, and calls for both greater individual responsibility and greater public accountability. In the Polish context, I argue, these ideals are imbued with additional moral weight by virtue of the widespread corruption, rogue privatization, and networks of political patronage that flourished in the wake of the Communist collapse. Overshadowing all branches of public office, this legacy of sleaze forces those in public service to form their claims to (moral) accountability in relation to it. Thus, while the idea of neoliberal intervention remains unpopular, bureaucrats and citizens alike nevertheless associate its core values with the virtues of greater public transparency.

This paradox is a particularity of the Polish post-socialist context. However, it is articulated in a very specific way by the complex moral position of my ethnographic subjects. As administrators of European subsidies, the men I spoke to were responsible for the allocation of public funding. And yet, they were not bureaucrats in the strictest sense of the word, in that they do not receive their wages from the state. Rather, their income (and that of their organizations) depended on their continued ability to attract and administer external funding streams. As such, they differed somewhat from many of the other actors studied in this book: unlike Balihar Sanghera's Kyrgyz elites, post-socialist liberalization had not freed them 'from social obligations to pursue their own self-interest' (ibid.), and neither had shifting political and professional values allowed them to privilege profit maximization over public duty like John Christensen's tax professionals. On the contrary, the neoliberal reform of the Polish public sector placed these administrators the somewhat precarious position of having to act as self-interested entrepreneurs, while also being subject to the measures of public accountability and scrutiny normally reserved for government officials. Indeed, as I show below, as the primary stakeholders in the Euroregion partnership, they were saddled with the task of introducing market rationality into public practice, while simultaneously being responsible for ensuring it was employed for the benefit of the greater good. Examining how they negotiate this apparently paradoxical position as enforcers of neoliberal value, and guardians of the public good, allows for a unique insight into the ways moral economies of fraud are produced (and re-produced) by the structures of contemporary bureaucracy (and the people who inhabit it).

Neoliberalism, post-socialism, and 'shadow elites'

Published shortly after Poland's second free elections in 1993, George Kolankiewicz's reflections accurately captured the experience of neoliberal 'shock therapy' for many ordinary citizens. Throughout the 1990s, the swift restructuring of the economy led not only to an explosion of the small to medium-sized businesses desired by reformers, but also to the loss of entire agricultural and industrial sectors, leading to rising unemployment, the casualization of labour, and a growing informal economy (Dunn 2004, Rakowski 2009, Stenning *et al.* 2010). The country's unions sided with the elites during this reform process, leading to a general sense of a loss of popular sovereignty amongst the urban and rural working classes (Kalb 2009, Ost 2005). In addition to economic and political privation, many working Poles thus felt they had suffered a particular kind of cultural dispossession: the strengthening of the power of capital vis-à-vis labour undermined established notions and structures of collective responsibility in favor of an individualist ideology (Pine 2007, Stenning 2005). In Michał Buchowski's words, neoliberal reform was accompanied by a 'restructuring of the perception of inequalities' in which not only elites viewed social and economic marginality as an index of individual laziness and lack of discipline, but ordinary citizens themselves appropriated liberal discourses to distance themselves from their less fortunate consociates (2006: 473–4). In other words, just a decade after the publication of Kolankiewicz's article lamenting the 'social redundancy' of one third of the working population, much of the Polish population were prepared to believe that they were responsible for their own plight.

Reading this stigmatization of disadvantaged groups as evidence of a moral restructuring of Polish society itself, Buchowski highlights the power of neoliberal reforms and rhetoric to function as a form of 'moral regulation' of institutions and identities (cf. Amable 2011, Muehlebach 2012). In the aftermath of the collapse of Communist rule, and the run-up to Poland's accession to the EU, such regulation was applied to private citizens and public organizations alike. In an effort to conform to EU and World Bank recommendations, policy-makers redesigned the existing health and welfare provisions from a universal system to one based on individual contributions. While general eligibility to social benefits was reduced and means testing introduced in the belief it would instil a novel sense of self-reliance in the populace, previously centrally handled tasks were delegated to local authorities, non-profit organizations, and volunteers in the name of economic efficiency (Cerami 2006). The same model of parsing out funds, functions, and decision-making capacities to public and private subnational 'stakeholders' was replicated across Poland's entire public sector. In this way, Europeanization introduced market rationality into administration via the principles of 'new public management', ushering in a new emphasis on the neoliberal values of enterprise, economic efficiency, and self-regulation (cf. Lane 2000). It opened up the space of public policy-making to a multitude of private–public partnerships, policy networks, and quangos – including the Euroregion studies in this chapter – which encouraged closer relationships between the state, capital, and non-governmental organizations.

Thought to promote higher standards of 'good governance', such entities have often been celebrated by academics and policy-makers alike as ideal mechanisms for providing 'the most effective response to public policy dilemmas' (Bache 2010: 58). Private–public partnerships, it is said, promote policy-making 'from below', ensuring a more democratic and economically effective solution than state-led development. They have also often been presented as a necessary step towards combating the proliferation of administrative and fiscal misconduct that is believed to have been embedded in the residual structures of the centralized, socialist-era public sector. Indeed, as Janine Wedel (2012) has pointed out, marketized discourses and practices of 'new public management' emerged with the end of the Cold War geo-political order in parallel with a renewed global commitment combating fraud (also Bukovansky 2006). Spearheaded by organizations like the World Bank and the International Monetary Fund, these anti-corruption initiatives focused on quantifying and combating discreet instances of rent-seeking by state officials, working on the assumption that malfeasance was primarily a problem of government. New democracies in Central Europe were encouraged to reduce incentives and opportunities for fraudulent behavior by shrinking the state and boosting the private sector (ibid.). At the same time, policy-makers faced new demands for increased accountability and transparency: those administering public funds were now expected to provide evidence of 'best practice' and document their performance using neoliberal practices of audit (Sampson 2010).

Such efforts to render public employees accountable were not entirely misplaced. In the decade following the fall of the Berlin Wall, post-Communist elites across Central Europe made use of their existing political connections to turn their political power into private economic assets (Vachudova 2009). In Poland, elite networks staged a partial capture of the state and its resources: while former managers of state enterprises used various tactics to acquire them as their own private property (*nomenklatura* privatization), state officials set up consulting firms that did business with their own ministries, or channelled state monies into their campaign funds through non-profit organizations (Wedel 1998, 2001). As Wedel (2009, 2012) has subsequently argued, such schemes were made possible not only by a lack of adequate regulation and corrupt judiciaries, but also by the particular biases inherent in the guidelines for fraud prevention described above. Developed by academics, supra-national organizations, and the third sector, these recommendations relied on a Weberian model of bureaucratic rationality that assumed a constitutional separation of the public and the private. Operating with a definition of fraudulent behavior as a diversion from formal norms, or as abuse of official position for economic gain, they ignored the 'complexity of local institutions and their make-up', as well as the 'the meanings and moralities' actors assigned to their activities (Wedel 2012: 474). More importantly, their assumption that privatization and public sector reform could act as a panacea for public malfeasance led them to overlook the fact that these processes carried their own incentives for corrupt behavior.

According to Wedel, in short, the parameters and prescriptions of globalized anti-corruption discourse rendered both scholars and governments blind to new patterns of fraud that emerged in the shadow of state-private entities created by neoliberal reform. The 'contracting out of government functions', Wedel explains, offered 'more opportunities for actors and entities … to surge beyond standard roles and responsibilities (2012: 477). It created a new class of money and power-brokers: individuals who were able to juggle multiple roles in the government, non-profit organizations, business, media, and the academic world while remaining answerable to neither. Rather than being engaged in 'classic' corrupt behavior (e.g. bribery), these shadow elites make use of their academic or political credentials to alternately (or simultaneously) advocate on behalf of corporations and industries, offer policy advice to government, and provide expert testimony. Like the Communist and post-Communist elites whom they openly condemn as corrupt, they 'personalize bureaucracy' and 'privatize information' by operating through personal relations within and across official structures. As such, shadow elites violate both 'the rules of the state (those of accountability) and the codes of business (those of competition)' by relaxing the rules of conduct at the interstices of official and private institutions (ibid.: 478–81). Indeed, precisely because they play a decisive role in processes of public policy-making they circumvent conventional means of accountability and transparency: they are able to evade accusations of fraud or questions about conflict of interest because they themselves define where public interest lies (ibid.: 481).

Wedel's observations are valuable on two accounts. First, they illustrate how ethics, as well as economics, have supplied the justification for neoliberal intervention into Central European society and politics. Second, they reveal how the very same moral interventions designed to introduce greater transparency into government have facilitated the creation of opaque power structures and fraudulent income streams for local elites. And yet, her insights fail to seriously challenge the very same Weberian distinction between private gain and public good that she states underpins the myopia of the contemporary anti-corruption industry. Thus, while Wedel points out that the roots and branches of business and government are rotten, her critique is (still) aimed primarily at exposing the 'bad apples' that exploit this decay. Uncovering the systemic roots of this 'greed corruption', she shows little interest in examining its moral universe, or the motivations of its inhabitants. This precludes Wedel from considering an alternative scenario: namely the possibility that the purposeful blending of private and public interests in contemporary bureaucratic structures may not only enable the fraudulent behavior of well-placed individuals, but actively undermine the performance of Weberian bureaucratic rationality itself. Or, to put it slightly differently, she fails to consider the possibility that the moral economy of modern quango culture regularly conflates the pursuit of private gain with the production of public good, rendering what she calls 'greed corruption' a routine side-effect of neoliberal policy-making (rather than the practice of a few rogue individuals).

In the following two sections, I pursue this second line of argument. Turning to my ethnographic material, I document how senior administrators in the cross-border Euroregion Těšínské Slezko-Śląsk Cieszyński justify their management of EU funding by making use of neoliberal ideas of audit and 'partnership'.[2] Evoking the ghosts of Communist rule and post-Communist corruption, they give additional purchase to such narratives of moral accountability by contrasting their actions and choices with the deviant behavior of other actors in the field. I suggest, however, that these narratives amount to little more than a re-description of the very same practices and relations along the line of neoliberal discourse. My approach is inspired in part by Laura Bear's recent observation that private–public partnerships place 'bureaucrats in a liminal, Janus-faced role, in which they act both to create and to cross the boundary between public and private action' (2011: 46). Neoliberal bureaucracy, she notes, allows for the articulation of licit and illicit forms of action while marking them as distinct, allowing 'techniques and inequalities previously associated with "the shadow state" or "corruption"' to become an integral part of the state project (ibid.: 57). Pushing Bear's ideas one step further, I suggest that the neoliberal blurring of state and society not only invites informal practices into the heart of formal government, but that certain genres of neoliberal discourse no longer pretend to their separation. As I argue below, claiming to establish the external validity of practices, the rationale of audit continues to adhere to Weberian notions of bureaucratic rationality. The rhetoric of 'partnership', in contrast, relies on a notion of internal validity that not only invites the collapse of private interest and public accountability, but justifies this conflation in moral terms.

Constructing moral accountability through audit

Located in the Czech-Polish cross-border town of Cieszyn/Český Tešín, the Euroregion was described to me by the general secretary of the Czech association Václav Laštůvka as 'an agreement on piece of paper … between two partners, one Czech partner, us, and a Polish partner'. His Polish counterpart, Bogdan Kasperek, used similarly blunt language to describe their administrative set-up, noting that Euroregions in general as essentially 'artificial' administrative constructs. And yet, both men felt that Cieszyn Silesia was one exception to this rule. They saw the local project as building on genuine, pre-existing cultural and linguistic affinities between Poles and Czechs on either side of the border. Noting that the Euroregion replicated almost perfectly the geo-political boundaries of the Habsburg Duchy of Cieszyn Silesa, Kasperek told me that 'History is a very strong element in our collaboration. The Euroregion Czieszyn Silesia … as one of the regions which have a certain thread running through their culture, which bring together micro-regions which were once a whole, is a little less artificial'. Across the bridge over the river Olza, which marked the border to the Czech part of the city, Laštůvka also outlined the confluence of the historical territory of the Duchy and that of today's Euroregion on a map in his office, and told me 'this is an exception, this is us … in other places it is not the case'.

Grasping at Cieszyn Silesia's Habsburg-era history, Laštůvka and Kasperek seemed eager to present the Euroregion as more than simply a bureaucratic fantasy of their own making. They had at least two reasons to worry about the integrity of the project in the eyes of local citizens (and visiting ethnographers). The first was the presence of certain local interest groups who viewed the Euroregion as a possible route to gaining funding projects of ethno-historical self-assertion; amongst them several associations and institutions that represented the

Polish-speaking minority in and around Český Tešín. Although they were eligible for financial support from the Euroregion, grants for cross-border projects celebrating minority culture often led to accusation of positive discrimination from the majority Czech population. The second reason was accusations of administrative incompetence and nepotism that had recently been levelled at neighboring partnerships on the Polish-German and Polish-Slovak borders (cf. Herschell 2011). In these places, Laštůvka explained, 'cooperation happened mainly to get money' resulting in a lack of public accountability and the funding of projects with no real impact on local business and society. Emphasizing that their own organizations were not in the business of 'buying cooperation for European [Union] money', both men were just as concerned with allocating funding to projects that would promote sustainable growth, as they were about dividing this funding along ethno-cultural lines.

Indeed, as if to pre-empt any questions of bias or profligacy, Václav Laštůvka started our first meeting by telling me that 'funding should not be given on the principle "give me money and I'll think about what to do with them"'. As joint members of Euroregion's steering committee, he and Kasperek oversaw the so-called 'Fund for Microprojects', a European funding stream that furnished most of the financial support for small-scale social, educational, and cultural projects in the region.[3] Noting that some mistakes had previously been made in the allocation of these monies, Laštůvka was eager to emphasize that only applicants with feasible project proposals received support from the Czech side of the cross-border partnership: 'We no longer support projects made "for devouring" – projects where we just ate our fill, drank our fill, and talked'. Any project now submitted for evaluation had to provide a plan for long-term development and adhere to 'clearly defined conditions' for project funding – what he called 'Czech rules'. Filtering existing tensions between the Czech and Polish partners through national stereotypes, he explained that while Czechs often erred on the side of caution, Poles had a tendency to make 'impulsive' decisions with the expectation that the parameters for funding could be renegotiated at a later date. Claiming that he made an effort to persuade his Polish partners to agree to 'do it according to the Czech principles', he hoped the implementation of hard and fast rules would instigate a culture change amongst the Euroregion's constituents.

Laštůvka, in short, saw greater sustainability and public accountability as achievable through the establishment of collectively held protocols for application and decision-making. Clearly defined rules and regulations would not only grant greater transparency to the network's internal proceedings, but also ensure financial equitability and counter cultural partisanship between the Euroregion partners. As such, he seemed to be reading straight from the rulebook of new public management, embracing its orthodox ideals of credibility through audit. According to Marilyn Strathern, these ideals have 'dual roots in moral reasoning and precepts of financial accounting', but have now been 'extended to become a new taken-for-granted process of neoliberal government' (2000: 2–3). Exercises of audit and assessment are understood to guarantee standards of 'good governance'. However, they are also the very technocratic tools by which accountability and transparency are manufactured: by gathering, organizing, and quantifying knowledge about the inner workings of an organization they promise unmediated access to an objective 'truth' external to themselves (Tsoukas 1997). Laštůvka's efforts to push an agenda of procedural clarity suggest that he was seeking to secure precisely such external validation for the Euroregion project. Indeed, his conviction that a 'culture change' was necessary amongst his Polish colleagues indicated that he saw himself making an ethical, as well as a technocratic, intervention into the partnership. By advocating for the implementation of 'Czech rules', he tried to claim moral leadership.

The British anthropologist Mary Douglas (1992) once remarked that rituals of verification (such as audits) arise primarily in situations of mistrust. Despite Laštůvka's somewhat light-hearted references to national stereotypes, he clearly felt some apprehension about the way his Polish partner organization operated. His misgivings seemed confirmed when I spoke to Bogdan Kasperek, who told me that 'we cannot do everything by the book'. Describing Laštůvka's attitude as unduly orthodox, he was reluctant to agree on hard and fast criteria for project management: in Poland's relatively poor funding environment, he explained, the administrative and financial demands of the application process alone often discouraged eligible members to apply for European funding. Long-term sustainability, Kasperek argued, was better fostered by accepting a certain amount of flexibility in the interpretation of the funding criteria. Over and above funding sustainable projects, it was important to draw applicants permanently into the structures of the Euroregion partnership: 'We have never funded a project which was just sort of "jump on the cash register" (*skok na kasie*), a type of project where the person has achieved what they wanted and disappeared'. Unlike Laštůvka, Kasperek worried that the implementation of rigid structures of procedure and audit would instigate a gradual 'etatization' of the Euroregion project, leading to the division and appropriation of ideas, money, and projects by either party. Indeed, rather than seeing Laštůvka's fondness of hard and fast rules as a sign of progressive reform, Kasperek associated it with his previous career 'in the other system' – that is, the Communist-era bureaucracy.

As we shall see below, Kasperek's distaste for what he saw as the over-bureaucratization of the Czech-Polish cross-border cooperation led him to pursue moral accountability through a different practical and discursive strategy, namely that of 'partnership'. And yet, their narratives did share certain fundamental communalities. The first was that both men framed their misgivings about the practices of the other a legacy of Communist rule, or post-socialist sleaze. Kasperek drew on the familiar link between socialism's tendency towards over-centralization and bureaucratic flexibility in order to present Laštůvka's enthusiasm for audit as the characteristic of an unreformed Communist. Laštůvka, however, evoked the endemic corruption of Poland's post-socialist public sector in order to present Kasperek's call for more 'flexibility' as a euphemism for the selective enforcement of eligibility criteria on favored candidates. A second, related communality was their mutual efforts to distance themselves from the unhealthy bureaucratic culture that had apparently flourished in other Euroregions nearby. Laštůvka's assertions that his organization was not in the business of 'buying' cooperation for European money, and Kasperek's statement that he had never funded a 'jump on the cash register', were clearly designed to make a decisive distinction between their practices and those of the profligate neighbors. Taken at face value, then, their narratives reflected a desire to maintain a strict separation between activities undertaken in the name of the public good (well-formulated, sustainable projects), and those motivated by personal connections and interests (projects made 'for devouring'). When subjected to closer scrutiny, however, this neat dichotomy often dissolved – particularly when the ethos of 'partnership' entered the frame.

Constructing moral accountability through partnership

Less wedded to the notion of rules and regulations, Bogdan Kasperek often took a more conciliatory view of instrumental requests for help and funding than his Czech colleague. 'We often find that someone comes to us for a consultation', Kasperek told me, 'and says, for example, "I would like to build an amphitheatre", help me write an application that will get me the money' (*wyciągnąć pieniądze* – literally 'pull out the money'). Explaining that such a project showed little promise of delivering any long-term, sustainable public good for the community in question, let alone the Euroregion network as whole, he noted that 'If someone were to present such a suggestion to my Czech partner, he would probably throw them out of his office'. Aware of the dearth of funding for local cultural projects, however, Kasperek took a more conciliatory view on the matter. In this case, the person seeking to gain funding from the Euroregion was the mayor of a local municipality on the Czech-Polish borderlands. Kasperek suspected that his plan to build an amphitheatre was little more than a vanity project designed to guarantee his re-election. However, rather than refusing the request outright, he helped the mayor to secure funding from the EU-sponsored Fund for Microprojects. He advised him to reformulate his request to suit the institutional and geographical remit of the Euroregion. Pointing out that the mayor's municipality already ran cross-border projects with a Czech partner municipality, he told him: 'Good, but then go to your Czech partner and create an agenda. Include what you want, but we have to justify the infrastructure by showing it is necessary in order for you to intensify your cooperation'.

Kasperek's story of the mayor and his amphitheatre can be read in several different ways. On the one hand, it appeared to illustrate his pragmatic attitude to the realities of the Polish context, where applicants neither understood nor cared about the stated goals of the Euroregion project. Indeed, acting in direct contravention to his own declaration that he never funded projects that were merely a 'jump on a cash register' (e.g. bids designed with the sole purpose was to extract funding), he encouraged the mayor to concoct a proposal that signalled sufficient adherence to the values of the Euroregion partnership to merit financial support, while granting him enough funds to fulfil his personal ambition. On the one hand, the story also illustrated Kasperek's conviction that flexibility and direct engagement with local actors, rather than strict enforcement of directives, led to sustainable projects and linkages between partners. Indeed, he insisted that what looked like the production of mere 'paper values' for a distant audience of European bureaucrats was in fact part of a re-education process that had the potential to turn the mayor (and his municipality) into a permanent, active member of the Euroregion network. Indeed, by making evidence of active collaboration, rather than the content of any proposed project, the foremost criteria for gaining access to funding, he seemed to want to convince the mayor that cross-border partnership could be more than simply an instrument for accessing European funding: 'I want there to come a certain moment when he says "Damn, well I have my amphitheatre and I have come to realise over the past five years that the amphitheatre is the least important thing"'.

Kasperek's efforts to shift the mayor's attitude from one of 'pulling out' money to creating an 'agenda for collaboration' thus appeared to reflect a genuine commitment to fostering long-term cooperation between Euroregion members. While Václav Laštůvka sought validation through mechanisms of audit, Kasperek attempted to establish his own integrity (and that of the Euroregion project as a whole) by recruiting the notion of 'partnership' to his cause. In line with much of the public policy teaching on partnership, he was convinced that cooperation not only created value, but *was itself a public good*, ensuring greater benefit and social merit by virtue of its collective nature (Mackintosh 1992). Thus, he saw the partnership principle as supplying the Euroregion project with its own internal validity that obviated the need for Laštůvka's bid for transparency through 'hard and fast' rules. As Janine Wedel has pointed out, auditing is an exercise that is primarily done for the benefit of outsiders and that relies on a type of accountability that is 'substantially removed from the internal ethics of a community it is supposed to apply' (2012: 486). Regarding the Euroregion network as a moral community shaped by the expectations, norms, and values of the social relationships between its members, Kasperek saw partnership itself as a potential source of such an 'internal ethic' that needed no external validation.

And yet, while the rhetoric of 'partnership' supplied his narrative with some moral integrity, certain aspects of Kasperek's story remained troublesome. By extending the mayor a helping hand, he not only invited him into the warm fold of the Euroregion network, but also trod a fine line between dispensing advice and what looked very much like advancing the interests of a favored consociate. In fact, Kasperek and the mayor were already well acquainted. Not only had the municipality in question already received Euroregion funding on a previous occasion, but the men had also met and collaborated on other matters already several years previously when Kasperek had worked as a civil servant in the Cieszyn County administration. Thus, when he took up his position as the general secretary, this collaboration was simply transferred into the Euroregion partnership, where the mayor became a fixture of the Polish organization's steering committee. Thus, what Kasperek presented as a necessary 'flexible' application of the rules to suit the needs of an applicant could very easily be construed by an outsider as favoritism resulting from a privileged relationship between the two men (cf. Ledeneva 1998). Indeed the mayor's very formulation of his request for help – that is, his open confession to wanting to 'pull out' money from the fund – suggested that he viewed the European funding system as a sort of closed 'gift economy' in which applicants with the right personal and professional relationships gained access to money unavailable to others. Successfully 'pulling out' money required an individual not only to find a source from which funding could be wrought, but more importantly, a well-placed personal connection (*znajomość*) that could facilitate access to this resource (Dunn 2004).

Rather than facilitating the open competition for funding, in short, 'partnership' appeared to reinforce existing relations and to privilege the priorities and goals of the existing membership. Indeed, Kasperek's own emphasis on the primacy of the network and its relations over the projects of individual members only serves to reinforce the impression that European funding could be used to build (and build on) connections between local elites. Studying Romanian consultants employed to construct and run European projects, Roxana Bratu (2012) observes that success thus relies on much the same skills of mediation and negotiation as those that characterize more questionable patron–client relations. While she emphasizes that this kinship does not automatically lead to malfeasance, she does note that the lines between mediation and the direct use of influence can blur in situations when the roles of individuals and institutions are fluid or opaque (ibid.: 210). In the case of Kasperek and the mayor, there seems not only to have been just such a blurring of roles and responsibilities, but a recategorization of personal connections that otherwise could have been deemed problematic under the more acceptable rubric of 'partnership'. Thus, while Bratu regards such opaqueness as the result of structural inequalities and outright corruption that exist beyond the client–consultant relationship itself, I would argue that in this case it is produced in part by the logic and rhetoric of neoliberal bureaucracy itself, and partnership discourse in particular. Indeed, by blending private and public interests, and promising to deliver internal goods for external funding, it naturalized the relationships between constituents by reframing the Euroregion network itself into a moral community of like-minded individuals.

Conclusions: bureaucracies, fraud, and moral economies

In their Introduction to this volume, David Whyte and Jörg Wiegratz argue that neoliberalism advances moral values which not only provide legitimacy for certain types of corrosive social and economic practices, but 'are conducive to fostering fraudulent motivation and practice' (Bratu 2012). Fraud, they contend, is 'a core feature of the structure of neoliberalism' (ibid.). Indeed, as several chapters in this book illustrate, the political and economic elevation of capital has allowed powerful groups to override older ideas of the public good in the name of self-interest; or rather, allowed them to define the public good as synonymous with their own self-interests. In the words of Steve Tombs, neoliberalism has been accompanied by the rise of the 'moral capital of capital' (see Chapter 3), and a depreciation of the public sector as 'wasteful, inefficient, and intrusive'. Designed to combat such impotence, the marketization of the public sector has generated a competitive environment where income, social status, and power have often become more valuable than a professional's excellence of practice, integrity, and worthiness (see Sanghera's Chapter 5). Thus, many of those actors whose roles traditionally included a duty to ensure the public interest, or at least adhere to its norms, now seemingly indulge in economic deviance and betray public trust with impunity. In a slight departure, my own chapter has explored the moral universe of a professional group that is a product of this neoliberal marketization of governance, but that is not able to extricate itself completely from the demands of public accountability; namely, those who administer and run the state–private mixes that increasingly form and implement policy today.

My ethnographic way into this moral universe came through an investigation of how two senior administrators in the Czech-Polish Euroregion Těšínské Slezko-Śląsk Cieszyński accounted for their management of EU funding streams flowing into the region. I showed how they made use of two staple concepts of neoliberal governance – audit and 'partnership' – in order to cement their moral accountability and the integrity of the Euroregion project itself. At the same time, I argued that their narratives of moral accountability were grounded not only in the language of neoliberal policy-making, but also emerged through a game of alterity that made implicit reference to the twin evils of Communist autocracy and post-Communist corruption. Indeed, Laštůvkas talk of 'rules' and Kasperek's apparent enthusiasm for the concept of 'partnership' were constructed in response to the conduct (or statements) of others. Thus, 'rules' were evoked in response to calls for greater flexibility, while 'partnership' was used to counter implicit accusations of patronage. During my conversations with Laštůvka and Kasperek, there was always a personalized or abstract other who conveniently carried the moral burden of corruption. And yet, upon deeper examination, these carefully constructed narratives of moral accountability quickly came undone. As illustrated by Kasperek's story of the mayor and his amphitheatre, neither practices of audit nor neoliberal concepts of 'partnership' provided real models for true accountability. Indeed, partnership discourse in particular appeared to reinforce, rather than to hinder, the reproduction of local elite networks. It institutionalized the relationship between Kasperek and the mayor, thus 'black-boxing' their personal and professional past, and making the success of the mayor's bid for funding (and his subsequent involvement in steering the Euroregion) appear to be a reflection of his actions, rather than his connections.

Such incidents of favoritism are hardly a new subject for scholars of Central and Eastern Europe. Since the fall of the Berlin Wall over a quarter century ago, they have struggled to explain why economic and political liberalization has not eliminated informality and economic deviance, but rather appears to have provided fertile ground for their proliferation. Scholars researching the formation of corrupt elite networks, as well as those studying the personal networks of ordinary citizens, have typically blamed fraudulent behavior on economic inefficiency, low levels of public trust, and a breakdown of the rule of law (Giordano and Hayoz 2014, Ledeneva 2013). Ethnographers of the region, in contrast, have often sought to re-embed semi-legal or illegal economic practices within the wider contest of local practices of exchange, seeking to construct culturally sensitive interpretations of action that capture a native perspective (see Sneath 2006). As such, they have often adopted moral relativism as a conscious methodological strategy, treating issues of fraud and corruption as a problem of moral economy, rather than simply the correct governance of market activity or public office. Here, I want to suggest an alternative approach that draws on neither tradition, but instead follows the arguments laid out by Whyte and Wiegratz in the opening chapter to this volume – that is, the idea that economic fraud is not a reflection of poor governance, but rather an endemic feature of a society in which neoliberal values of individualism, self-interest, and enterprise have become embedded in structures of power, public culture, and private practice alike.

As a result, I view narratives of moral accountability like those presented by Laštůvka and Kasperek not simply as narratives of self-justification that should be understood in terms of their professional culture or personal circumstances, but rather as reflecting the contours of a much wider neoliberal moral economy that has penetrated Polish society (and indeed, other societies in Central Europe and beyond). These stories without a doubt help these men negotiate their somewhat paradoxical (and morally precarious) position as both enforcers of neoliberal values and guardians of the public good, but their real value lies in what they can tell us about the ways moral economies of fraud are produced (and reproduced) by the structures of contemporary bureaucracy (and the people who inhabit it). The most important of these lessons is perhaps the fact that the development of private–public partnerships and the growth of quango culture have led to the routine conflation of the pursuit of personal gain with the production of public good, rendering instances of what Wedel calls 'greed corruption' a routine side effect of neoliberal policy-making. The purposeful blurring of state–society relations, and the marketization of the bureaucracy under the guise of fraud prevention, has remodelled bureaucratic structures in ways that not only accommodate and legitimize private interests, but also present them as public virtues. As such, it presents a serious challenge to conventional approaches to fraud that understand corrupt behavior as rooted in self-interest, and self-interest as often (though not always) conflicting with the public good. Indeed, as Laura Bear argues, it suggests that 'we can no longer assume that personal verbal promises, patronage, and private agendas are used only to capture and divert the power and resources of state institutions', but that such practices may in fact be productive of state ends (2011: 57–8).

Notes

1 A Euroregion carries no independent legislative powers. The analysed Euroregion carried out activities under the EU PHARE (pre-2004) and INTERREG III A (post-2004) programs.

2 The ethnographic material was gathered over the course of a total of six interviews with the Bogdan Kasperek and Václav Laštůvka between 2011 and 2013. In addition to these conversations, interviews were conducted with several local interest groups, regional development offices, and municipal actors involved directly or indirectly in

the Euroregion partnership. The material from these interviews is not included here, but informs the narrative presented.

3 The Fund for Microprojects taps into a funding stream for Czech-Polish cooperation allocated under the National Regional Policy Framework with means from the European Regional Development Fund (until 2004 PHARE CBC, then INTTERREG III A and INTERREG IV A).

References

Amable, B. (2011) 'Morals and politics in the ideology of neo-liberalism'. *Socio-Economic Review*, 9(1): pp. 3–30.

Bache, I. (2010) 'Partnership as an EU policy instrument: A political history'. *West European Politics*, 33(1): pp. 58–74.

Bauman, Z. (2000) *Liquid Modernity*. Cambridge: Polity Press.

Bear, Laura. (2011) 'Making a river of gold: Speculative state planning, informality, and neoliberal governance on the Hooghly'. *Focaal – Journal of Global and Historical Anthropology*, 61(3): pp. 46–60.

Buchowski, M. (2006) 'The spectre of orientalism in Europe: From exotic other to stigmatized brother'. *Anthropological Quarterly*, vol. 79(3): pp. 463–482.

Bukovansky, M. (2006) 'The hollowness of anti-corruption discourse'. *Review of International Political Economy*, 13(2): pp. 181–209.

Bratu, R. (2012) Actors, Practices and Networks of Corruption: The case of Romania's Accession to European Union Funding. PhD thesis. London School of Economics and Political Science. Available at: http://etheses.lse.ac.uk/891/1/Bratu_Actors%20 practices%20and%20networks%20of%20corruption.pdf.

Cerami, A. (2006) *Social Policy in Central and Eastern Europe. The Emergence of a New European Welfare Regime*. Berlin: Lit Verlag.

Douglas, M. (1992) *Risk and Blame: Essays in Cultural Theory*. London and New York: Routledge.

Dunn, E. (2004) *Privatizing Poland. Baby Food, Big Business, and the Remaking of Labour*. Itahaca: Cornell University Press.

Giordano, C. and N. Hayoz. (2014) *Informality in Eastern Europe: Structures, Political Cultures, and Social Practices*. Bern: Peter Lang Publishers.

Harvey, D. (2007) 'Neoliberalism as creative destruction'. *Annals of the American Academy of Political and Social Science*, vol. 610: pp. 22–44.

Herschell, T. (2011) *Borders in Post-socialist Europe: Territory, Scale, Society*. Farnham: Ashgate.

Kalb, D. (2009) 'Conversations with a Polish populist: Tracing hidden histories of globalization, class, and dispossession in postsocialism (and beyond)'. *American Ethnologist* 36(2): pp. 207–223.

Kolankiewicz, G. (1994) 'Elites in search of a political formula'. *Daedalus*, 123(3): pp. 143–157.

Lane, J.-E. (2000) *New Public Management*. London: Routledge.

Ledeneva, A. (1998) *Russia's Economy of Favours*. Cambridge: Cambridge University Press.

Ledeneva, A. (2013) *Can Russia Modernise? Sistema, Power Networks and Informal Governance*. Cambridge: Cambridge University Press.

Mackintosh, M. (1992) 'Partnership: Issues of policy and negotiation'. *Local Economy*, 7(3): pp. 210–224.

Muehlebach, A. (2012) *The Moral Neoliberal. Welfare and Citizenship in Italy*. Chicago: The University of Chicago Press.

Ost, D. (2005) *The Defeat of Solidarity: Anger and Politics in Postcommunist Europe*. Ithaca, NY: Cornell University Press.

Pine, F. (2007) 'Dangerous modernities? Innovative technologies and the unsettling of agriculture in rural Poland'. *Critique of Anthropology*, 27(2): pp. 183–201.

Rakowski, T. (2009) *Łowcy, zbieracze, praktycy niemocy*. Gdańsk: Wydawnictwo słowo/obraz terytoria.

Sampson, S. (2010) 'The anti-corruption industry: from movement to institution'. *Global Crime*, 11(2): pp. 261–278.

Sneath, D. (2006) 'Transacting and enacting: Corruption, obligation, and the use of monies in Mongolia'. *Ethnos*, 71(1), pp. 89–112.

Stenning, A. (2005) 'Where is the post-socialist working class? Working class lives in the spaces of (post) socialism'. *Sociology* 39(5): pp. 983–999.

Stenning, A., Smith, A., Rochovska, A. and Szwątek, D. (2010) *Domesticating Neoliberalism: Spaces of Economic Practice and Social Reproduction in Post-socialist Cities*. Oxford: Wiley.

Stiglitz, J. (2010) 'Moral Bankruptcy. Why are we letting Wall Street off so easily?'. *Mother Jones*, January/February. Available at: www.motherjones.com/politics/2010/01/joseph-stiglitz-wall-street-morals.

Strathern, M. (2000) *Audit Cultures. Anthropological Studies in Accountability, Ethics, and the Academy*. London: Routledge.

Swader, C. (2013) *The Capitalist Personality: Face-to-Face Sociality and Economic Change in the Post-Communist World*. London: Routledge.

Tsoukas, H. (1997) 'The tyranny of light. The temptations and the paradoxes of the information society'. *Futures*, 29(9), pp. 827–843.

Vachudova, M. (2009) 'Corruption and compliance in the EU's post-Communist members and candidates'. *JCMS: Journal of Common Market Studies*, 47(s1): pp. 43–62.

Wedel, J. (1998) *Collision and Collusion: The Strange Case of Western Aid to Eastern Europe, 1989–1998*. Basingstoke: Macmillan.

Wedel, J. (2001) 'Clans, cliques, and captured states. Rethinking "transition" in Central and Eastern Europe and the Former Soviet Union'. *Discussion Paper no. 2001/58. United Nations University*. Available at: www.econstor.eu/bitstream/10419/52751/1/333456785.pdf.

Wedel, J. (2009) *Shadow Elite: How the World's New Power Brokers Undermine Democracy, Government, and the Free Market*. New York: Basic Books.

Wedel, J. (2012) 'Rethinking corruption in an age of ambiguity'. *Annual Review of Law and Social Sciences*, 8: pp. 453–498.

Wedel, J. (2015) 'High priests and the gospel of anti-corruption', *Challenge*, 58(1): pp. 4–22.

Wiegratz, J. (2010) 'Fake capitalism? The dynamics of neoliberal restructuring and pseudo-development: The case of Uganda'. *Review of African Political Economy*, 37(124): pp. 123–137.

Wright Mills, C. (2000) *The Power Elite. Oxford*: Oxford University Press.

Zigon, J. (2010) *Making the New Post-Soviet Person: Moral Experience in Contemporary Moscow*. Leiden: Brill.

16 Fraudulent values

Materialistic bosses and the support for bribery and tax evasion

Christopher S. Swader

Introduction

Are capitalists more likely than others to justify 'immoral' acts such as bribery or tax evasion? This chapter investigates the conditions under which this is the case. While qualitative studies continue to document the nuances, mechanisms, and practices of cheating and fraud among capitalists, quantitative work that tests the presence of fraud in modern economic life across a wide range of societies is scarce. Using recent survey data representing 47 countries (World Values Survey 2005–2009 wave; 66,500 individuals), this chapter aims to rectify this gap.

I proceed by presenting two alternative views about the role of fraud within capitalism: one supposing that fraud stems from a dysfunctional form of capitalism and another supposing that fraud is intrinsic to capitalism. I then combine some ideas from these approaches by investigating both stable and variable components of capitalism in relation to fraud. Namely, I suppose that structural incentives within capitalism to maximize profit are universal, while individual support of fraud would be variable, depending on an individual's materialistic values. Following this, four ideal-types are established that combine these two dimensions in order to test their empirical interplay with fraud support. Thereafter fraud support is tested across a wide sample using logistic regression models. Results indicate that the justifiability of fraud is driven by an aspect of capitalist culture that is malleable: the adherence to materialistic values. Fraud support does not emerge only from having a key position in the capitalist class.

Fraud and the 'nature' of capitalism

Fraud is often depicted as the result of 'bad apples', lone individuals who violate a set of well-recognized, well-policed, and functional norms. Yet such labeling of white-collar crime, for instance in the media, tends to ignore the institutionally fraudulent nature of some corporations (see Benediktsson, 2010). More broadly, explaining fraud through 'bad apples' sidesteps the question of whether or not modern businesses as a whole tend to function with fraud as an underlying norm. In contrast to the 'bad apple' view, fraud can be seen as an everyday business practice, but one that is seldom caught and not systematically reported upon.

Yet even among scholars who agree that the normative structure of neoliberalism is to blame for fraud, there are contrasting ways in which fraud is linked to capitalism. For instance, fraud can be seen as either the result of an 'incomplete' or undeveloped capitalism or as a natural byproduct of a pure, unfettered capitalism. In the first case, it is argued that modern capitalism has taken a neoliberal turn that results in a more fraud-supportive normative structure. Such claims suggest that neoliberalism may be an inauthentic form of capitalism (Wiegratz, 2010; 2012). This implies that fraudulent outcomes may therefore be reduced by 'repairing' fraudulent capitalism, fixing its socio-cultural structure, for instance by rolling back neoliberalism. In the second case, in contrast, scholars claim rather that neoliberalism is not merely a corrupt mutation; rather it is the epitome of a capitalism that is exploitative and fraudulent at its core because its ethos of profit maximization tends to align practices and expectations toward its fulfillment using any means available, including fraud (Swader, 2013). If the latter case is correct, fraud cannot be reduced by 'fixing' capitalism; instead, fighting fraud implies the regulation of, rolling back of, capitalism itself.

The above discussion raises three important questions about the links between capitalism and fraud: (1) the extent to which *variations* in capitalism (see Hall and Soskice, 2001) can be linked to fraud, (2) whether there are *common* fraud-conducive features across capitalist systems as a whole, and (3) the long-term intrinsic *tendency* of capitalism toward fraud. This chapter addresses questions one and two empirically and speculates on the third question in the conclusion based on these empirical results. Regarding common features, I suggest that the structural demands on a capitalist enterprise, and thus, of those who are in charge of it, to *achieve profit through the most efficient techniques available* is a universal. However, I also suggest there is cultural variability in the *individual profit motive*. In other words, although capitalist systems may universally reward profit maximization, even when it is achieved through undetected fraudulent means, the likelihood of individuals to be personally invested in profit maximization can vary substantially. I will outline how these two features may interact in producing fraud.

Structural rewards for profit maximization: the capitalist class

A capitalism-intrinsic view of fraud assumes that the capitalist mode of economic action and production implies an inherent exploitation: extraction of surplus value of some kind. This core 'mission' is housed in a class of people, the owners of productive capacities (see Marx, 1961). If they are successful in their surplus extraction work, made possible by their ability to direct the means of production they own and manage, members of this class are rewarded with more surplus capital for their enterprises and for their personal share in such enterprise activity. In their work, they make use of techniques – the capitalist 'tricks of the trade', *which include cheating and fraud* – in order to achieve the maximum possible gain. Fraud is seen here as an additional technique of profit enhancement that will reward those who implement it successfully and disadvantage those (through denying maximum profit) who do not. Profit can almost always be further increased through various forms of covert cheating, to include deception. If fraud is indeed intrinsic to capitalism's incentive structure, then those who are 'in charge' of capitalist enterprises should be more likely to justify it.

There is indeed evidence that members of the capitalist class learn to cultivate economic success through adopting a moral flexibility (such as lying, cheating, or stealing) (Swader, 2009) that helps them to achieve it. Some examples of moral flexibility are illustrated in *The Capitalist Personality* (Swader, 2013), wherein former-Communist businessmen (from Eastern Germany, Russia, and China) talk about having transformed their former value of 'open honesty' into something called 'trader's honor' during their adaptations to capitalist culture in the post-socialist setting of the 1990s and early 2000s. Their former value of 'open honesty' prescribed telling their associates everything they knew as well as keeping their promises within the context of trade relations. This became problematic for salespersons because they also knew their own product was overpriced and the competitor's was of better quality. However, the new 'trader's honor' only demanded that you 'keep your word'. In this way, it was more functional than open honesty for business exactly because it imposed *fewer* moral restrictions. These businessmen also learned to pay their workers 'less than they were worth' in order to maximize their profits, thus dispatching (not without qualms) with another moral restriction that impeded profit maximization: that of non-exploitation. If, by 'morality', we refer to the rules of proper conduct in interactions with other people, the above changes signify a neoliberal normative system that equates to a *reduction* in the scope of morality. Individuals are still governed by norms, but these self-focused norms become less restrictive in terms of how people should conduct themselves *in relation to others*. In this way, such norms are, analytically speaking, less moral.

Therefore, theoretically the bosses of capitalist enterprises are particularly likely to have internalized the value set most useful for the 'capitalist' role, including any values of deviance that may be profitable, such as support for fraud. I use the term bosses to describe those survey respondents who are 'employers' and 'office managers', and I contrast them with professionals, manual workers/supervisors, farmers, or those in the armed forces. I label managers alongside employers as 'bosses' because both have the same institutional incentives and tools to maximize profit for their enterprise. Moreover, the inclusion of managers in the 'boss' category does not change the empirical relationship between bosses and fraud. These bosses represent the 'capitalist class' by virtue of their occupying structural roles within workplaces in economies in various stages of capitalist development. They are the ones who are most often directing the capital-enhancing activities within modern enterprises.

The individual profit motive: psychological materialism

Fraud potential is not merely a result of one's structural class position as the head of an enterprise – it is not only reducible to the capitalist 'tricks of the trade'.

Modern capitalism also has a culture that encourages personal profit, consumption, and material luxury, which are far removed from the now obsolete Weberian ascetic ethic (Swader, 2013; Veblen, 2004; Weber, 2003). This culture can be called psychological materialism, and it refers to the personal drive to acquire wealth.

In social psychological literature, such materialism has been linked to egoism, the 'Machiavellian' manipulation of other people for personal gain, relationship instability, and competitiveness (Kasser *et al.*, 2003). This 'Machiavellianism' arises because materialist values involve a mode of valuation that tends to be means-ends oriented, instrumental, with an ultimate value, *material gain*, which hierarchically arranges other values and other people, and especially the prosocial moralities governing the interaction between people, beneath it. Therefore, materialists should be more likely to have anti-social traits or to commit deviant acts in order to achieve their aims.

In comparison to the class-based, structural dimensions of capitalist involvement, being materialistic supplies an internal personal drive and temptation to commit fraud *in order to become rich*. If I am correct, support for fraud does not depend merely on one's location within the economic structure; it also depends on the extent to which a person has internalized materialistic values.

Fraud support and four ideal-types

By fraud, I refer to illegal business practices that employ deception for the purpose of financial gain. However, instead of measuring fraudulent *behavior*, I measure pro-fraudulent *attitudes*. This is because it is very difficult to get accurate self-reports of wrongdoing within an interview or survey context. I observe fraud support through a survey question asking whether respondents think 'cheating on taxes' is justifiable. This is equivalent to tax fraud. However, I also make use of a question dealing with corruption more broadly: whether respondents justify the payment of bribes. Bribery fits into the wider category of 'cheating the public', and more particularly, deceiving the public through undermining formal and transparent processes (such as allocation of procurement contracts). Moreover, both tax fraud and bribery are means for businesses to cheat in order to maximize profit. In this sense, fraud is seen as an additional, albeit illegal, technique for further maximizing profit extraction.

How might such 'fraud support' differ according to a person's 'boss' status and their values? A good way to demonstrate the interaction between class position (the 'tricks of the trade') and materialist values (the desire to become rich) is by comparing the two dimensions within a two-by-two table (see Table 16.1). This leads to four different ideal-types: 1) the traditional, intrinsic valuators, 2) the unmotivated capitalists, the 3) disempowered materialists, and 4) the 'fraudsters'. Such types give us a theoretical linchpin against which to test the effects of class position and materialistic values in different combinations. By comparing the empirical reality with these types, we can judge the adequacy of the theoretical constructs.

Table 16.1 Ideal-types combining class position and materialism

	Non-materialist	*Materialist*
Non-boss	Traditional, intrinsic valuation	Disempowered materialist
Boss	Unmotivated capitalist	Fraudster

The combination of the socialized, technical, class-based fraud knowledge possessed by bosses and the personal materialistic drive to accumulate wealth may reach its maximum potential in the materialistic boss, which I call the 'fraudster'. Materialistic bosses would theoretically have both the technical means (e.g. profit calculation, extraction techniques) and the incentive (material gain) to engage in fraud.

In comparison, bosses who are not materialistic might not be as driven to commit fraud in order to get a 'piece of the economic pie'. Such bosses can be labeled 'unmotivated capitalists'. They may be seen as professionally ineffective, as they lack the personal desire to accumulate wealth that might harmonize with their profit extraction at work.

Other people may be materialistic, but they lack the institutional support, ties, position, and technical mastery to commit fraud. They may be called 'disempowered materialists'. Since they do not occupy a businessperson position, they lack the technical knowledge and capital access to successfully accumulate profit on a large scale that could be further enhanced through fraud.

Finally, many people neither occupy positions as owners or managers nor are materialistic; these are our ideal-typical 'traditionalists'. They are neither materialistic nor have the technical know-how or access to commit fraud. Such persons could be seen as traditional, intrinsic valuators (as opposed to instrumental, profit-oriented ones).

I also aim to determine whether fraud support varies across more and less advanced capitalist societies; I control for the level of economic development by classifying societies as OECD (Organisation for Economic Co-operation and Development), post-Communist (hereafter known as 'PC'), or developing. Overall, PC societies should have the highest levels of fraud support because of 'over-adaptation' to capitalism, the pendulum effect by which they adapted to an essentialized (neoliberal) image of capitalism (Swader, 2013) amid high overall corruption and low institutionalization of rule of law. Fraud support should be weakest in developing countries in keeping with a lower degree of capitalist development, and the fraud degree in the OECD should be high but still less than in the PC states.

Testing fraud support

I use logistic regression modeling to predict individual likelihoods to highly justify fraud support (defined as the top 35 percent of justifying bribery and cheating on taxes) based on a variety of characteristics, such as the individual's boss status, materialism, income, the importance of helping others, country type, age, and gender.

The broadest set of quantitative data available, comprising the most countries, for such an analysis is the World Values Survey. I use the recent 2005–09 wave (66,500 individuals sampled from 47 countries) because it contains adequate indicators of materialistic values, professional status, and fraud support. The countries represented in this analysis are displayed with their exact sample sizes in Table 16.2.

Descriptive data for each of the variables used in the analysis can be found in Table 16.3. The following represent operationalizations of key concepts and expectations linked to them.

The *justifiability of bribery and of cheating on taxes* are chosen to represent the outcome (dependent variable) of fraud support. These were combined into one additive index. The distribution, as for most deviant beliefs and actions, is highly abnormal, with the majority (56 percent) of people ranking both items with a '0 out of 10 in justifiability. I dichotomized the index to compare those who are in the top 35 percent (2 or higher on a scale of 0 to 18) of deviance justifiability on this index with those who are not. This indicator represents a 'moderately high' level of fraud support for these two serious deviant acts. Stricter and more liberal operationalizations of fraud support have both been tested, and the results are not substantially different from this 'moderately high' version.

I measure *position in the capitalist structure, the 'boss' role*, through the respondent's profession as either an employer or white-collar manager. Employers and managers have the same mandate to implement the principles of capitalist business management. I expect such bosses to be more likely than non-bosses to justify deviant acts, such as cheating on taxes or committing bribery, because such under-the-table dealings may provide additional technical means for them to achieve success through maximizing profit.

Psychological materialism is measured through a variable asking to which extent the individual sees her/himself as someone for whom 'being rich is important'. This item was split into those who agree with this statement and those who do not. This is superior to Inglehart's 'materialism/post-materialism index' (Inglehart and Welzel, 2005) for my purpose, because that index involves questions about one's ideal society rather than about one's own individual goals. Materialism should represent the personal profit-incentive for committing fraudulent acts. Therefore the 'importance of being rich' should predict fraud support.

Boss-materialist types: I constructed four class-materialism ideal-types based on the materialism and boss dimension interplay (see again Table 16.1). I suppose that the highest fraud support is found among materialistic bosses, the 'fraudsters', and the least among non-materialistic non-bosses, the 'traditionalists'. I do not have preconceptions about the fraud support rates of the 'unmotivated capitalists' or the 'disempowered materialists', except that they should embody greater fraud support than the traditionalist.

As a representation of prosociality, I control for the *importance of helping others*. I expect it to negatively correlate with anti-social varieties of deviance,

Table 16.2 Countries and sample sizes

Country/region	*Developing*	*Country type* *post-Communist*	*OECD*
Argentina	1,002	0	0
Brazil	1,500	0	0
Burkina Faso	1,534	0	0
Cyprus	1,050	0	0
Egypt	3,051	0	0
Ethiopia	1,500	0	0
Ghana	1,534	0	0
India	2,001	0	0
Indonesia	2,015	0	0
Iraq	2,701	0	0
Jordan	1,200	0	0
Malaysia	1,201	0	0
Mali	1,534	0	0
Morocco	1,200	0	0
Rwanda	1,507	0	0
Serbia and Montenegro	1,220	0	0
South Africa	2,988	0	0
Thailand	1,534	0	0
Trinidad and Tobago	1,002	0	0
Uruguay	1,000	0	0
Zambia	1,500	0	0
Bulgaria	0	1,001	0
China	0	1,991	0
East Germany	0	1,076	0
Georgia	0	1,500	0
Hungary	0	1,007	0
Moldova	0	1,046	0
Poland	0	1,000	0
Romania	0	1,776	0
Russia	0	2,033	0
Slovenia	0	1,037	0
Ukraine	0	1,000	0
Viet Nam	0	1,495	0
Australia	0	0	1,421
Canada	0	0	2,164
Chile	0	0	1,000
Finland	0	0	1,014
France	0	0	1,001
Great Britain	0	0	1,041
Japan	0	0	1,096
Mexico	0	0	1,560
Netherlands	0	0	1,050
Norway	0	0	1,025
Sweden	0	0	1,003
Turkey	0	0	1,346
United States	0	0	1,249
West Germany	0	0	988
Total	33,774	15,962	16,958

Source: World Values Survey 1981–2014 Longitudinal Aggregate v.20150418.

because it should limit the commission of crimes that may hurt the wider society. Respondents were asked whether they consider themselves to be people for whom helping others is important. In contrast, I did not control for religiosity because the importance of helping others variable is a more direct measure of the prosociality I expect religiosity to potentially impart. In addition, 'helping others' is empirically more successful than religiosity as a negative predictor of fraud support (WVS Longitudinal Aggregate v.20150418). Typically, authors such as Inglehart and Welzel refer to this prosocial dimension as 'post-materialist' (Inglehart and Welzel, 2005), indicating a focus away from survival and more on self-expression and creativity seated in modern societies. I prefer the 'prosocial' label because it is less biased in its relationship to economic development.

Country type is measured as either *OECD, PC, or Developing* ('others' were not kept in the dataset; societies that are members of both OECD and PC categories were coded as PC). I presume that fraud support patterns may be different in societies at different stages of economic development. Research (Swader, 2013, Chapter 9) supports a hypothesis that class and materialism in PC societies should equate with the highest levels of fraud support because of over-adaptation to capitalism, and this effect should be weakest in developing countries.

A respondent's *income* is measured on a 1–10 scale. Income is a measure of economic success and thereby also of the tools, such as fraud, that may be necessary to achieve such success. Therefore, I control for it and expect it to correlate with greater fraud support.

Values research on the *gender* question shows women to be more compassionate, less competitive, and less materialistic than men (Beutel and Marini, 1995; Swader, 2013, Appendix C). In addition, women are much less likely to

Table 16.3 Descriptive statistics of key variables

	N	*Minimum*	*Maximum*	*Mean*	*Std. deviation*
Age centered at 41	80,239	–26	57	0.22	16.52
Female	80,396	0	1	0.51	0.50
Income	73,524	0	9	3.55	2.33
Helping others	70,292	0	5	3.72	1.14
Disempowered materialist (vs. traditionalist)	55,760	0	1	0.35	0.48
Ineffective capitalist (vs. traditionalist)	55,760	0	1	0.06	0.23
Fraudster (vs. traditionalist)	55,760	0	1	0.03	0.18
PC (vs. Developing)	80,493	0	1	0.20	0.40
OECD (vs. Developing)	80,493	0	1	0.28	0.45
Top 30 % fraud support	73,433	0	1	0.35	0.48

Source: World Values Survey 1981–2014 Longitudinal Aggregate v.20150418.

commit crimes. I therefore control for gender, expecting women to be less supportive of fraud.

Finally research shows that almost all forms of deviance *decline with age.* I control for age in order to take this into account, with the expectation that older respondents are less supportive of fraud.

I employ logistic regression modeling (using SPSS 22 software) to predict the likelihood of an individual having a high (top 35 percent of sample) justifiability of cheating on taxes and bribery, based on the above characteristics. I calculated four models: one analysis for all individuals pooled together and three separate analyses for individuals from OECD, PC, and developing countries in order to assess different dynamics.

Results

Bivariate analysis

When comparing various predictors directly with fraud support, without taking other variables into account, bosses have only a slightly higher degree of fraud support than non-bosses. This difference is statistically significant but quite small in scale.

Moreover, in all societies fraud support rises steeply with income only to drop off slightly within the highest income group. PC societies start with the lowest level of fraud support but have the steepest rise with income. Developing societies start off with higher fraud support, but the income-related rise is more moderate. The OECD starts with lower fraud support levels, and this rises moderately with income, but the 'taper off' in the OECD is minor compared to PC and developing societies. A similar trend is observed with psychological materialism; each step higher in materialism equates to a greater mean in fraud support until the highest levels of materialism. Fraud support diminishes slightly at the highest two degrees of materialism, although it is still much higher than among those who are not materialistic at all. Developing countries start off with higher fraud support at lower levels of materialism, but country types become indistinguishable at the higher levels of materialism.

What happens when the boss and materialism variables are combined into four ideal-types and fraud support is analyzed across them? I find that (see Table 16.4) fraudsters have the highest degree of fraud support, followed by disempowered materialists, followed by traditionalists and unmotivated capitalists, and the latter two are indistinguishable (these results are statistically significant and confirmed by ANOVA). Moreover, these results are the same whether we consider bribery support, tax evasion support, or both.

Multivariate analysis

The above bivariate analyses do not account for all relevant factors simultaneously. For instance, the income effect could be due to the fact that those with

Table 16.4 Fraud support by boss-materialism types

	%	N	Std. deviation
Traditionalist	34	30,227	.47
Disempowered materialist	42	18,794	.49
Unmotivated capitalist	34	3,094	.47
'Fraudster'	47	1,868	.50
Total	37	53,983	.48

Source: World Values Survey 1981–2014 Longitudinal Aggregate v.20150418.

higher incomes are more materialistic, and the real effect is from materialism. I can control for this within logistic regression models, which show the likelihoods of deviance support after controlling for all recognized factors.

Results of this more sophisticated analysis (see Table 16.5) demonstrate, in terms of our controls, a significant age effect across all models, whereby older age is equivalent to lower support for fraud. This is in keeping with strong findings on deviance, which recognize that deviance diminishes with age. Being female in OECD countries is also strongly linked to lower fraud support, but this effect is not found in developing or PC countries. Also higher income in our sample is strongly and directly linked to a higher support for fraud. The final control, representing the prosociality of the respondent, the importance of helping others, is very strongly linked to less fraud support, as expected. This is true of all country types.

Table 16.5 Logistic regression results: likelihood of being in the top 35 percent of justifiability of bribery and cheating on taxes

	Overall (Pooled)		*PC*		*OECD*		*Developing*	
	B	*Exp(B)*	*B*	*Exp(B)*	*B*	*Exp(B)*	*B*	*Exp(B)*
Constant	0.32	1.37	0.24	1.27	0.00	0.00	0.42	1.52
Age (centered at 41)	–0.01	0.99	–0.01	0.99	–0.01	0.99	0.00	1.00
Female (0–1)	–0.09	0.91	0.00	0.00	–0.34	0.71	0.00	0.00
Income (0–9)	0.04	1.04	0.06	1.06	0.02	1.02	0.03	1.03
Help others (0–5)	–0.25	0.78	–0.30	0.74	–0.18	0.84	–0.27	0.77
Disempowered materialists (vs. traditionalist)	0.22	1.24	0.36	1.44	0.37	1.45	0.09	1.09
Unmotivated capitalists (vs. traditionalist)	0.00	0.00	0.00	0.00	0.00	0.00	0.00	0.00
Fraudster (vs. traditionalist)	0.41	1.50	0.68	1.98	0.54	1.71	0.23	1.26
PC (vs. developing)	–0.09	0.92						
OECD (vs. developing)	–0.20	0.82						

Note: All results with a B and Exp(B) other than zero are significant at the .05 level or better.

Source: World Values Survey 1981–2014 Longitudinal Aggregate v.20150418.

Regarding this study's main explanatory variables, the class-materialism ideal-types, indeed the main hypothesis about these is supported. Being a 'fraudster' (materialistic boss) raises fraud support drastically in every sample; the likelihood for this group is nearly double that of traditionalists in PC and OECD societies, and it is 25 percent higher than for the traditionalists in developing societies. Traditionalists, as expected, have the lowest degree of fraud support.

Moreover, the materialist value set matters much more than class position ('being a boss') in all samples. Although less fraud supportive than 'fraudsters', disempowered materialists (materialists who are not bosses) are much more likely than traditionalists to support fraud in every sample. In contrast, being a boss in of itself (an 'unmotivated capitalist') has no effect. Therefore, disempowered materialists support fraud more than traditionalists, but traditionalists and unmotivated capitalists are equal in fraud support.

In terms of country type, the PC societies have a slightly exaggerated 'fraudster' effect. This is in keeping with findings (Swader, 2013) indicative of a pendulum effect of excessive moral flexibilization in some spheres in PC societies. However, the impact of materialism alone ('disempowered materialists') is equally strong in the OECD and PC countries. Overall, developing societies display much weaker boss-materialism ideal-type effects on fraud support. In other words, the materialistic-boss and fraud support link is most established within the OECD and PC countries. Finally, the OECD does have slightly lower levels of fraud support, but these country-type indicators' effects are very small compared to other factors. There is substantially more variation between individuals within country types than between country types. In other words, values matter much more than country type in predicting fraud support.

Reframing of results

A practical way to illustrate these findings is to compare the model's estimates for people of various characteristics. For instance, across country types I can predict the fraud support of (a) poor, older, non-materialistic women; with (b) male fraudsters; with (c) 'disempowered materialist' males who have other middle-range characteristics; with (d) 'unmotivated capitalist' males; with (e) prosocial male fraudsters (see Table 16.6). These results show how likely each of these subpopulations is to support fraud. They illustrate that fraud support can vary drastically, from our low estimate, of a poor, prosocial, and older woman in a developing country (18 percent) to a young, fraudster male in a PC country (84 percent). One of the more vivid results is the importance of prosocial values. They may greatly reduce the likelihood of even a young, rich, 'fraudster' male to support fraud (from 84 percent for an 'anti-social' person to 53 percent for a fully prosocial person).

Discussion

To summarize, materialistic bosses ('fraudsters') are indeed the most supportive of bribery and tax evasion. However, being a boss only enhances fraud

Table 16.6 Predicted fraud support based on logistic regression results

Type	*Percent expected to be in top fraud-support category* PC	OECD	Developing
61 year old, female, poorest, prosocial, traditionalist	18	19	27
21 year old, rich, male, antisocial, fraudster	84	72	74
41 year old, mid income, female, mid-prosociality, disempowered materialist	50	40	47
41 year old, mid income, female, mid-prosociality, unmotivated capitalist	41	32	45
21 year old, rich, male, prosocial, fraudster	53	52	42

Source: World Values Survey 1981–2014 Longitudinal Aggregate v.20150418.

justification in connection with the individual desire to become rich. In contrast, traditionalists and non-materialistic bosses ('unmotivated capitalists') have the weakest degree of fraud support. Non-boss materialists ('disempowered materialists') exhibit greater fraud support than traditionalists but less than fraudsters. Therefore, the 'class' component of capitalism activates toward fraud support only in combination with psychological materialism. This implies that a variable feature of capitalism (materialistic values) contributes the most to the support for fraud. In addition to this, fraud support is substantially offset by the prosocial values spurred by economic development processes.

In terms of overall fraud support across country types, on the surface, developing countries display the highest, PC countries have mid-range, and the OECD has the lowest fraud support. Why is this the case? There is very little difference in prosociality between countries, so this is an unlikely cause. There are differences in the size of the 'fraudster' class, but PC countries surprisingly have the fewest fraudsters, while developing countries have the most. Rather the biggest gap across country types is in materialism. Ineffective capitalists are three times more common in the OECD than in developing or PC states, and disempowered materialists are half as common in the OECD compared to other two. This means the OECD is less materialistic as a whole, which may slow the spread of fraud. There is evidence that OECD societies developed their reserve of post-materialist values (Inglehart and Welzel, 2005) in the course of, or in reaction to, economic development. These values appear to provide a counterforce to the sharper edges of capitalism. In addition, the OECD has a more substantial and functioning legal infrastructure that may better work to catch particular forms of fraud. PC states, by comparison, in adapting to an essentialized capitalism, embraced materialism wholeheartedly without establishing welfare states that may spur a value set distinct from materialism. At the same time, PC state institutions only poorly regulate fraudulent business practices.

While OECD and PC societies have slightly lower fraud support levels overall, fraud support in these countries increases substantially with materialism and the materialistic-boss status. In comparison, traditional societies have slightly higher starting levels of fraud support, but this is less affected by materialism and class position. In other words, despite the average fraud levels, the effects of the class-materialism ideal-types are strongest in PC countries, followed by the OECD, followed by developing countries. Thus fraud can be predicted by the same model despite country type. This ability of class-materialism combinations to predict fraud support in diverse societies suggests that fraud operates according to a common underlying dynamic, a background structural-cultural capitalist logic that unifies how fraud is incentivized.

Most importantly, the data make very clear that country types really do not matter that much in predicting fraud support. Individual characteristics – income, prosocial values, and the boss-materialism relationship – are far more powerful predictors.

These data do not directly represent fraudulent *behaviors*. Rather I analyzed the *justifiability* of fraud, which is something different. However, individual self-reports in surveys about actual criminal behaviors cannot be trusted, which is why fraud-support measures are used instead. Moreover, I analyze an outcome of moderately high (the top 35 percent) fraud support for the quite serious crimes of tax evasion and bribery. It is reasonable to assume that some of the individuals in this high support category are more inclined to actually commit fraud than those who are not.

A zone for further research surfaces in our gender findings. In contrast with expectations that females should have a lower degree of fraud support, after controls we have found that this holds true only in the OECD. Women are less likely to support fraud, but our model has successfully explained *why* in PC and developing countries. For instance, women are much more likely to be prosocial, which explains much of the 'female effect' on lower fraud support. However, some other unidentified gender difference remains in the OECD that makes women less likely to support fraud. This is also indicated by the fact that women in the OECD especially are much less likely to belong to the 'fraudster' ideal-type (66 percent of OECD fraudsters are men, compared to 50 percent in PC countries, and 56 percent in developing countries).

Conclusion

This chapter's empirical results now allow me to address the question of capitalism's intrinsic 'tendency' in relation to fraud. I claim that this tendency is woven into the neoliberal normative culture, because it is precisely this culture that symbolizes the 'unencumbered' core of capitalism and that at the same time promotes the activation of fraud support (through materialistic values). At the same time, a defiant response to this tendency is also revealed in the form of cultural and political movements (such as the growth of prosocial values and the state regulation of markets) that successfully resist neoliberal culture. This interplay can be seen as part of Karl Polanyi's (2001) 'double movement': the first movement is characterized by market-driven cultural disembedding, and the second movement is where social forces respond to, and against, the most destructive possibilities of economic transformation, less society be fully uprooted. In this sense, these findings highlight the simultaneous need, and possibility, for counteracting materialistic culture.

The outcome of this chapter is optimistic: the negative repercussions of one dominant aspect of modern economic culture, materialistic values, may be at least partially offset by highlighting another subordinate aspect – prosocial values – *even within the capitalist class*. Because values are malleable, these findings provide a point of intervention that could allow us to counterbalance potentially undesirable normative changes in relation to capitalism. The continuous nurturing, at the grassroots, of values – whether creativity/arts, family, spirituality, or simple leisure – that may compete with psychological materialism is one central mode of accomplishing this. The state may also play out an intentional value-policy role by fighting poverty, encouraging equality, supporting families, fostering spirituality, or promoting the arts. The resulting prosocial values may have a large impact in keeping capitalists from cheating based on their own moral prohibitions. Naturally, the above interventions assume hybrid forms of capitalism that recognize that market societies must continue to be politically regulated in the first place.

References

Benediktsson, M. O. (2010) 'The Deviant Organization and the Bad Apple CEO: Ideology and Accountability in Media Coverage of Corporate Scandals', *Social Forces*, 88 (5), pp. 2189–2216.

Beutel, A. M. and Marini, M. M. (1995) 'Gender and Values', *American Sociological Review*, 60, pp. 436–448.

Hall, P. A. and Soskice, D. (eds) (2001) *Varieties of Capitalism: The Institutional Foundations of Comparative Advantage*. Oxford: Oxford University Press.

Inglehart, R. and Welzel, C. (2005) *Modernization, Cultural Change and Democracy*. Cambridge: Cambridge University Press.

Kasser, T., Ryan, R. M., Couchman, C. E., and Sheldon, K. M. (2003) 'Materialistic Values: Their Causes and Consequences', in Kasser, T. and Kanner, A. D. (eds) *Psychology and Consumer Culture: The Struggle for a Good Life in a Materialistic World*. Washington, DC: American Psychological Association, pp. 11–28.

Marx, K. (1961) *Capital: A Critique of Political Economy*. Frederick Engels (ed.). London: Lawrence and Wishart.

Polanyi, K. (2001) *The Great Transformation*. Boston: Beacon Press.

Swader, C. S. (2009) 'Adaptation as "Selling Out"? Capitalism and the Commodification of Values in Post-Communist Russia and Eastern Germany', *Journal of International Relations and Development*, 12, pp. 387–395.

Swader, C. S. (2013) *The Capitalist Personality: Face-to-Face Sociality and Economic Change in the Post-Communist World*. New York: Routledge.

Veblen, T. (2004) *The Theory of the Leisure Class: An Economic Study of Institutions*. Whitefish, Montana: Kessinger Publishing.

Weber, M. (2003). *The Protestant Ethic and the Spirit of Capitalism*. Mineola, NY: Dover Publications.

Wiegratz, J. (2010) 'Fake Capitalism? The Dynamics of Neoliberal Moral Restructuring and Pseudo-development: The Case of Uganda', *Review of African Political Economy*, 37(124), pp. 123–137.

Wiegratz, J. (2012) 'The Neoliberal Harvest: The Proliferation and Normalization of Economic Fraud in a Market Society', in Winlow, S. and Atkinson, R. (eds) *New Directions in Crime and Deviancy*. New York: Routledge, pp. 55–70.

World Values Survey Association (1981–2014) *World Values Survey 1981-2014 Longitudinal Aggregate v.20150418*. World Values Survey Association (www.worldvaluessurvey.org). Aggregate File Producer: JDSystems, Madrid SPAIN.

17 The moral economy of neoliberal fraud

David Whyte and Jörg Wiegratz

In this conclusion we draw upon the various analyses of fraud in this book to establish a more coherent and schematic approach to locating fraud in the moral economy of neoliberalism. Before we turn to addressing some of the substantive aspects of the relationship between moral economy, fraud and neoliberalism, we offer some comments that develop our approach to 'neoliberalism' set out in the introduction to this book. Building on this approach, the chapter then outlines how a particular moral economy supports the neoliberal project generally and the production of 'fraud' specifically.

Neoliberalism as a set of fraudulent ideas

It is important to recognise that neoliberalism is not a type of social 'system' as such. Neoliberalism is an analytical category (Harrison, 2010) that we use to identify, describe and make sense of a system of sometimes interconnected and sometimes disparate, but always contradictory, truth claims about the way human societies should be structured. Crucially, what we call neoliberal ideas are always connected to the promotion of particular economic and public policies. Those policies generally promote the commodification of all forms of social provision, consumption and distribution. In this sense, neoliberalism seeks the intensification of commodified social relationships in which the social domination of finance, and more generally, capital is sought.

Neoliberalism seeks to achieve this in several important ways that break with the post-war consensus model of capitalism that dominated many of the largest economies of the Global North until the 1970s. It promotes a model of economic growth (and a respective social order) based upon: the removal of capital controls; supply-side economic policies (including tax reductions for the rich and for corporations); national economic policies fixated on wage and inflation control; the removal of collective rights for workers; the concentration of power in large corporations; and the privatization of public services. In this sense, neoliberal societies can be categorised 'simply' as societies shaped by this set of marketisation policies and related discourses, agendas and programmes that are advanced by state and capital and its 'civil society' allies.

In pursuing this model of growth – and related societal restructuring – a huge amount of government energy is corralled into assisting, cajoling and promoting its efforts (Tombs, 2015). Of course, this is not actually what neoliberal theorists say about this approach. Neoliberal rhetoric is full of platitudes about the importance of 'free' markets, 'flexible' workers and open societies. Neoliberal theorists actually say very little about the institutionalization of state–capital connections, deepening inequalities or the concentration of power. They therefore say little about neoliberalism as a concerted effort to maintain a particular social system or as a particular strategy of social domination. This is the first point to grasp about neoliberalism: the individuals and groups that promote neoliberal ideas from above selectively represent the social rationale for and impact of neoliberalism; they selectively project how neoliberalism is experienced by the majority. The following two points help illuminate this disjuncture between what neoliberalism is and what neoliberals say it is.

First, neoliberal ideas make major claims in defence of economic freedom. This claim is generally made from an anti-state and anti-collectivist position and stresses the economic freedom of individuals. Collective trade union freedoms and social rights are, from this perspective, constructed as the enemies of 'freedom'. State interventions in markets on behalf of the broader social or public interest (as well as more specific social values such as income equality) are similarly rejected as 'anti-freedom'. Second, and related, is the claim that 'freeing' the market of government interference allows business to be efficient. It has become received wisdom that providing services and selling things involves fewer 'transaction costs' when they are done by the private sector as opposed to the public sector. In other words, the costs of research and development, of managing workers or of transporting goods from factory to shop are less when the costs of these things are kept low by 'market forces'. Those claims are normative, since they seek to position neoliberal policies as being in the public interest (defined for example, in relation to competitiveness, growth, exports), making a contribution to the 'good' society and so on. Thus, neoliberal constructions of market freedom simply equate the 'public interest' with the interests of the 'market' and of the private sector (especially where business owners are assisted in the maximisation of profit rates).

Both moral arguments ignore and disguise the material realities of the moral-economic structure, and of the real costs of neoliberal capitalism. For instance, the fact that it is governments, acting on behalf of taxpayers, that pay for many of the largest costs of doing business is generally absent in public understandings of how the relationship between public and private works. Governments establish the national infrastructure. This includes road, rail and air transport systems, and telecommunications and media systems. Governments fund and subsidise education systems that provide businesses with highly trained employees. Governments provide legal and regulatory structures that enable businesses to function. More than a third of all research and development expenditure in the UK comes from government funds (Office of National Statistics, 2012). Of course, private companies play a major role in providing infrastructure, but ultimately this infrastructure is planned and put in place by governments. Although companies pay taxes, the contribution that an individual company makes to public spending is minimal when compared to the value it derives from the total public investment in transport, health and education infrastructure. Finally, the state is a major 'customer' of business (e.g. via outsourcing) and thus a source of corporate profit (Bowman *et al.*, 2015; Hildyard, 2013; Mazzucato, 2013; Whyte, 2015a).

The degree to which businesses rely on government support normally only becomes obvious in moments of crisis when governments are required to intervene and bail out vulnerable businesses or to underwrite whole markets. Most recently this process of 'bailout' occurred in the wake of the 2008 financial crash. In the UK alone, the immediate value of the bailout for the banks was £550 billion across 2008 and 2009. And this huge burden on the taxpayer continues, long after the 'emergency' bailout. In 2011 and 2012, UK government banking subsidies exceeded more than £30 billion.[1] This form of 'corporate welfare' has been clearly positioned as a matter of public rather than private interest – we are all saved when the banks are saved.

In fact, the political and moral-economic principles behind the bank bailout are operationalised in everyday politics routinely. One study has estimated that 'corporate welfare' or the value of government handouts to business (including tax benefits, the value of cheap credit made available to business, government marketing support and public procurement from the private sector) in the UK adds up to a total of £85 billon year (Chakrabortty, 2014). What we see here is one of the several key neoliberal moral constructions of the good, proper, desirable: this construction that repackages corporate welfare as public interest – as investment in British innovation, exports and growth and gains-for-all futures and so on – is reinforced time and time again by politicians across parties and is simply taken for granted by most media and think tank commentators. But this construction is never juxtaposed with that other fundamentally moral discourse of 'market freedom'. The 'corporate welfare equals public interest' claim is arguably one of the most powerful and crucial normative constructions for the advancement of the neoliberalisation of society: it promotes and legitimises the ordering of society around corporate wellbeing, especially profit making of large, dominant companies, and the advancement of a type of societal restructuring that fosters this agenda (for example, corporate tax reduction, outsourcing of state services to companies, the removal of social protection or the flexibilisation of labour markets).

In the sense that the essence of the neoliberal representation of capitalism is regularly or significantly based upon fanciful claims that are impossible to sustain or evidence, but have reached the status of 'common sense', neoliberalism is based on a series of myths that themselves are fraudulent. The idea that markets can exist in their current form *and* be autonomous, 'free' or efficient (and even 'just' in distributional terms according to liberal criteria, i.e. rewarding individual ability, effort etc.) without a very high level of intervention by states is one of the core assumptions promoted in neoliberal discourse and policy. And yet, it is entirely false and constitutes a very widespread and fraudulent set of moral claims that reap major material rewards for both political and corporate elites (Whyte,

2015b). But neoliberalism is not only based on blatant lies (i.e. misrepresentations or misrecognitions) about economic relations, processes and outcomes and related causalities (say, concerning wealth production and the respective distribution of gains and harms) but also on a number of abstractions, disguises and fetishes (see, for example: Marx and Engels, 1987; Zizek, 1989; Carrier and Miller, 1998; Hedges, 2009; Mirowski, 2013) that allow for and support the reproduction of the false narrative and claim-making about matters of 'the economy'. In short then, the representation in mainstream analysis and debates of the moral economy of neoliberalism is shaped by the operation of a number of key abstractions, disguises, fetishes and frauds that are produced and reproduced as part of the power structure underpinning 'neoliberalism'. We would therefore argue that there is a lot of work to be done to fully understand and analyse the moral-economic and moral-psychological repercussions of this central feature of neoliberal society.

The end of neoliberalism? Or the 'final' lock-in?

Values that are typically linked with neoliberalism generally advance self-interest and self-interested practice, individualism, egoism, a disposition and behaviour to maximise utility, instrumental rationality, opportunism and cunning, low other-regard and empathy, and disregard for the common good (Slater and Tonkiss, 2001; Harrison, 2005; Ferguson, 2006; Giroux, 2008; Streeck, 2009; Wiegratz, 2010). Through its moral project, neoliberal restructuring therefore targets not just the economy, but also the polity, society and culture, in its ambition to recreate capitalist market societies. As Thatcher rather chillingly observed: 'Economics are the method, but the object is to change the soul' (quoted in Harvey, 2007: 23).

Neoliberal political interventions have always sought to alter dominant ways of thinking, feeling, reasoning and acting. However, the societal repercussions of neoliberal policy and reform in terms of moral structure and moral economy remain understudied. There remains a lack of research into how neoliberalised material conditions (for instance high levels of poverty, precarity, insecurity, inequality) have affected how people feel, reason and act concerning matters of money, career, income or livelihood and related moral tensions and conflicts (Wiegratz and Cesnulyte, 2016).

That said, in the aftermath of the 2007/2008 financial 'crash' it has been widely suggested that neoliberalism is a bankrupt and dying system that has been 'proven wrong' (not least in terms of policies of 'light touch' regulation of corporations generally and the banking and finance sector in particularly) and is now losing its credibility as a prescriptive method of governance. It is further argued that post-neoliberal times have arrived in at least some parts of the world (for example, Davies, 2012; Grugel and Riggirozzi, 2012). There also seems to be some desire to leave behind and abandon neoliberalism as an analytical category (Clarke, 2008). We would contest this. The neoliberal market society project (Harrison, 2005) has not been abandoned by the rulers and elites in many countries around the world; market society is in the making *and* in operation, its repercussions are unfolding (Wiegratz, 2014).

Indeed, what Tombs (2001) called the moral capital of capital has, in many respects since 2008, become even more institutionalised in the dominant economies of the world. Thus, the moral claims that capital uses to cajole and discipline governments that seek to control the economy in particular ways – and more generally the moral dominance and near-hegemony of the logic of capitalism (see also Fisher, 2009; McGuigan, 2009; Cremin, 2011; Konings, 2015) – have not been significantly undermined in the period following 2008. Indeed, in recent years, corporations have continued to win most arguments against restrictive practices, social regulation or more stringent tax regimes. Restrictive regulation in fraud-ridden sectors tends to be implemented often only in very limited forms and after years of scandals, public outrage and activism and resulting increase of political pressure to 'do something'; banking and tax havens are good case studies in this regard. In other words, respective governments have acted as if the social and moral dominance of capitalism is something that must be nurtured and expanded rather than controlled and contained. Indeed, the dominant cultural position of the institutions in which the power of capital is realised – corporations - has in many ways remained unshaken, despite overwhelming evidence of routine corporate deception and corporate crime across all advanced capitalist states (Tombs and Whyte, 2015). This suggests, first, that key political economic actors have been able to sustain their general commitment to defend and advance neoliberal social order and its political-economic and normative apparatus. The establishment has acknowledged the public concern and debate about the moral character of todays' capitalism in light of not only fraud but also escalating inequality and environmental degradation, and has responded with (partly symbolic-populist) discourses and initiatives around responsible capitalism, prosperity for all, inclusive development, inclusive states, zero-tolerance-to-corruption and the like (Wiegratz, 2015a; see for an example Montgomerie, 2015). Second, the post-crash moral power of neoliberal capitalism suggests that some of the key normative pillars of this order – corporate welfare, materialism, individual advancement and enjoyment, social hierarchy, inequality, the primacy of the private – constitute part of the common sense and are taken-for-granted (though not necessarily loved or cherished) as necessary or as normal practice by significant sections of neoliberal society (Tombs, 2015). Yet again, capitalism has been able to reproduce to a significant extent 'its' core moral infrastructure (and regularly contained and neutralised moral competitors, e.g. critical/anti-capitalist protest movements), even in times of acute crisis.

This raises the simple but crucial question: What type of events or social dynamics will, can or could destabilise, undermine and reduce this moral capital? Full-scale economic and ecological 'collapse' in the imperial centres (as dystopian novels and movies suggest)? Large parts of the Global South 'under water'? The last man standing?

We don't want to dismiss the crucial dynamic that large-scale corporations in sectors ranging from tobacco to oil, pharmaceuticals, banking and agribusiness, are being challenged around the globe for their fraud and criminality as well as social harm, on legal, economic, social, political and cultural grounds. And this has undermined some of their legitimacy. At least temporarily (we write this is in a year that has seen the exposure of the fraud-ridden mighty VW and Deutsche Bank for instance). We would observe, however, that the political and moral power of the anti-fraud critics and activists is yet insufficient to produce a 'tipping point' (Gladwell, 2000) in the moral confrontation and moral resistance against capital. Maybe we are in a transition phase towards a new, non-liberal settlement with capital, in which the moral power of capital has been shrunk, but that kind of scenario seems rather many years than months ahead, at least for the political economies of the Global North. In any case, it seems then that the long-term and deeper-level political-economic and socio-cultural repercussions of the unfolding of the neoliberal 'project' are not behind us, but remain with us. To actually undo the various lock-ins of neoliberalism – to de-facto de-neoliberalise, to move society off the market society track, economically, socially, politically, culturally (Wiegratz, 2015c) – is a mounting task, especially given, first, the opposition of capital and its backers and beneficiaries within the state and beyond to such an undertaking, and second, the condition of human and ecological crisis that remains the likely political-economic context for this conflict-ridden process. To de-neoliberalise, including to de-neoliberalise the current structure of moral power, means to significantly change the current power arrangements of social order and domination, in short, to make powerful neoliberals 'lose' properly and sufficiently (ibid.; Whyte, 2015b).

The neoliberal moral economy

Together, the chapters in this book have taken a major step forward in understanding neoliberal morality, especially in relation to the economy. In what follows, we argue that a synthesis of the evidence and arguments developed in this book offer us a schematic way of understanding the *processes* of neoliberal moral restructuring (Wiegratz, 2010) that allow us to identify key aspects of the deeper political-economic and socio-cultural repercussions of the neoliberal project. In the analysis that follows, we focus on five distinct processes of neoliberal moralisation. First, we set out how the moral representation of markets, or the way that claims about what markets are and should be – that we have begun to discuss in this conclusion – seek to impact upon economic practice (see also Callon, 1998; Carrier and Miller, 1998). Second, we discuss how class power and inequality is mystified, or disguised by moral messages and claims about the nature of markets and social relations. Third, we identify a process we describe as a 're-moralisation of politics', in which sets of moral assertions support a reconfiguration what is possible in political terms. Fourth, we set out how neoliberal moralisation reproduces particular forms of subjectivity, disciplining and incentivising individuals into particular modes of thinking and acting. Fifth, we argue that a process of disguising and legitimising fraudulent practice is a key effect of the implementation of neoliberal policies.

The moral representations of markets

All of the chapters in the book either point directly to, or allude to, the normative constructions, evaluations and claims that stand behind economic practice. In this sense, a core of the moral economy approach taken here is that markets must be seen, represented and interpreted normatively by all economic actors – whether the actor is an overpaid corporate chief executive officer (CEO) or an underpaid employee. To study the moral economy of neoliberalism (or indeed other forms of social and economic order) is to search for key normative assumptions – the particular conceptions of the normal, proper, good, desirable and just – that underpin social practices especially around matters of economic order, process and outcome. Thus, ways of making money and accumulating individual material wealth, social surplus and social power are processes that are always morally justified in specific ways. To investigate 'neoliberal moral economy', then, means to analyse amongst others the neoliberal mode of 'talking economy', of legitimation and justification, and thus normative ordering (see Carrier, 1997; Boltanski and Thevenot, 2006) with regard to the specificities of these economic relationships, practices and outcomes (Wiegratz, 2016).

James Carrier makes a key statement on what he sees as a key shift in the representation of markets that the early liberal scholars have in common with the ideologues of the 'neoliberal' era. He argues, following Polanyi, that the separation of social and economic domains was a core part of the project of liberal scholars like Adam Smith, and argues that this tendency, which holds that the economic realm and the people in it should operate free from social constraint, is also a core organising principle in neoliberalism. It is this principle, he argues, that that creates the impetus for widespread and normalised deviance in the banking and financial sectors. There is no shortage of evidence for this in the circumstances that led to the 2007/2008 financial crisis. His analysis thus prompts a call for dissent analogous to E.P. Thompson's crowd; a demand to recouple the social and political to the economic realm and to restrict (more extensively than is currently the case) the range of social and economic practices that are permitted for normative or socio-cultural reasons (Thompson, 1971). Steve Tombs' detailed analysis of the aftermath of the 2007/2008 financial crisis reveals how a series of 'morality plays' enabled blame to be attributed in ways that have ultimately stabilised the structures and practices of financial institutions and have preserved the sanctity of the market. As various explanations moved from a vague market-centered responsibility to highly individualised rotten apple models of blame, the causes of the crisis have been repacked at a multitude of levels, but always in ways that ensure the impunity of the most powerful individuals and institutions in the financial world and thus the reproduction of the status quo and the key normative constructions including legitimacy claims in and about that sector (see also Fourcade *et al.*, 2013; Münnich, 2015a, 2015b). Those chapters show how the circulation of a series of classical liberal (Carrier) and neoliberal (Tombs) normative claims and discourses provided ideological support to the practices that led to the crisis itself, as well as to the futility of state responses and public outrage to the crisis. The (structural) power of finance has, in a de-facto sense, largely remained unrestrained; a few fines had to be paid, a handful of 'rogue professionals' face the dock while regulation that is necessary to limit the power of finance has not been implemented significantly anywhere in the 'core' economies, now some eight years after the crisis erupted (Barak, 2015; Will *et al.*, 2013).

The moral economy of masking class power

Most of the chapters in the book, whether concerned with Global North or Global South economies, provide evidence of the relationship between class power, moral economies and fraud. In uncovering a fraudulent claim that mystifies the real structure of capitalist property relations, Andrew Sayer argues for the recognition of a distinction that has fallen out of use in political economy analysis: the distinction between *earned* and *unearned* income. The former is income generated from waged and salaried employees and is income that self-employed people get for producing goods and services. It is dependent on people working in ways that contribute directly or indirectly to producing use values. The latter is income generated by those who control an already-existing asset, such as land or a building or equipment, that others lack but need or want, and who can therefore be charged for its use. Unearned income is generated not by working in ways that produce use value, but in ways that generate income regardless of whether the owner is working or not. Unearned income does not, therefore, create wealth. Rather, it is purely wealth extraction. Our inability to make such a distinction allows the process of profiting from such assets (that Sayer terms 'improperty'), without making any other social contribution, to remain unchallenged. According to Sayer, a central feature of neoliberal policies is that they encourage unearned income based upon assets and at the same time present these 'earnings' as wealth creation (see also Van Der Pijl and Yurchenko, 2015). This is an example of the moral-economic operation of neoliberalism; or the particular moralisation of economic activity, and the material relations and outcomes this advances. Respective policies as well as professional and public discourses, amongst others, are key ingredients of this neoliberal moral work of legitimisation, of rendering 'improperty' proper. It is a process that insists on the moral worth of an activity, *and* the moral worth of a social actor type (for example, the property mogul or absent landlord/property owner), that sections of the public regard as immoral (Wiegratz, 2016).

Using the case study of contemporary Kyrgyzstan, Balihar Sanghera offers an analysis of the moral economy of post-socialist capitalism. He sheds light on how the changes in the public sector (divestment, underfunding, marketisation) and economy (deindustrialisation, financialisation) bring about a society where material self-interest, trickery and wealth extraction – rather than non-material professional goals, honesty, decency and wealth creation – have become more dominant. Sanghera shows that the emerging moral economy of wealth extraction becomes legitimised via the employment of normative neoliberal theory and discourse, while the actual moral outcomes of its operation – massive wealth and power concentration and large scale harms across society, and the organisation of fraudulent capital flight – become morally disguised and normalised. At the same time, the neoliberalisation of the state brings professional cultures in sectors ranging from teachers to doctors closer to this culture, legitimising the concentration of power and heightening the financial orientation of those professions. In those accounts, the circulation of classical liberal and neoliberal normative claims provides ideological support to the class domination and the concentration of wealth in a small minority who engage in unearned wealth extraction.

It is a normative structure, both in its classical liberal (Sayer) and neoliberal (Sangera) guises that reinforce phenomenal concentrations of wealth and embed class inequalities at unprecedented levels. The case analyses show that neoliberal material and normative changes interact closely and produce the conditions for and (subsequent) realities of increased class dominance along political-economic and socio-cultural lines. In short, the normative processes described here constitute part of the removal and undermining of socio-cultural 'barriers' to anti-social practices in a mode that is compatible with and supportive of advanced capitalist society. Sangera's study highlights that one of the preconditions of this process of barrier re-movement is the increased material pressure on subaltern groups (aka the intensification of conditions of poverty and precarity in neoliberal economies). This process, it can be argued, has lowered the resistance against neoliberal moral economic change; instead, across societal subsectors we see a general and popular compliance with or endorsement of the advancement of neoliberal-capitalist culture (self-interest, materialism, philanthropy) (see also Wiegratz, 2010, Wiegratz and Cesnulyte, 2016).

Together, the contributions to the book show that the dominance of neoliberal moral culture of earning a living, including the neoliberal moral economy of fraud, is an outcome of the process of materially destabilising the prevalence of key values and norms that are in the way of self-interest, materialism and exploitation of weaker counterparts (for example non-material professional norms, or generally norms of honesty, solidarity and equality). The political-economic and socio-cultural power of moral norms and attitudes that are somewhat anti-exploitation, anti-instrumentalism, anti-gain maximisation, anti-social-harm or anti-capitalist has been diminished in many of the cases presented here. The dominance of neoliberal moral economy – and of the related fraud-conducive morals – is a significant achievement of societal restructuring, in the sense of the successful (1) crowding out of competitor morals (the norms that are dominant in less materialist and more socialist or social-democratic societies) and (2) suppressing, neutralising or responding to the core moral divisions, conflicts, crisis and counter-pressures that could have otherwise derailed the significant embedding and institutionalisation of a neoliberal moral economy that we have witnessed in so many countries in recent years. Thus the dominant class appears to have found it relatively easy to build the normative support processes it requires for the material practice of power.

The re-moralisation of politics

All of the chapters discussed so far point out in different ways the normative claims that support a particular vision and *modus operandi* of a 'market society' (and thus the labelling of particular economic practices as necessary, good and proper). Policies that are realised in the interests of a wealthy elite are consistently portrayed by governments either as inevitable (there is no alternative) or desirable (as the only means to secure investment and growth for all). In this sense, our case study-based analyses suggest that in neoliberal social formations there is no apparent conflict of interest between political and corporate elites. Instead, they have been significantly aligned or merged. We see a joint interest of capital and state in operation; powerful state actors apparently seek a strong and expansive corporate sector in order to reproduce a capitalist social order that allows for the continued and increased control and capture of resources by both, state and corporate elites. Thus, the expansion of neoliberal moral economy has rewarded elites handsomely through incomes, bonuses, fees and profits, a process indicated by obscene ratios of income inequality within advanced economic and between different economies (Sayer, 2015). The major state and government actors have been the key promoters of the neoliberal moral economy in general and the moral capital of capital in particular (see in particular chapters by Mair and Jones, Ellis, Quiroz, Christensen, Tombs and Sanghera)

In short, neoliberal moral economy has beneficiaries, allies and supporters who have advanced this moral structure and are likely to continue to defend it, or slight variations of it, as a permanent moral base into the foreseeable future (i.e. keep neoliberal society locked-in). Crucially, the material incentive structure is aligned to this purpose not just because of the material rewards for 'playing the game' (and all of us working in universities in the UK for instance are aware of a growing number of colleagues who shape status quo-preserving agendas in order to attract official funding and recognition), but also because the exposure and critique of capital and the corporate state can be costly, in personal, professional, material terms, as numerous radical industry critics, whistle-blowers and activists can testify to (see for example Hedges, 2015).

In his analysis of data derived from interviews with tax professionals, John Christensen analyses why and how fraud in the tax advice industry (illegal and near-illegal products in the area of tax avoidance, evasion, dodging etc.) has seen rapid expansion, formalisation and routinisation in the sector. This case study of fraud-as-big-business shows the role of large companies – and the business associations they dominate and state agencies they partner with – in setting the pace and character of the radicalisation of a pro-profit business culture. Furthermore, his analysis highlights how professionals justify and legitimise their products and practices – referring to constructs and discourses such as competition, efficiency, cost reduction, clients' interests, wealth creation, innovation, freedom, hostility to the state and giving priority to private interests over public interests. Perhaps most tellingly, Christensen shows how this has unfolded with the active support of government regulators and policy makers. Indeed, no matter how dodgy and anti-tax the industry has become – it remains a close and influential ally and adviser to politicians and public officials on matters of 'tax' and related legislative reform.

In these cosy state-capital set ups, state sanctions against criminal capital (and wealth creation) are generally token, and in any case, seek to encourage the growth of corporate power rather than limit it (Bernat and Whyte, 2015; Tombs, 2012; Whyte, 2016). Thus, in moral economy terms, in neoliberal society criminal and/or harm-producing capital remains the partner of the state; indeed corporate criminality is at best tacitly, and at worst explicitly, endorsed by states (Whyte, 2014). It is only when we compare the structure of impunity protecting the perpetrators of corporate frauds with those that punish the poor that we fully understand the effect of this relationship as a form of naked class power. For instance, the doubling of the UK prison population since the 1980s is largely accounted for by in custodial sentences handed down by the courts for property-related crimes (burglary, robbery, theft, handling stolen goods, fraud and forgery). To take one example of those property crimes, on average, the Crown Prosecution Service prosecutes around 40,000 burglars. By contrast the UK Serious Fraud Office (SFO) prosecutes 20 individuals per year, and around 400 individuals are prosecuted for tax offences every year. Benefit fraud, which is probably worth less than 2 per cent of all detected fraud,[2] generates around 10,000 prosecutions per year. All of this raises profound questions about the extent to which neoliberal moral economies encourage the extension of class bias in law. The neoliberal period has experiences very explicitly political strategies that secure the decriminalisation of white-collar and corporate criminal at the same time as criminal justice and prison systems are rapidly expanded in the mass criminalisation of the poor (Coleman *et al.*, 2009).

Yet why should we realistically expect the corporate state to chase down, punish and in any way restrict criminal capital (beyond, say, politically necessary levels) (Tombs and Whyte, 2010, 2013)? A core theme that we find in many of the contributions to this book is that impunity for criminal and socially harmful economic activity is not merely a side-effect of power, but plays a key role in advancing elements of neoliberal moral economy: the mix of imperatives of amongst others self-interest, careerism, materialism and profit maximisation can expand and escalate the routine use of (quasi-)illegal and ever more harmful practices. The neoliberal moral economy is largely 'blind' to rising harm levels: if hardly any tax is paid by corporations and the wealthy then so be it (until, perhaps, sufficient political pressure mounts to force some adjustments). What this means for the provision of state services to 'the poor', children, elderly and otherwise vulnerable is of less concern than ensuring that the system of accumulation maintains a steady rate of growth. This is really the key question for the form that the state regulation of markets and market actors takes: how far does the form of regulation guarantee a stable and routinised form of accumulation and growth (Whyte, 2004)? This is the core logic of regulatory policy: that controls on capital and on corporations should not interfere fundamentally with the maintenance of systems of accumulation – and indeed that they should encourage accumulation above other social goals – that encourages and institutionalises the criminal and fraudulent practices of corporations and powerful individuals (Whyte, 2014).

Paul Jones and Michael Mair's chapter shows how supermarkets in the UK increasingly play out a 'community building' role that, in other national contexts, they do not. Their expansion into communities (especially poorer communities) advances the power of supermarkets and facilitates the growth of predatory and parasitical moral economies vis-à-vis suppliers, workers, customers and tax payers. Supermarket growth constitutes a particularly effective anti-politics and anti-morality machine. This machine is itself based on the deception that corporate agendas and practices are not political, that corporate dominance over workers and communities is inevitable and even desirable, and that this dominance is a matter of economy (efficiency, growth, jobs) not of social order and power. This machinery works effectively to 'submerge' political decisions and priorities, obscuring their status as moral and political matters that could be open to collective deliberation, critique and struggle. This process is clearly summed up in their analysis of the proposed scrapping of the tax credit regime. The effect of this policy will be to undermine social welfare as a collective matter, thus forcing responsibility for the 'safeguarding' of the welfare of employees into employers' hands. In this scenario, corporations assume moral responsibility for workers, not governments. It is here that a new moral economy emerges in which workers are not to be guaranteed protection against exploitation. Jones and Mair's contribution reflects a theme across several of our analyses: that the state (and dominant political-economic logics and imperatives typically prevalent in neoliberal society) open and set up communities for increased domination, exploitation and dispossession by capital in general, and fraudsters, parasites and squeezers in particular (from the UK to Kyrgyzstan, South Africa and Benin). All of the chapters here show how states have played a key role in the re-moralisation of politics along neoliberal lines. This process has unfolded to enable for instance large oligopolies to gain near-complete control of two disparate but crucial public functions: the production and distribution of food, and the design of corporate tax regimes. In those contexts, local and national political practices draw upon neoliberal normative rationales and precipitate policies that fundamentally change the moral structure of those societies. It is to the process of changing the moral structure of those societies that the chapter now turns.

The production of neoliberal subjects

Changing the moral structure of a given society requires an attempt to change the values and attitudes of individuals. By this we mean that neoliberal policies, programmes and discourses have an impact upon the way that individuals construct and understand their own identities, attitudes, roles, values and functions as economic (and more broadly social) actors; capitalist systems of social organisation construct the socio-economic conditions through which people are able to function as employees, entrepreneurs, consumers, investors and so on, and structure their subjectivities, as well as the norms that they are materially and socially encouraged to adopt in order to fit into their economic function.

Steve Hall and Georgios Antonopoulos uncover how a specific type of 'illegal marketer' – the entrepreneur operating in the legal market economy who has become involved in illegal activities related to the legitimate business – is an inevitable product of the current period of economic crisis. They argue that the strengthening and reproduction of neoliberal hegemony does not require an overall shift in core societal values but simply an increased acceptance of the logic and culture of competition that is a fundamental, core, value of capitalism (Coleman, 1987). Through a case study of a chocolate maker situated on a large island in southern Greece they show how markets are able to give a false impression of moral regulation (one that is characterised by apparently benign self-interest and produces low levels of fraud) when times are sufficiently prosperous for the majority of traders to be profitably selling things to each other (echoing Hirschman's notion of 'doux-commerce'). In times of hardship, the system's supposed moral core is exposed as a myth. Thus, Hall and Antonopoulos argue, the 'new' and relatively more brutal norms that seem to prevail in the neoliberal era can be used to justify particular practices ideologically, but that initial drives and encouragement towards such actions are pre-moral and are located in a more fundamental set of subjectivities that are shaped by the imperatives of economic survival. In this sense, Hall and Antonopoulos' argument deviates from our general perspective: they argue that the relationship between 'morality' and capitalism is shaped by neoliberalism's specific mode of stimulation, rather than its bid for ideological hegemony.

In her analysis of a study of justice workers, members of the military and police officers in Lubumbashi, Democratic Republic of Congo, Maritza Felices-Luna finds a synergy between the values and reasoning underpinning corruption and the moral claims made by proponents of neoliberalism in state, private sector and donor sections. She identifies three 'moral orders' in which this synergy manifests itself and acts to promote particular forms of economic practice, to create new financial subjects and ultimately legitimise a predatory economy based on appropriation through dispossession. Crucially, those moral orders offer their proponents a way of legitimately challenging Western anti-corruption initiatives as hypocritical, but in the end they have the same effect: to promote neoliberal structural adjustment. Thus, even where there is an apparent normative conflict between the subjective understandings of the world that justify fraud and corruption, and those that promote anti-corruption policies, they combine to maintain the same socio-economic conditions that promote corruption. The moral orders that she identifies in her respondents are therefore consistent with international structural adjustment policies (see our discussion in the introduction to this book).

Across those chapters, we find a consistency in the relationship between the structural imperatives of capitalist social orders that (particularly in times of crisis and scarcity) enables fraudulent and corrupt practices to be incorporated into the moral worlds of public servants and small business people alike. In so far as this precipitates some change in social and cultural practice (if not the material basis of the social order), we might call this a process of re-moralising the individual. And it is this process that is revealed, amongst others, in some complexity by Erik Bähre's case study of the insurance industry in post-apartheid South Africa. Bähre shows that the prevalent debate in the country about the (im-)morality of the industry has a race and class specific character: white, middle-class clients of insurances are concerned with matters of fraud, corruption, illegality and profit orientation in the industry, while black, poor clients are especially concerned with the disruptive effect of the spread of insurance industry into poor communities on personal relationships. His study also unveils a concern in the latter communities, of anti-social, egoistic and competitive values at the heart of this industry; a moral concern with the idea that people can materially gain from a fellow human being's misfortune, for example get the life insurance pay-off when a neighbour or family member has died (without the latter knowing and/or agreeing to take out an insurance on her/his life). It is a concern with the socio-cultural impact of (1) the 'hidden' structure of material interests and gain-making in capitalist society; (2) a for-profit, abstract, expansive market for human suffering such as illness or death that extends into communities and families (also Zelizer, 1979); and (3) an economic system that materially rewards those that can (in a quite instrumental fashion) identify, deepen and exploit the vulnerabilities of others (also Wiegratz, 2016).

The moral neutralisation of fraudulent practice

We began this thematic review of the chapters in the book as a means of unveiling the process of neoliberal moralisation. And our starting point was that all of the chapters in the book either point directly to, or allude to, the moral views and claims that stand behind *fraudulent* economic practice; that the moral economies identified and studied here encourage, permit and reproduce fraudulent practice. Indeed, we argue that the promotion of individualised capitalist norms – especially in the neoliberal period – have led to the proliferation of fraudulent practices. Some profound questions about the anti-social and fraudulent character of capitalist market societies are therefore raised by the chapters here. The development of fraudulent cultures and practices as part and parcel of normal economic activity in a given locality or sector is especially clear in the chapters we turn to discuss now.

In his study of payment protection insurance (PPI) frauds in the UK in the 2000s, David Ellis uncovers an irresolvable contradiction: in dealing with evidence of routine and pervasive fraud – practices that were produced ostensibly from policies that sought to improve market competitiveness – state regulators had to argue that tough action was needed to enhance the 'competitiveness of markets'. Hence, the fraudulent rhetoric of contemporary capitalism itself can be found as a rhetorical support to both the causal factors that underpinned those frauds and their cure. For Ellis, the neoliberal state played a key role in the development of a moral economy that sought to 'responsibilise' subjects as financialised citizens, even when this pushed them into a position in which their victimisation by fraudulent corporations is more or less inevitable. In other words, Ellis reveals an intimate connection between the re-moralisation of politics and the production of neoliberal subjects in ways that make large-scale frauds structurally inevitable. More generally, elites promote ideas around individual aspiration, ambition, growth and expansion and thereby contribute to individual actors taking on and investing in often 'impossible' schemes (see also the chapter by Quiroz). This quick-and-high-growth-is-good mantra that shapes many organisations, communities, households and individuals in neoliberal society is, our analyses show, conducive to fraud.

Although he is studying a very different context, Matias Dewey's research, on the ways in which the state promotes informality and illegality in Argentina's sweatshop industry reveals a very similar connection. The state-implemented 'shadow policy', as Dewey calls it, effectively suspends law enforcement in order to encourage particular forms of (illegal) production and trade-related illegalities ranging from counterfeiting to informal employment, sweatshops, robbery and fraud. His analysis shows that illegal state practices – an informal money collection or taxation system run for years by the police to 'protect' illicit textile markets – are in various ways beneficial for a range of actors including local officials, state administrations at the provincial and municipal level, businesses and workers and, thus, the reproduction of a capitalist social order: after all, this illegality-condoning structure secures competitiveness, growth, jobs, income, consumption, taxes, state legitimacy and election gains in tough times and therefore helps mediate global economic pressures and crises at local level. Large-scale illegal markets have thus become integral to local economic, political and social structures (and thus the reproduction of the capitalist state and economy). Chris Holden's analysis of the role of tobacco companies in smuggling and tax evasion similarly reveals the routine legitimation of *corporate* activities in unambiguously illegal markets. In his case, tobacco companies operate within a set of moral understandings of their business that permits explicitly illegal behaviour and empowers executives to publically defend their unambiguously illegal practices. Indeed, it is the material conditions that we find in the industry – a fiercely competitive market dominated by a small number of very powerful producers – that makes fraud and tax evasion inevitable. Indeed, this behaviour, he argues, is not unique to the tobacco industry, but is entirely consistent with the broader moral economy of the corporation, especially in the neoliberal period.

Sitna Quiroz's study of the development of a major Ponzi scheme in Benin shows how the moral economy of fraud is embedded in and co-constituted by a number of social relations, principles and imperatives from across relevant economic, religious and political spheres that in both their form and interaction are shaped by, amongst others, neoliberal reform. This analysis highlights precisely how neoliberalism produces social dynamics that require expansive economic activity – intense investment, organisational growth and so on – in order to act out its prevailing logics. Fraud in this context became not only inevitable but 'necessary' in order to reproduce and advance these growing organisations (see also Spiegel, 2015 for data about similar dynamics in the German context). Quiroz also shows that it is not 'greed' but a series of moral and social discourses (for example the pursuit of prosperity and a good life for one's family), obligations and expectations as well as religious imperatives that legitimise the need for and drive practices of money investment and redistribution. In all of this, the role of the state and political elites, including international financial insitiutions, is crucial in shaping the conditions in which particular subjectivities are created to enable fraudulent activities to flourish.

Neoliberal reform has reformed the state and related discourses and practices in the name of making the public sector more market-like, efficient, transparent and accountable, as well as open to the interests and concerns of both, private sector and civil society. Public–private partnerships (PPPs) and audit programmes are two of the formats being used in this context to officially advance this sort of agenda. Nicolette Makovicky's analysis of a Polish-Czech PPP programme funded by the European Union shows that the discourse and practice of a 'partnership' between public and private entities is de-facto a legitimisation vehicle (and window-dressing) for a continuation and reinforcement of a (often pre-existing) cosy set up of elite-level give-and-take relationships and deals. The construct of 'partnership' now allows a range of bureaucratic, political and economic actors (e.g. consultants, experts, mayors) to claim they and the networks they set up and control are working in the interest of the public good when in fact they chiefly pursue or support self-interested agendas. Furthermore, those 'partnerships', set up as a neoliberal tool set for accountability, turn out to (re-)produce and institutionalise de-facto opaque inter-institutional links that however have the outward appearance of transparency. The partnership discourse is in Makovicky's words 'black-boxing'; it conceals personal connections and power relationships, and disguises related private interests as major drivers of partnership funding decision (as opposed to mere public good interests and respective project worthiness). The 'beauty' of this neoliberal moral construction is that our prototype PPP champion can carry out (largely) self-interested action but claim to produce and advance public goods and pro-social values (in this case, cross-border cooperation). This is because in a neoliberal market society the notion of public good is to a significant degree aligned (via discourse etc.) with the self-interest of (liberally minded) 'entrepreneurs' and agents who define the realm of the public good and thus shape public culture, discourse and practice in line with a narrow set of private interests. Marketised bureaucracies, as Makovicky shows, thus accommodate and legitimise private interest and present them as public virtue.

Fraud as socially constituted

That said, the chapters in this book provide ample evidence that the commonly reproduced claim that fraud is simply a product of greed (and thus a result of the actions a few 'bad' individuals) is false and misleading and another powerful neoliberal myth. We have significant evidence across the book that fraud is socially constituted: an outcome of mainstream political, social, economic and cultural structures, relations and processes. Fraud then is a product of a particular social order not of individual's irrationalities, inhumanities, miscalculations and the likes. Fraud is driven and underpinned by – thus, again, a product of – a mix of political, economic, social, cultural logics and imperatives. Commentators and scholars that single out 'greed' as an explanation for fraud, and economic crisis more generally, misconceive the empirical phenomenon in question (Wiegratz, 2015b).

Moreover, Quiroz and Dewey amongst others show that fraud is not always or necessarily anti-social and destructive, but, to the contrary, also can in various ways be socially productive, i.e. fraud can help reproduce capitalist social order and ensure growth, jobs and tax incomes (at least for a certain period of time). Fraud, yet again, functions as a 'necessary' part of current capitalist order, an order that requires and desires ever more expansion, surplus and material success (both personal and organisational) to 'stabilise' and reproduce itself, however temporarily (see on related matters Neckel, 2008; Goda and Lysandrou, 2014). It can be argued retrospectively that without corporate fraud and criminality the rapid market expansion in the neoliberal 1990s and 2000s would have slowed down in major industry ranging from banking to properties, food, oil and car production (with telling cases from the US subprime mortgage expansion to VW cars sales) with respective repercussions for incomes, bonuses, profits, shareholder payments and taxes. Judging by their actions, honesty, propriety and decency are bad for competitiveness, growth and wealth (and thus power), as many of our captains of industry and democracy seem to have concluded for years during the height of neoliberalism (see for example Taibbi, 2010; Will *et al.*, 2013).

Fraud then, we can argue, was needed to-date to satiate neoliberalised subjectivities including material ambitions, anxieties and expectations as well as the organisational imperatives of various actors in competitive capitalist order, in both the economy and the state. In short, fraud – and its corresponding moral disguises and fetishes – helped to keep the show on the road (despite occasional 'scandals' and disasters). Fraud in the capitalist societies studied here, then, is both at the same time: pro-social and anti-social, socially harmful and socially productive. It produces losers and winners. Actors in the top echelon of society that benefit directly and indirectly from the proceeds of fraud (and generally socially harmful corporate practice) use the material gains to defend and reproduce neoliberal society and thus keep market society on track.

Uniquely, Chris Swader shows the possibility and usefulness of using quantitative data to assess the likelihoods of the 'winners' to engage in fraudulent practice. His examination of a large set of quantitative data from the World Values Survey indicates that the personal desire to acquire wealth – what Swader terms 'psychological materialism' – can make people more fraudulent, especially if given the opportunity. The data reveal that owners and managers of companies who have internalised materialistic values are most likely to consider fraud as a technique of profit maximisation. Actor types that are less interested in material riches and more inclined to prioritise pro-social values are less likely to justify fraud. The crucial message of Swader's analysis of the relevance of the values dimension in matters of fraud is that the neoliberal cultural emphasis on individual materialism, achievement and advancement – coupled with what Swader calls enhanced moral flexibilisation – has promoted a value system that is prone to fraud. The repercussions of this embedding and/or deepening of a materialistic culture are likely to haunt many neoliberal societies for foreseeable future, in both Global North and Global South.

Conclusion

The evidence assembled in this book leaves us in no doubt that the way that norms and values develop and change in a given society is a *political* matter. Norms and values are part of the panoply of class domination; conflicts over norms and values are part of the class antagonisms and struggles that shape capitalist society (Sayer, 2005). Morals matter in terms of political economy. Moral claims and assertions are always present in bids for 'common sense' on all kind of issues related to economic activity, not least the production of fraud.

All of the studies published here show that capitalist states are accomplices to criminal and fraudulent capital. In political, economic and socio-cultural terms, fraud then is the product of a cynical state–corporate relationship. Anti-fraud initiatives and movements for a moral move in opposition to neoliberal principles and strategies therefore need to face up to the structural tendency within the current neoliberal-capitalist state and society to produce pro-fraud moral economies.

Of course, as we stress in this conclusion, and in the Chapter 1 of this book, none of this is new or unique to the neoliberal period. Indeed, the coterminous development of capitalist surplus accumulation and rampant fraud has its high-points throughout history, from the corporate corruption that was rife in the mid-colonial period, to the late nineteenth century of the US robber barrons and the rise of white-collar fraud in European banking, and then to the rise to dominance in US cities of a troika of legitimate capital, organised crime syndicates and corrupt city officials in the mid-twentieth century (Pearce, 1976; Whyte, 2009). Fraud has been a core feature at key periods in the in the long history of capitalism. Just as each of those periods has required distinctive analysis and explanation, so the apparently intensifying levels of fraud in the contemporary period require our attention and analysis. In many ways, the contradictions that capitalism reproduces in the current period bring with them a more demanding and difficult challenge.

To be against corporate fraud in current times, we argue, means to be against neoliberal moral economy and its corresponding political economy. To combat fraud in any serious sense means also combatting the moral supremacy of capital. In today's world this means, amongst other things, strengthening cultural and political-economic resistance to neoliberal politics. The current neoliberal moral economy, we have shown, is an outcome of a particular form of political and economic domination; the question of its demise is therefore linked to the question of this specific dominance. Thus, opposition – given current trends in the core states – will likely be monitored, if not made illegal at some point.

Those observations, for us, raise the following key questions: Who of the principle actors in neoliberal market society are decisively standing against corporate fraud and harm? Who actually fights for a shift in moral order, against pro-status quo capital and the state? Who is willing to endorse the material consequences of a radical de-neoliberalisation (including the lower incomes, bonuses etc. for current middle- and high-earners that are likely outcomes of closing down on the channels of easy, quick, dodgy profits for capital)? Who is prepared to pursue the measures that would precipitate a serious moral economy of anti-fraud?

The data assembled in this book at least suggest that in many countries neither state institutions and governments nor the institutions of capital can currently be trusted to take seriously and mount a meaningful challenge to the neoliberal moral economy of fraud.

Debates about the future sustainability, and indeed viability, of capitalist societies, neoliberal or otherwise, are intensifying in a range of contexts across the globe. Increasingly, we see not just the open expression of concerns about the political-economic but also the cultural aspects of the crisis of contemporary capitalism; concerns that are generally not specific to the current era alone but have occupied capitalist societies for a very long time, and have not simply preoccupied academics, but have been a theme in popular commentary and in literature (for example Brecht *et al.*, 1979, 1991; Terkel, 2001, 2004; Dickstein, 2009). Generations before us have articulated the need for a challenge to processes of commodification, marketisation and class domination; often with overall little effect, especially in the core countries.

In other words, the cultural shift desired by sections of the polity has proven very difficult to achieve in any meaningful sense. In these times, a cultural shift away from market society – including a de-neoliberalisation of our contemporary moral-economic structure – is, without question, a highly challenging undertaking, not least since anti-status quo cultural change goes to and challenges the core of politics and the social order. Many commentators on the crisis and the way forward have underplayed the significance of the political-economic and moral-economic stalemate. In short, they pay too little attention to the extent and character of the 'lock-in' of capitalist logics in (advanced) market societies. Thus, a number of post-crash debate entries suggest implicitly or explicitly a 'return' to a pro-social compromise with capital, aka a return to the 'golden age' of post-World War II Western capitalism with 'embedded capitalism', a welfare state, more tight regulatory arrangements and so on. In other words, what is envisaged is a future of a responsible, ethical, civic capitalism (see for example Hay and Payne, 2015). We are sceptical that given current turbulences and trends in the global political economy – and an in many countries ever more authoritarian, undemocratic, violent neoliberalism (Crouch, 2004; Bruff, 2014; Evans and Giroux, 2015; Giroux, 2015; Springer, 2015) – such an easy and linear 'way out' can be negotiated with capital. The history of *significantly* and lastingly 'taming' the political economy but especially the culture of capitalism in the core countries (and beyond) suggests pessimism not optimism in this regard; and the history of fraud (and its cultural-economic drivers) in capitalism is a case in point.

This scepticism or sobering realism concerning the enormity of 'the problem' can however shape our awareness and understanding of the size and type of analytical and political tasks and allow us to pay more attention to the drivers, characteristics and repercussions of capitalist moral economy, its enduring power (and political importance for system reproduction) and its vulnerabilities (in other words, the most fruitful points of attack).

We seek in this book to play a small part in identifying the vulnerabilities of contemporary capitalism and expand our understanding of the interaction between political economy and moral economy. But we know that an intellectual challenge to contemporary capitalism needs more than simply critique and understanding. Increasingly, we need to engage in work that supports cultural resistance and localised attempts of people to 'free' their community or society from the cultural forces of contemporary capitalism. The task for a new generation of intellectual workers will be to develop support for efforts in which our societies can be genuinely de-neoliberalised, however small or big in terms of scale. It is only by working through workable and practical challenges to capital that we will find the possibilities and preconditions for humans to co-exist in a way that differs from the market society 'script'. The study of efforts to build alternatives – and there is no shortage of the emergence of such examples across the globe – or how communities have achieved that change, the nature of the change, and what sort of moral economies they produce in their 'new' setting, is going to be a vital ingredient in refuelling the political and analytical energy to expand our intellectual horizons.

If we take one message that emerges collectively from the chapters in this book it is not merely that capitalism's morality can be socially destructive, but that there is no shortage of critique of the dominant moral economy. Yet, despite the fraudulent and socially destructive practices that this moral economy perpetuates, pro-social morals continue to coexist alongside other moral values, also in market societies. It remains to be seen how the current crisis will ultimately affect this clash of moral systems. But whatever the future holds, the various norms that shape what is acceptable and unacceptable practice in the economy are likely to continuously change and be contested. If one thing is certain it is that the prevailing norms are too socially important to be left to the morality politics of financiers, politicians and the business-owning class.

Notes

1 See the NEF report online at: www.neweconomics.org/blog/entry/37.7bn-reward-for-britains-biggest-banks.

2 Analysis derived from National Fraud Authority estimates, available online at: www.gov.uk/government/uploads/system/uploads/attachment_data/file/118530/annual-fraud-indicator-2012.pdf.

References

Barak, G. (2015) Introduction: on the invisibility and neutralization of the crimes of the powerful and their victims, in Barak, G. (ed.) *The Routledge International Handbook of the Crimes of the Powerful*, London: Routledge.

Bernat, I. and Whyte, D. (2015) Entendiendo Los OríGenes Del Crimen Estatal-Corporativo: un análisis de los desastres del Prestige y Morecambe bay, *Revista Critica Penal y Poder*, 9, September: 255–278.

Boltanski, L. and Thévenot, L. (2006) *On Justification. The Economies of Worth*, Princeton, Princeton University Press.

Bowman, A., Ertürk, I., Folkman, P., Froud, J., Haslam, C., Johal, S., Leaver, A., Moran, M., Tsitsianis, N. and Williams, K. (2015) *What a Waste: Outsourcing and how it goes wrong*, Manchester: Manchester University Press.

Brecht, B., Willett, J. and Manheim, R. (1979) *Collected Plays Vol 2: The Threepenny Opera (Methuen Modern Plays)*, Methuen Drama.

Brecht, B., Willett, J. and Manheim, R. (1991) *Saint Joan of the Stockyards (Methuen Modern Plays)*, Methuen Drama.

Bruff, I. (2014) The rise of authoritarian neoliberalism, *Rethinking Marxism*, 26(1): 113–129.

Callon, M. (1998) Introduction: The embeddedness of economic markets in economics, in Callon, M. (ed.) *The Laws of the Markets*, Oxford: Blackwell.

Carrier, J.G. (1997) Introduction, in Carrier, J (ed.) *Meanings of the market: The Free Market in Western Culture*, Oxford: Berg.

Carrier, J.G. and Miller, D. (eds) (1998) *Virtualism: A New Political Economy*, Oxford: Berg.

Chakrabortty, A. (2014) Cut benefits? Yes, let's start with our £85bn corporate welfare handout, *The Guardian*, 6 October, available at: www.theguardian.com/commentisfree/2014/oct/06/benefits-corporate-welfare-research-public-money-businesses.

Clarke, J. (2008) 'Living with/in and without neo-liberalism', *Focaal*, 51: 135–147.

Coleman, J. (1987) Toward an integrated theory of white-collar crime, *American Journal of Sociology*, 93(2): 406–439.

Coleman, R., Sim, J., Tombs, S. and Whyte, D. (2009) 'Introduction', in Coleman, R., Sim, J., Tombs, S. and Whyte, D. (eds) *State, Crime, Power*, London: Sage.

Cremin, C. (2011) *Capitalism's New Clothes: Enterprise, Ethics and Enjoyment in Times of Crisis*, London: Pluto Press.

Crouch, C. (2004) *Post Democracy*, Cambridge: Polity.

Davies, W. (2012) The emerging neocommunitarianism, *The Political Quarterly*, 83(4): 767–776.

Dickstein, M. (2009) *Dancing in the Dark: A Cultural History of the Great Depression*, New York: Norton.

Evans. B. and H.A. Giroux (2015) *Disposable Futures: The Seduction of Violence in the Age of Spectacle*, San Francisco: City Lights Books.

Ferguson, J. (2006) *Global Shadows*, Durham: Durham University Press.

Fisher, M. (2009) *Capitalism Realism – Is there no alternative?*, Hants: O Books.

Fourcade, M., P. Steiner, W. Streeck and Woll, C. (2013) Moral categories in the financial crisis, *Discussion Forum with Socio-Economic Review*, 11(3): 601–627,

Gladwell, M. (2000) *The Tipping Point: How Little Things Can Make a Big Difference*, Boston: Little, Brown and Company.

Giroux, H. (2008) *Against the Terror of Neoliberalism*, Boulder: Paradigm.

Giroux, H.A. (2015) *Dangerous Thinking in the Age of the New Authoritarianism*, London: Routledge.

Goda, T. and P. Lysandrou (2014) The contribution of wealth concentration to the subprime crisis: a quantitative estimation, *Camb. J. Econ*, 38(2): 301–327.

Grugel, J. and Riggirozzi, P. (2012) Post-neoliberalism in Latin America: rebuilding and reclaiming the state after crisis, *Development and Change*, 42(1): 1–21.

Hay, C. and Payne, A. (2015) *Civic Capitalism*, London: Polity

Harrison, G. (2005) Economic faith, social project, and a misreading of African society: the travails of neoliberalism in Africa, *Third World Quarterly*, 26(8): 1303–1320.

Harrison, G. (2010) Practices of intervention: repertoires, habits, and conduct in neoliberal Africa, *Journal of Intervention and Statebuilding*, 4(4): 433–452.

Harvey, D. (2007) *A Brief History of Neoliberalism*, London: Oxford University Press.

Hedges, C. (2009) *Empire of Illusion: The End of Literacy and the Triumph of Spectacle*, New York: Nation Books.

Hedges, C. (2015) *Wages of Rebellion: The Moral Imperative of Revolt*, New York: Nation Books.

Hildyard, L. (2013) Huge executive salaries are vital to UK competitiveness: Mythbusters, London: NEF and High Pay Centre, available at: http://b.3cdn.net/nefoundation/7718a56aff19fffa76_4em6beezp.pdf.

Konings, M. (2015) *The Emotional Logic of Capitalism*, Stanford: Stanford University Press.

Marx, K. and Engels, F. (1998) *The German Ideology: Introduction to a Critique of Political Economy*, London: Lawrence and Wishart.

Mazzucato, M. (2013) *The Entrepreneurial State – Debunking Public vs. Private Sector Myths*, London: Anthem Press.

McGuian, J. (2009) *Cool Capitalism*, London: Pluto.

Mirowski, P. (2013) *Never Let a Serious Crisis Go to Waste: How Neoliberalism Survived the Financial Meltdown*, London: Verso.

Montgomerie, T. (2015) *Prosperity for All*, London: Legatum Institute.

Münnich, S. (2015a) Readjusting imagined markets. Morality and institutional resilience in the German and British bank bailout of 2008, *Socioecon Rev*, S. mwv014.

Münnich, S. (2015b) Thieves, fools, fraudsters, and gamblers? The ambivalence of moral criticism in the credit crunch of 2008, *European Journal of Sociology*, 56(1), 93–118.

Neckel. S. (2008) *Flucht nach vorn - Die Erfolgskultur der Marktgesellschaft*, Frankfurt/Main: Campus.

Office of National Statistics (2012) *UK Gross Domestic Expenditure on Research and Development*, London: ONS.

Pearce, F. (1976) *The Crimes of the Powerful*, London: Pluto.

Sayer, A. (2005) *The Moral Significance of Class*, Cambridge: Cambridge University Press.

Sayer, A. (2015) *Why We Can't Afford the Rich*, Bristol: Policy Press.

Slater, D. and Tonkiss, F. (2001) *Market Society: Markets and Modern Social Theory*, Cambridge: Polity Press.

Spiegel (2015) Unternehmensberater-Umfrage: Foulspiel gehört in Firmen immer häufiger zum Alltag, available at: www.spiegel.de/wirtschaft/unternehmen/unternehmen-foulspiel-gehoert-immer-haeufiger-zum-alltag-a-1065876.html.

Springer, S. (2015) *Violent Neoliberalism: Development, Discourse, and Dispossession in Cambodia*, Basingstoke: Palgrave.

Streeck, W. (2007) Wirtschaft und Moral: Facetten eines unvermeidlichen Themas, in Streeck, W. and Beckert, J. (eds) *Moralische Voraussetzungen und Grenzen wirtschaftlichen Handelns*, Forschungsbericht aus dem MPIfG 3. Cologne: Max Planck Institute for the Study of Societies.

Streeck, W. (2009) Institutions in history: bringing capitalism back in, in Morgan, G. *et al.*

(eds) *The Oxford Handbook of Comparative Institutional Analysis*, Oxford: Oxford University Press.

Taibbi, M. (2010) *Griftopia: A Story of Bankers, Politicians, and the Most Audacious Power Grab in American History*, New York: Spiegel & Grau.

Terkel, S. (2001 [1970]) *Hard Times: An Oral History of the Great Depression*, New York: The New Press.

Terkel, S. (2004 [1972]) *Working: People Talk About What They Do All Day and How They Feel About It*, New York: The New Press.

Thompson, E. (1971) The moral economy of the English crowd in the eighteenth century, *Past and Present*, 50: 76–136.

Tombs, S. (2001) Thinking about white-collar crime, in Lindgren, S. (ed.) (2001) *White Collar Crime Research. Old Views and Future Potentials*, BRA-report 2001:1, Stockholm: The National Council for Crime Prevention.

Tombs, S (2012) State-corporate symbiosis in the production of crime and harm, *State Crime*, 1(2): 170 – 195.

Tombs, S. (2015) *Social Protection After the Crisis: Regulation Without Enforcement*, Bristol: Policy Press.

Tombs, S. and Whyte, D. (2009) The state and corporate crime, in R. Coleman, J. Sim, S. Tombs and D. Whyte (eds) *State, Crime, Power*, London: Sage.

Tombs, S. and Whyte, D. (2010) *Regulatory Surrender: Death, Injury and the Non-Enforcement of Law*, London: Institute of Employment Rights.

Tombs, S. and Whyte, D. (2013) The myths and realities of deterrence in workplace safety regulation, *British Journal of Criminology*, 53(5): 746–763.

Tombs, S. and Whyte, D. (2015) *The Corporate Criminal*, London: Routledge.

Van Der Pijl, K. and Yurchenko, Y. (2015) Neoliberal entrenchment of North Atlantic capital. From corporate self-regulation to state capture, *New Political Economy*, 20(4): 495–517.

Whyte, D. (2004) Corporate crime and regulation, in Muncie, J. and Wilson, D. (eds) *The Student Handbook of Criminology and Criminal Justice*, London: Cavendish.

Whyte, D. (2009) *Crimes of the Powerful: A Reader*, Maidenhead: Open University Press.

Whyte, D. (2014) Regimes of permission and state-corporate crime, *State Crime Journal*, 3(2): 237–246.

Whyte, D. (2015a) *The Myths of Business*, London and Liverpool: Institute of Employment Rights and Centre for Labour and Social Studies.

Whyte, D. (2015b) Introduction, in Whyte, D (ed.) *How Corrupt is Britain?* London: Pluto.

Whyte, D. (2016) The criminal corporate veil, in Spicer, A. and Baars, G. (eds) *The Corporation: A Critical, Interdisciplinary Handbook*, Cambridge: Cambridge University Press.

Wiegratz, J. (2010) Fake capitalism? The dynamics of neoliberal moral restructuring and pseudo-development: the case of Uganda, *Review of African Political Economy*, 37(124): 123–137.

Wiegratz, J. (2014) The arrival of the new normal, *Le Monde diplomatique*, 9 April.

Wiegratz, J. (2015a) No country for dirty money: behind Britain's populist promise on corruption, *The Conversation*, 6 August.

Wiegratz, J. (2015b) Book review of 'The price of civilization: reawakening virtue and prosperity after the economic fall', by J. Sachs, *Review of African Political Economy*. DOI: 10.1080/03056244.2015.1113657.

Wiegratz, J. (2015c) Locked-in culture? The challenge of de-neoliberalising 'the social',

Inclusive Societies Annual Meeting, University of Sheffield, 6–7 July.

Wiegratz, J. (2016) *Neoliberal Moral Economy: Capitalism, Socio-cultural Change and Fraud in Uganda*, London: Rowman Littlefield International.

Wiegratz, J. and Cesnulyte, E. (2016) Money talks: moral economies of earning a living in neoliberal East Africa, *New Political Economy*, 21(1): 1–25.

Will, S., Handelman, S. and Brotherton, D.C. (eds) (2013) *How They Got Away With It: White Collar Criminals and the Financial Meltdown*, New York: CUP.

Zelizer, V. (1979) *Morals and Markets: The Development of Life Insurance in the United States*, New York: Columbia University Press.

Zizek, S. (1989) *The Sublime Object of Ideology*, London: Verso.

Index

Helping you to choose the right eBooks for your Library

Add Routledge titles to your library's digital collection today. Taylor and Francis ebooks contains over 50,000 titles in the Humanities, Social Sciences, Behavioural Sciences, Built Environment and Law.

Choose from a range of subject packages or create your own!

Benefits for you

» Free MARC records
» COUNTER-compliant usage statistics
» Flexible purchase and pricing options
» All titles DRM-free.

REQUEST YOUR **FREE** INSTITUTIONAL TRIAL TODAY

Free Trials Available
We offer free trials to qualifying academic, corporate and government customers.

Benefits for your user

» Off-site, anytime access via Athens or referring URL
» Print or copy pages or chapters
» Full content search
» Bookmark, highlight and annotate text
» Access to thousands of pages of quality research at the click of a button.

eCollections – Choose from over 30 subject eCollections, including:

- Archaeology
- Architecture
- Asian Studies
- Business & Management
- Classical Studies
- Construction
- Creative & Media Arts
- Criminology & Criminal Justice
- Economics
- Education
- Energy
- Engineering
- English Language & Linguistics
- Environment & Sustainability
- Geography
- Health Studies
- History
- Language Learning
- Law
- Literature
- Media & Communication
- Middle East Studies
- Music
- Philosophy
- Planning
- Politics
- Psychology & Mental Health
- Religion
- Security
- Social Work
- Sociology
- Sport
- Theatre & Performance
- Tourism, Hospitality & Events

For more information, pricing enquiries or to order a free trial, please contact your local sales team: **www.tandfebooks.com/page/sales**

The home of Routledge books

www.tandfebooks.com

For Product Safety Concerns and Information please contact our EU representative GPSR@taylorandfrancis.com Taylor & Francis Verlag GmbH, Kaufingerstraße 24, 80331 München, Germany